Medieval Mothering

THE NEW MIDDLE AGES
VOLUME 3
GARLAND REFERENCE LIBRARY OF THE HUMANITIES
VOLUME 1979

THE NEW MIDDLE AGES

BONNIE WHEELER
Series Editor

The New Middle Ages is dedicated to transdisciplinary studies of medieval cultures, with particular emphasis on women's history and feminist and gender analyses. The series includes both scholarly monographs and essay collections.

Clothes Make the Man: Female Cross Dressing in Medieval Europe
by Valerie R. Hotchkiss

Medieval Mothering
edited by John Carmi Parsons and Bonnie Wheeler

Fresh Verdicts on Joan of Arc
edited by Bonnie Wheeler and Charles T. Wood

Medieval Mothering

EDITED BY
JOHN CARMI PARSONS
BONNIE WHEELER

GARLAND PUBLISHING, INC.
NEW YORK AND LONDON
1996

First paperback edition published in 1999 by
Garland Publishing Inc.
A Member of the Taylor & Francis Group
19 Union Square West
New York, NY 10003

10 9 8 7 6 5 4 3 2 1

Library of Congress Cataloging-in-Publication Data

Medieval mothering/ edited by John Carmi Parsons and Bonnie Wheeler.
       p.   cm. — (Garland reference library of the humanities ; vol.
1979.
The new Middle Ages ; vol. 3)
    Includes bibliographical references.
    ISBN 0-8153-3665-9(alk. paper)
    1. Motherhood—Europe—History. 2. Mothers—Europe—His-
tory. 3. Europe—Social Conditions—To 1492. I. Parsons, John Carmi,
1947- . II. Wheeler, Bonnie. III. Series: Garland reference library of the
humanities ; v. 1979. IV. Series: Garland reference library of the humanities. New Middle Ages ; vol. 3.
HQ759.M432 1996
306.874'3—dc20   96–12073
                                                     CIP

Printed on acid-free, 250-year-life paper
Manufactured in the United States of America

For

Olivia Louise Franklin
Patricia Avis McCaslin
Deborah Wilson

CONTENTS

ix   *Introduction*: MEDIEVAL MOTHERING, MEDIEVAL MOTHERERS
John Carmi Parsons and Bonnie Wheeler

xviii *Abbreviations*

3   NURTURING DANGER: HIGH MEDIEVAL MEDICINE AND THE
       PROBLEM(S) OF THE CHILD
       William F. MacLehose

25   THE MILK OF CHRIST: HERZELOYDË AS SPIRITUAL SYMBOL IN
       WOLFRAM VON ESCHENBACH'S *Parzival*
       Patricia Ann Quattrin

39   THE PREGNANT QUEEN AS COUNSELLOR AND THE MEDIEVAL
       CONSTRUCTION OF MOTHERHOOD
       John Carmi Parsons

63   THE OCCLUSION OF MATERNITY IN CHAUCER'S *Clerk's Tale*
       Allyson Newton

77   THE MATERNAL BEHAVIOR OF GOD: DIVINE FATHER AS
       FANTASY HUSBAND
       Pamela Sheingorn

101   JOSEPH AS MOTHER: ADAPTATION AND APPROPRIATION IN
       THE CONSTRUCTION OF MALE VIRTUE
       Rosemary Drage Hale

117   IS MOTHER SUPERIOR?: TOWARDS A HISTORY OF FEMININE
       Amtscharisma
       Felice Lifshitz

139   MATERNITY IN AELRED OF RIEVAULX'S LETTER TO HIS SISTER
       Susanna Greer Fein

157   *In the Meydens Womb*: JULIAN OF NORWICH AND THE
POETICS OF ENCLOSURE
Maud Burnett McInerney

183   THE INVERTED METAPHOR: EARTHLY MOTHERING AS *Figura*
OF DIVINE LOVE IN JULIAN OF NORWICH'S *Book of Showings*
Andrew Sprung

201   OLD NORSE MOTHERHOOD
Jenny Jochens

223   THE VIKING'S MOTHER: RELATIONS BETWEEN MOTHERS AND
THEIR GROWN SONS IN ICELANDIC SAGAS
Stephan Grundy

239   FEMALE NETWORKS FOR FOSTERING LADY LISLE'S
DAUGHTERS
Barbara A. Hanawalt

259   LOOKING FOR GRANDMOTHER: THE PASTONS AND THEIR
COUNTERPARTS IN LATE MEDIEVAL ENGLAND
Joel T. Rosenthal

279   THE EMPRESS MATILDA AND HER SONS
Marjorie Chibnall

295   PUBLIC LIVES, PRIVATE TIES: ROYAL MOTHERS IN
ENGLAND AND SCOTLAND, 1070–1204
Lois L. Huneycutt

313   ADELA OF BLOIS AS MOTHER AND COUNTESS
Kimberly A. LoPrete

335   BERENGUELA OF CASTILE'S POLITICAL MOTHERHOOD: THE
MANAGEMENT OF SEXUALITY, MARRIAGE, AND SUCCESSION
Miriam Shadis

359   THE FAMILY ROMANCE OF GUIBERT OF NOGENT: HIS STORY/
HER STORY
Nancy F. Partner

381   *Contributors*

Introduction:

MEDIEVAL MOTHERING,
MEDIEVAL MOTHERERS

John Carmi Parsons and Bonnie Wheeler

M*edieval Mothering*: the very title suggests a fluid, graceful sculpture of a Gothic Madonna nestling her babe in her arms, exuding tranquil reassurance, providing the comfort of the "mother-bond" to all believers. Yet this stereotype has its harrowing profane shadows, for "medieval mothering" also conjures highly-charged alternatives, among them that of the medieval mother as a careless aristocrat who callously rejects her children, sending them into fosterage, monastic life, and warfare. This other mother—that mere incubator, according to some theorists, whose procreativity is appropriated by a patriarchal culture—may have economic or political "interests" in her children, but lacks any profound emotional bonding with them. And what about the frequent invocation of the mother from all social classes who is malignant, beating her children until she bends them to her will? Which of these images most accurately reflects mothering in the Middle Ages?

In her compelling and contested *Death without Weeping: The Violence of Everyday Life in Brazil*, the anthropologist Nancy Scheper-Hughes warns us against any simple conclusion:

> …perhaps there is a middle ground betweeen the two rather extreme approaches to mother love—the sentimentalized maternal "poetics" and the mindlessly automatic "maternal bonding" theorists, on the one hand, and the "absence of love" theorists, on the other. Between these is the reality of maternal thinking and practice grounded in specific historical and cultural realities and bounded by different economic and demographic constraints. Maternal practices always begin as a response to "the historical reality of a biological child in a particular social world."[1]

Scheper-Hughes reminds us that all mothering begins as a *practice*. Even we medievalists, we hope, do not need to be reminded that motherhood itself is a sex-bound role exclusive to women. Men are not mothers. Only once did a child have a father as sole parent: she was the goddess Athena who sprang from the head of Zeus, and hers is not a medieval story. Though contemporary cultures have destabilized previously static notions, norms, and claims of gender, and though the terms "femininity" and "masculinity" spend some time these days cross-dressing, "mother" remains feminine. That literal, utterly and appropriately *essentialized* womanly status of "mother" does not necessarily apply to the practice of "mothering," however. Maternity is a biological fact, rooted in the female body through birth, yoked to breast-nurture through infancy. But mothering is an activity. As an activity, mothering is culturally constructed, "grounded in specific historical and cultural practices," and the subject of this collection.

We speak therefore mostly of mothers and their mothering, but also of mother*ers*—some women (and all men) who, though not biological mothers, participated in what their cultures considered maternal practices. We start from the premise that most of the voices currently available to us on this subject, and thus represented in this volume, are filtered through medieval men. Julian of Norwich is here a predictably major exception. Medieval women's own discourse is being recuperated at a rapid rate, although our information about all medieval family roles remains fragmentary. Can we yet pinpoint with confidence, for example, a moment by which the Roman *paterfamilias* assumed the different role of the typically bourgeois father? Furthermore, how do we differentiate medieval practices of "mothering" from "fathering"? The present collection sensibly suggests one must look for fathers as well as children if one is to understand maternal activities, and that one must ask whether these family roles marked a moment of experience or a distinct stage in human development. Several of these essays, for example, address current debate on medieval understandings of childhood as a distinct stage in human development, showing that such awareness existed and implicitly concluding that medieval societies did perceive children as beings who needed mothering. The presence and emotions of the child are therefore crucial to considerations of medieval mothering. But we cannot look for medieval children in neatly delimited zones in our sources, and the same is true for medieval mothers and motherers. To conduct such a search we must first define medieval contexts of mothering carried out against a patriarchal background in which women were shuffled or traded among male lineages and bore children of whose lineages they themselves might never really be members. We must examine the full continuum of medieval motherer's experience throughout their lives in the full range of their activities. Several essays here map new theoretical ground as well as new materials for the consideration of medieval mothering, but all stay rooted in the particulars of those maternal practices.

The essays in this volume move from medieval to contemporary theories about mothering, providing the reader in each instance with case studies of medieval maternal practices. These essays are not ordered by space or time, and they make no claim to be exhaustive, comprehenisve, or representative. We begin with the dangerous territory of the body and the bodily, of pregnancy and nursing. William MacLehose's "Nurturing Danger: High Medieval Medicine and the Problem(s) of the Child" shows the prevalence in medieval medical thought of the notion that, since biological mothers or wetnurses (surrogate mothers) were unable to control their own bodily fluids, they were potentially fatally dangerous to the child: their blood or milk could be toxic. This stands in contrast to the rich, frequently religious literature also mentioned by MacLehose containing positive imagery of maternal milk if not blood. This use is exemplified by Patricia Quattrin's "The Milk of Christ: Herzeloydë as Spiritual Symbol in Wolfram von Eschenbach's *Parzival*," that shows us bodily images of Herzeloydë, first as expectant mother and then as wetnurse and protective, instructive nurturer. Herzeloydë experiences a powerful metamorphosis from biological mother to nurturer and teacher even before her son's birth, however, when she sees an explicit connection among her milk, the waters of baptism, and Christ's spiritual nourishment: she is reminded that the Virgin nursed Christ just as Herzeloydë herself will nourish and teach Parzival.

If MacLehose and Quattrin establish the essential contours of medieval motherhood as biological event and nurturing behavior, the essays by Allyson Newton and John Parsons suggest that motherhood in the Middle Ages was primarily seen, at least in the male imagination, as cocooning, warmly supportive nurture. As

Parsons shows in "The Pregnant Queen as Counsellor and the Medieval Construction of Motherhood," the contrasted reproductive roles of male rulers and their consorts affected the construction of images of rulership to suggest that men envied women's reproductive capacities and found them threatening to male royal authority. This fear was often neutralized by ritually emphasizing queens' nurturing intercession, which thus also allowed the king to manifest his magnanimous care for his subjects. A childless or aging queen might, moreover, substitute an intercessor's nurturing role for that of a parturient mother and "labor" to ensure order and concord in the kingdom. In "The Occlusion of Maternity in Chaucer's *Clerk's Tale*," Newton considers the perverse and sad case of the "patient Griselda" and provides a fundamental background to the ideas Parsons puts forward. Succinctly stated, the male powerholder, unable to participate in the reproduction of the species as intimately or visibly as the female, is consequently envious and fearful of women's reproductive power. Therefore, women's biological role is decentered in favor of the nurturing role, which can be shared by men and women alike. This touches on the inherent threat that women pose to activities regarded as prestigious and honorable: such activities are pre-empted by men—"occluded" is Newton's term—to become associated with male behavior.

All agree that nurture was a particular cultural positive in the Middle Ages. Thus it is not surprising that mothering imagery, especially of the mother-nurturer, was so frequently appropriated by male figures. The emphasis on nurturant mothering allowed patriarchy to assert a share in the processes it could not biologically claim. In "The Maternal Behavior of God: Divine Father as Fantasy Husband," Pamela Sheingorn shows how the "maternal" figuration of the divine was deployed in the later Middle Ages to support one ideology of patriarchy—that young girls should happily consent to idealized marriages with old men. Rosemary Hales' "Joseph as Mother: Adaptation and Appropriation in the Construction of Male Virtue" further instantiates the lack of gender specificity attached to mothering activity in the late medieval period. Both these essays deal with religious imagery, closely related to the Marian cult that celebrated virginity, occluded sexual maternity, emphasized nurturant behavior, and disseminated this viewpoint to society at large. Felice Lifshitz' essay on the abbess' position in early medieval monastic

Rules reveals that the role of gender in the construction of female monastic authority was also complicated. If medieval women attempted to "father," Lifshitz argues that they lost claims to authority; in her words, "a female responsibility to nurture does not imply a maternal authority to command." Lifshitz' conclusions about the lack of necessary gender specificity in religious writings about mothering also appear in Susanna Fein's essay on Aelred of Rievaulx' *De institutione inclusarum,* a close study of the metaphorical appropriation of physical maternity by Cistercian monastic writers such as Aelred. In its metaphorical practice—or in its literal absence—as all these essays show, mothering was a convenient way to suppress female authority precisely in order to absorb it into male patriarchal ideologies and thus exploit it for patriarchy's own self-promoting purposes.

Maud McInerney's and Andrew Sprung's essays on Julian of Norwich echo the gender-crossing tendencies even of the womb in the Middle Ages. No writer more famously yokes the procreativity and kindness of the Divine to notions of maternity than does Julian, the supreme enunciator of the motherhood of God. Both McInerney and Sprung note Julian's evocation of Christ's salvific "labor" to bring forth Christianity, a symbolic travail like that of the barren but interceding queen. McInerney further shows that it is precisely Julian's imagery of fluids, and the permeable bodily boundaries it implies, that allows her to confirm Jesus' motherhood—a particularly neat reversal to the Arabic medical traditions that found such fluids dangerous, as MacLehose has informed us. Sprung stresses that Julian represents God's fatherhood and motherhood not oppositionally but complementarily. Sprung sees in Julian's writings the longing for a mothering protection that offers both emotional reassurance and an intellectually educating presence. Though this mirrors the representation of Herzeloydë in Wolfram's *Parzival,* it does so darkly, for Julian's child-before-the-mother stance is that of a woman standing before a male divinity.

The next essays address current debate on the quality of the medieval mother-child relationship. In "Old Norse Motherhood," Jenny Jochens finds a coolness between mothers and their children in pagan Germanic traditions; only late in the pagan period does Jochens see traces of a more intimate side to mother-child relations; she argues that Christian traditions may have encouraged warmer parental affection. Stephan Grundy comes to Icelandic materials from another perspective, arguing in "The Viking's Mother: Relations between Mothers and Their Grown Sons in Icelandic Sagas" that this adult relationship was intensified by the combination of women's explicit legal and physical powerlessness and implicit social and personal power. In the instances Grundy cites, mothers' actions both reinforce social norms of mothering and call attention to their boundaries. The two subsequent essays amplify our vision of these norms and practices. In "Female Networks for Fostering Lady Lisle's Daughters," Barbara Hanawalt shows that medieval parents' recourse to surrogate caregivers need not imply indifference or lack of emphatic, positive, emotional engagement with their children. Hanawalt presents new perspectives on the much-maligned stepmothers of our fairy tales, and further shows that fostering arrangements frequently had significant positive results. Here and in Joel Rosenthal's "Looking for Grandmother: The Pastons and Their Counterparts in Late Medieval England," surrogacy itself is the subject: how are maternal roles encoded through the generation of grandchildren? how are maternal roles expressed to surrogate children? Rosenthal examines an often-neglected aspect of medieval life, the place and roles of the aging grandmother within the family after her childbearing years are over. Rosenthal focuses our attention on fresh aspects of the Paston family, directing our attention away from the much-emphasized violence of some Paston mothers to the agendas of the Paston grandmothers.

These studies of particular mothers and motherers continue to address issues of how mothers set goals and agendas for their children within prevailing sociocultural norms. Marjorie Chibnall, Lois Huneycutt, Kimberly LoPrete, and Miriam Shadis contribute detailed studies of aristocratic mothers, the actual medieval mothers most readily observed in conventional surviving sources. Individually and collectively, these essays reveal a group of politically prominent women actively engaged not only with their children's futures as public figures but also with their physical, material, and spiritual well-being—with their persons and their personalities. In each case we are required to assume new cultural lenses: despite what we might be led to suspect by the patriarchal attitudes that dominated the ruling classes of medieval Europe, aristocratic women were by no means overwhelmed by any sense of displacement as they were traded in marriage to further the interests of a patrilinear milieu. If anything, aristocratic mothers were experts in liminality, for their negotiations of divided loyalties between paternal and affinal lineages were fundamental to their careers and self-understanding. Mothering was an essential element in their ability to negotiate the boundaries of the natal and marital families. Unlike a patriarchal spouse, mothers— as non-members of affinal lineages—were able to consider the well-being of all their children even if they concentrated their energies on their eldest sons. Medieval mothers, however shaped by patriarchies with which they themselves colluded, often exploited those systems for the benefit of all their children.

The final essay, Nancy Partner's "The Family Romance of Guibert of Nogent: His Story/Her Story," gives us an actual medieval person speaking about his dead mother, creating her maternity before our curious eyes. Medieval mothers and sons, we remember, lived in shadows cast not only by the figure of Christ and Mary, but also by Augustine and Monica. In this psychoanalytic reading, Partner uncovers Guibert's ambivalent rhetorical and narrative strategies in his imitation of Augustine's *Confessions* as he recollects his mother's maternity, femininity, and power. In Partner's reading, they live timelessly in a psychodrama of family romance.

These essays combine to lay emphasis on nurturant behavior rather than strict sexual reproduction as the dominant theme in medieval mothering. Patriarchal thinkers appropriated the imagery of mothering in attempts to usurp or participate in the maternal function, but so too did other writers, including Julian of Norwich. These essays suggest therefore that it is possible to amplify our notion of mothering beyond its usual gender bond without merely reinscribing and thereby reinforcing noxious patterns of authority. After considering these esssays as a whole, we realize anew the need to interrogate mothering and motherers in precise cultural contexts. What and where are the gaps between maternal and paternal roles? What did "nurture" mean for medieval persons? Can we reasonably read back into the Middle Ages our modern cultural expectations that mothering equals warm nurturing? Scheper-Hughes captures part of our problem:

> Whenever social scientists involve themselves in the study of women's lives—especially in practices surrounding sexuality, reproduction, and nurturing—they frequently come up against theories of human (and

maternal) nature that have been uncritically derived from assumptions and values implicit in the structure of the "modern," Western, bourgeois family. I refer to theories proposing essential, or universal, womanly scripts, such as Marshall Klaus and John Kennell's (1976) "maternal bonding," Sara Ruddick's (1989) "maternal thinking," Nancy Chodorow's (1978) "feminine personality," and Carol Gilligan's (1982) "womanly ethos," all of which can be found to be both culture and history bound....

Contemporary theories of maternal sentiment—of mother love as we know and understand it—are the product of a very specific historical context. The invention of mother love corresponds not only with the rise of the modern, bourgeois, nuclear family...but also with demographic transition: the precipitous decline in infant mortality and female fertility....mother love as defined in the psychological, social-historical, and sociological literatures is far from universal or innate and represents instead an ideological, symbolic representation grounded in the basic material conditions that define women's reproductive lives. [2]

If, as Scheper-Hughes says, even "emotions are discourse; they are constructed and produced in language and in human interactions... without our cultures, we *simply would not know how to feel* "(431), then larger-than-life emotions allocated to "Mother" in contemporary culture may burden our capacity to examine the mothering of the past. Our modern yearning for mothering has been cast as timeless by psychological theorists. Is it possible that it is as culture-induced, perhaps even as unhealthy, as our yearning for refined sugar? The range of essays in this book offer a wide informative base from which to ponder how medieval western Europe regarded nurturant mothering. This topic has, especially as a result of the work of Clarissa Atkinson, begun to attract notice, and remains open to theorizations for which these essays constitute an early foundation. These essays do not uniformly assume that mothering had special ontological status, or that there was one way for a mother or motherer to be. Instead, they begin to make us aware of the wide range of medieval maternal behaviors and emotions, and the varying agendas that shape them, so that we can conclude, in the words of Sara Ruddick, that, in some sense, all mothers are adoptive.

[margin note: This is the grant of breastfeeding (one point): it triggers biological responses that assist the mother to care successfully for the child.]

NOTES

1. Nancy Scheper-Hughes, *Death Without Weeping: The Violence of Everyday Life in Brazil* (Berkeley and Los Angeles, CA, 1992), p. 356, quoting Sara Ruddick, *Maternal Thinking: Towards a Politics of Peace* (Boston, 1989), p. 348. She further argues (p. 354) that "[h]istorians, anthropologists, philosophers, and the "public" at large are influenced by old cultural myths and stereotypes about childhood innocence and maternal affection as well as by their opposites....Whenever we try to pierce the meanings of lives very different from our own, we face two interpretive risks. On the one hand, we may be tempted to attribute our own ways of thinking and feeling to "other" mothers....But the alternative is to cast women as passive "victims" of their own fate, as powerless, without will, agency, or subjectivity. Part of the difficulty lies in the confusion between *causality* and *blame*."

2. Scheper-Hughes, *Death Without Weeping*, p. 402.

LIST OF ABBREVIATIONS

AASS   Jean Bolland, Godfrey Henshenius, Daniel Papenbroch *et al.*, eds., *Acta sanctorum quotquot toto orbe coluntur...* , 70 vols., 2nd edn.(Paris, 1863-1940)

CCCM   Corpus Christianorum, Continuatio Mediaevalis

CF   Cistercian Fathers (Institute for Cistercian Studies, Kalamazoo, MI)

CS   Cistercian Studies (Institute for Cistercian Studies, Kalamazoo, MI)

EETS   Early English Text Society

EHR   *The English Historical Review*

GEC   George Edward Cokayne, *The Complete Peerage of England, Scotland, Ireland, Great Britain and the United Kingdom*, rev. edn., 13 vols. in 14 (London, 1910-56)

JMH   *Journal of Medieval History*

MGH   Monumenta Germaniae Historica (AA = Auctores Antiquissimi, SS=Scriptores)

PL   *Patrilogia Cursus Completus, Series Latina*, ed. J. P. Migne, 221 vols. (Paris, 1841-64)

RS   Rolls Series

Medieval Mothering

NURTURING DANGER:
HIGH MEDIEVAL MEDICINE AND THE
PROBLEM(S) OF THE CHILD[1]

William F. MacLehose

Medical literature of the High Middle Ages reveals concern for children's health that derived from and reinforced anxieties over women's bodily fluids which were transformed from slightly hazardous nourishment into toxic liquids.

> It is asked, why are children not nourished by menstrual blood, as is asserted by certain people? *Answer:* Menstrual blood is corrupt, [and] ought to generate corrupt and fluid humors. Therefore children are not nourished by menstrual blood because it is corrupt, since if they were nourished from thence they would be quickly corrupted.[2]

This statement from *The Prose Salernitan Questions*, a late twelfth-century natural philosophical collection, addressed a question of interest to high medieval writers on physiology: humanity's sustenance in the earliest stages of life. High medieval medical writers believed that the child in its earliest stages of growth was inherently fragile and susceptible to disease and could succumb quickly to physical ailments. As twelfth- and thirteenth-century medical and natural philosophical writers considered the child's problematic condition and sustenance, they revealed concern for the child's survival and for women's bodies, social roles, and actions: a major cause of pathology was located in the physiological functioning of mothers and nurses.[3] What were the implications of the belief that food and child alike could be "corrupted?" What socio-cultural concepts of childhood and nurturing lay explicitly and implicitly behind such beliefs?

The history of high medieval pediatric literature parallels and is closely linked to gynecological issues. In analyzing this literature, I focus primarily on perceived causes of pediatric pathology and on changes in the understanding of its etiology. Medical literature written and read in France from 1100 to 1250 continues and heightens classical concern for the child's safety as a fetus, newborn, and infant. The denial of menstrual blood as the child's food source before and after birth at once contradicted and reinforced common physiological theories. In discussing embryology and neonatal care, many western medical writers followed Arabic medical knowledge and devoted equal space to each actor most closely involved: mother, nurse, and fetus/newborn/infant.[4] Such writers thus explored, extended, and altered prevailing opinions on menstrual blood as the source of fetal nourishment and on milk as the infant's sustenance, and they expressed anxiety for the child's health that derived from, and reinforced, underlying apprehension and ambivalence toward women's bodies as sources of pathology and danger.

Thirteenth-century medical writers reformulated and recombined disparate ancient traditions. In the fifth century B.C., the Hippocratic corpus included texts on embryological development and the appropriate length of pregnancy.[5] Aristotle stressed the double importance of the menses as matter and as the fetus' sustenance. Continuing the Hippocratic tradition in the second century A.D., Galen defined the child according to his humoral theories as warm and humid. At the same period, Soranus included in his *Gynecology* much practical advice for pregnant, birthing, and lactating mothers.[6] Isidore of Seville (d. 636) incorporated in his *Etymologies* a discussion of fetus and child that drew on early patristic and late Roman natural philosophical writings.[7] Increasingly well-known in the West in the High Middle Ages, Arabic traditions—deeply influenced by Galenism—provided practical advice and theoretical insight into child-rearing.

Medical understanding of childhood and motherhood appeared in a variety of sources in this period. William of Conches, in the first half of the twelfth century, incorporated Galenic and Hippocratic ideas to explain the sensory world; he thus placed the human being's creation and development in a wide context of natural phenomena in *De philosophia mundi* (1125–35) and in its revision, the *Dragmaticon* (1146–49).[8] William's interest in fetal development is echoed in the

Prose Salernitan Questions, shaped by classical and early medieval *quaestiones disputatae*.[9] During the thirteenth century, competing medical and physiological ideas were introduced by the New Aristotle—i.e., the reintroduction of his biological texts—and the Arabic Galenic encyclopedists, Rhazes (d.c. 932), Haly Abbas (d. 994) and Avicenna (d. 1037).[10] The thirteenth-century Latin encyclopedists represented a dynamic process of compilation, careful selection, reevaluation, and transformation: Bartholomaeus Anglicus,[11] Thomas of Cantimpré,[12] and Vincent of Beauvais[13] began an often-contradictory and only partly-successful assimilation of these traditions. In *Le Régime du corps* (1256), Aldobrandino of Siena continued the integration of Arabic medical views on childhood.[14] In the same period, there appeared several examples of a medical genre devoted exclusively to pediatric illness, etiology, and remedies. All of these writers expressed concerns for the health of the fetus and newborn and particularly for their nourishment.

To grasp high medieval views on fetal nourishment and the changes such views underwent, we must first understand classical and medieval views of embryology and female physiology. Medical writers concerned themselves with the physical well-being of the child from the moment of conception onward. The Hippocratic (two-seed) theory of conception, prevalent in early twelfth-century Europe, rested on the idea that the fetus was formed by the heat and moisture of the father's and mother's seeds, which provided warmth to the mother's womb to create a boiling sensation through which the child's materials coalesced.[15] Perhaps the most common image used by medical writers since antiquity to describe the fetus' existence was that of fruit hanging from a tree:[16] the gravid woman's body contained various substances harmful to the child *in utero*, above all its food, which could cause it to fall from the womb like fruit from a tree.

Medical writers thus gave particular attention to fetal sustenance. Apart from the passage quoted at the beginning of this essay, medical authors concluded that the menses fed the child *in utero*. In *De philosophia mundi*, William of Conches drew on a long tradition of natural philosophical questions and asked "why man does not walk, when he is born." Other animals were able to walk at birth; William claimed man could not because "he is nourished in the womb by menstrual blood" and in *Dragmaticon*, he added that the blood was "menstrual and corrupt."[17] The idea that menstrual blood was corrupt and debilitating did not begin with William; his novelty lay in placing his discussion in the midst of his embryological narrative. Earlier natural philosophers such as Adelard of Bath, in *Quaestiones naturales*—written a decade before *De philosophia*—discussed the same question but not in the context of an organized study of human development.[18] The association of embryology with a negative view of menstrual blood distinguished William's work from prior discussions of embryology and set a precedent for writers over the next century.

Arabic medical authors identified several kinds of menstrual blood. Vincent quoted Avicenna's trifunctional division of gravid women's menses: one fed the fetus *in utero*, another was raised to the breasts to become milk, and a third remained in the womb as a superfluity— the amniotic fluid, discharged with the fetus.[19] Such beliefs were typical of Arabic medical writers, who had few negative ideas about menstrual blood but focused rather on its positive functions. This situation is partly explained by the fact that Galenic and Hippocratic writings, the Arabic doctors' main sources, ascribed few negative attributes to the menses.[20] Yet the western medical tradition, even before the integration of Arabic learning and increasingly during the thirteenth century, almost unanimously perceived the menses as at the least problematic if not harmful to the fetus.[21] What attributes troubled western medical writers? And, given the frequency of menstrual taboos in western culture, from what traditions did these ideas stem?

William of Conches' embryological narrative first mentioned menstrual blood after discussing conception. The menses arose from women's cold nature; they could not "digest well, and a superfluity remained which [was] purged every month. Upon conception, heat [was] doubled from the fetus, whence better food was digested, and such superfluities did not arise as before. Again, because the fetus is nourished by the blood from the womb, it does not need a purging."[22] Based on a Hippocratic inequality of the sexes, such statements presented the menses not as harmful but as the result of feminine inferiority and an inherent lack of heat. Later writers, however, saw the menses' superfluousness as an indication of their harmful nature.

Immediately after defining the menses and their utility in feeding the fetus, William put the question about man's inability to walk at birth, his answer to which suggested that the menses were less innocuous than previously stated. Unlike later writers, William never directly asked why the menses caused such complete disability in newborns. Like his definition of menstrual blood, however, William's ideas on sexual differentiation pointed to a connection between temperature and quality of nourishment. The fetus would be male if the seed "remains on the right side, because the liver is close to the left side of the womb, [thus] the fetus is nourished by better and warm blood and is made male." If the seed lay in the left part "distant from the font of heat, that is the liver," the result would be a girl.[23] Although its primary purpose was to explain the origin of the sexes, the passage reveals that menstrual blood needed improvement, and heat provided it.

Such statements echoed Galenic ideas of contrary qualities—hot/cold, dry/moist. They thus reinforced medical views of gender inequality and paralleled notions central to Aristotelian natural philosophy as understood and expounded in the century following William of Conches.[24] Writers who incorporated the New Aristotle in the thirteenth century's first decades, David of Dinant in particular, stressed women's physical inferiority and especially their comparative lack of heat. According to the Aristotelian (one-seed) theory of conception, a mother provided only menstrual blood as unformed matter, to which the sperm brought heat and the power (*vis operatiua*) to transform that matter into a human body: "the woman appears like a child or an imperfect male, and her menses like undigested sperm, retaining its bloody shape due to the weakness of heat."[25] David added that sperm and menstrual blood were superfluities, but women's fluids were more numerous than men's and retained the color of blood, again due to a "defect of digesting heat."[26] William and the neo-Aristotelian system alike defined women and their bodily functions as irrevocably incomplete (*imperfectus*), weaker copies of a male physiological model; menstrual blood was inherently flawed, at least in relation to its male counterpart. Nevertheless, its defective nature did not necessarily imply inherent pathology.

A crucial problem for medical authors lay in women's retention of superfluous menstrual blood, which had potentially harmful consequences. *The Prose Salernitan Questions* contained several references to women's increased desire for food and intercourse due to the menses' retention: "Why do women in the first and second months from conception desire those things which must not be desired, such as coal and the like; in the other months however their appetite is not so irrational."[27] Related questions suggested that a mother's unusual and excessive desires could have negative consequences for the fetus. The power of her imagination began a physiological process; it transformed the fetus' nourishment, and in the process changed its shape; her inability to satisfy cravings thus entailed physical deformities to the fetus.[28] Such claims implied that the menses were at least potentially dangerous, working in a "vicious circle" in which they were both cause and effect. It was this process that high medieval medical writers scrutinized.

All medical writers agreed that the umbilicus carried food from mother to fetus. In considering how the child was fed in the womb, Conches described the blood's descent from liver to fetus through nerves in the umbilicus. Blood from this path was "pure" and digested or concocted;[29] the liver again acted as a purifying agent by boiling off the superfluities. Here was an implicit belief that menstrual blood had to be refined through heating in order to provide sustenance. Later authors quoted and continued William's account of the blood's journey. Citing Constantinus' *Pantegni*, Bartholomaeus thought the umbilicus consisted of veins, nerves, and arteries, through which "the fetus attracts and sucks fine blood (*sanguinem subtilem*) and receives breath...."[30]

The danger posed by raw, undigested menstrual blood was emphasized by many authors, based in part on Conches' statements. William stressed the seed's active role, in particular its heat, in forming the fetus' body, which became differentiated by both parents' heat. Early on, the dryness produced by heating and thickening "creates a little sack (*folliculum*) containing within itself the conceived, lest some superfluities, by mixing with that one, corrupt [the fetus]."[31] Heat in William's text played a double role in sheltering the fetus, by purifying blood for nourishment and by creating a protective shell.

Thirteenth-century encyclopedias more clearly articulated exactly how and why menstrual blood was harmful. Bartholomaeus discussed the menses in book five of *De proprietatibus rerum*, not in the chapter "On Blood" but in a section on "the bad property of blood" (V.8: *De sanguinis mala proprietate*). In discussing this "less praiseworthy" blood, Bartholomaeus quoted Galen on the menses' retention as "the cause and occasion of the worst illnesses."[32] Yet Roman and early medieval encyclopedic material, the natural philosophical traditions that most plainly condemned menstrual blood, only re-entered medical literature in the early thirteenth century. Bartholomaeus and, a decade later, Vincent, quoted a famous passage from Isidore of Seville's *Etymologies*, now first repeated in high medieval physiological writings: "on contact with this blood, crops do not germinate, new wines go sour, grasses die, trees lose their fruit, iron is corrupted by rust, air and copper are blackened; which, if dogs should eat from it, they are made rabid..." Isidore had taken the passage from the second-century Roman encyclopedist Solinus, who in turn had borrowed from Pliny's *Natural History*.[33] None of the dangers here attributed to menstrual blood were deleterious to human beings; in the same section as this passage (11.1.139–145), Isidore twice briefly mentioned menstrual blood in relation to reproduction and fetal development but suggested no inherent pathology.[34] Thirteenth-century medical discussion of the menses based on Pliny, moreover, rarely referred to theological (ultimately Levitical) representations of menstrual blood as unclean and polluting.[35] Both traditions agreed that contact with menstrual blood led to negative consequences, but while Levitical tradition emphasized spiritual uncleanness, medical writings stressed physical or material dangers.[36] By including only the Pliny passage in their texts, the thirteenth-century encyclopedists explained in a purely physiological sense the negative attributes found in William of Conches' writings. Medical writers thus regarded menstrual blood as problematic not through spiritual or physical pollution but because of its mutability and propensity toward "corruption" : the menses provided a needed purge of the non-gravid woman's body but were volatile rather than inherently unclean.

In the 1240s, Thomas of Cantimpré incorporated his embryological narrative into the final sections of the first book, on anatomy, of *De natura rerum*, immediately after discussing male and female genitalia. His treatment of conception and embryological development combined ideas from Aristotle and William of Conches and quoted extensively from the latter. After repeating verbatim William's account of the liver's purifying power and the amnion, Thomas gave his own version of the fetus' relations with menstrual blood. Thomas (and Vincent, who quoted this passage) made more explicit the role of liver and placenta as intermediaries between the menses and fetus. In the blood's transformation into the embryo's sustenance, the liver's natural heat acted as a purifying agent necessary to fetal survival:

> Therefore, as all the philosophers say, the child lives by menstrual blood, but by the best and purest digested blood, mediated of course by a more pleasant and more agreeable part of the body, that is, the liver. Indeed if there were no intermediary or not the best intermediary, the menstrual blood would pass through to the child, and through its malignity [the blood] would kill more than nourish [the fetus]. This is evident in some people born with stains on their faces or on another part of the body. Truly this arises from menstrual blood, which, when there is too great an abundance, falls upon the child in the mother's womb. And unless the little sack [*folliculus*] of the placenta is the intermediary between the falling blood and the child, [the blood] by penetrating would kill him who is exposed. Nevertheless from this there remains on the child a stain, which can never be destroyed, even when his skin has been stripped.[37]

Thomas made explicit what harm the menses could inflict if the body did not create defenses against them. He combined the two aspects mentioned by William but showed that liver and amnion existed to the same end: to protect the fetus from the fluid that surrounded and nourished it. The passage underscored the danger by identifying the menses as a mortal threat.[38] Thomas (and Vincent) thus added to the medical mythology on menstrual blood extensive new discussions of the potential for the nourishment's negative impact. The danger was no longer to external, non-human objects but to the internal and human, the fetus. Direct contact with the menses meant certain death to the child.[39]

Resolution of the paradox of the menses' simultaneous threat and necessity involved the regimen a gravid woman was to observe. There existed an extensive literature on the regimen of pregnancy dating back to late antiquity, particularly in Latin translations of Soranus' *Gynecology* by Mustio (Moscio) and Caelius Aurelianus, but high medieval writers did not borrow from them. Vincent of Beauvais, more than the other encyclopedists, included within the *Speculum maius* (ca. 1250) much practical medicine from the Arabic encyclopedists Haly Abbas, Rhazes, and Avicenna.[40] Vincent provided a chronological study of human life from conception and fetal development to death, which he began by stating that "it is necessary that infants and the old have their own regimen, since their strength (*virtus*) is weak [and] their natural heat is weak. Therefore we will begin the regimen of infants with the regimen of pregnant women."[41] He listed complications from which mother and fetus could suffer: all the Arabic writers agreed that improper food could harm the child and singled out bitter or sharp foods and any that might induce a menstrual flow and sudden miscarriage (*aborsus*).[42] These sections included material on pregnancy's physical or emotional dangers (exercise, lack of sleep, anxiety), but in each case the focus was on proper maternal nourishment. Haly Abbas, the only Arabic medical writer to ascribe negative attributes to the menses, linked the mother's nutrition with fetal health by noting the fetus' extreme weakness in the first four months and hence the need for food, without which the fetus would die.[43] The Arabic writers listed prohibited foods so the mother could avoid the damaging effects such a diet might produce in the child through impurity or lack of fetal nourishment. While calls for regulation of the mother's habits predated the High Middle Ages, thirteenth-century anxieties over menstrual blood validated and reinforced the need for such precautions.

Medical writers dwelled extensively on the dangers of miscarriage, birth, and the first hours of the child's life when it faced a variety of dangers, particularly the many incorrect positions which could prove fatal to mother and/or child were the midwife inexperienced.[44] If less fragile than the fetus, the newborn was weak and soft "by nature," and had not yet undergone solidification, the result of heat and swaddling clothes. A constant site of anxiety to the medical writers was the infant's nourishment. Every high medieval source of pediatric material contained at least some reference to, if not a detailed analysis of, the source and quality of milk. The space devoted to testing the milk and curing imperfect lactation indicates that medical writers considered the subject to be of the highest importance. They viewed the child's food, as they viewed fetal nourishment, as a source of both sustenance and pathology.[45]

High medieval writers connected negative views of menses to their concern over milk through the belief in the western natural philosophical tradition that milk was menstrual blood that had been heated, coagulated, and whitened by hot air.[46] The Galenic, Hippocratic, and Aristotelian traditions agreed on this and on the belief that the mother's milk was most appropriate for the child, strengthening the parallel of menses and milk. All concurred, however, that such milk posed considerable danger to a newborn. Mustio's text, known to the high medieval scholastic world, argued in chapters devoted to the feeding process that maternal milk could not provide sufficient nourishment after the strain of labor; though Avicenna advocated maternal feeding, he held (and was quoted by Vincent) that the mother should not feed the child "until [her] complexion...is made temperate."[47] The possibility of the milk's corruption at the outset of lactation paralleled the belief that external forces could effect negative changes in its quality. Unlike the menses, too potent unless mediated, the mother's or a nurse's milk was considered malleable and easily transformed into a pathological substance. Medical writers identified many causes of corruption in maternal milk and thus allowed greater understanding of what was believed about the intricacies of yet another aspect of female physiology.

Discussions of the transformation of blood into milk restated medical misgivings about menstrual blood. Aristotle, quoted by Bartholomaeus, stressed that milk was a superfluity of the menses (already a superfluity), which became milk by being boiled (*decoctus*) in the breasts. This purified blood was then regarded as "digested and uncorrupted."[48] Borrowing from Galen, medical writers perceived the metamorphosis from red liquid to a thicker white substance as part of a process whereby blood was transformed into something closer to the nature of the breasts themselves.[49] As with fetal nourishment, the active agent was the breasts' heat. Bartholomaeus summarized, again quoting Aristotle: "The breast therefore is a necessary member for the nourishment of the fetus [sic] which takes up menstrual blood for the creation of milk; which purifies the impure blood; which digests, changes, whitens, sweetens, thickens;...which shows corruption, is round, oblong, full of nerves, fleshy, is exposed to the teeth of little children, and is full of cavities or porous."[50] In the *Pantegni*, Constantinus traced a slightly different path for the milk's journey, locating the transformation in the veins to and from the heart. Constantinus and Vincent stressed that the blood remained in the veins "until it is boiled most perfectly."[51]

Given their apprehension over the maternal body's inability to transform blood into milk just after birth, medical writers agreed a wet-nurse was needed. There is a considerable literature on a nurse's appropriate attributes; she was responsible for many aspects of neonatal care, most obviously with lactation—hence *nutrix*, "she who nourishes." Descriptions of an ideal nurse's physical and moral attributes revealed medical writers' concern with this apparently common social practice.[52] By definition socially inferior to the biological mother, the nurse had to simulate the mother's good health and qualities; Aldobrandino even urged that "the woman resemble the mother as best she can."[53] A child's survival depended on the correct physiological functioning of a body foreign to it (and likely unknown to the mother). Thus the encyclopedists, particularly Vincent, blurred the distinctions between choosing a wet-nurse and maintaining her health by a strict regimen: both demanded excellent judgement.[54] The late-classical Soranian and Arabic literatures detailed the identification of a healthy lactating nurse by focusing on her physical appearance: her weight (neither too thin nor too fat), her age (twenty-five to thirty), her habits, the shape of her breasts, the quality of her milk, and the time since her last parturition (one or two months), all received attention. The sources agreed that, as a sign of the nurse's fertility and good health, she must have given birth to a son.[55] Aldobrandino's *Régime du corps* largely paraphrased Avicenna in discussing the choice of a wet-nurse, but he did add several new worries to his occasional rewriting of material from the *Canon*. Thus he added to the *Canon*: "You ought to look at the woman so that she [...] is as healthy as any you can find, since sick nurses kill children."[56] He saw direct links between a nurse's health and the possibility of extreme danger to the child's life.

After initial inspection, medical writings urged continued vigilance of the nurse's habits to protect her milk. Every aspect of her regimen described by Arabic and western writers focused on the blood's successful transformation into milk: choice of foods (nothing spicy or bitter, no emmenagogues, little wine), exercise (neither too much nor too little), and emotional state (minimal anxiety, no anger, sadness, fear, foolishness). It was imperative that the nurse have and retain the ability to effect this transformation, which depended upon several internal and external variables. The connection between regimen and bodily functioning stemmed from the fact that the health of nurse, milk, and child was more easily identifiable than that of the fetus in pregnancy. Only negative results were visible in pregnancy: the release of blood from the womb or milk from the breasts signaled danger to the fetus.[57] The embryological literature stressed that menstrual superfluities contained an excess of powerful qualities; neonatal writings emphasized the danger of too little nourishment, exemplified in Avicennian discussions of a lack of good milk.

Thus the quality of the milk was the focus of concern in a genre of medical literature that evolved in the High Middle Ages. Three independent treatises survive, offering practical solutions for common pediatric illnesses. The first, *De curis puerorum*, is ascribed to Rhazes in most copies. The entry for each disease in *De curis* includes a description of symptoms, a try at etiology, and a cure. It provides three types of remedy: anointment of the child's head, a mild medicinal drink, and most often a purging or "correcting" of the nurse.[58] *De curis* states that in many cases the cause of illness lay in the milk's corruption.[59] Two shorter Latin works on pediatric pathology, from the twelfth century and later, declare clearly that problem and cure could be found in the nurse's milk. The older, the *Practica puerorum* (*Passiones puerorum*), begins by stating that "first one must consider the milk from which the child is nourished, if it is good."[60] The work claims one can see milk's malign aspects and moves on to its testing and "qualities." From Soranus and the Arabic writers came a much-varied tradition of investigation that involved four of the senses. Some texts suggested using a piece of glass, a rock, or sword, others a fingernail upon which a drop of milk was placed and inspected for thickness, smell, taste, and color. To correct any deficiencies in these qualities, the texts suggested changes in the nurse's regimen.[61] Another text, the *Liber de passionibus puerorum Galieni* (*Ut testatur Ypocras*), dealt with milk before ailments. The child's health told of problems in the nurse's physiology: "In the first place, whatever the child's illness, caution must be imposed upon the nurse's diet and so exact a diet must be observed, as if the nurse were suffering from the ailment of the little infant, because nurses' milk derived from contrary foods generates an ailment in little infants previously not existing and aggravates one already found."[62]

Texts concerning the nurse's regimen provided extended discussions of reasons for her milk's corruption. Even were the milk good in the woman's breast, the child's body could still be damaged thereby if, for example, the nurse rocked the child too violently and caused the milk to curdle. Similarly, Avicenna suggested the newborn be made to cry before nursing to release noxious superfluities.[63] But the potential for corruption at the milk's source received the closest attention. The nurse's regimen to a large extent followed that of the pregnant woman, at least after she was selected. Physical, dietary, and emotional aspects of the nurse's life were thought to affect the production and quality of her milk; doctors urged light exercise and minimal anxiety. Foods to be avoided repeated the prohibitions for gravid women: salty, sharp, or bitter foods, onions, garlic, or "foods of this sort which corrupt milk."[64] Avicenna's *Canon* insisted that the nurse not have intercourse while nursing lest, if she should conceive, blood essential to feed the newborn or to nourish the fetus would be lessened, thus weakening the born and the unborn alike. Vincent acknowledged the importance of Avicenna's caveats. Aldobrandino heightened this concern for the child's safety by again reworking a passage from Avicenna and stressing the child's vital interest. In advising against allowing the nurse to have intercourse while feeding, he claimed that "one should beware that she should not sleep with a man, since it is the thing which most corrupts the milk…because a pregnant woman kills and destroys the child when she breast-feeds."[65] What was simply a danger (*nocumentum*) of corruption in the *Canon* was transformed into something with inevitably fatal consequences.

Distrust of women's bodies as sources of neonatal nourishment and concern over nursing women's habits were linked to moral worries about women's actions and their consequences for children.[66] Despite emphasis on the dangers of bad milk and views of the woman's body as detrimental to the child, however, medical writers did express the belief that, were the regimen followed, either mother or nurse could produce healthy milk to preserve the child and promote its growth. Medical writers thus suggested feasible, practical solutions to the vulnerability of child and fetus to women's bodily fluids. This literature nonetheless left the women involved in childcare in an ambiguous position. While pregnant, the mother played a clearly essential part in the fetus's growth; yet she could harm it in many ways, intentionally or otherwise. Similarly, after the child's birth mother and nurse brought both necessary sustenance for life and the possibility of death to the child. Medical literature here expressed a profound ambivalence toward women, essential yet dangerous nurturers.[67]

In high medieval medicine, this ambivalence appeared in the intellectual context of the integration and extension of contradictory strands of knowledge: the Greek concept of women as physically weaker than men and the Roman natural philosophical claim that women's bodies were powerful due to their potential threat. We must, however, distinguish paradox from contradiction. The paradox of women as nurturers and corruptors, creators and destroyers, epitomized high medieval medical authors' ambivalence toward women. There is no contradiction when these claims are understood within medical discourse. The female role in childcare left fetus and newborn vulnerable to a threat that lay in women's inability to control their bodily functions and fluids. Women's weakness was synonymous with their threat: their lack of control. Women's strength and threat, also synonymous, lay in the claim that menses and milk were not weak but all too potent. Thirteenth-century medical writers followed in a misogynist tradition of medical thought (Hippocratic theories of the wandering womb; Aristotelian ideas of women as imperfect men) in which they tried to biologize the female threat as women's inability to control nutritive yet dangerous bodily fluids. There was thus an irresolvable impasse between the necessity of female nourishment for the child, and the danger in that nourishment.

High medieval medical literature centered on the child's inherent disposition to illness and sought to explain infant and fetal illness and death. Given the reality of high rates of miscarriage and infant mortality, this literature suggested that women's bodies were the source not only of puerile pathology but of the child's weak and vulnerable nature. Given the necessity of women's bodies in generation, before birth, and up to weaning, and the belief that other animals did not menstruate and were not so helpless at birth, blame for the child's weakness attached to women's physiological inadequacies or imperfections, particularly the menses. The high medieval problematizing of the female body, particularly of the sources of nourishment for fetus and child, heightened concern for the health of mother and child alike.

NOTES

1. For comments on this paper, I wish to thank John Baldwin, Jerome
Bylebyl, Susan Ferry, Monica Green, Lynn Gorchov, Christine Reno,
Walton Schalick, and Gabrielle Spiegel and her seminar on the Production
of History. Special thanks to the staff of the Institute for the History of
Medicine, Baltimore, and the National Library of Medicine, Bethesda.
Earlier versions of this paper were presented to the Johns Hopkins
University Medieval History Seminar and to the 29th International
Congress on Medieval Studies, Kalamazoo.

2. *The Prose Salernitan Questions*, ed. Brian Lawn (Oxford, 1979)
B306, p. 144. I am indebted to Giulia Sissa and Andrew Kelly for assistance
with this passage.

3. Luke Demaitre, "The Idea of Childhood and Childcare in Medical
Writings of the Middle Ages," *History of Childhood Quarterly*, 3 (1976), 461–
490, emphasizes later medieval sources. See also Jean-Noël Biraben, "La
médecine et l'enfant au moyen-âge," *Annales de démographie historique*
(1973), 73–75, and Eduard Seidler, "L'enfant dans la médecine du moyen-
âge," *Colloque international d'histoire de la médecine médiévale* (1985), 44–
54.

4. Terminology used by authors cited in this paper was not as fixed
as modern translations may suggest. *Fetus* and *embryo* most often indicated
prenatal stages (with no sense of the modern distinction between them);
the former could refer to a child in the first stages after birth. *Puer* could
refer to any stage of development from embryo to young adult (not to
mention its meaning as "slave," "serf," etc.). Many medical writers clearly
differentiated between stages of life and often divided the earliest stages into
infantia and *pueritia*; see Elizabeth Sears, *The Ages of Man: Medieval
Interpretations of the Life Cycle* (Princeton, 1986).

5. See treatises on the seven- and eight-months' child in E. Littré,
Oeuvres complètes d'Hippocrate (Paris, 1853), 7:432–61. The *Aphorisms* contain
pediatric material, while the treatises on "The Nature of the Child" were
devoted to embryology; see G. E. R. Lloyd, ed., *Hippocratic Writings,* trans.
J. Chadwick and W. N. Manse (Harmondsworth, 1978), pp. 214–27, 317–
46. See also Pearl Kibre, *Hippocrates Latinus: Repertorium of Hippocratic
Writings in the Latin Middle Ages* (New York, 1985).

6. On translations, Monica Green, "The Transmission of Ancient
Theories of Female Physiology and Disease through the Early Middle Ages"
(Ph.D. diss., Princeton University, 1985), chap. 3. For the texts, *Sorani
Gynaeciorum vetus translatio latina*, ed. V. Rose (Leipzig, 1882), hereafter:
Mustio; and *Caelius Aurelianus, Gynaecia: Fragments of a Latin version of
Soranus' Gynaecia*, eds. M. and I. Drabkin (Baltimore, 1951).

7. Isidore of Seville, *Etymologiarum sive originum libri XX*, ed. W.M.
Lindsay (Oxford, 1911).

8. There is no modern edition of *De philosophia mundi*; see *PL* 172:39–102, ascribed to Honorius of Autun, and *PL* 90:1127–1178, ascribed to Bede. The *Dragmaticon* [hereafter: *Drag*] also has no modern edition; see *Dialogus de substantiis physicis: Ante annos ducentos confectus, a Vuilelmo Aneponymo philosopho*, ed. Guillelmus Guatarolus (Argentorati: Iosias Rihelius, 1567; rpt. Frankfurt am Main, 1967).

9. On the *quaestio*, B. Lawn, *The Rise and Decline of the Scholastic "Quaestio disputata"* (Leiden, 1993).

10. Helen Lemay, "Arabic Influences on Medieval Attitudes toward Infancy," *Clio Medica*, 13.1 (1978), 1–12. For reception of Arabic medicine, Heinrich Schipperges, *Die Assimilation der arabischen Medizin durch das lateinische Mittelalter*, Sudhoffs Archiv, Beihefte 3 (Wiesbaden, 1964); D. Jacquart and F. Micheau, *La médecine arabe et l'occident médiéval* (Paris, 1990).

11. Bartholomaeus Anglicus, *De proprietatibus rerum*, ed. George Barthold (Frankfurt: Wolfgang Richter, 1601; rpt. Frankfurt am Main, 1964), hereafter: Bart. On his sources, G. Se Boyar, "Bartholomaeus Anglicus and His Encyclopaedia," *The Journal of English and Germanic Philology*, 19 (1920), 168–189, and M. C. Seymour, *Bartholomaeus Anglicus and his Encyclopedia* (London, 1992). Michael Goodich translates pediatric sections of bk. 6, "Bartholomaeus Anglicus on Child-Rearing," *History of Childhood Quarterly*, 3.i (1975), pp. 75–84.

12. There are two editions of the sections used here: Christoph Ferckel, *Die Gynäkologie des Thomas von Brabant: Ein Beitrag zur Kenntnis der mittelalterlichen Gynäkologie und ihrer Quellen* (Munich, 1912) and *Thomae Cantimpratensis liber de natura rerum*, ed. H. Boese (Berlin and New York, 1973).

13. *Bibliotheca mundi Vincentii Burgundi... Speculum quadruplex, naturale, doctrinale, morale, historiale* (Douai: Balthazar Bellerus, 1624). See R. K. Weber, "Vincent of Beauvais: A Study in Medieval Historiography" (Ph.D. diss., University of Michigan, 1965), esp. chaps. 1–2.

14. *Le Régime du corps de maitre Aldebrandin de Sienne: texte français du XIIIe siècle*, ed. L. Landouzy and R. Pépin (Paris: H. Champion, 1911); J.-B. Soalhat, "Les idées de maistre Alebrand de Florence sur la puériculture" (Dissertation, Faculté de Médecine, Paris, 1908).

15. Joseph Needham, *A History of Embryology* (New York, 1959), pp. 31–37; Prudence Allen, *The Concept of Woman: The Aristotelian Revolution, 750 BC–AD 1250* (Montreal, 1985), pp. 83–85, 95–103.

16. See Avicenna's *Canon* bk. 3, fen. 21, tract. 2, ch. 10. I have used two early printed editions: *Avicenne Liber canonis medicine Cum castigationibus Andree Bellunensis* (Bruxelles, 1971, rpt. of Rome, 1524) and *Avicennae principis et philosophi sapientissimi Libri in re medica omnes qui hactenus ad nos pervenere* (Venice: Vincentius Valgrisius, 1564). An English translation from the Arabic is Mazhar Shah, *The General Principles of*

Avicenna's Canon of Medicine (Karachi, 1966). See, too, Aldobrandino, *Régime*, p. 71.

17. Conches, *Phil* 4.14 (*PL* 172:89 or 90:1171); idem, *Drag*, ed. Guatarolus, p. 243.

18. *Die Quaestiones naturales des Adelardus von Bath*, ed. Martin Müller, *Beiträge zur Geschichte der Philosophie und Theologie des Mittelalters*, Bd. 31, Heft 2 (Münster, 1934), pp. 41–42.

19. Vincent, *Speculum naturale*, 31.34 (col. 2318), hereafter: *SN*.

20. L.A. Dean-Jones, *Women's Bodies in Classical Greek Science* (London, 1994), pp. 125–26; A. Hanson, "The Medical Writers' Woman," in *Before Sexuality,* eds. D. Halperin, J. Winkler, and F. Zeitlin (Princeton, 1990), pp. 309–37.

21. Of recent studies, J. Delaney, M.J. Lupton, and E. Toth, *The Curse: A Cultural History of Menstruation* (New York, 1977), pp. 33–42; for medieval views, Charles Wood, "The Doctor's Dilemma: Sin, Salvation, and the Menstrual Cycle in Medieval Thought," *Speculum* 56.4 (1981), 710–27. For early modern ideas, Ottavia Niccoli, "'Menstruum Quasi Monstruum': Monstrous Births and Menstrual Taboo in the Sixteenth Century," in *Sex and Gender in Historical Perspective,* eds. E. Muir and G. Ruggiero (Baltimore and London, 1990), pp. 1–25. Compare Clarissa Atkinson, *The Oldest Vocation: Christian Motherhood in the Middle Ages* (Ithaca, NY, 1991), pp. 39–46. For Helen Lemay's *Women's Secrets: A Translation of Pseudo-Albertus Magnus' De secretis mulierum with Commentaries* (Albany, NY, 1992), see note 39.

22. Conches, *Phil* 4.8–12. William allied himself with the two-seed theory more clearly in his later work (*Drag*, ed. Guatarolus, pp. 239–240).

23. Conches, *Phil* 4.15 (*PL* 172:90). See Joan Cadden, *Meanings of Sex Difference in the Middle Ages* (Cambridge, 1993), pp. 170–73, and G.M. Nardi, *Problemi d'embriologia umana antica e medioevale* (Florence, 1938), pp. 105–12.

24. On transmission of the Aristotelian physiological works, A. Birkenmajer, "Le rôle joué par les médecins et les naturalistes dans la réception d'Aristote au XIIe et XIIIe siècles," *Studia Copernicana I: Etudes d'histoire des sçiences et de la philosophie au moyen-âge* (Warsaw, 1970), pp. 73–88, and Sibyl Wingate, *The Mediaeval Latin Versions of the Aristotelian Scientific Corpus, with Special Reference to the Biological Works* (London, 1931).

25. *Davidis de Dinanto Quaternulorum fragmenta*, ed. M. Kurdzialek in *Studia Mediewistyczne* (Warsaw, 1963), p. 24; Enzo Maccagnolo, "David of Dinant and the Beginnings of Aristotelianism in Paris," in *A History of Twelfth-Century Western Philosophy*, ed. P. Dronke (Cambridge, 1988), pp. 428–42.

26. Dinant, *Quaternulorum fragmenta*, ed. Kurdzialek, p. 23.

27. Lawn, *Prose* B294, p. 140; the response here is very clear.

28. Lawn, *Prose*, B35, p. 19 and P80, pp. 236–37. For the phenomenon beyond the medieval period, Marie-Hélène Huet, *Monstrous Imagination* (Cambridge, MA, 1993).

29. Conches, *Phil* 4.16 (*PL* 172:90), and *Drag*, ed. Guatarolus, p. 147; the *Prose Salernitan Questions* repeated this phrasing, ed. Lawn, B25, p. 15.

30. Bart 5.47, ed. Barthold, p. 103, from Constantinus Africanus, *Pantegni* 1.3, in *Opera* (Henricus Petrus, Basel 1536–39) 2:72. On Constantinus and the Salernitan school, Paul Kristeller, "The School of Salerno: Its Development and Its Contribution to the History of Learning," in *Storia e letteratura: Raccolta di studi e testi*, 54: *Studies in Renaissance Thought and Letters* (Rome, 1956).

31. Conches, *Phil* 4.15 (*PL* 172:90B).

32. Bart 4.8, ed. Bartholdus, p. 105.

33. Isidore, *Etymologiae*, 11.1.141. My translation is based on William Sharpe, *Isidore of Seville: The Medical Writings*, in *Transactions of the American Philosophical Society*, n.s. 54.2 (1964); cf. Bart, 4.8. On Isidore's sources, *C. Iulii Solini collectanea rerum memorabilium*, ed. T. Mommsen (Berlin, 1864), p. 17. Pliny was more expansive on menstrual blood's detrimental effects: *C. Plini Secundi Naturalis historiae*, ed. C. Mayhoff (Stuttgart, 1967), 7.15.64–65 (vol. 2:22–23); one theme in his list, menstruating women's power to darken mirrors, appeared in Aristotle's *On Dreams*, 459b–460a. The mirror motif appears in the section on human generation in Arnoldus Saxo's early thirteenth-century encyclopedia; Emil Stange, *Arnoldus Saxo, der älteste Encyklopädist des dreizehnten Jahrhunderts* (Halle a.S., 1885), pp. 50–51.

34. Isidore, 11.1.139 and 142. The second reference declared that pathology (in this case, the inability to conceive) would occur *without* the menses.

35. The only reference I have found of medical writing linking menstruation and original sin is Hildegard of Bingen, *Causae et Curae*, ed. P. Kaiser (Leipzig, 1903), p. 102, paralleling Eve's actions in the Garden and menstrual cycles; Eve's temptation, "the flow of cupidity," directly caused women's menstrual flow, "a river of blood." Michael Scot in the early thirteenth century referred in *De secretis naturae* to original sin without remarking menstrual blood *per se*; see part 1, ch. 8 (*Forma foetus generati in matrice*) in *Alberti Magni De secretis mulierum libellus* (Strasbourg: Lazarus Zetznerus, 1601), p. 271. The influential (though non-medical) *De miseria humane conditionis* by Lothar dei Segni (later Innocent III), saw a link between Pliny's physical danger and Levitical uncleanness (*Lotharii cardinalis De miseria humane conditionis*, bk. 1, chap. 4, ed. Michele Maccarrone [Lugano, 1955], pp. 11–12). His combination of "unclean" children and mad dogs connects the traditions, but medical literature does not.

36. Lev. 15.19–33 dealt with the physical acquisition (through touch, sexual intercourse, etc.) of spiritual *immunditia*. The *Glossa ordinaria* did not elaborate on physical aspects of this uncleanness, but explicated menstruation as indicative of human sinfulness or as comparable to other types of physical illness Christ could cure; see the gloss on Lev. 15.21; for theological dimensions of menstruation, Wood, "Doctor's Dilemma."

37. Thomas of Cantimpré, *De natura rerum*, 1.73, ed. Boese, p. 74; Ferckel, *Die Gynäkologie des Thomas von Brabant*, p. 28; Vincent, *SN* 31.51 (col. 2330). Thomas solves the dilemma of the menses' destructive and nurturing properties by describing the fetus's nourishment as *purissime digesto*, while Leviticus saw the menses as by definition impure.

38. Soranus, *Gynecology* (1,58) suggests a threat from the womb's liquids, the remaining urine excreted by the embryo. The sack closest to the fetus (the amnion) protected the fetus from the "pungent and destructive" urine, described as excess material. See Soranus, *Gynecology*, ed. Rose, p. 226, and *Soranus' Gynecology*, trans. O. Temkin (Baltimore, 1956), p. 60. Soranus expressed scepticism over the amnion's existence, though no Latin version included this detail; for Mustio, see Rose, p. 19: ("*55. Quid est amnion?*"); for Caelius Aurelianus, see *Gynaecia*, ed. Drabkin, p. 33. The translation known as *Liber geneciae ad soteris obsetrix* [sic], ed. Rose, p. 134, only hinted at mortal danger to the child; the translator did not discuss the urine.

39. Lemay, *Women's Secrets*, intr. pp. 35, 37, notes thirteenth-century "condemnation of" the menses (pp. 35, 37). I argue not for condemnation but for suspicion and suggest that increased elaboration on menstrual blood stemmed from ideas present before the New Aristotle appeared. I do not see William of Conches' writings as "dispassionate" but interpret his statements as an extension of Isidore's views on menstrual blood's dangerous effects (combined with Aristotelian ideas on women's inherent imperfection), moving from the nonhuman to the human. I concur that there was a thirteenth-century heightening of interest in women's bodily fluids.

40. Many medical sections of the *Speculum naturale* appear in abbreviated form in the *Speculum doctrinale*. On Vincent's organization, Michel Lemoine, "L'oeuvre encyclopédique de Vincent de Beauvais," *Cahiers d'histoire mondiale*, 9.iii (1966), 571–79.

41. Vincent, *Speculum Doctrinale*, 12.25 (col. 1088), hereafter: *SD*. See Claude Thomasset, "Quelques principes de l'embryologie médiévale (de Salerne à la fin du XIIIe siècle)" in *L'Enfant au moyen–âge*. Senefiance 9 (Aix-en-Provence/Paris, 1980), pp. 107–21.

42. Vincent, *SN* 31.116 (col. 2385) from Rhazes, *Ad Almansorem* 4,27; see *In hoc volumine continentur Liber Rasis ad almansorem…* (Argentorati: George Ulricher, n.d.), f. 20vb; Avicenna, *Canon* bk. 3, fen 21, tract. 2, ch. 2; and Haly Abbas, *Liber totius medicine necessaria… regalis dispositionis nomen assumpsit* (Lyon: Jacobus Myt, 1523), Practica, 1.19 (ff. 151ra– va). On

Arab sources see John Riddle, *Contraception and Abortion from the Ancient World to the Renaissance* (Cambridge, MA, 1992), pp. 118–34.

43. Vincent, *SN,* 31.116 (col. 2385); Haly Abbas, *Regalis dispositionis,* Practica 1, chap. 19 (fol. 151ra).

44. In this period there was particular concern over midwives' ignorance of obstetrics and, of more importance to thirteenth-century writers, of baptism should the newborn be in danger. Thomas of Cantimpré demanded that midwives be trained by priests to perform the rite; *De natura rerum* 1.74 (*De virtute nascitiva*), ed. Boese, pp. 75, 76; Ferckel, *Gynäkologie des Thomas von Brabant,* pp. 29, 32.

45. I do not imply that the writers considered here viewed all women's milk as necessarily harmful. There is a considerable literature on milk's image as healthful and important. Caroline Bynum refers to the importance of milk imagery in high medieval culture, with little indication of pathological possibilities; see *Jesus as Mother* (Berkeley and Los Angeles, 1982) and *Holy Feast and Holy Fast* (Berkeley and Los Angeles, 1987). Most literary sources discuss positive aspects of milk as nourishment; Ferdinand Fellinger, *Das Kind in der altfranzösischen Literatur* (Göttingen, 1906), pp.104–12 and D. Berkvam, *Enfance et maternité dans la littérature française des XIIe et XIIIe siècles* (Paris, 1981), pp. 50–54. Shulamith Shahar, *Childhood in the Middle Ages* (London, 1990), pp. 53–70, discusses medieval breastfeeding but includes little medical material. Compare Atkinson, *Oldest Profession,* pp. 58–61.

46. Dinant, *Quaternulorum fragmenta,* ed. Kurdzialek, pp. 13, 32.

47. Mustio, ch. 88, ed. Rose, p. 31. Mustio did not note that milk's corrupting power originated in menstrual blood. For Vincent, Avicenna, *Canon,* 1.3.2, and Vincent, *SN,* 31.78 (col. 2336).

48. Bart. 4.8, ed. Barthold, p. 106.

49. Bart. 5.34, ed. Barthold, p. 179, quoting Constantinus, *Pantegni, Loci medici* 3, chap. 34: *De mammillis* (ii, 77).

50. Bart. 5.34, ed. Barthold, p. 180. This passage does not easily match any Aristotelian passage, and is most likely Bartholomaeus' abbreviation.

51. Constantinus, *Pantegni, Loci medici* 3, ch. 34, ii, 77, and Vincent, *SN* 28.83 (col. 2050).

52. Shahar's *Childhood,* pp. 55–76, gives few references to twelfth- and early thirteenth-century practice. Despite their prevalence in vernacular literature, there are few nonliterary examples of the practice in this period. One famous case involved Hodierna, her biological son Alexander (likely Alexander Neckam), and her nursling, the future Richard I of England (b. 1157); even after Richard's death, English sources mention Hodierna's yearly pension (R.W. Hunt, *The Schools and the Cloister: The Life and Writings of Alexander Nequam (1157–1217)* [Oxford, 1984], pp. 1–2). Nobles generally employed lower-class wet-nurses, though as Shahar adds, nurses must have had their own unweaned child(ren) nursed by others.

53. Aldobrandino, ed. Landouzy and Pépin, p. 76. Note the stress on visual inspection.

54. The texts provide few clues as to who the judge might have been; the doctor was the likely choice but possibly also the parent(s). We have little indication of the extent to which any of these texts was used in reality. Save for Aldobrandino's *Regime du corps*, which he claimed was written for the countess of Provence, we know little about their production and use.

55. That a son implied better health for the mother than a female referred to the Hippocratic Aphorisms (5.38); see Constantinus Africanus' translation, and the *Articella* (Pavia: Bartholomeus de Morandus, 1506), 5.42.

56. Aldobrandino, *Régime,* ed. Landouzy and Pépin, p. 76.

57. The enlarging belly could be a sign of fetal health, but few attributes of the gravid woman indicated the fetus' vitality unless one included "nonevents," such as the lack of menstrual flow or of milk at the breasts.

58. *De curis* has no modern edition. My readings are from two MSS in the Yale Medical Historical Library, Medieval Medical MSS 4 (N. Italy, XIV), fols. 151v–153v, and 28 (Paneth Codex, Bologna, ca. 1300), fols. 332v–336v; and the early printing reproduced in Karl Sudhoff's *Erstlinge der pädiatrischen Literatur* (Munich, 1925), Tafeln 2–7. See translations in V.T. Passalacqua, "La 'Practica Puerorum' di Rhazes," *Pagine di storia della medicina*, 3 (1959), 26–53 and Samuel Radbill, "The First Treatise on Pediatrics," *American Journal of Diseases of Children*, 122.5 (November 1971), 369–76.

59. There is no Arabic version of this text, though sections of Rhazes' *Liber ad Almansorem*, Haly Abbas' *Practica* and Avicenna's *Canon* contain similar (not identical) material. The text is certainly of Arabic origin, as its incipit (*Sahafati accidit*) and many non-Latin words suggest.

60. Karl Sudhoff, "Die Schrift des Cornelius Roelans von Mecheln über Kinderkrankheiten und eine ihrer handschriftlichen Quellen," *Janus*, 14 (1909), 467–85, at 476.

61. Glass: Haly Abbas, *Practica* 1.21: *De electione nutricum*, in Vincent, *SN* 31.79 (col. 2337). Rock or sword: *Passiones puerorum*, p. 476. Fingernail: Rhazes in Vincent, *SN* 31.78 (col. 2336).

62. Sudhoff, "Nochmals Dr. Cornelis Roelants von Mecheln," *Janus*, 20 (1915), 443–58, and John Ruhrah, *Pediatrics of the Past* (New York, 1925), pp. 22–23.

63. Avicenna, *Canon* bk. 1, fen 3, doctrine 1.2, also in Vincent, *SN* 31.78 (col. 2336).

64. Haly Abbas, *Practica*, 1.21 (f. 153ra), quoted in Vincent, *SN* 31.79 (col. 2337). Rhazes included a similar list in *Liber ad Almansorem*, tract. 4, ch. 30 (f. 21rb).

65. Aldobrandino, *Régime*, ed. Landouzy and Pépin, p. 77.

66. Aldobrandino, ed. Landouzy and Pépin, pp. 76–77, stated that the nurse's *coustumes* (apparently her emotional state or habits) could adversely affect the child. There is no clear indication that such emotional states affected a child via the milk; the nourishment generally brought physical corruption, not moral.

67. In this regard, my thesis echoes the twelfth-century ambivalence toward women found by Penny Schine Gold, *The Lady and the Virgin: Image, Attitude and Experience in Twelfth-Century France* (Chicago, 1985), esp. ch. 1.

THE MILK OF CHRIST:

HERZELOYDË AS SPIRITUAL SYMBOL IN WOLFRAM VON ESCHENBACH'S *Parzival*

Patricia Ann Quattrin

In Wolfram von Eschenbach's Parzival, Herzeloydë *prepares her son,* Parzival, *for his life's work, the search for the Grail. Her effect on his understanding of the two sides of his existence—knighthood and the Grail—produces her importance in the poem.*

In the Middle High German Romance *Parzival* by Wolfram Von Eschenbach, the practical interest of Lady Herzeloydë in the welfare and training of her young son, progeny of the dead knight-errant Gahmuret, takes a different turn from what we might expect of the typical medieval mother who prepares her son to contribute to the family economy, protect her dower property, and advance family interests. Then again, Lady Herzeloydë is unlike any other queen or courtly lady in medieval romance. Although she appears only in Book II and briefly in Book III, her influence on her son throughout the remainder of the narrative is not only that of a natural mother but also a spiritual mother.

In the few short lines that Wolfram gives her, Herzeloydë appears in three distinct roles: queen of Waleis and Norgals, wife of Gahmuret, and mother of Parzival.[1] Before her marriage to Gahmuret, Herzeloydë assumes control over events in her life and takes the initiative in her relationship with Gahmuret. Having lost her betrothed while yet a virgin, she arranges a tournament after which she will give herself and her inheritance, Waleis and Norgals, to the knight who prevails in the contests. Herzeloydë is immediately smitten when Gahmuret rides into Kanvoleis to participate in the tourney—for the *aventure*, not to win a bride, for he is already married to the heathen queen Belecane. After Gahmuret defeats the

other knights, Herzeloydë goes to his tent and convinces him of the
morality and the legality, according to Christian law, of his becoming
her husband:

> The Mooress you should be leaving
> And to my love be cleaving.
> In the Christian cross more power lies.
> Now rid yourself of heathen ties
> And love me as good Christians do,
> For I am sick for love of you.[2]

That Herzeloydë is a baptized Christian and Belacane is not imbues
Gahmuret's potential marriage to the former with a religious and
spiritual significance that lies at the heart of Wolfram's poem.[3]

Herzeloydë succeeds in her desires: this courtly lady, who we later
learn holds a special place in the Grail family, is united in matrimony
to the chivalric knight, who combines *minne* and *strit* with such
unsurpassed prowess that his fame outlives his death. She must only
agree to allow Gahmuret the right to participate in tournaments.
He explains his position:

> If jousting be to me refused,
> I still can play the trick I used
> What time I fled and left my wife:
> Her too I'd won in chivalrous strife.
> When joust and tournament she banned
> I let her have both folk and land. (96.29–97.4)

Despite the lack of marital commitment that Gahmuret's statement
suggests, Herzeloydë accedes to his conditions as a small price for
the joy and happiness she now enjoys as his wife and queen. Wealth
and virtue are hers; as queen of Waleis, Norgals, and Gahmuret's
lands of Anjou, she has won the world's admiration and favor. Love,
says Wolfram, makes her like the sunlight, for she attained the aim
of all her desires.[4]

Unfortunately, however, as the narrator repeatedly points out to
the reader, such worldly joy soon turns to sorrow: "*Alsu ver diu
mennischeit.*"[5] Forewarned by what Wolfram describes as a dream
so terrifying that it brought her anguish seldom if ever felt by a
woman in her sleep (104.1–30), Herzeloydë learns of her husband's
death and collapses into unconsciousness. Her insensate state can
be seen not only as a physical reaction to Gahmuret's death but also
as the symbolic death of the courtly lady who had been a worldly

wife and queen.[6] Subject to the fatal consequences of human nature, which in Herzeloydë's case turned her love for Gahmuret into a preoccupation with the secular aspects of courtly life, she now dies to that nature that chose the world over God.

Upon regaining consciousness, however, Herzeloydë experiences a rebirth into a new role, the role of motherhood, a role also pregnant with symbolic meaning. She at once recognizes herself as that container of nourishment that provides life:

> The little breasts, soft and white,
> Now engaged her care and sight
> And to her crimson lips were pressed:
> Her womanhood was manifest.
> Then said this woman wise and good,
> "Thou dost contain an infant's food:
> The child has sent it on ahead
> Since its life in me was heralded."
> For thus she saw her wish come true,
> That o'er her heart its food now grew.
> The lady with her fingers pressed
> The infant's milk out of her breast.
> Said she, "Thou'rt born of loyalty.
> Had they not once baptized me,
> I'd take thee for my christening." (110.25–111.9)

As her milk flows forth, she reflects on its association with the waters of baptism and her own entrance into the Christian life. Fourteen days later, at the birth of her son, she identifies herself with a spiritual purpose beyond that of human mother and child:

> Directly the queen took those small
> brownish-pink buds of hers—
> I mean the tips of her little breasts—
> and pressed them to his tiny mouth,
> she who had born him in her womb
> was also his nurse.
> She who fled from all womanly misconduct
> clasped him to her bosom.
> ....
> Wisely Lady Herzeloydë said,
> "The supreme Queen gave her breasts to Jesus,
> Who afterwards for our sake met
> bitter death in human form upon the Cross
> and Who kept faith with us."[7]

Herzeloydë nourishes her child with milk from her own breasts and identifies that milk first with the living waters of baptism and then with the spiritual nourishment that is Christ. What is the significance of these associations? What meaning do they have for Herzeloydë, for her son Parzival, and for the poem as a whole?

The Christian Church has long metaphorically associated milk, coming from the breast and nourishing the child, with the food of Christ, and the mother who furnishes that milk with the maternal care of God.[8] Examples of the metaphor are found in the Old and New Testaments and in the writings of the early Church fathers.[9] In an article that explores St. Augustine's use of this metaphor, Marsha Dutton points out:

> In the *Confessiones*, … Augustine utilizes the now-familiar metaphor to enunciate a doctrine of the role of the Incarnation in humankind's spiritual growth. He declares that Jesus is the milk for the spiritually immature, nourishing and sustaining them in their infancy, preparing them for an adult knowledge of God, and bringing them through himself to that maturity, where they can eat at last of solid food.[10]

For Augustine, maternal action "both demands that the infant soul come to maturity in the faith and brings it there." As Dutton explains these words of Augustine:

> The preparation for maturity is accomplished, says Augustine, through the soul's slow drinking "of the milk of Christ" [XIII.xviii.23], sustained by the language of Scripture "as a mother cradles an infant in her bosom" [XII.xxvii.37]… . But once spiritual infancy is completed, the soul must be weaned in order to be brought finally and completely to God.[11]

Continuing the metaphor, Augustine identifies four spiritual stages through which each human being must proceed: *primordia* to *infantia*, *pueritia*, *adulescentia*, and *iuventus*.[12] In the *Confessiones*, he uses his own experience of growing up as a paradigm for the transition that must take place in all Christians as they move from spiritual infancy to spiritual adulthood, as they journey from hearing about God to truly knowing Him in their heart.[13]

When Herzeloydë regains her senses and her life, she makes the associations noted earlier between her milk, the living waters of baptism, and the spiritual nourishment that is Christ, associations a Christian audience would have understood. Her statements seem to suggest that she as well as her son must begin at the stage that

Augustine calls spiritual infancy. In her spiritual rebirth and through her spiritual guidance, she images the milk of Christ which will bring her and her young son, the progeny of courtly life at its best and worst, from an overdependence on the world of the flesh to an understanding of the spiritual life to which both have been ordained, as we learn later from Trevrizent. Forsaking all contact with courtly life and the wealth associated with it, Herzeloydë moves with her new son to live in the pure and simple wilderness forest of Soltane. Identifying Herzeloydë as a woman who lives out her faith in a life of poverty, Wolfram praises the life she chooses, saying that poverty endured for the sake of faith will bring the soul to God (116.5–117.6). Through this humble life of penance, Herzeloydë attempts to influence her son's spiritual growth. In so doing, she follows the pattern of life stages that Augustine describes in his spiritual autobiography. At the same time, she provides a paradigm for her son to follow; thus, like Augustine in the *Confessiones*, Herzeloydë is both living pattern and patternmaker.

Having acknowledged her necessary role as provider of spiritual as well as literal milk for her newborn son, Herzeloydë attempts to protect him from worldly contamination. She moves from Augustine's *primordia* to *infantia*: with love and skill she rears Parzival in isolation, warning all the servants never to speak of knights or knighthood:

> "If my dear child were ever told
> Of knights and knightly station,
> Twould be my ruination.
> I bid you now, be keen and shrewd
> And tell him naught of knightlihood."
> With care they did as bidden,
> Such things from him were hidden.
> In bleak Soltane reared, he heard
> Of Royal pomp no single word. (117.24–118.2)

As these lines indicate, Parzival, whose destiny it is to be Grail King, begins his life nourished by his mother's milk and protected from the secular world that Herzeloydë now believes kills, both physically and spiritually. In this stage of spiritual infancy, Parzival's identity is dependent upon and identical with that of his only universe, his mother Herzeloydë. What she perceives to be his food from God is the milk he will receive. While his spiritual nature at this stage is outside himself and incomplete, he is satisfied, for the healthy infant requires and desires no more than the healthy mother has to provide. Augustine says of this period in his own life, "The comfort of human milk nourished me,...By an orderly affection they willingly gave me what they possessed so abundantly from you."[14]

When Parzival moves into boyhood, Augustine's *pueritia*, he develops the power of speech and engages in rational self-conscious activity.[15] Tendencies innate in him from both father and mother burst forth with little or no prompting. He is skilled with bow and arrow and teaches himself to hurl the javelin: "Many a stag he thus destroyed,/ Which queen and servants much enjoyed" (120.3–4). When he hears the birds' song, his heart swells. In courtly love lyrics, the image of singing birds represents the secular love associated with court life; thus Parzival's childhood, though through his mother's tutelage not typical of a courtly knight, reveals his innate courtly heritage from his father, those interests and skills that will qualify him for the court of Arthur. He cannot be diverted from this secular legacy. At the same time, Herzeloydë teaches him about God. While watching his heart stir at the birds' song and knowing what that signifies, Herzeloydë wishes to destroy their song. She realizes, however, that killing them will not destroy Parzival's awakened, indistinct yearnings that are as yet neither *caritas* nor *cupiditas*. Instead, she attempts to direct those longings away from the carnal world toward the spiritual:

> "What right to thwart [God's] will have I,
> Since He's the mighty God on high?
> Should birds for my sake give up joy?"
> Then said to her the little boy,
> "O Mother, what is God, I pray?"
> "My son, I'll tell thee straightaway.
> The sun itself is not so bright
> As He, who forfeited His might
> To take the shape of humankind.
> Son, this teaching bear in mind:
> Pray to God in need and dearth:
> His love helps all who dwell on earth." (119.13–24)

In this way, Herzeloydë taught her son the "difference twixt light and dark" (119.30). Parzival's questions about the birds and about God suggest that he has entered the second stage of the spiritual journey, whereby one begins to know oneself and God through speech, drawing on intelligence and memory. He questions his mother, beginning to experience a separation from, if not an opposition to, that which previously had been his identity. Augustine describes this stage in his own maturation:

> We discovered, Lord, that certain people prayed to you
> and we learned from them, and imagined you, as far as
> we could, as some sort of mighty one who could hear us
> and help us, even though not appearing before our
> senses...and in praying to you I broke the knots that
> tied my tongue. (*Conf.* I.viii.13, I.ix.14)

As the authority in Parzival's life, Herzeloydë uses human language fitting to his childish state to point him away from the secular world of the court toward the only love that is everlasting, the love of God, that light that brings help and refuge. The young boy is only at the beginning of his moral development, however, and interprets everything on the level of the senses. He remains bound by the immediate and the particular. Like Augustine, Parzival is unable to fix his gaze on invisible things (*Conf.* I.xx.31). Thus, when Parzival meets the knights from King Arthur's court, he mistakes each for a god, responding in awe to their courtly splendor the way his mother may once have done. He identifies the secular world as that which merits adoration and love:

> Three knights approach, a handsome sight,
> From head to foot in armor dight.
> The lad conceived the notion odd
> That each of them must be a god.
> No longer then he stood at ease:
> In the path he fell upon his knees
> And loud he cried upon the Lord:
> "Help God! Thou canst help afford." (120.25–121.2)

Parzival identifies such beauty and brightness with that which, in his immature state, is yet inconceivable. The knights fit Herzeloydë's description of God. As David Yeandle points out, her religious instruction to her son contains three basic tenets about God's being: "God is brighter than the day (119,19); He took human form upon Him (119,20f); His *triuwe* ("loving faithfulness") has always offered assistance to mankind (119,24f)."[16] Parzival, in his simplicity and spiritual innocence, deduces that these resplendent worldly knights are the spiritual life about which his mother has taught him.

When later Parzival declares to his mother that the life of knighthood and the Arthurian Court is what he wants, he enters the spiritual stage Augustine calls *adulescentia*. Herzeloydë had spent her reborn life sheltering Parzival from the ways of the world. Much as she tries to resist reality, her son now will leave his mother and journey alone. She tries to nourish him one last time with the only milk she now has for him, words of guidance. Like Augustine at this stage of his spiritual life, Parzival's moral guidance comes from his mother's words and tears (*Conf.* II.iii.7). In terms of the narrative, Herzeloydë's instruction can be seen simply as generating the narrative action of the poem, but on another level, her instruction prepares Parzival for the world. She offers him counsel and advice about the three arenas of life that every human being must acknowledge and balance. She instructs him on his spiritual, emotional, and physical life, in the order in which she believes they are important to his well-being.

First, Herzeloydë admonishes Parzival to listen to the advice of an older and wiser man.

> And when a man who's wise and gray
> Would teach decorum, as he may,
> Show zeal in him obeying,
> Rude anger not displaying. (127.21–24)

Perhaps she has in mind her brother Trevrizent, the man who will teach Parzival how to take his place as the Grail King. Or she may mean any holy man who teaches about God; the forests of courtly romance are filled with such hermits. Her words, though simple, stress the importance of obeying those teachings that are given through wisdom and obeying them with enthusiasm, for such words may point him toward the way of life that is his destiny. Through listening and obeying such teachings, Parzival may come to understand his spiritual purpose.

Knowing from her own experience the temptations of courtly life and especially of the love that can overshadow God, Herzeloydë next cautions Parzival about loving too much a woman who will turn him from his "transcendental obligations,"[17] as she herself may have done. She tells him to look for a good and chaste woman. Only such a woman's "ring" will bring him contentment.[18]

> If thou a goodly woman's ring
> Canst win from her with her consent,

> Take it: that's cure for discontent.
> To give her kisses make all haste,
> Her body tightly be embraced:
> That gives thee joy and gladsome mood,
> Provided she is chaste and good. (127.26–128.2)

Such a "goodly woman" will be not only his joy but also his call to transcendence. For Wolfram, it seems, such a love is synonymous with marriage and is profoundly good and meaningful in itself.

Finally, Herzeloydë tells Parzival about the lands which were once hers but have been taken by "proud and haughty Laeheline," who killed or took captive the people of the land (128.3–12). These lands, as Trevrizent explains to Parzival later, were destined to be ruled by the Grail family. The lands are Parzival's inheritance from his mother, and he vows to win them back for the Grail family.

Because Parzival is at the beginning of his moral development and has no experience to draw upon, he misinterprets the ethical meaning behind Herzeloydë's simple words of guidance. His value system is limited and his understanding is rooted in sensuality; therefore, he retains only tangible ideas. Herzeloydë's instructions are given to him on his level, that is on the level of the senses; however, the ideal state of understanding toward which she aims, Augustine's *iuventus*, is not a sensual state but a spiritual one. It is the stage of spiritual adulthood, that stage in which the soul knows God intuitively, without any intermediary, without the mother's milk. This last stage, however, the soul must travel alone. Thus Parzival has reached that point in his spiritual maturity where, equipped with the moral and spiritual teaching provided by and through his mother, he must move toward understanding God for himself; he must come to "know" God experientially, on his own terms, in his own heart.

Though often confused about his purpose, as Parzival meets the knights and ladies of Arthur's court and the family who serve the Grail, he reinterprets and ingests as adult food the instruction provided by his mother. He had not previously understood its significance but now experiences her words as speaking to his own spiritual needs and to his needs as the future Grail King. Linda Parshall argues, I believe, rightly:

> The Gral is the binding motif throughout Parzival's story. Though
> not overtly expressed in the first two books of the poem, it is
> symbolically present in Herzeloydë's genetic bequest to her son.

Parzival has inherited ties to two worlds. His mother joins him to the Gral kinship and his father to the courtly world of chivalric prowess. Herzeloydë and Gahmuret thus represent the two realms in which Parzival slowly matures and which finally commingle in him.[19]

But Parshall's statements that Parzival's quest for the Grail is "a continuation of the search for his mother" and that his relief of Anfortas' suffering "can be seen symbolically as atonement for having caused his mother's sorrowful death,"[20] seem to miss the mark. Wolfram's text makes it clear that Parzival outgrows his physical need for his mother, as he mentally and emotionally matures through his adventures and experiences. When the narrative is read on the symbolic level that I have been suggesting, he also outgrows, as did Augustine, his spiritual need for his mother. Although Herzeloydë's influence and guidance are not expendable, for neither is Christ as example and teacher expendable, for Parzival to continue in search of her would be to regress to infancy rather than progress toward spiritual adulthood. The adult Christian leaves his or her dependence on Christ as mediator to experience the Word of God as equal with God.

Parzival's quest for the Grail symbolizes his search for spiritual perfection. Although it could be argued, as the narrator strongly suggests, that Herzeloydë reaches spiritual perfection for herself by the time Parzival leaves her, her perfection cannot be his. Herzeloydë operates on one level in this poem as that spiritual milk that the spiritually uninitiated need at the first three stages of spiritual life. Although Parzival will feel the influence of his mother for the rest of his life, that spiritual perfection for which he now searches will be found in another symbol, one identified with God the Father—the Grail.

Spiritually, Herzeloydë's death has a purpose, the end of Parzival's childish spiritual state. When her son chooses to leave her for "knightly doing," however, the mother invents a stratagem to keep him with her. She dresses Parzival in "fool's attire" and provides him with an unchivalric nag so that if others "pound and pummel him/ He may come back to me again" (126.11–29).[21] Then, when he mounts his nag to leave, "She kissed him and after him she ran."

> This faithful loving woman fell
> To earth, where grief, a savage knife,
> So cut her that it took her life. (128.16, 20–22)

Like Augustine's mother Monica, Herzeloydë acts according to the pattern for spiritual motherhood by cooperating with God's plan and yet on the physical level failing to understand the full consequences of that cooperation (*Conf.* V.vii.15).[22] Since Herzeloydë's understanding of God's plan for Parzival is limited, God appears to act against what she desires, which is to keep her son with her. On the symbolic level, however, Parzival's leaving and Herzeloydë's death must take place, for Parzival has reached that spiritual stage at which he can no longer rely upon his mother's nourishment. His soul must be weaned in order to come to spiritual maturity. His journey, a literal following after his earthly father Gahmuret, can also be seen as a spiritual movement away from his mother Herzeloydë, who symbolizes his spiritual birth and nourishment, and toward a deeper relationship and fidelity with God the Father, as found in the paternal symbol of the Grail. As Christ cast off in death the mortal flesh received in His mother's womb in order to become one with His Father, so the maternal aspect of Parzival's spiritual life must die in order for him to come to a true relationship with God the Father.[23] The journey will now consist of learning how to ingest and digest as an adult the spiritual food of God, how to commingle within himself the *aventure* of Arthurian knighthood with the spiritual perfection expected of the Grail King.

Even though Herzeloydë appears only briefly in the narrative, the thematic resonances of her presence are felt throughout the poem. Her character and influence as giver of life and nurturer pervade the work as Christ pervades the life of every maturing Christian. The literal as well as the symbolic influence of this woman on her son allows his quest to take on a spiritual dimension. Although the author intrudes upon the narrative at this point to take issue both with the traditional values of courtly love and with the wiles and duplicity of the women of his own time, his depiction of Herzeloydë and his narrative commentary in these sections draw her as a distinct contrast. She is a strongly developed character, very much an individual, not a type. At the same time, she can be seen as a significant symbol for her son's spiritual life. Her internal strength and character as well as her image as a spiritual mother are presented as the ideal over and against what Wolfram seems to perceive as the real. Parzival leaves his mother to live out the statement made in the opening lines of Book I, that this is a tale of a hero who is *ar kuene traecliche wis*—a brave man slowly wise. With her death begins his ascent into true malehood and spiritual perfection:

> Each woman true, each faithful wife,
> Should bless this stripling bold and fair
> Who now forsakes his mother's care. (129.2–4)

NOTES

1. In this three-stage division I agree with David Blamires, *Characterization and Individuality in Wolfram's* Parzival (Cambridge, MA, 1966), p. 67, rather than David Yeandle, "Herzeloydë: Problems of Characterization in Book III of Wolfram's *Parzival*," *Euphorion* 75 (1981), 1–28, who identifies these stages as: queen of Waleis up to her marriage, wife of Gahmuret and mother of a new baby, and (after withdrawal to Soltane) mother of the young Parzival. As I will show, Herzeloydë's role as mother is the crucial one for the development and meaning of the theme of the work as a whole. Apparent inconsistencies between the three roles remain one of the problems with which critical readers of Wolfram's work must contend; a possible solution, as I suggest here, is to read the character of Herzeloydë on more than one level.

2. *The Parzival of Wolfram Von Eschenbach*, trans. Edwin H. Zeydel and Bayard Quincy Morgan, University of North Carolina Studies in the Germanic Languages and Literatures 5 (Chapel Hill, 1951), 94:11–16. Unless otherwise indicated, all quotations are from this translation, whose spelling I maintain.

3. Blamires argues that the relationship between Herzeloydë and Gahmuret does not follow the expected code of courtly love as found in most medieval romances, where unrequited love and service by the knight to the lady prevails. Wolfram reverses the roles, resulting in a relationship whereby the woman takes the initiative, love is consummated in marriage, and the lovers participate in mutual service one to the other (Blamires, *Characterization and Individuality*, pp. 82, 85).

4. In describing Herzeloydë's relationship with Gahmuret, the narrator emphasizes her abundant love for her husband and her successful life as his queen. Later in the text, we learn of her kinship to the Grail family, knights and ladies of the highest quality, chosen by God for a special purpose, who enjoy a favored relationship with Him. Blamires maintains that "the Grail had no significance whatsoever in Herzeloydë's life" (*Characterization and Individuality*, p. 67); Sidney Johnson, however, argues convincingly that Herzeloydë's relationship to the Grail does affect her and may determine her decision after her son's birth to forsake courtly life: "Wolfram actually tells us very little about Herzeloydë's married life, but…

[w]e gain the impression that she is an able, popular, wealthy, virtuous ruler in the eyes of the world. It seems possible that her success in the world and her love for Gahmuret could produce a situation in which she might well have forgotten her higher obligations to God. When she forsakes the world to raise her son in the forest, she does so as if in penance, suffering poverty and the loss of all the joys of the world willingly" (Johnson, "Herzeloydë and the Grail," *Neophilologus* 52 (1968), 148–55).

5. "Such is the way of the world." *Wolfram von Eschenbach*, ed. Karl Lachmann, rev. ed. Eduard Hartl, vol. 1: *Leider, Parzival and Titurel* (Berlin, 1952), 102.23–103.24.

6. Sidney Johnson describes Herzeloydë's life with Gahmuret as "too great a preoccupation with things that are *only* of the courtly world and a consequent neglect of transcendental obligations" ("Herzeloydë," 155). Johnson's discussion supports my argument that in her love for Gahmuret, Herzeloydë chooses the world over God.

7. Lachmann, *Leider, Parzival and Titurel*, 113.5–12, 17–22 (my translation).

8. See, e.g., Caroline Walker Bynum, *Jesus as Mother: Studies in the Spirituality of the High Middle Ages* (Berkeley, CA, 1982); Rita Marie Bradley, "Patristic Background of the Motherhood Similitude in Julian of Norwich," *Christian Scholars Review* 8 (1978), 101–13; Sallie McFague, *Models of God: Theology for an Ecological, Nuclear Age* (Philadelphia, 1988).

9. E.g., Isaiah 49.15, 66.9–13; 1 Cor 3.1–2; Hebrews 5:12–14; 1 Peter 2.2–3; Clement of Alexandria, *Paedagogus*; Tertullian, *De corona militis*; Augustine, *Enarratio in Psalmum*.

10. Marsha L. Dutton, "'When I Was a Child': Spiritual Infancy and God's Maternity in Augustine's *Confessiones*," *Collectanea Augustinea, Augustine: Second Founder of the Faith*, eds. Joseph C. Schnaubelt and Frederick Van Fleteren (New York, 1990), pp. 113–40, 117, 118.

11. Dutton, "Spiritual Infancy," p. 118.

12. Augustine distinguishes *primordia*, the life in the womb until birth (*Confessiones*, I.vi.10); *infantia*, from birth to boyhood (*Conf.* I.vi.10); *pueritia*, from the power of speech to puberty (*Conf.* I.viii.13); *adulescentia*, from puberty to maturity (*Conf.* II.iii.6); *iuventus*, maturity (*Conf.* VII.i.1). See also P. Courcelle, *Recherches sur les Confessions de Saint Augustin* (Paris, 1969), p. 63.

13. No evidence supports the premise that Wolfram knew Augustine's *Confessiones* or that he consciously used the saint's ideas in his work, but St. Augustine's influence on medieval thought and literature was pervasive, often not visible but always ubiquitous. He was, in Douglas Gray's words, "in a real sense one of the 'founders of the Middle Ages,' who helped to form the 'mentalities,' the ways of seeing the world, of succeeding generations" ("Saint Augustine and Medieval Literature," in *Saint Augustine and His Influence in the Middle Ages*, eds. Edward B. King and Jacqueline

T. Schaefer, Sewanee Mediaeval Studies 3 [Sewanee TN, 1988], pp. 19–58).
Thus similarities in pattern, imagery and language would seem to justify
a closer look at the significance of Augustine's influence on the poem.

14. Augustine of Hippo, *Confessiones*, trans. John K. Ryan (New York,
1960), I.vi.7. All Augustine quotations are from this translation.

15. "Rational self-consciousness" is used by Colin Starnes in his
article, "Saint Augustine on Infancy and Childhood," *Augustinian Studies*
6 (1975), 15–43.

16. Yeandle, "Herzeloydë," p. 19.

17. Sidney Johnson uses "transcendental obligations" to describe that
which Herzeloydë neglects when she becomes too obsessed with Gahmuret
and her life as his queen (see above, notes 4 and 6).

18. In Norse and Germanic myth and legend, the ring represents the
female vagina, a fact of which Wolfram would undoubtedly have been
aware. Such an interpretation of the "goodly woman's ring" suggests advice
to Parzival from Herzeloydë of a more sensual and erotic nature.

19. Linda B. Parshall, *The Art of Narration in Wolfram's* Parsival *and
Abrecht's* Jungerer Titurel (Cambridge, MA, 1981), p. 134.

20. Parshall, *Art of Narration*, p. 135.

21. The dressing of the young boy in fool's clothing has been
identified with the Dümmling motif; however, another motif associated
with the fool that bears a closer study as it relates to *Parzival* is that of the
fool for God, which crops up in many medieval works.

22. For a description of Monica's role in Augustine's spiritual journey,
see Dutton, "Spiritual Infancy," pp. 123–29.

23. For an interesting discussion of the maternal body as a metaphor
in *La Queste del Saint Graal* see Rosalyn Rossignol, "The Holiest Vessel:
Maternal Aspects of the Grail," *Arthuriana* 5 (1995), 52–61.

THE PREGNANT QUEEN AS COUNSELLOR AND THE MEDIEVAL CONSTRUCTION OF MOTHERHOOD

John Carmi Parsons

The implications of juxtaposing the queen's roles as dynastic mother and intercessor are examined in fourteenth-century literary works that depict the queen in an advanced state of pregnancy when she intercedes with her husband.

O f the many ways in which the study of medieval queens and queenship differs from that of kings and kingship, among the more significant is that while the king swore a coronation oath that defined his obligations to the realm and accepted oaths of fealty in return, his wife neither gave nor received such promises. The lack of constitutive oaths for the queen put no formal restraints upon her relationships with either the king or the realm. From her standpoint this left her power usefully undefined, but it also left unlimited the grounds from which her subjects observed, praised, and criticized a woman now established in a most intimate relationship to the center of magisterial authority in the realm. A vast range of expectation, experience and expression thus informed society's definition, construction and observation of the queen's office; limits on her access to, and exercise of, power were implied through a like variety of means. To fathom the processes by which this came about, the modern scholar must sift a commensurate amount of richly varied material. I have elsewhere examined the imagery of queenship in medieval England, first in the rituals that displayed the queen to the realm and at the same time steered her toward informal arenas and then examined in the record evidence illustrating popular reactions to the image created by her ritual behavior.[1] This essay will examine literary sources' imagined scenarios to see whether such works support or dispute conclusions from that earlier research, especially those on the relationships between queenly maternity and intercession.

After some eight decades of contraction from the mid-twelfth century, the English queenship experienced a resurgence in wealth and prominence following Henry III's 1236 marriage to Eleanor of Provence. The queen's renewed eminence coincided with the rapid expansion of royal bureaucracy that distanced the king from his subjects and his consort from the routine conduct of official business. It also coincided with the full flowering of devotion to the Queen of Heaven as intercessor, veneration that soon came to shape the queen's image in the rituals and ceremonies that were increasingly important to the conduct of royal government. The consequent assimilation of intercession by the earthly and Heavenly queens—identifiable in both ecclesiastical and popular thinking by the late thirteenth century—further encouraged the queen's role as intercessor. Paul Strohm notes the frequency with which English queens appear as intercessors in fourteenth-century literary works. Some texts, however, embellish this image by depicting the queen in an advanced state of pregnancy when she asks the king to grant a pardon or favor. The best-known case is unquestionably that of Edward III's wife Philippa of Hainaut at Calais in 1347 when, according to the chronicler Jehan Froissart, she threw herself, great with child, on her knees to beg Edward's pardon for the townsmen:

> Then the noble queen of England, who was heavily pregnant [*durement enchainte*], humbled herself greatly and wept so tenderly from pity that none could bear it. The valiant and good lady threw herself on her knees before her lord the king and said, "Ah, my dear lord, since I came across the sea in great peril, as you well know, I have asked nothing of you nor required any favor. Now I humbly pray and request of you a favor, that for the Son of Holy Mary and for love of me, you shall wish to have mercy on these six men." The king waited a little before he spoke and he looked upon the good lady, his wife, who was very pregnant and wept so tenderly on her knees before him. A change of heart came over him as she knelt there before him; and when he spoke, he said, "Ah, lady, I would have much preferred you were anywhere but here. You have prayed so strongly that I dare not refuse the favor you ask of me."

While no evidence confirms all Froissart's details, there is no reason to reject the idea that Philippa interceded at Calais. But there is one major flaw in Jehan's story: while Calais fell on August 5, 1347, royal

household records show that Philippa's next child was born in May
1348, nine months later. Just possibly she had reason to suspect a
pregnancy at Calais—already the mother of ten, she would have
known the early signs well—or afterwards calculated that she might
very recently have conceived then. But clearly she was not "extremely
pregnant." [2]

The Calais incident, with Philippa's pregnancy embellished if not
fabricated, finds a pendant in the Middle English romance *Athelston*,
probably written in the reign of Richard II (1377–98). Told by a
jealous noble (the king's sworn brother) of the disloyalty of his sister's
husband, King Athelston orders sister, husband (also his sworn
brother), and their sons put to death. A squire takes this news to
Athelston's unnamed wife, who now appears for the first time in the
work:

> Garlands of cherries off she cast,
> Into the hall she came at last,
> Long ere it were noon.
> "Lord king, I am before thee come
> With a child, daughter or a son;
> Grant me my favor,
> My brother and sister that I may succor,
> Until next day at morrow,
> Out of their strong pains;
>
> That we may know by common assent
> In the full parliament...."
> "Lady," said he, "go from me;
> Thy boon shall not y-granted be;
> I give thee to know.
> For, by Him Who wears the crown of thorns,
> They shall be drawn and hanged tomorrow,
> If I am king of the land."
>
> And when the queen heard these words,
> As though she were beaten with a rod,
> The tears she let downfall.
> On her bare knees down she fell,
> And prayed again for them all.
> "Ah, lady," he said, "verily,
> Have you broken my commandment?
> You shall suffer full dearly."
> With his foot (he would not abide)

He slew the child right in her womb;
She swooned amongst them all.
Ladies and maidens that were there,
The queen unto her chamber bare,
And there was grief enough.
Soon, within a little space,
A boy-child y-born there was,
As bright as blossom on bower.
He was both white and red;
Of that blow he was dead—
His own father had him slain.

From her bed the queen summons the archbishop of Canterbury, whose counsel is also rejected, but after a threatened revolt by his barons Athelston is convinced that the charges are false when his sister and her husband miraculously survive the ordeal of hot ploughshares; he frees his sister's family and recognizes her newborn son as his heir.[3]

It would be hard to imagine a more powerful counterpoise to Froissart's handling of Philippa's pregnancy. Indeed, it would be hard to find a more powerful image of male versus female or one that more forcefully opposes the power to give life and the power to take it away—a conflict as epochal and eternally tragic in its way as that of Cain and Abel.[4] Despite divergent responses to queenly pregnancy, these two texts underline a close connection between a queen's intercession and maternity that was mapped explicitly for an English king's wife at the moment she became queen. Intercession and childbearing were the two functions of her office upon which her coronation *ordo* dwelled most intently. The opening blessing, which has been called a fertility charm, patently aligned the new queen's childbearing with that of women of the elect Davidic lineage, including the Virgin Mary. At the same time, however, the service inscribed limitations on her conjugal relations with her husband, exhorting her to observe such chaste behavior as to merit the palm next to virginity so she might, like the five wise virgins, be worthy of the Celestial Bridegroom. As the *ordo* thus sought to reconcile the Church's ideal of virginity with childbearing's sexual aspect, a later prayer evoked the story of Esther to urge the new queen to assume the role of intercessor with the king; English practice, indeed, called for her to perform an act of intercession with the king amid her coronation festivities. Other rituals that constructed her image also linked intercession and childbearing, for example the appeals for royal favor or pardon that medieval English queens made after childbirth. These two functions were, moreover, the aspects of the queen's behavior constructed by those rituals that were most heavily invested with Marian imagery, imagery more explicitly developed in the later medieval entry pageantry that welcomed and instructed a new queen upon arrival in the kingdom. The Marian image, at once celebrating and confining, allowed society to see the king's wife as a humble intercessor even as she was exalted as his anointed consort, and to imagine her as chaste, if not virginal, even as she was consecrated and exhorted to bear his children.[5] This reiterated alignment of queenly intercession and maternity resonantly echoes their juxtaposition in Froissart and *Athelston*. Froissart's exaggeration of pregnancy and its brutal rejection in *Athelston* pose questions that may open new paths to understanding a queen's role in the kingdom and the medieval construction of motherhood in general.

I begin, then, by considering queenly pregnancy within the parameters suggested by these two texts. Medieval perceptions of gestation do little to modify the observation that, even today, pregnancy is for men a time of mystery. Medieval medical works dealt in detail with a hypothetical sequence of intrauterine events during pregnancy, but we may wonder how far such writings affected popular awareness; John Baldwin notes, for example, that vernacular literature makes very few references to events between coitus and birth. It seems clear, in any event, that for the most part the mysteries of caring for pregnant women and those in labor were left to other women.[6] Medieval sources, moreover, often cast pregnancy as a time of wonder and enigma. Gestational miracles, mostly Biblically inspired, included conception after long sterility, saintly intervention to decide a child's sex, relief of labor pains, and dreams or visions experienced by the mothers of future saints, Thomas Becket's mother being perhaps the best known.[7] Pregnancy as a wondrous state was also manifest in the Church's blessing for the preservation of a fetus in the womb: at the Visitation, the child in St. Elizabeth's womb miraculously witnessed the Messiah's presence in the Blessed Virgin's womb.[8] The child *in utero*, then, of this world but not yet in it, might act as a messenger between two worlds and so add to the moral weight of a pregnant queen's message. Athelston's wife explicitly asserts an air of mystery, stating that she knows not whether her child is male or female; the promise and enigma she thus claims can be tellingly compared with Edward I of England's 1306 effort to guarantee for himself the sex of his unborn child by making an offering for "Lord Richard, the child now in the queen's womb" (who, as things turned out, had to be named Eleanor instead).[9]

That Athelston's wife's hidden child is male makes his destruction of it more incredible, for a queen's ability to bear a lawful heir to the throne was the chief reason for her presence in the realm and in the king's life. Many queens were repudiated for infertility; failure to produce an heir elicited elaborate excuses, extending to claims of chaste marriage.[10] A knowing queen advertised the proof of her fertility, and English practice gave her ample opportunity to do so: she, not the king, formally announced her children's births, and, remarkably, English queens appear to have named their children (if only daughters).[11] The pomp surrounding English royal childbirth focused primarily on the queen; the king had no part therein except to grant the favors his wife might request from childbed.[12]

No queen was ever "just" pregnant, nor was she merely a mother; she was the matrix of future kings—in Janet Nelson's words the guarantor of the realm's survival and integrity and so of peace and concord.[13] The queen thus shared in the processes by which the king's physical powers were projected onto the realm to assure its welfare, a theme familiar since James Frazer's *Golden Bough* and for which evidence does exist from the Christian Middle Ages—Alcuin, for example, wrote in 793 to King Aethelred of Northumbria, "...the king's virtue equals the welfare of the whole people, victory by the army, good weather, fertility, male offspring, and health."[14] But without a queen to give licit proof of his powers' survival, a Christian monarch had no legitimate way to manifest them. His wife's role in perpetuating the royal lineage was thus subject to intense scrutiny. In England, the Marianizing rituals of royal childbearing suggest that the queen could have been assimilated to the elements of a fertility cult implicit in medieval veneration of the Virgin; she might even have come to be something of a fertility figure herself. Queens' bodies were thus invested with immense significance; society projected onto them hopes and anxieties that were sexual as well as political, as Louise Fradenburg and Abby Zanger show in other contexts.[15] But a royal couple's ideal fertility only reminds us again that Athelston deprives himself of the living proof that his powers are intact and harnessed for the realm's benefit.

The scenarios imagined in Froissart's account of the Calais incident and in *Athelston* thus only skim the surface of a complex of meanings that requires further attention. On a primary level, the association of pregnancy and intercession would appear likely to enhance the emotional as well as the moral impact of a queen's plea. Froissart's exaggeration of Philippa's pregnancy is echoed, for example, in an account of the death of the heir of Louis IX of France in 1260 in a gossipy, moralizing, and overtly entertaining contemporary chronicle by a "minstrel of Reims" who, with the obvious intent of emphasizing the parents' grief, states that Queen Margaret of Provence "was pregnant with a child, very near her time." The king announced his son's death on January 12; but an original archiepiscopal register reveals that Margaret's daughter Agnes was born on August 9, seven months after the heir died. If Margaret was almost certainly pregnant in January 1260, like Philippa in August 1347 she was plainly nowhere "near her time"—another royal pregnancy overstated for effect.[16] A second historical case that clearly points in the same direction, and by coincidence in identical tragic circumstances, is the solace offered Henry VII of England by Elizabeth of York after the death of their son Arthur in April 1502. After Henry broke the news, Elizabeth noted that his mother had but one child, himself, yet God had preserved him to the throne, and Henry and she still had another son and two daughters. She then reminded him that "God is still where He was, and we are both young enough," obviously implying that they could have more children. Here the mere promise of conception and birth served to enhance queenly counsel, and indeed Elizabeth must have conceived very quickly thereafter, for she died in childbirth in February 1503.[17]

The image of the pregnant interceding queen chosen by both Froissart and *Athelston*'s author thus carried strong emotional overtones, but it is this added emotional tinge pregnancy gives the queen's advice, this intensification of much that the Middle Ages associated with the woman and the queen, that carries the undertones of danger to the king to which *Athelston*'s kick seems to be a reaction. It is precisely the emotional, intuitive aspect of a queen's power to attract petitioners and to persuade the king that menaces the male hierarchy he originates, embodies, and supports. Pregnancy might increase this threat by sharpening the emotional and, unavoidably, sexual edge to the scenario: as Julia Kristeva notes, motherhood is the only female function to which men can attribute existence—a reality that may of itself menace a king, especially if compounded by pregnancy's aura of mystery, that fruitful enigma evoked by Athelston's wife.[18] The fictive virginity with which Marian imagery ritually invested the queen was one way to control her sexual threat; pregnancy could do the same by signifying the king's subjection of his wife's body—her sexual function—to the interests of his lineage, limiting her capacity to exploit her sexuality to sway him. By taking an intercessor's ideally submissive posture, moreover, the queen affirmed the superiority of male authority and so strengthened hierarchy. The king in turn profited from the goodwill aroused by her kindness and, should she intercede when pregnant, he might well appropriate a greater aura of goodness and virtue. Again, however, this only deepens the conundrum of Athelston's kick.

Resolution is suggested by both a marked difference and a momentary resemblance between Froissart's tale of Philippa at Calais and the queen's appeal to Athelston. To deal first with the difference: Philippa does not speak of her condition openly and so does not assert her sexual self to sway the king—she displays only her intercessory, nurturing self. He silently notes her pregnancy but does not mention it, nor does he grant her request because of it—only because she asks him "so strongly." (Like the chronicler who overstated Margaret of Provence's pregnancy, Froissart exploits Philippa's to affect his readers, not his characters.)[19] The accounts are momentarily similar in that when Philippa begs Edward to spare the men of Calais, he answers "I would have much preferred you were anywhere but here"; Athelston's response is "Lady, go from me." A comparable picture of male perplexity when faced with unexpected female intervention appears in a monastic chronicler's account of an English queen's behavior when the townspeople of Saint-Albans in April 1275 sought to lay their complaints against the abbot before Edward I's wife Eleanor of Castile as she neared the town in her coach: the abbot tried to keep her away from the mob by entering the abbey through a far gate, but she scolded him and listened to the people.[20]

Froissart's Philippa and Athelston's wife dart from margin to center; Eleanor is called in by the crowd.[21] Their intrusions clearly are unwelcome, and in all three cases, the initial male response is to re-marginalize them. In fact the overall picture of queenly intercession in England suggests that such intrusions were rare. Documentation for a queen's intercession almost always reflects a sedate and discreet sequence of events: a petitioner seeks her help, usually in the king's absence, and she furthers the request by consulting him or his officers, who decide the matter. All of this is handled with little fanfare. In essence, the petitioned and interceding queen exerts no narrative powers. She accepts a petition but cannot act upon it; she may add a *pro forma* request for assistance but for all practical purposes merely forwards the petitioner's words to a male who can act upon them. The few occasions on which queens did intercede publicly (their coronations, for example, or such obviously staged events as Katherine of Aragon's plea for the London apprentices after the 1517 May Day riots) were in David Loades' words "designed to impress" and were undoubtedly devised in advance. Spontaneous queenly interventions are even rarer, confined for the most part to literary works like those examined here.[22]

A former intimate of the English court, Froissart would have known well the etiquette observed at such times, but we cannot say whether *Athelston*'s author was aware of the tactful protocol the king's wife was expected to observe when she asked a favor of him. The prominence of her intercessory role had grown from the thirteenth century, however, and as Strohm notes, the queen who shared the English throne when *Athelston* was written was known and praised for her public—and hence probably well-rehearsed—mediation with Richard II. The association of Marian imagery with the queen's intercession, moreover, and conventional artistic representations of interceding queens as submissive, kneeling women, would implant images of submissive queenly behavior in the popular mind. There is thus great meaning in the depiction of Athelston's wife, who unabashedly abandons decorum and dignity: from her chamber she darts into the king's hall, openly refers to the mystery of her pregnancy, and asks that counsel be taken in parliament—a venue with which queens are rarely associated and one which implies limits on royal power to judge and condemn that Athelston does not welcome (it is precisely at this point in her speech that he interrupts to order her out of his presence). In these imagined cases, moreover, one crucial element is missing from the sequence that can be documented when historical queens interceded: neither Froissart's Philippa nor Athelston's wife is first solicited by a petitioner. Rather, both women intuitively discern a situation in which they can act and do so without any prompting. (Note the interpenetration of images in Eleanor of Castile's Saint-Albans encounter: she is approached by petitioners, albeit in peculiar fashion as a male authority figure is present, and listens to them though the abbot tries to prevent it. The chronicler ends by silencing queen and people alike: Eleanor, who evidently speaks no English, has to rely on a bilingual courtier, and in her presence the town's spokes*woman* is—the monk smugly notes— unable to say anything against the abbot.)[23]

In the ideal submissiveness it inscribes, the queenly-intercessory scenario is a script for female behavior, imposed on the king's wife; as Strohm notes, there is nothing exclusively male or female about intercession, but a patriarchal society made it a script for female behavior, real or imagined. Hedged about with restrictions as the queen's behavior might be, however, the essential informality of her intercession did allow room for maneuvering. Provided the proprieties were observed, queens could (and did) exploit their intercession for their own ends—to win supporters, to create networks of mutual obligation and, as will be seen, to shape popular opinion of themselves and the king.[24] The fictional or fictionalized queens discussed here, however, like the historical Eleanor of Castile at Saint-Albans seize upon that prescription and seek to turn it to their own self-enabling ends, to the evident confusion of male authority.

As has been seen, the emotional appeal of pregnancy might enhance a queen's ability to sway the king, but that same appeal menaced the hierarchy the king embodied. It is necessary, then, to ask how pregnancy might hinder her exploitation of the role, as it does for Athelston's wife. The Aristotelian view of woman's role in conception, as accepted by the Middle Ages, is pertinent here: a female only passively receives the active male principle, contributing to prenatal development only the matter shaped by the active male principle and the environment in which the fetus is nourished. As a queen's child is thus, as it were, only an emanation of the king, pregnancy again signifies subjection to him: in justifying her intrusion by her pregnancy, Athelston's wife seeks to appropriate something not really hers to claim.[25] Closely related to this point is the commonplace that medieval noblewomen were seen as commodities, traded to confirm alliances among male rulers.[26] Athelston's wife does not meekly accept her socio-biological destiny; she appropriates the role by which she is expected to support the male order and uses it to assert her own agency, in the process trying to reverse a male decision. (Of the cases discussed here, only Elizabeth of York submits her sexual self to the king by offering to preserve his lineage.)

As noted earlier, the pomp surrounding royal childbirth in medieval England focused on the queen, and at first glance this would appear to enhance her gestational role to give her a strong claim to power. The foregoing discussion, however, suggests fresh distinctions to refine our understanding of this ritual context. First, these events took place not during a queen's pregnancy but only after her delivery. Second, her role in these rites, however prominent, was almost entirely passive (as in her churching, for example). Third, the ceremonies took place in or from that most domestic and feminine of spaces, the queen's chamber where her child was conceived and born—that chamber Athelston's queen abandons and to which she is returned, injured and in travail.[27] Finally, like the plea Athelston's wife sends the archbishop, the intercessory appeals English queens made from childbed reiterated that even at a time when the king might be unusually susceptible to his wife's requests, she could only forward petitions from others to solicit his authority, not overturn his judgments. In effect, then, the drift of medieval English royal childbearing ritual emphasized a queen's passive role in postpartum events and her nurturing intercession, thus decentering the sexual side of her maternity. This masking of maternity's sexual element and the exaltation of its nurturing aspect by linking queenly motherhood with intercession echoes the coronation incantations which sought to control the threat the queen's sexuality posed to the king's pursuit of his duties, to enlist her fertility in the service of his lineage, and to recruit her intercession for the benefit of his rule. It also affirms distinctions between the tragic initial failure of Athelston's wife, and Philippa's success at Calais.[28]

A pregnant Philippa also occurs, by implication, in a remarkable work that underlines the points argued here. *Le voeu du héron* is a mid-fourteenth-century Picard poem on the origins of the Hundred Years' War: during a feast at Edward III's court, the exiled Robert of Artois urges an attack on France and brings into the hall a dish of herons, on which he asks king and nobles to swear to accomplish the endeavor. They do so in terms patently over the top: the earl of

Salisbury vows to keep one eye shut until the war is won, while his
beloved swears that if he forgets his vow she will never couple with
him or any other man. At the climax, Edward's unnamed queen
adds her vow:

> "Vassal," said the queen, "speak to me no more of this.
> While she has a husband a woman cannot swear,
> For if she vows anything, her lord, who has the power,
> Can well revoke whatever she shall swear;
> And shamed be the body who shall ever think of it,
> Before my dear lord command me."
> And the king said, "Swear everything that shall please you;
> Whatever you vow, my body will accomplish,
> To the last extent that it can be done;
> Swear boldly, and God will help you."
> "Well, then," said the queen, "I have known for some time
> That I am with child; my body has sensed it,
> Though the child has yet barely turned within my body.
> And I vow and promise to God, Who created me and
> Was born of the Virgin without damaging her body,
> And Who died on the Cross where they crucified Him,
> That this fruit shall not issue from my body
> Until you have taken me to that country over there,
> To accomplish the vow you have sworn.
> And should it desire to come forth, if need be,
> I will slay myself with a great knife of steel,
> And so have my soul lost, and the child perish."
> When the king heard this, he stoutly forbade her
> And said, "Surely, none shall swear anything more."

The royal couple then journey to Antwerp, where the queen bears a
son, Lionel.[29] Though its details are all but certainly imagined, *Le
voeu*'s historical basis is inarguable. Artois' presence at the English
court has long been seen as one factor that led to the war's 1337
outbreak; Edward's first base of operations on the Continent was at
Antwerp, where Philippa indeed bore Lionel in November 1338. (As
Lionel arrived a full year after the onset of hostilities, however, the
queen's pregnancy in *Le voeu* is—hey presto!—advanced in time for
dramatic effect.)[30]

   The poem's nineteenth-century French editors decried the queen's
vow, but their disgust did not prevent them suggesting parallels in
John of Joinville's account of the plea by Louis IX's pregnant wife
that a knight should kill her if the Saracens took Damietta after

Louis' defeat at Mansurah, and a fourteenth-century countess of Flanders' threat that if her son married his daughter to the English king's son, she would cut off the breasts with which she had suckled him.[31] In contrast to Froissart's tale, Le voeu's queen refers openly to her pregnancy—indeed, her emphasis on her body is remarkable and seems to give the king a forcible demonstration that she can give life and take it (thus claiming both male and female powers).[32] But the context here is less confrontational than Philippa's intercession with Edward at Calais or Athelston's encounter with his queen, and as the child has barely moved within her, the queen's pregnancy in Le voeu is not as visible as in Froissart or Athelston. In any case, she uses her condition not to contest male authority but to urge the king to keep his vow. She first openly submits to him, refusing to swear without permission; he ends by silencing her, revoking her oath as she admits he has the power to do. She mentions her pregnancy with one aim, to bear her child on French soil—clearly supporting the claims of Edward's lineage to the French throne, since her child will be French by birth. (She thus forecasts Elizabeth of York's offer of her biogenetic self to Henry VII after Prince Arthur's death.)

Le voeu's queen uses her pregnancy to prompt the king to take what is his by right, to do his chivalric duty and preserve his honor and, with it, hers and their child's. Here is the link between Le voeu's and Joinville's queens: both are willing to destroy self and child to preserve honor. Such support of male honor was seen as appropriate female behavior since the heyday of the chansons de geste, which often portrayed women, safe in their castles, urging their menfolk to return to battle and uphold the honor on which women's status depends— as Froissart has Philippa hearten Edward's commanders before the battle of Neville's Cross—and then praise their victory.[33] Despite her submissiveness and Edward's silencing, then, his wife offers him significant support and appears in a favorable light. Just as her pregnancy serves to uphold the honor of the king's lineage, of course, her absurd claim to control the length of gestation and her double threat of suicide and infanticide are reinforced by juxtaposition with the Virgin's compliant acceptance of maternity and Christ's loving self-sacrifice. Her oath has been further prepared by that of John de Fauquemont: "Thus will I spare neither monastery nor altar/Pregnant woman nor child that I may find." [34] By contrasting herself with

Mary and Christ and aligning herself with a male warrior who sees no fault in killing pregnant women, the queen inverts ideal female and maternal roles and so doubly inscribes her passivity and biogenetic submission to the king's lineage.

It was suggested earlier that examination of literary sources might support, dispute, or augment earlier conclusions on relationships between a queen's childbearing and intercession. The last has proved to be the case, for the ritual associations between childbearing and intercession have indeed been refined: such associations less explicitly evoked a biological maternity than they exalted a nurturing motherhood. And as we are now in a sense back where we started—with an allegedly pregnant Philippa ready to do her duty to king and country—we can pursue some of the further ramifications for queen and people.

The prominence of images of royal pregnancy is explained by a queen's embodiment of the realm's hopes for secure succession to the throne and of its fears of her sexual sway over the king. It is not surprising that such astonishing images of pregnancy should constellate around Philippa, as the mother of twelve one of the two most prolific of English medieval queens. Nor is it an accident that like that most fruitful queen, Eleanor of Castile (the mother of sixteen), Philippa has enjoyed the best press in recent centuries—queenly fecundity was more safely extolled when she was in her tomb than when she was in bed with the king. If a good posthumous press proves a queen's success, however, we must admit to Philippa and Eleanor's company one who was not fertile. *Athelston* probably dates from the reign of Richard II, whose wife, Anne of Bohemia, was, like Athelston's wife, childless, but she did exert herself as mediator between king and people, who deeply appreciated her efforts though she never labored in childbirth.[35] If, like Anne, Athelston's wife cannot assure the survival of the realm by bearing a son, she can still "labor" to assure order and concord by seeing to it that the king reverses an unjust decree.

Athelston is not swayed by his wife's pregnant physical body; she succeeds by tactfully exercising her intercessory self—her official body, so to speak, as distinct from her physical frame. We may say, then, that the queen had two bodies, though not in the sense Ernst Kantorowicz posited for a king.[36] A queen did not enter her office in the same manner as a king, nor did one consort succeed another as a king succeeds his predecessor. Thus there is a sense in which a queen "dies" while the king does not, but certain of her attributes and duties could be seen to adhere to her office, not her person: if her biological maternity was limited in time by natural physiological processes, her role as a nurturing mediator was not and could be identified with her official self. Long after her natural body ceased to manifest the king's physical powers, intercession allowed her to continue a maternal function and reveal his ideal paternal magnanimity. Some queens, like Henry III's wife Eleanor of Provence, may well have substituted nurturing intercession for biological maternity as they ceased to bear children or reached widowhood; others, like Edward I's second wife, Margaret of France, or Edward II's wife, Isabella, perhaps exploited mediation to win popular favor or to create the image of an intimate royal union.[37] In most cases in medieval England, a queen's official body was exalted by unction and coronation; to become a model of regal feminine behavior, however, that body had to be abased to the intercessor's ideal passivity and silence.[38] Likewise, a queen's physical body, like any woman's, was denigrated as a site of sin and pollution and, in a queen's case, feared especially as a means whereby she might sway the king. Her sexual role was of central importance to the realm, but just as her official body was silenced, her sexual maternity was hidden and her nurturing mothering emphasized through association with her intercession. As with queens who exploited intercession when biological maternity was past and the barren Anne, the tragedy of Athelston's wife affirms that a queen's nurturing, official body could substitute for her physical, reproductive body.

If the study of queenly intercession tells us anything, it is that the regal behavior of a king and queen together formed a continuous unity, popular observation of which was critical to shaping the official face of each partner. Hence, both Froissart and *Athelston* are fundamentally attentive to behavior proper to either spouse. Thus consideration is elicited here of the role a female figure played in the construction of Western images of sovereignty and the implications for a male ruler's image of the responses of Athelston and Edward III to their wives' appeals. The king shared in a kind of doubled discourse prompted by his wife: properly exercised—as in Philippa's appeal at Calais—a queen's prudent intercession manifested the superiority of the king's power yet allowed him to change his mind gracefully to appear just and clement. There was no lack of good reasons why he should listen to her counsel and act upon it. Churchmen urged queens, indeed all wives, to work even amid intimate embraces to improve their husbands' behavior; like any husband, a king was exhorted to treat his conjugal partner with respect and hear out her advice. It is easy to say that Athelston's rejection of his wife's plea marks him as a brutal and tyrannous ruler, but an analogous historical case shows that the interplay of gendered roles was rather more complex. Save for the 1275 incident at Saint-Albans, Eleanor of Castile figures in no dramatic intercession scenes; in fact, she appears only infrequently as a mediator with Edward I. Indeed, from an early date in his reign, Eleanor won a reputation for avarice unique among medieval English queens and thereby evidently was not looked for by those who sought a mediator. Perhaps she simply did not care to do so, but at any rate, her appearances in that role are noticeably fewer than those by Edward's mother or his second wife. Whatever underlay Eleanor's sporadic mediations, by thus denying Edward opportunities to manifest his willingness to allow a woman's beneficial counsel to modify his magisterial decisions, she very likely contributed to popular opinion of him as a harsh ruler: in fact Archbishop John Pecham of Canterbury warned in 1283 that she was blamed for the severity of Edward's rule. As Athelston's wife offers him just the kind of opening Eleanor appears not to have given Edward, Athelston's kick doubly advances the construction of his tyrannous persona. In contrast, Froissart's Philippa helps to reveal Edward III as a prince magnanimous in victory.[39]

Athelston's rejection of his wife's plea does not devalue her roles as mother and intercessor. But it does return both to a properly discreet, domestic arena and insists that she work to modify royal judgment without confronting the king—and without arguing pregnancy's mysterious and emotional connotations.[40] If this prescription affects a queen as wife, it could also affect her as mother. As Charles Wood notes, medieval society allowed greater political leeway to a royal mother than a wife, and the lives of Eleanor of Aquitaine, Blanche of Castile or Isabella of France show that a queen could reap immense political profit from motherhood. That medieval England never recognized any queen as regent for her son, however, asks us to look further.[41] Ritual might suggest limits on a queen's relationship with the king, but no rite of queenship implied any controls on her relations with her son, save in the sense that her influence with him must, like the Virgin's, be intercessory or supplicatory. Royal maternity's construction as domestic or nurturing—not political—could thus serve a potentially critical multigenerational purpose.

When the younger Agrippina saw that her son Nero's men had come to kill her, she urged them to strike at the womb that bore him;[42] a medieval countess of Flanders threatened rather to cut off the breasts that nourished her son. Queens were not the archetypal women of the Middle Ages; but they were medieval women writ large. The works examined here invite wider reflection on the medieval construction of motherhood as a nurturing role, not a sexual event or biological process. Clerics reminded queens that the enacting of subjection to husbands and modest behavior set an example for the realm and told them to regard Church and realm as their households—and thus themselves as housewives.[43] Advice to be submissive to husbands, not to contradict them in public, to make requests of them prudently and to counsel them attentively was common in the lives of medieval women of all classes as was intergenerational mediation between husbands and children. A queen's capacity to exploit the intercessory role as well as other "domestic" duties like the education of children held true for other women, too.[44] Julia Kristeva notes that the modern age has had no discourse of motherhood after the Virgin, a reminder that the Marian construction of the queen's image could help convey these ideas and notions of mothering to women who, if they could never attain Mary's virginal gestation, might at least emulate her mothering.[45] Royal maternity rituals, replete with Marian imagery that focused on postpartum nurturing, imply a palpable link to the paucity of medieval depictions of Mary as visibly pregnant.[46] A more familiar Marian image was the mother nursing her Son or, as she intercedes with Him, baring her breast to recall that nurturing role. Thus the Marian cult might well secrete human conception and pregnancy, too, and as a queen was the most eminent and visible of women, the construction of her maternity as chiefly nurturing or intercessory could also impart an asexual maternal imagery to society. Ironically, then, a highly visible and much-scrutinized royal pregnancy could serve to conceal just as much as it promised.

NOTES

A portion of this material was presented at the International Congress on Medieval Studies, Kalamazoo (May 1995). This article owes much to Paul Strohm, who generously corresponded with me while working on his article cited below, and to a conversation with Andrew Taylor. David Townsend and Bonnie Wheeler kindly offered many valuable suggestions. Of course all conclusions are my own responsibility.

1. John C. Parsons, "Ritual and Symbol in the English Queenship to 1500," in *Women and Sovereignty*, ed. Louise O. Fradenburg, *Cosmos*, 7, (Edinburgh, 1992), 60–78, and "The Queen's Intercession in Thirteenth-Century England," in *Power of the Weak. Essays On Medieval Women*, eds. J.E. Carpenter and S. B. Maclean (Urbana, IL, 1995), pp. 147–77. The latter is not cited further here, but the reader must remain aware that it is fundamental to the present discussion.

2. Jehan Froissart, *Oeuvres*, ed. J.M.B.C. Kervyn de Lettenhove, 25 vols. (Brussels, 1867–77), 5:205 (3rd redaction), 215 (4th redaction); my translation differs from Paul Strohm's, "Queens as Intercessors," in idem, *Hochon's Arrow: The Social Imagination of Fourteenth-Century Texts* (Princeton, 1992), pp. 99–105. As Strohm notes, Froissart's text derives from Jehan le Bel's chronicle, in which Philippa's pregnancy is not stressed; Froissart's early version (*Oeuvres*, 5:198) omits it. On Philippa's child, see Henry M. Lane, *The Royal Daughters of England and Their Representatives*, 2 vols. (London, 1910), 1:63 note 72.

3. A. McI. Trounce, ed., *Athelston. A Middle English Romance*, EETS, O.S. 224 (Oxford, 1951), pp. 75–76 (ll. 253–314); I owe the reference to Patricia Eberle. This episode represents only a brief portion of the romance.

4. On the gendered power to give life and take it away, see Peggy Reeves Sanday, *Female Power and Male Dominance: On the Origins of Sexual Inequality* (Cambridge, 1981), pp. 184–211; cf. Marilyn Arthur, "From Medusa to Cleopatra: Women in the Ancient World," in *Becoming Visible: Women in European History*, eds. R. Bridenthal, C. Koonz and S. M. Stuard (New York, 1987), pp. 82–83.

5. Parsons, "Ritual and Symbol"; Leopold G. W. Legg, ed., *English Coronation Records* (Westminster, 1901), pp. 37–39; Ernst H. Kantorowicz, "The Carolingian King in the Bible of San Paolo fuori le Mura," in *Selected Studies by Ernst Kantorowicz*, eds. M. Cherniavsky and R. Giesey (Locust Valley, NJ, 1965), pp. 88–89. All Biblical women named in the initial blessing (Legg, p. 37) did not miraculously conceive after long sterility, and the mothers of Samuel, Sampson and John Baptist are omitted. As the one common link among the women named is the Davidic lineage, the blessing's focus is a specifically *dynastic* fertility.

6. John Baldwin, *The Language of Sex: Five Voices from Northern France around 1200* (Chicago, 1994), pp. 206–10; M. C. Seymour, ed., *On the Properties of Things. John Trevisa's Translation of Bartholomaeus Anglicus De Proprietatibus Rerum: A Critical Text* (Oxford, 1975), pp. 263–66, 294–97; Barbara Hanawalt, "Conception through Infancy in Medieval England: Historical and Folklore Sources," *Folklore Forum*, 13 (1980), 127–57. On pregnant women, M. Green, "Women's Medical Practice and Health Care in Medieval Europe," in *Sisters and Workers in the Middle Ages,* eds. Judith M. Bennett *et al.* (Chicago, 1989), pp. 39–78; L. Pinto, "The Folk Practice of Obstetrics and Gynecology in the Middle Ages," *Bulletin of the History of Medicine,* 47 (1973), 513–23; Beryl Rowland, *Medieval Woman's Guide to Health: The First English Gynecological Handbook* (Kent, OH, 1981); Merry E. Wiesner, "Early Modern Midwifery: A Case Study," in *Women and Work in Preindustrial Europe,* ed. Barbara Hanawalt (Bloomington, IN, 1986), pp. 94–113.

7. Michael E. Goodich, *Violence and Miracle in the Fourteenth Century* (Chicago, 1995), pp. 86–91; *Vita S. Thomae auctore Edwardo Grim,* in *Materials for the History of Thomas Becket,* ed. J.C. Robertson, 7 vols., RS 67 (London, 1875–85), 2:356–57.

8. M. Andrieu, ed., *Le pontifical romain au moyen âge,* 4 vols. (Vatican City, 1938–41), 3:678–80.

9. Pierre Chaplais, "Some Personal Letters of Edward I," *EHR,* 77 (1962), 81 note 3; Michael Prestwich, *Edward I* (London and Berkeley, CA, 1988), p. 131.

10. John Carmi Parsons, "Family, Sex, and Power: The Rhythms of Medieval Queenship," in *Medieval Queenship,* ed. John Carmi Parsons (New York, 1993), pp. 4–5.

11. John C. Parsons, *Eleanor of Castile: Queen and Society in Thirteenth-Century England* (New York, 1995), pp. 67, 280 note 216. J.F. O'Sullivan, ed., S. M. Brown, trans., *The Register of Eudes of Rouen* (New York, 1964), p. 419, notes Agnes of France's birth as that of Louis IX's wife's child, implying she announced it. On English queens naming daughters, see references in J.C. Parsons, "The Year of Eleanor of Castile's Birth and Her Children by Edward I," *Mediaeval Studies,* 46 (1984), 257–65.

12. Walter Ullmann, ed., *Liber regie capelle: A Manuscript in the Biblioteca Publica of Evora,* Henry Bradshaw Society, 92 (London, 1961), pp. 72–73.

13. Janet L. Nelson, "Inauguration Rituals," in *Early Medieval Kingship,* eds. P.H. Sawyer and I.N. Wood (Leeds, 1977), p. 71, repr. in Nelson, *Politics and Ritual in Early Medieval Europe* (Ronceverte, 1986), p. 304.

14. The classic study of sacred kingship and the king's physical links to the realm's prosperity is E. E. Evans-Pritchard, *The Divine Kingship of the Shilluk of the Nilotic Sudan* (Cambridge, 1948). See also James G. Frazer,

The Golden Bough. A Study in Magic and Religion, 2 vols. (London, 1890); the quote is from *Alcuini Epistolae*, ed. E. Dummler (MGH Epistolae, 4 [Berlin, 1895]), no. 18.

15. Parsons, "Family, Sex, and Power," pp. 4–5, and "Ritual and Symbol," p. 66. English examples seem to be lacking, but mothers of future kings were represented as having dreams or visions like saints' mothers (e.g., Gábor Klaniczay, "The Paradoxes of Royal Sainthood as Illustrated by Central European Examples," in *Kings and Kingship in Medieval Europe*, ed. Anne Duggan[London, 1993], pp. 352–53). On Marian veneration and fertility, see Rosemary R. Ruether, *New Woman, New Earth: Sexist Ideologies and Human Liberation* (New York, 1975), p. 50; Pauline Stafford, *Queens, Concubines and Dowagers: The King's Wife in the Early Middle Ages* (Athens, GA, 1983), p. 27; Marina Warner, *Alone of All Her Sex: The Myth and Cult of the Virgin Mary* (London, 1976), pp. 273–84; B.C. Pope, "Immaculate and Powerful: The Marian Revival in the Nineteenth Century," in *Immaculate and Powerful. The Female in Sacred Image and Social Reality*, eds. C.W. Atkinson, C.H. Buchanan and M.R. Miles (Boston, 1985), pp. 173–200. Emmanuel Le Roy Ladurie, *Montaillou, village occitan de 1294 à 1324* (Paris, 1975), pp. 493–94, rather overdoes the point. Cf. L. Fradenburg, "Sovereign Love: The Wedding of Margaret Tudor and James IV of Scotland," pp. 78–100, and A. Zanger, "Fashioning the Body Politic: Imagining the Queen in the Marriage of Louis XIV," pp. 101–20, both in Fradenburg, *Women and Sovereignty*.

16. *Chronique de Reims*, *RHF*, 22:301 ("Et estoit la roine ençainte d'enfant, près de l'agésir"). On young Louis' death and Agnes' birth, O'Sullivan, *Register of Eudes of Rouen*, pp. 403–04, 419.

17. S.B. Chrimes, *Henry VII* (London, 1972), pp. 285, 302–03.

18. Julia Kristeva, "Stabat Mater," in eadem, *Tales of Love*, trans. L. S. Roudiez (New York, 1987), p. 234. On male fear of female sexual powers and disruptive influence on male solidarity, see H.R. Hays, *The Dangerous Sex: The Myth of Feminine Evil* (New York, 1964); Wolfgang Lederer, *The Fear of Women* (New York, 1968); and Edward Harper, "Fear and the Status of Women," *Southwestern Journal of Anthropology*, 25 (1969), 81–95; the perceived threat to high-status male activity is noted by Sherry B. Ortner and Harriet Whitehead, eds., *Sexual Meanings: The Cultural Construction of Gender and Sexuality* (Cambridge, 1981), pp. 20–21. See also Parsons, "Queen's Intercession," pp. 159–61; Elizabeth A. Rowe, "The Female Body Politic and the Miscarriage of Justice in *Athelston*," *Studies in the Age of Chaucer*, 17 (1995), 79–98.

19. Strohm, "Queens as Intercessors," pp. 101–02, sees Philippa's reference to "great peril" when crossing the sea as an evocation of pregnancy—a plausible interpretation but not the only one: Anglo-French hostilities could have menaced her in the Channel.

20. *Gesta Abbatum Sancti Albani*, ed. H.T. Riley, 3 vols. as one, RS 28.4 (London, 1867–69), pp. 411–12, dated April 11, 1275. Eleanor had borne a child on March 15 (Parsons, "Year of Eleanor of Castile's Birth," 262). Did childbirth-intercession links thus enhance her appeal as an intercessor on this occasion?

21. Cf. Strohm, "Queens as Intercessors," p. 101.

22. David Loades, *The Tudor Court* (London, 1986 and Totowa, NJ, 1987), pp. 4–5. In August 1331 a platform from which Philippa and her women were watching a parade collapsed under them; "precibus et genuflexionibus," she won the king's pardon for the carpenters, but it is unclear whether she did so at once or later (*Chronica Galfridi le Baker de Swynebroke*, ed. E. M. Thompson [Oxford, 1889], p. 48; notably fewer details in *Annales Paulini, in Chronicles of the Reigns of Edward I and Edward II*, ed. W. Stubbs, 2 vols., RS 76 [London, 1882–83], 1:355, and *Chronica Adae de Murimuth*, ed. E.M. Thompson, RS 93 [London, 1889], p. 63).

23. The squire who tells the queen of Athelston's decree does not ask her to act. Her garlands stress the feminine, domestic space she occupies; casting them off affords her actions an impulsive color. On the queen and parliament, see Rowe, "Female Body Politic," 97; on Eleanor, *Gesta Abbatum Sancti Albani*, ed. Riley, p. 412. Cf. criticism of women as leaders of resistance to male monastic authority in R.H. Hilton, "A Thirteenth-Century Poem on Disputed Villein Services," *EHR*, 56 (1941), 90–97.

24. Strohm, "Queens as Intercessors," p. 105. This passage has been influenced by E. Jane Burns, *Bodytalk. When Women Speak in Old French Literature* (Philadelphia, 1993), though the double sense in which queens used intercession is also implied by Joan M. Ferrante, "Public Postures and Private Maneuvers: Roles Women Play," in *Women and Power in the Middle Ages,* eds. M. Erler and M. Kowaleski (Athens, GA, 1988), pp. 213–29.

25. I owe this observation to Sharon Farmer. Aristotelian ideas on conception were current by the early thirteenth century and thereafter co-existed and contended with Hippocratic-Galenic views (Vern L. Bullough, "Medieval Medical and Scientific Views of Women," *Viator*, 4 (1973), 485–501).

26. Concise exposition in Carla Freccero, "Marguerite de Navarre and the Politics of Maternal Sovereignty," in Fradenburg, *Women and Sovereignty*, pp. 132–33.

27. On noblewomen's spatial isolation in medieval households, see Roberta Gilchrist, "Medieval Bodies in the Material World: Gender, Stigma and the Body," in *Framing Medieval Bodies,* eds. S. Kay and M. Rubin (Manchester, 1994), pp. 49–59; on the gendering of space, Barbara Hanawalt, "At the Margins of Women's Space in Medieval Europe," in *Matrons and Marginal Women in Medieval Society,* eds. R.R. Edwards and V. Ziegler (Woodbridge, 1995), pp. 1–17. Particular meanings of the queen's bedchamber are noted in Parsons, "Ritual and Symbol," pp. 67–68.

28. Concern for the queen's sexual dominance was not limited to ritual expression; cf. Pauline Stafford, "The Portrayal of Royal Women in England, Mid-Tenth to Mid-Twelfth Centuries," in Parsons, *Medieval Queenship*, pp. 150–51, 154, 157.

29. *Le voeu du héron: poème publié d'après un manuscrit de la bibliothèque de Bourgogne*, eds. R.G.H. Chalon and C.J.B. Delecourt, Publications de la Société des bibliophiles de Mons, 8 (Mons, 1839), ll. 398–424 (pp. 19–20, my translation).

30. Édouard Perroy, *The Hundred Years War*, trans. W.B. Wells (New York, 1965), pp. 92–93; Christopher Allmand, *The Hundred Years War. England and France at War c.1300–c.1450* (Cambridge, 1989), p. 12. For Lionel's birth, GEC, 3:257.

31. *Le voeu du héron*, pp. xi–xii.

32. Cf. Sanday, *Female Power and Male Dominance*, pp. 184–211; Burns, *Bodytalk*, p. 143. Aristotelian views on conception would, of course, deny a mother any such powers.

33. Penny S. Gold, *The Lady and The Virgin. Image, Attitude, and Experience in Twelfth-Century France* (Chicago, 1985), pp. 4–18, stressing women's peripheral and domestic space in the *gestes*. For Philippa at Neville's Cross, see Froissart, *Oeuvres*, 5:333.

34. *Le voeu du héron*, ll. 326–41 (p. 16). On Mary's acceptance of pregnancy, as opposed to Eve for whom it was a punishment, see G.E. Brereton and J.M. Ferrier, eds., *Le Ménagier de Paris* (Oxford, 1981), 1.6.13 (pp. 74–75).

35. Froissart stresses Anne's childlessness (*Oeuvres*, 15:137); her acts of intercession seem more often "designed to impress" than other queens noted here (Strohm, "Queens as Intercessors," pp. 105–19). On Eleanor, see Parsons, *Eleanor of Castile*, chap. 4.

36. Ernst H. Kantorowicz, *The King's Two Bodies. A Study in Medieval Political Theology* (Princeton, 1957).

37. Parsons, *Eleanor of Castile*, pp. 152–53, 251.

38. Cf. the silencing of Enide as queen in Chrétien's *Erec* (Burns, *Bodytalk*, pp. 191–93) and the silence of English queens at their coronations. On Erec's wife as a queenly model, Lewis Jillings, "The Ideal of Queenship in Hartmann's *Erec*," in *The Legend of Arthur in the Middle Ages*, eds. P.B. Grout et al., *Arthurian Studies*, 7 (1983), pp. 113–28.

39. In general, see Fradenburg, *Women and Sovereignty*. See also Jillings, "Ideal of Queenship;" Sharon Farmer, "Persuasive Voices: Clerical Images of Medieval Wives," *Speculum*, 61 (1986), 517–43; Parsons, *Eleanor of Castile*, pp. 45–46, 113–17, 149–53.

40. Esther approaches Ahasuerus on his throne with dread, for anyone who does so unbidden is worthy of death; even when he welcomes her she does not entreat him then and there, in public, but only at a banquet in her apartments (*Esther* 4:11, 5:1–9, 7:1–6).

41. Charles T. Wood, "The First Two Queens Elizabeth," in Fradenburg, *Women and Sovereignty*, p. 128; Parsons, "Family, Sex and Power," pp. 4–5.

42. P. Cornelius Tacitus, *Annales*, 14.8, in *P. Cornelii Taciti opera. Editio nova et auctior*, ed. G. Brotier, 5 vols. (London, 1812), 2:181.

43. E.g., *PL*, 207:448–49; Matthew Paris, *Chronica majora*, ed. H.R. Luard, 7 vols., RS 57 (London, 1872–84), 4:349; *Roberti Grosseteste episcopi quondam Lincolniensis epistolae*, ed. Luard, RS 25 (London, 1861), pp. 271–72; *Registrum epistolarum Fratris Johannis Peckham Archiepiscopi Cantuariensis*, ed. C.T. Martin, 3 vols., RS 77 (London, 1882–86), 2:555, 619–20, and 3:937–38.

44. David Herlihy, *Medieval Households* (Cambridge, MA, 1985), pp. 120–22. In Erler and Kowaleski, *Women and Power*, see Judith M. Bennett, "Public Power and Authority in the Medieval English Countryside," pp. 18–36; JoAnn McNamara and Suzanne F. Wemple, "The Power of Women Through the Family in Medieval Europe, 500–1100," pp. 83–101; and Ferrante, "Public Postures," pp. 213–29. See also M.Y. Offord, ed., *The Book of the Knight of the Tower Translated by William Caxton*, EETS s.s. 2 (London, 1971), chaps. 17 (p. 35), 74–77 (pp. 105–07); Parsons, "Mothers, Daughters, Marriage, Power: Some Plantagenet Evidence, 1150–1500," in idem, *Medieval Queenship*, pp. 63–78.

45. Kristeva, "Stabat Mater," p. 262.

46. Even when Mary's pregnancy is implied, as at the Visitation, its divine origins are clearly manifest. See Gregor M. Lechner, *Maria Gravida. Zum Schwangerschaftsmotiv in der Bildenden Kunst* (Zürich, 1981), a reference I owe to Rosemary Hale.

THE OCCLUSION OF MATERNITY IN
CHAUCER'S *Clerk's Tale*

Allyson Newton

Chaucer's Clerk's Tale *charts an anxious trajectory set by Aristotelian and Aquinian theories of motherhood, in which the paternal structures of lineage and succession appropriate, and thereby occlude, the role of the mother.*

Before she is cast out of Walter's manor to "make room" for his new "wife," Griselda turns to her husband and says, "'Naked out of my fadres hous... / I cam, and naked moot I turne agayne.'"[1] Critics of Chaucer's *Clerk's Tale* highlight this crystallization of the implicit analogy between Griselda and Job, whose words Griselda echoes: "Naked came I out of my mother's womb, and naked shall I return thither."[2] One striking revision of Job's words effected by Griselda's lines, however, is largely unnoticed: the displacement of the "mother's womb" by the "father's house." What happens to these lines mirrors the *Clerk's Tale* as a whole: the maternal—the "mother's womb"—is appropriated by processes of patriarchal continuance and paternal succession—the "father's house"—that occlude the maternality upon which lineage and succession are dependent. Dominant medieval theorizations of reproduction, as formulated by Aristotle, Augustine, and Aquinas,[3] served also as a paradigm for literary production. Within their frame, Griselda's passivity and inertia about the loss of her children may be celebrated as responses that constitute proper maternity. The displacement of the mother's womb by the father's house suggests the degree to which paternal structures of lineage and succession absorb, and thereby cause to disappear, the maternal on which such structures depend: "My child and I with hertely obeisaunce/ Ben youres al, and ye mowe save or spille/ Youre owene thing" (502–504).

Griselda's own language persistently identifies herself with mothers at the nexus of medieval theorization of femaleness, Eve and Mary. When Griselda laments that "I have noght had no part of children tweyne/ But first siknesse, and after wo and payne"(650–651), she evokes the sorrow with which Eve was cursed to conceive and bring forth children, even as her words convey the limits of her role beyond bearing Walter's children. The occlusion of the maternal, which Griselda here yokes with allusions to Eve, resurfaces in a similar linguistic context when the Pardoner refers offhandedly to "Adam oure fader and his wyf also" (192). The Pardoner syntactically unnames Eve, just as he subverts the expected parallelism of Eve as mother, instead casting her as wife. Such elisions and displacements create gaps between maternal and paternal roles that run through the *Canterbury Tales* and particularly marked in the language of the poem's clerical speakers.

The linkage of motherhood with biblical curse against Eve in Griselda's language is mitigated by persistent imagery that figures her as the Virgin.[4] As Utley points out, like Griselda, the Virgin was "both a shepherdess and a spinster ... the paragon of industry, enemy of idleness ... with the Virgin Mother, Griselda takes on immense stature, that of the Universal Mother."[5] But the imaging of Griselda as Mary engages not only the power and stature of the Mother of God but also the paradox of power yoked to humility and obedience.[6] For, as Elizabeth Robertson asserts, Mary's "image did little to alter male views of woman's essential nature,"[7] especially the female role in reproduction. Not even the redemptive power of Mary's motherhood alters the valorization of the paternal that pervades medieval theories of reproduction.

Scholars additionally emphasize the similarities between the surrender of Griselda's children and the biblical narrative of Abraham and Isaac,[8] an analogy complicated by its equation of the largely powerless, maternal Griselda with the supreme patriarch of the Hebraic and Christian faiths. Griselda is further imaged as Rebekah, the wife of Isaac: the description of Griselda "sett[ing] down hir water-pot anoon/ Bisyde the threshold in an oxes stable" (290–291) alludes to Rebekah going "down to the well, and fill[ing] her pitcher."[9] Like Griselda, who "knew wel labour, but non ydel ese"(217), Rebekah receives praise for her willingness to serve as she draws water not only for Isaac's servant but also for his camels "until they

[had] done drinking."[10] Imaging Griselda as the exemplary Rebekah carries subversive possibilities: Rebekah subverts her role as servant to her husband when she becomes an accomplice in her younger son Jacob's scheme to obtain the rights of the firstborn from Esau. Mother conspires with son against both father and rightful heir, threatening lawful succession and disrupting the smooth transmission of patriarchal power. Masculine anxieties generated by fears of subversive interruptions of phallic power saturate the *Clerk's Tale*. Such anxieties seem rooted not only in the perceived threat to the transmission of phallic power by the mother, as the biblical narrative of Rebekah and Isaac suggests, but also in the father's own dread of his displacement by even a lawful heir.

The *Clerk's Tale* begins with an anxious assertion of Walter's own unimpeachable lineage: "A markis whylom lord was of that londe,/ As were his worthy eldres him before" (64–65). The Clerk stresses that Walter is a lord "of linage,/ The genilleste y-born of Lumbardye," who dwells "wher many a tour and toun thou mayst biholde/ That founded were in tyme of fadres olde" (60–72), and emphasizes the continuum of paternal succession that firmly links Walter with the "fadres olde," for this kingdom has enjoyed uninterrupted transmission of power. [11] Walter's own hesitancy to marry and secure his place in the distinguished line by producing an heir threatens to disturb this idyll of patriarchy, and this refusal fills his subjects with a "bisy drede"; they confront him with the fear that "thrugh your deeth your lyne sholde slake,/ And that a straunge successour sholde take/ Youre heritage" (137–138).

Walter's puzzling distaste for the marital yoke has often been explicated in psychoanalytic terms as a "fear of life itself." Thus, the "creative sexual act may seem to Walter a kind of dying and a confession of the necessity of having an heir an admission of mortality."[12] But if the necessity of having an heir produces an anxious "admission of mortality," then the necessity of procuring a woman to perform the maternal role also forces an equally anxiety-provoking admission of patriarchy's inability to reproduce itself autonomously. Walter's seemingly perverse choice of the socially inferior Griselda, then, gestures toward the Aristotelian devaluation of the maternal role in reproduction: the inferiority of the mere matter to be shaped is irrelevant, given the paramount, inherent superiority of the active, formative male principle.[13] Walter's choice of Griselda as the mother of his children not only tests his own maxim that "Bountee comth al of God, not of the streem/ Of which they been engendred and y-born" (157–158) but also the idea that this "bountee" comes, as Aristotelian and Aquinian theories of reproduction assert, solely from the paternal contribution to that "engendering."

Walter's covert attempt to limit maternal influences on lineage and succession meets with its first obstacle when a daughter, rather than the desired male heir, is the firstborn. This disappointment saddens even Griselda, who asserts "Al had hire levere have born a knave child" (244); the Clerk nevertheless maintains, however, that "Glad was this markys and the folk therefore,/ For though a mayde child coome al bifore, / She may unto a knave child atteyne/ By lyklihede, syn she nys nat bareyne" (445–448). But if the "mayde child" attests to her mother's fruitfulness, she also casts doubt on Walter's potency: if the male principle of reproduction indeed forms and shapes, then how does one explain the birth of a daughter when a male heir is so sorely required? One can condemn the "matter to be shaped," the mother, and this is Walter's course of action. Aristotle postulated that the "production of the female [comes] from a defect in the active force or from some material indisposition,"[14] and such medieval theologians as St. Albert concurred: "the sex of the child [is] determined during conception and if the seed material [is] well digested and strong it [leads] to males but if it [is] poorly digested and weak it [results] in a 'femalization' and the birth of a girl."[15] Thus, the birth of a daughter produces anxiety about the masculine ability to form and shape the embryonic matter provided by the mother; attempts to explain the seeming disparity between masculine intention and "defective" femaleness exacerbate Walter's already obsessive need to secure and maintain complete control.

Walter projects this anxiety onto his subjects when, in the course of "tempt[ing] his wyf, hir sadnesse for to knowe," he claims that "They seyn, to hem it is greet shame and wo/ For to be subgetz and ben in servage/ To thee, that born art of a small village./ And namely sith *thy* doghter was y-bore/ Thise wordes han they spoken, douteless" (481–485, my emphasis). As Deborah Ellis says, "[Walter's] use of the pronoun—'thy doghter'—signals to us that it is Griselda who is expected to pay the price of her husband's 'reste and pees.' Walter, in fact, is expert at stabbing with pronouns that casually signal dispossession and exile."[16] More importantly, Walter's pronouns disclaim his own role in his daughter's conception and blame Griselda for the lack of a male heir. Walter's language elides the lowly Griselda's own parentage: he refers to her as "born out of a small village"; the discomfiture Walter attributes to his subjects of being "in servage" to Griselda reflects and enlarges his anxiety about his dependency on his wife for a male heir. Though this anxiety is sometimes viewed as Walter's refusal to accept his own mortality, when Lavers says that "[Walter] has symbolically denied his paternity, and so denied his mortality…Walter has also denied Griselda's maternity,"[17] the critic's grammatical subordination of the denial of Griselda's maternity to Walter's denial of his own paternity misconstrues how patriarchal structures *first* deny the maternal in order to absorb it into illusory, autonomous male succession. Walter's language does not similarly divest itself of claims to paternity when speaking to Griselda about their son, for he maintains that "My peple sikly berth oure marriage,/ And namely, sith *my* sone y-boren is" (625–626, emphasis mine). Walter's language claims not only sole possession of the male heir but also proprietary interest in the community at large—"my peple"—that is absent from the seemingly parallel previous utterance, full of distancing, ambiguous "they's," about his daughter. The process of consolidation enacted in Walter's language actively requires the elimination of Griselda, and thus the occlusion of the maternal, to restore the relationship between the King and his "people" that had seemed on the verge of dissolution at the very beginning of the *Clerk's Tale*.

Walter's language occludes Griselda's maternal role even more decisively when he remarks, "Now sey they thus, "Whan Walter is agoon,/ Thanne shall the blood of Janicle succede/ And been our Lord" (631–633), not only eliminating Griselda entirely from the line of succession but also voicing the fear that somehow the maternal line will eclipse his own impeccable blood line.[18] Walter's symbolic murder of the children, then, is not so much a denial of paternity or mortality as it is an attempt to purge the maternal. Walter consolidates the paternal power by removing the children from Griselda's care and entrusting them to his own sister; this consolidation culminates in Walter's final speech to Griselda, an attempt at explanation that does less to explain Walter's perverseness than to seal the occlusion of Griselda's maternity:

> 'This is *thy* doghter which thou hast supposed
> To be my wyf; that oother feithfully
> Shal be *myn* heir, as I have ay disposed;
> Thou bare him in thy body trewely.
> At Boloigne have I kept hem prively;
> Taak hem agayn, for now maystow nat seye
> That thou hast lorn noon of thy children twey...
> ...I have doon this deede...
> ...for t'assaye in thee thy wommanheede,
> And nat to sleen *my* children—God forbede'
>   (1065–1076, my emphasis)

Walter's language carefully discriminates between "thy doghter" and "myn heir," asserts the King's sole claim to the male heir, and absents Griselda from that process of succession. Walter admits Griselda's maternity with "[t]hou bare him in thy body trewely," but his language accords with the Aristotelian model of woman as vessel. While Walter's language would seem to offer Griselda some claim to the children with the reference to "thy children tweye," mutuality is nullified by the couching of the statement in the negative and by the fact that Walter is only ventriloquizing the words of Griselda: "now nastow not seye/ That thou hast born non of they children tweye." By this speech's end, Walter's pronouns again lay sole claim to the children that Griselda has borne: "And nat to sleen *my* children, God forbede."

Griselda's own language has already anticipated Walter's possessiveness in striking ways, particularly in her request for a smock to cover her nakedness before Walter casts her out of the manor:

> 'Ye coude nat doon so dishonest a thing
> That thilke wombe in which youre children leye
> Sholde biforn the peple, in my walking,
> Be seyn al bare ...
> ... swich a smock as I was wont to were,
> That I therwith may wrye the wombe of here
> That was youre wyf' (876–888).[19]

Griselda seems always to agree with Walter, but she manages here to resist Walter's linguistic mystifications. Griselda's language identifies her with her womb only to underscore her dispossession and distance from that womb. Her maternal role is plangently collapsed into the "womb" that has borne Walter's children, even as her insistent repetitions of the word stab at the mystifications of the maternal that pervade Walter's language.[20] Griselda's subsequent plaint that "I have noght had no part of children tweyne/ But first siknesse, and after wo and peyne" speaks her own pained sense of maternity and reveals deeply-felt cost in the human terms of "wo and peyne."

For the most part, Griselda's despair remains locked in her silence but physically apprehended in the swooning grip that she maintains on her children when they finally return to her: "And in her swough so sadly holdeth she/ Hire children two, when she gan hem t'embrace, / That with greet sleighte and greet difficultee/ The children from hire arm they gonne arace" (1100–1103). No sooner are the children returned to Griselda than they are once more, literally, torn from her arms. This scene reenacts the earlier separations from her daughter: "When that this child had souked but a throwe" (450), and from her son: "When it was two yeer old and fro the breast/ Departed of his norice" (617–618). The *Clerk's Tale* thus constructs the separation of Walter's male heir from Griselda's arms as a natural act of weaning: patriarchal succession itself is thus mystified as "natural." Walter's decision to entrust childrearing to his "suster deare," rather than to Griselda, signifies more than just his "feel[ing] that the peasant Griselda cannot rear his children in true noble fashion"[21] and something other than his "unconscious wish that [his sister] were actually having children by him."[22] This decision is a concentrated effort to consolidate paternal influence while diminishing maternal influence.

Whether or not Walter "consciously" attempts to attenuate what little maternal influence Griselda may exert on her children is not my concern; I focus rather on the patriarchy that ensures the smooth, uninterrupted transmission of phallic power in lineage and succession. Attempts to explicate the seemingly incomprehensible Walter and Griselda in terms of individual psychologies are unsatisfactory because they divorce the characterological from the structural. Such readings miss the implications throughout the tale that it is the system of patrilineage which appropriates the maternal, denies its significance, and then attempts to exclude it, so accounting for the tale's pervasive cruelty. To brand Griselda a "bad mother" for surrendering her children complacently[23] fails to acknowledge the systemic culpability of a patriarchy that devalues and denigrates the maternal. The Clerk himself, as narrator, is the first to insinuate the possibility of a less-than-exemplary Griselda:

> This markys wondred evere lenger the moore
> Upon hir pacience, and if that he
> Ne hadde soothly knowen therbifoore
> That parfitly hir children loved she,
> He wolde have wend that of som subtiltee,
> And of malice, or for crueel corage,
> That she had suffred this with sad visage.
> But wel he knew that next himself, certayn,
> She loved hir children best in every wyse (687–695).

Excess in this elaborate denial emphasizes the possibility it ostensibly dispels: perhaps Griselda's "sad visage" masks a deep-seated "malice" and "cruel corage." Walter's fleeting but disturbing doubts about Griselda seem almost to confirm those of the Clerk himself, who has interjected earlier in the Tale his own suspicion that

> I trowe that to a norice in this cas
> It had been hard this reuthe for to se;
> Wel myghte a mooder thanne han cryd 'allas!'
> But natheless so sad stidefast was she
> That she endured al adversitee (561–565).

Griselda's very passivity seems more disturbing to both Walter and the Clerk than open defiance, however provoked, would be; there seems to be some trace of resistance to Griselda's steadfastness that problematizes her seeming complacency.[24] Even critics sympathetic with Griselda's plight often seem compelled to ward off this specter of the "bad mother"; their attempts entail the same nervous denials that structure the language of Walter and the Clerk.[25]

Griselda's almost excruciating patience is the essence of the maternal as defined in Aquinas's sense of "the two distinct operations, that of the agent and that of the patient" and by his insistence that "the entire active operation is on the part of the male and the passive on the part of the female."[26] The problem is not that Griselda is a bad mother but rather that she exemplifies Aristotelian passivity and inertia of the maternal all too well. The passivity which causes uneasiness about the quality of Griselda's mothering represents perfectly one medieval image of proper motherhood.

Griselda is represented as being all too aware of her own maternal role, of her objectification as the vessel that carries Walter's child and heir. Again and again she rejects Walter's mystification of the children as "hers":

'My child and I, with hertely obeisaunce,
Been youres al, and ye mowe save or spille
Youre owene thyng: werketh after youre wille' (502–504).

'Ye been oure lord; dooth with youre owene thyng
Right as you list' (652–653).

'Ye coude nat doon so dishonest a thyng
That thilke wombe in which youre children leye
Sholde biforn the peple, in my walking,
Be seyn al bare' (876–879).

Griselda's language functions not to deny her own role as mother
but to insist on the degree to which that role has been appropriated
and absorbed by interests of the patriarchal structures of lineage and
succession that Walter serves. The effect of her language on the
character's own seeming awareness of this appropriation renders more
wrenching the series of possessives with which she embraces her
children in a moment of unguarded expression: "'Graunt mercy,
lord, God thanke it you,' quod she,/ 'That ye han saved me my
childred dere!/ ... O tendre, o dere, o yonge children myne'" (1088–
1093). Griselda's dispossession of her children is also underscored in
the terms of Walter's ownership of their children, again signalling
the exclusion of Griselda:

And richely *his* doghter marryied he
Unto a lord, oon of the worthieste
Of al Ytaille; and then in pees and reste
His wyves fader in *his* court he kepeth,
Til that the soule out of *his* body crepeth.
His sone succedeth in his heritage,
In reste and pees, after *his* fader day
                    (1130–1136, emphasis mine).

The proliferation of masculine pronouns in these lines suggests that
the tale closes firmly in the realm of the patriarchal: the acceptance
of Griselda's father into Walter's court seals the absorption of the
maternal into the patrilineal and the safe passage of the "heritage"
from Walter to his son and heir seems at last secured.

I have referred here to the different languages of Griselda, Walter,
and even of the tale. This acknowledges one aspect of the tale and
occludes another: the language of the characters is theirs, but it is
also fictionalized as that of the Tale's narrator, the Clerk. If it is
language that speaks character into being, then what about the

narrator who speaks that language into being? What is the Clerk's relation to his Tale? Is he allied with Griselda, as Carlyn Dinshaw suggests,[27] or is he complicit with Walter's masculinist impulses? Grennen argues that the tales' readers must "try to fathom the nature of the Clerk's struggle...." [28]

Medieval theories of maternity accommodate the complex relation of the Clerk's relation to his Tale. The Aristotelian notion of an active, masculine force that acts upon and gives form to passive, feminine material became a medieval model not only for the reproductive process but also for the literary process. The Clerk, in giving shape and form to the received narrative of Petrarch, occupies not only a masculine but also a paternal position in relation to the feminized, embryonic matter of Petrarch's narrative. This relation is established in the Tale by analogies between Petrarch and Griselda with which the Tale both begins and ends. At the very opening of the Tale, the Clerk asserts that Petrarch "is now deed and nayled in his chest," (29)[29] by the close of the Tale, it is Griselda who "is deed, and eek hire pacience, / And both atones buried in Itaille" (1077–1078). These echoes position the *Clerk's Tale's* received narrative of Petrarch in the same passive, inert role of the maternal formulated by Aristotle and Aquinas; the Clerk establishes himself as the active, shaping force of the paternal as he exerts his own narrative capabilities on Petrarch's "formless matter." The Clerk may seem sympathetic in his portrayal of the long-suffering, exemplary Griselda, but he is actually closer to Walter, assuming the role of the father who is the active, superior force in shaping Petrarch's now-feminized material.

Another crucial dimension concerns the Clerk's position in relation to the Wife of Bath. Does the Clerk rebut her assertion of female "mastery" by countering with the submissive Griselda, or does he in fact support her contention that it is women who are most worthy to exercise such mastery? By resituating the terms of this long-standing debate within the context of medieval theories of the maternal, one can partially escape from this critical impasse to see some complex ways in which the Clerk "quittes" the Wife. The Clerk counters by opposing the exemplary Griselda to the rebellious Wife and by resituating the female sexual desire celebrated by the Wife back into the realm of the maternal. The Clerk reappropriates the energy of female sexuality released by the Wife's exuberance and returns it to the service of reproducing patriarchy. The *Clerk's Tale* would thus nullify the Wife's exuberant interruption of the largely masculine enterprise of tale-telling, would reestablish the "lineage" of literature as a patrilineal enterprise, occluding not only the maternal but also the feminine in the interest of maintaining the illusion of autonomous reproduction. It is not in Petrarch's chest, but in the womb of the mother that we find once more the house of the fathers.

NOTES

1. Geoffrey Chaucer, "The Clerk's Tale," in *The Canterbury Tales*, ed. V.A. Kolve and Glending Olson (New York, 1989), lines 871–872. All further references will be cited in the text.

2. Job 1:21. Douay translation. The Latin Vulgate reads, "Nudus egressus sum de utero matris meae et nudus revertar." Readings of the tale that emphasize the analogy between Griselda and Job include John P. McCall, "The Clerk's Tale and the Theme of Obedience," *Modern Language Quarterly* 27 (1966), 260–69; Donald H. Reiman, "The Real Clerk's Tale: or, Patient Griselda Exposed," *Texas Studies in Literature and Language* 5 (Autumn 1963), 356–76; and Charlotte C. Morse, "The Exemplary Griselda," *Studies in the Age of Chaucer* 7 (1985), 51–86.

3. For a helpful summary of this synthesis of Aristotelian science and medieval theology, see Vern L. Bullough's "Medical and Scientific Views of Women," *Viator* 4 (1973), 485–501. See also George H. Tavard's *Woman in Christian Tradition* (Notre Dame: 1973), especially Chap. One, "The Two Traditions" ; Kari Elisabeth Borresen's *Subordination and Equivalence: The Nature of Women in Augustine and Thomas Aquinas* (Washington, D.C., 1981); Prudence Allen's *The Concept of Woman: The Aristotelian Revolution, 750 B.C. to A.D. 1250* (Montreal, 1985); and Elizabeth Robertson's *Early English Devotional Prose and the Female Audience* (Knoxville, 1990), especially Chap. Three, " Medieval Views of Female Spirituality."

4. Francis L. Utley, " Five Genres in the *Clerk's Tale*," *Chaucer Review* 6 (1972), 217.

5. Utley, " Five Genres," pp. 220–25.

6. The nature of Mary's maternal role in the incarnation was itself a paradox for medieval theologians. Augustine does not limit Mary's role by the physical requirements of birth, which necessitated the very fullness and inclusiveness of the redemptive process: "It was necessary that the liberation of man should be made manifest in both sexes. Therefore, since it was fitting that He should take the human nature of man, the more honorable of the two sexes, it remained for the deliverance of the female sex to be shown by the fact that this man should be born of a woman" (*De diversis quaestionibus octoginta tribus*, as quoted in Borresen, *Subordination and Equivalence*, p.

74). Aquinas filters Mary's role through the lenses of Aristotelian physiology, truncates Augustine's emphasis on Mary's spiritual as well as physical fruitfulness. As Borresen explains, the "presence of a female element in the mystery of the incarnation, itself ordered to the liberation of all humankind, is realized within the limits of the passive role played by woman in human propagation" (p. 233). Thus, even the position of privilege accorded to Mary is as much a function of female passivity and inferiority as a transvaluation of them.

7. Robertson, *Early English Devotional Prose*, p. 39.

8. See especially E. Pearlman, "The Psychological Basis of the 'Clerk's Tale,'" *Chaucer Review* 11 (1977), 248–57.

9. Genesis 24:16; the Vulgate reads, "Puella...descendant autem ad fonten, et impleverat hydriam, as revertebatur."

10. Genesis 24:19; the Vulgate reads, "donec cuncti bibant."

11. See Thomas A. Van, "Walter at the Stake: A Reading of Chaucer's *Clerk's Tale,*" *Chaucer Review* 22 (1988), 215.

12. Norman Lavers, "Freud, the *Clerkes Tale,* and Literary Criticism," *College English* 26 (December 1964), 183. More recent psychoanalytic readings, like that by Patricia Cramer, stress the "infantile solipsism" that dominates Walter's premarital existence: "Walter enters marriage under the sway of an infantile fantasy of omnipotence as indicated by the description of his premarital freedom....This psychological state parallels the infant's early autoeroticism and the fantasies of self-sufficiency characteristic of this state" ("Lordship, Bondage, and the Erotic: The Psychological Bases of Chaucer's *Clerk's Tale,*" *Journal of English and Germanic Philology* [1990], p. 496).

13. In the *Generation of Animals*, Aristotle argues that "If, then, the male stands for the effective and active, and the female, for the passive, it follows that what the female would contribute to the semen of the male would not be semen but material for the semen to work upon" (729 A, 25–34), trans. A.L. Peck, The Loeb Classical Library (Cambridge, MA, 1953).

14. Aristotle, *Generation of Animals*, 729 A 25–34, trans. A.L. Peck.

15. St. Albert, as quoted in Bullough, "Medieval Medical and Scientific Views of Women," p. 491.

16. Deborah S. Ellis, "Domestic Treachery in the *Clerk's Tale,*" in *Ambiguous Realities: Women in the Middle Ages and Renaissance*, eds. Carole Levin and Jeanie Watson (Detroit, 1987), pp. 99–113. The lines actually create, through the nervous repetitions of "They seyn" and "han they spoken," together with the over-compensatory "douteless," not Walter's "reste and pees," but rather his mounting anxiety.

17. Lavers, "Freud, the *Clerkes Tale*, and Literary Criticism," p. 186.

18. And, incidentally, eliminating any traces of Griselda's own mother, who is noticeably absent from the tale.

19. The issue of Griselda's "consciousness" of her objectification, of these lines as an ironic rendition of her own role, emerges here for some readers. The presence of ironic language need not require the speaker's ironic consciousness, whether that of Griselda or of the Clerk who "speaks" her.

20. Griselda's claims that the children are Walter's seem profoundly ambivalent, in that they both affirm Walter's possessiveness toward his male heir and counter his insistent dispossessions of his daughter.

21. Patrick Morrow, "The Ambivalence of Truth: Chaucer's " Clerk's Tale," *Bucknell Review* 16 (1968), 80.

22. Lavers, "Freud, the *Clerkes Tale*, and Literary Criticism," p. 186.

23. Utley, "Five Genres," p. 226.

24. Linda Georgianna's "The Clerk's Tale and the Grammar of Assent," *Speculum* 70 (1995) recuperates the "active willing" seemingly belied by Griselda's passivity, but I do not concur with Georgianna's claim for the "eager activity of Griselda's willing." It may be that the *Clerk's Tale* attempts to transvalue passivity, but to construe that phenomenon as oppositional "activity" reinscribes the oppositions that the *Tale* twists anxiously between.

25. Utley, "Five Genres," p. 213.

26. St. Thomas Aquinas, *Summa Theologica*, trans. Roland Potter, O.P. (New York, 1972), Part 3, question 32, "De conceptione Christi quoad Activum Principum," Article 4.

27. In *Chaucer's Sexual Poetics* (Madison, 1989), Dinshaw reads the *Clerk's Tale* as a locus for "the intersection of hermeneutics with the question of the feminine" (p. 135) and argues that the Clerk "sympathizes, in the telling of his tale, not with the translator but with the translated, not with Walter but with Griselda, not with the man but with the woman" (p. 135). Although my understanding of the relationship between Aristotelian models of reproduction and medieval models of literary production remains heavily indebted to Dinshaw's work, I disagree with her about the Clerk's allegiances. The Clerk remains allied with the clerical tradition stretching back to Aquinas and Augustine and, through them, all the way back to Aristotle, and does not "explicitly oppose[s] himself to other clerks" (p. 135).

28. Joseph E. Grennen, "Science and Sensibility in Chaucer's Clerk," *Chaucer Review* 6 (Fall 1971), 89.

29. The Clerk's language may even allude to the womb with the image of the "cheste" within which Petrarch lies.

THE MATERNAL BEHAVIOR OF GOD:
DIVINE FATHER AS FANTASY HUSBAND

Pamela Sheingorn

The medieval association of maternal behavior with God the Father shared in the construction of His masculinity even as it communicated an image of male "tenderness and attentive concern." This buttressed normative heterosexuality and female submissiveness.

Can men mother? Motherhood has traditionally been seen as "natural, universal, and unchanging" and therefore restricted to females. But one of the many contributions of feminism has been to distinguish between birthing and mothering by separating the behavior called mothering from biological reproduction. As a result, mothering becomes a socially constructed set of behaviors available to both males and females. In this essay I use Evelyn Nakano Glenn's definition of mothering as "a historically and culturally variable relationship 'in which one individual nurtures and cares for another.'"[1] Caroline Walker Bynum's groundbreaking work has shown that the Middle Ages offers powerful evidence of mothering as socially constructed: the mothering individuals she discusses, Jesus and abbots who imitate him in nurturing and caring for others, are male.[2] I focus here on another figure and different social milieux to consider mothering within the constellation of gender characteristics ascribed to God the Father in the later Middle Ages. Specifically, I examine here the representation in later medieval culture of the love relationship between the Father-God and the Virgin Mary in the context of patterns of marriage between older men and young women in the same period. I am especially interested in the ways representation forwarded the ideology of patriarchy by idealizing such marriages and thereby urging young women to consent to them.

I argue this point by analogy from a twentieth-century analysis of a similar phenomenon in contemporary culture, the romance, which I see functioning in the way that pictorial representation functioned in later medieval culture. Just as Janice Radway undertook her study of romance partly to understand what women gain from reading romances so intensively, I undertook this inquiry to explore the impact on women of the proliferation of representations of a masculinized God the Father in later medieval art.

The idea of Jesus as mother is firmly based in the theology of mystics like Julian of Norwich. Julian saw the first person of the Trinity as the Father who created the human soul and the second person as the Mother, the creator of the flesh, in accordance with the common medieval association of the female with the material.[3] Julian further assigned to Jesus three maternities: the first, his motherhood in creation; the second, in the Incarnation, which begins "the motherhood of grace"; and the third, the "motherhood at work." With regard to the first of these maternities, Jesus' role in the embodiment of the human soul, Denise Nowakowski Baker traces from the Neoplatonism of Plotinus, through Augustine, and into the thought of later medieval theologians, the notion Julian developed of "two phases of human creation: God the Father's formation of the substance [or soul, 'the higher part'] and Jesus the Mother's embodiment of the substance in the sensuality."[4] As Baker notes, Julian's personification of the Logos as a mother "conformed to the association of the female with the material and corporeal in the scientific and theological discourse of the Middle Ages."[5] The Incarnation or "motherhood of grace" is "his taking of our nature" or taking on a body. At work here is also the tradition that identified Jesus with Sophia or Wisdom, a female manifestation of God. In the words of another mystic, Meister Eckhart, "Wisdom is a name for a mother. The characteristic of a motherly name is passivity, and in God both activity and passivity must be thought. The Father is active, and the Son is passive because of his function as the one being born. For the Son is Wisdom born from eternity in which all things are distinct."[6] Jesus' third maternity has to do with his nourishing of the human soul with the sacraments. Thus, Jesus' Incarnation embodied him in his mother's female flesh and his nourishing of the human soul with the sacraments made him "a protective but enabling mother."[7]

Scholars have argued that "the frequent depiction of Christ as female in devotional literature and art mitigated the misogynistic clerical tradition."[8] Perhaps this is true, but this depiction did not challenge the gender hierarchy that places the masculine above the feminine. Because Jesus gives birth to the universe and then takes on human flesh as well, he acquires not only the social behavior of mothering that belongs to the female but also other feminine qualities such as passivity, leaving masculine characteristics for the male Father-God. These constructions preserve gender characteristics as separate clusters by assigning to one set the name "father" and to the other the name "mother" and, by so doing, maintain gender hierarchy. In this way of thinking the metaphor of gender inflects the first two persons of the Trinity, replicating both the gender difference and the gender hierarchy of medieval society itself.

A further impact of Jesus' assimilation of the female body is to elide the physical bodies of medieval women. Jesus' pure "feminized" flesh is inscribed over the messy, leaky bodies of the women who actually gave birth.

Explicating one of her visions, Julian of Norwich cautioned that although God's manifestation assumes the male form, "we ought to know and beleue that the Father is not man."[9] Such a nuanced understanding may have been possible for mystics like Julian, but those not inclined to theological reflection on the persons of the Trinity may well have drawn different conclusions. I have argued elsewhere that God the Father's increasingly frequent representation in a male body in later medieval art corresponds closely with the assignment to him of the behavior understood to belong to a man, masculine behavior.[10] Such behavior in secular medieval society could include the quality of nurturing. For example, in his "Willehalm," Wolfram von Eschenbach creates a knightly hero who finds Vivanz mortally wounded and holds him in his lap during his death throes.[11] Given the prevalence of the Pietà as a subject in later medieval art, we think of the ritual gesture of embracing the body of the dead in one's lap as strongly gendered but, as Uta Schwab demonstrates, it belongs as well to the milieu of the Christian hero. The gesture also belonged to an older male in a different context: representations of the Last Judgment frequently show the patriarch Abraham, whose fatherhood is central to the Hebrew Bible and whose luxuriantly full beard demonstrates his masculinity, clasping the souls of the

Figure 1. "Nativity," illustration to Primer of the Hours of the Virgin, *Book of Hours by the Master of the Munich Golden Legend, fol. 52v, ca. 1430 (Baltimore, Walters Art Gallery MS W 288).*

blessed to his bosom in paradise. As God the Father took on human form in later medieval art, he acquired Abraham's role of nurturer of souls. The representation of God the Father with dove, crucifix, and a cloth of souls, which I have called the "Bosom of Abraham Trinity," appeared frequently in alabaster sculptures that probably functioned as cult objects.[12] The cloth of souls signals the caring protection of the male god just as Mary's sheltering cloak attributes similar qualities to her as "Mother of Mercy." God the Father also acquired the gesture of embracing the dead in the subject called the *Notgottes*, which shows the Father-God cradling the body of his dead son. The *Notgottes* is the compositional and emotional equivalent of the Pietà in that both express parental love and grief.

This essay explores the impact of combining God the Father's nurturing and caring behavior with his masculinity in the specific context of his heterosexual love relationship with Mary. Especially concentrated in Books of Hours, representations of this couple would have been easily available to women of the upper classes, but their realization in more accessible media such as carved and painted altarpieces and even in the multiple editions of woodcuts suggests that this aspect of patriarchal ideology was presented to women across classes. Such representations normalize the idea of caring protection as an integral part of a love relationship between an old man and a young woman and expand our understanding of medieval masculinities. Thus we see him gazing at her with loving concern in representations of the Annunciation.[13] He blesses her and wraps her in his radiant light at the Nativity (Fig. 1).[14] As parents, they suffer the pain and death of their Son together, as is especially clear in the Crucifixion in the *Bedford Hours*, where their intimacy is revealed by the shared blue color of their clothing and even more by their glances, which focus on Christ but also appear to meet one another.[15] He mourns with her over the body of their son.[16] After her death he eagerly awaits her Assumption and crowns her his eternal queen in heaven.[17] He even supervised the transfer of her house from its original site in Nazareth to its present location in Loreto (Fig. 2).[18]

Such late medieval representations of an embodied Father-God with the Virgin Mary participated in the construction of his masculinity and buttressed the ideology of male dominance as I have shown elsewhere. They allayed the anxiety of the older man

Par les anges de paradis et sur ladicte eglise. Sans les fondemens les quelx sont encores en Nazareth
Pour perpetuelle est signee et portee es parties de la Domme au quenlx Lieulx ladicte Eglise
fut long espace de Temps mais pource que les Chrestiens prochains de ce Sainct lieu.
Nen Tenoint pas grant Compte gens incognulz et des Poyriens de Sens.

Figure 2. "The Transportation of the Holy House of Loreto," woodcut
made in Savoy, France, dated 1494 (Rosenwald Collection, National
Gallery of Art, Washington).

by emphasizing his paternity and the power of the male gaze to control a young wife, an especially pointed issue because of the increased number of marriages between older men and young women in the later Middle Ages. Here I shift the point of view to that of the female audience and ask a different question: How might women have responded to these representations? Did they function to urge young women to marry older men? There was a dearth of marriageable women due to higher female mortality resulting from death in childbearing; young mothers were especially vulnerable to the recurrent waves of plague in the fourteenth and fifteenth centuries. One man could live through several wives and continue to select virginal young women to bear his children. Representations of a nurturing God the Father construct such a relationship as beneficial to women and thus operate as part of the ideological system that transmitted the values of patriarchy.

To explore ways in which the nurturing Father-God offered an appealing husband-model for young women, I turn to a psychoanalytic model of the formation of female identity offered by object relations theory. Crucial to my use of this model is the social fact that both in medieval Europe and in our own society women have primary responsibility for the parenting of babies and young children. The many representations of the Holy Kinship, that is, of Saint Anne and her daughters surrounded by their children, provide visual analogues.[19] In both medieval and contemporary societies, "women are the primary love object and object of identification for [children]."[20] According to object relations theory, male children come to recognize their difference from the mother and negotiate a switching of identity to claim the father and heterosexual masculinity, but female children may assume heterosexual femininity without psychic separation from the mother and may never be forced to deny their need for nurturing care.

This theory became crucial for Janice Radway when she was analyzing the data collected in her study of women as romance readers, published in 1985.[21] Radway was searching for a model that would help her understand why the women she interviewed "apparently felt an intense need to be nurtured and cared for....[T]he heroines they most appreciated were virtually always provided with the kind of attention and care the... women [themselves] claimed to desire and further...the hero's ministrations were nearly always linked metaphorically with maternal concern and nurturance."[22] Radway saw in these women "an ongoing, unfulfilled longing for the mother....[S]o much of what the women consciously said and unconsciously revealed...pointed to the centrality of the fact that in ideal romances the hero is constructed androgynously. Although the women were clearly taken with his spectacularly masculine phallic power,...they emphasized equally that his capacity for tenderness and attentive concern was essential as well."[23] For Radway, Nancy Chodorow's theories "seemed helpful because of their capacity to explain what [she] thought of as the twin objects of desire underlying romance reading, that is, the desire for the nurturance represented and promised by the preoedipal mother and for the power and autonomy associated with the oedipal father. Romance reading... permitted the ritual retelling of the psychic process by which traditional heterosexuality was constructed for women...."[24]

I want to suggest here that the life of the Virgin Mary as represented in late medieval visual culture also offered a ritual retelling of this process. When Mary's mother Anne conceived after many years of childlessness, she promised to "bring [her child] as a gift to the Lord," according to the *Protevangelium of James*.[25] Reluctant to give her up at the age of two, Anne acquiesced when Mary was only three and presented her at the temple, a scene that is repeatedly represented in later medieval art. This separation from her nurturing mother enabled Mary's years of education in the temple but, in psychoanalytic terms, intensified her need to find a new source of loving care. The next event in her life is her marriage to the elderly Joseph, a reluctant husband. The late Middle Ages is, of course, the period when the representation of Joseph was being explored, with varied results. As Ruth Mellinkoff puts it in her recent book, *Outcasts*, "Joseph was on the one hand treated with reverence as saintly spouse, as protector and nourisher of Christ and the Virgin, as tender and loving, trusting and consoling, prayerful and unselfish, and as fully aware of his noble mission. But on the other hand, Joseph was belittled as a doddering old man, a grumbling, disgruntled husband, a fool, a cuckold and comic, a crude rustic fit only for household chores, and a man so unaware of his role that he was indifferent to Christ's birth."[26] Mellinkoff cites many examples in which Joseph is denigrated by the denial of a halo, even when minor figures such as a nursemaid have them, as in a painting of the Nativity dated about ca. 1390 (Fig. 3). Mellinkoff also shows that Joseph was identified

Figure 3. "Nativity," Antwerp-Baltimore triptych, ca. 1390 (Antwerp, Museum Mayer van den Bergh).

with the Old Law and with Synagoga by the use of specific visual signs such as the Jew's hat. This ambiguity about Joseph's suitability, as well as the lack of any sign of sexual potency, represented him as lacking the "power and autonomy associated with the oedipal father" that romance readers seek. That power and autonomy belong, of course, to God the Father who, from the Annunciation onward, remained a steady presence in Mary's life. On the other hand, Joseph in his fallible humanity resembles the actual husband of the medieval female viewer and is pushed into the background so that the fantasy husband of romance can take his place (Fig. 4). Like the romance hero, God the Father's behavior toward the heroine displayed both his "spectacular phallic power" and his "capacity for tenderness and attentive concern." When this most powerful of males threatens humankind with the arrows of his wrath, Mary can deflect them (Fig. 5).[27] Like Beauty with the Beast, she comprehends his gentle nature as he watches over her, compensating for the inattentiveness of her human husband.

In its rehearsal of the process by which female identity is shaped by the continued need for nurturing as well as for the power of the father, the romance of the Virgin Mary and God the Father yields to a psychoanalytic reading that, as Radway says of contemporary romances, "explain[s] why the story hails these readers, why they believe it possible to pursue their own pleasure by serving as witness to the romantic heroine's achievement of hers."[28]

Another quality shared by the contemporary romance and the romance of the Virgin Mary reminds us that mythic stories, whether those of the past or the present, meet genuinely felt needs. Radway notes that the women in her study were remarkably familiar with the genre of romance fiction because they read numbers of romances each week.[29] Similarly the iconographically fixed story of Mary, repeated in both pictorial arts and vernacular texts, must have produced a remarkable familiarity for the medieval audience. Judith Butler's concept of gender performativity offers a way of understanding the need to repeat what is already familiar. Gender performativity is "the reiterative and citational practice by which discourse produces the effects that it names."[30] In the case of the contemporary romance and the romance of the Virgin Mary, the effect being produced is that of normative heterosexuality. As Radway writes:

Figure 4. "Annunciation and Nativity," Altar of Knight of Stauffenberg, 1450-60 (Colmar, Musee d'Unterlinden).

Figure 5. "Madonna in a Wreath of Roses," woodcut made in Augsburg 1490-1500 (Rosenwald Collection, National Gallery of Art, Washington).

What the psychoanalytically based interpretation reveals is the deep irony hidden in the fact that women who are experiencing the consequences of patriarchal marriage's failure to address their needs turn to a story that ritually recites the history of the process by which those needs are constituted. They do so, it appears, because the fantasy resolution of the tale ensures the heroine's achievement of the very pleasure the readers endlessly long for. In this reading of the story of a woman who is granted adult autonomy, a secure social position, and the completion produced by maternal nurturance, all in the person of the romantic hero, the... women [readers of romance] are repetitively asserting to be true what their still-unfulfilled desire demonstrates to be false, that is, that heterosexuality can create a fully coherent, fully satisfied, female subjectivity.[31]

But the psychoanalytic theories on which my interpretation has thus far rested have been justly critiqued for their lack of cultural or historical specificity. Thus, I want now to inflect the more "universal" analysis I have just given by conjoining it with an analysis that will begin historically and culturally to locate the subjectivities of the medieval female audience I posit.[32] In spite of the centuries separating Radway's women from those of the later Middle Ages, there are some parallels that justify the use of Radway's study to understand representations of the nurturing God the Father. Here I specifically want to consider an audience of women who were not mystics, not especially adept at or interested in spiritual exercises, and were accepting of the conventional teachings of Christianity they heard from parish priest or family confessor, including those detailing the responsibilities of women for home and family. And I want to suggest a parallel between these women and the women of today whose lives seem to me to be similarly positioned in relation to their societies.

According to Radway's study, romances have a particular appeal to young women: "romance reading apparently correlates strongly with the years of young adulthood and early middle age."[33] Young women are also one of the target audiences for cultural constructions of the nurturing divine husband. Romances assume heterosexuality and patriarchal marriage. As Radway notes, "even the most progressive of recent romances continue to bind female desire to a heterosexuality constructed as the only natural sexual alliance, and thus continue to prescribe patriarchal marriage as the ultimate route to the realization of a mature female subjectivity."[34] Similarly, conduct books for medieval women assume marriage to be a "natural" role. Frequent childbearing meant that medieval women lived surrounded by children. Radway found that "it is precisely this emotional drain caused by a woman's duty to nurture and care for her children and husband that is addressed directly by romance reading at least within the minds of the women themselves."[35]

The contemporary romance, then, both reinscribes patriarchy and can be appropriated by women to meet their own needs: Radway calls it "a profoundly conflicted form."[36] The life of the Virgin Mary can also be understood as "profoundly conflicted," since it functioned both as part of the ideological system of late medieval patriarchy and as a site where women could claim some autonomy. Later medieval representations of the Virgin Mary construct her as a woman whose life experiences resonate with those of women in medieval society. The next section of this essay explores how representations of scenes from Mary's life were interpreted and inserted into culture by a male-dominated Church that was indoctrinating girls so that, as women, they would assume the prescribed ideological positions. I demonstrate that such representations could have been differently received by medieval "resisting readers."

For an example I turn to a little girl's primer, her first reader, *The Primer of Claude of France* (Fig. 6).[37] Its "text begins with the ABC and proceeds with the Lord's Prayer, the Creed, Grace before Meals, the Creation Story, Adam and Eve, the Hail Mary, Nativity and Adoration of the Shepherds and other basic religious matters."[38] The opening miniature shows Claude and the Virgin Mary as equals in age and position, presented by Saint Anne, who includes both girls in her maternal protection, to the Bishop of Besançon, also named

Claude, who was both the child Claude's patron saint and a representative of the male authority of the Church. The girl can see clearly the image of the Virgin and Child embroidered on the orphrey band of the bishop's cope. The motto at the top of the page, the beginning of the "Hail, Mary," both glorifies Mary and reminds of her fate: "The Lord is with you" ("Dominus tecum"). The obsessive repetition of these words on the architectural elements of the design corresponds to their repeated perform-ance as part of the girl's devotional practices. This reiterative performance participates in the construction of Claude's sex

Figure 6. Claude of France before Her Patron Saint Claude, "Primer of Claude of France," p. 1 (Cambridge, Fitzwilliam Museum, MS 159).

and gender and is, in that way, performative.   Claude's repetition of the "Hail, Mary" produces her sexed and gendered body as one prepared to accept her "lord." The repetition also reminds us of Judith Butler's observation that the adaptation to normative heterosexuality is never satisfactory; the struggle is never fully ceded because it is founded on ambivalence. Such ambivalence may, in fact, be crucial to understanding the medieval woman's (hypothetical) reception of the culturally central narrative that constructs a female character who accepts God the Father's nurturing. Claude needed to adapt, because she was also destined to have a "dominus," a lord, as soon as possible. She was the elder surviving child of Anne of Brittany and Louis XII and "[n]egotiations for [her] marriage…with [Emperor] Maximilian's grandson the Archduke Charles (the future Emperor Charles V) began when both infants were scarcely out of their cradles."[39] Claude was officially betrothed to the heir to the French throne when she was seven and married when she was fourteen. In addition to teaching her to read, an important function of her primer was to present her with the model of the Virgin Mary so that she would similarly insert herself into the prescribed role of wife and mother.

Madeline Caviness provides another example of a Book of Hours performing this function. In her analysis of the *Hours of Jeanne d'Evreux*, Caviness shows that the opening for Matins in the Hours of the Virgin is one of the sites in this book where a "girl-bride" is instructed in proper behavior in her marriage with an older man. As Caviness observes, "Embedding didactic images in the devotional text that was in constant use would keep the lessons in mind, and prayer and visual exempla worked together toward the same end, the construction of gender."[40] These materials aimed at young girls parallel the comics aimed at twentieth-century girls that have been analyzed by Valerie Walkerdine. She argues that "young girls of primary school age are presented with, and inserted into, ideological and discursive positions by practices which locate them in meaning and in regimes of truth.…[C]ultural products for girls…may serve to prepare the ground for the insertion of the little girl into romantic heterosexuality."[41]

The *Taymouth Hours*, a book made for an English noblewoman between 1325 and 1335, uses a negative exemplum to underscore the wisdom of adapting to the prescribed role. Linda Brownrigg notes that a woman making use of this book in her devotions would see in a very important location, the opening of the Hours of the Virgin, an exemplum "which she could apply to herself, which indicates correct behaviour."[42] After an opening miniature that shows the Virgin in her house, crowned by the hands of God (fol. 59v), the marginal illustrations on fols. 60v-68v, complete with narrative captions, tell the story of a young woman rescued from a "wodewose" or wildman by an elderly knight. Instead of expressing her gratitude, the demoiselle goes off with a young knight and suffers an unhappy fate as a result.[43] This negative exemplum is clearly an object lesson for the young woman courted by an old man; its pairing with the story of Mary, a young woman who accepted and was subsequently crowned by an old man, strongly suggests that Mary is the intended model to which the young woman should turn. Representations like these functioned to further the interests of the dominant ideology of patriarchy.

Figure 7. "The Expectant Madonna with Saint Joseph," oil and tempera on wood, fifteenth century (Samuel H. Kress Collection, National Gallery of Art, Washington).

On the other hand, as Valerie Wayne concludes from her reading of Raymond Williams, "a dominant ideology is never either total or exclusive."[44] Thus we should consider the uses women made of these images, uses that might differ from those prescribed by patriarchy. "Within an apparent hegemony...there are not only alternative and oppositional formations…but, within what can be recognized as the dominant, [there are] effectively varying formations which resist any simple reduction to some generalized hegemonic function."[45] Women could and did appropriate these representations for their own uses. In 1399 Christine de Pizan wrote of the Virgin Mary, "The Father paid her great honor, for he wished to make woman his spouse and his mother, the temple of God conjoined to the Trinity. Women should really be joyful and cognizant that they have the same body that she did."[46] Radway reports that Dorothy Evans, author of an informational newsletter called "Dorothy's Diary of Romance Reading" as well as "many of the writers and readers of romances, interpret them as chronicles of female triumph …[They] believed a good romance focuses on an intelligent and able heroine who finds a man who recognizes her special qualities and is capable of loving and caring for her as she wants to be loved."[47]

Thus one might suggest that medieval women could derive pleasure from fantasizing about the Virgin Mary's divine husband, who never battered or abused her, sent his angelic servants to watch over her, elevated her to a higher station than she ever could have expected, and made her his queen (Fig. 7). For them as for the women in Janice Radway's study, contemplation of such images could have functioned as "a form of individual resistance to a situation predicated on the assumption that it is women alone who are responsible for the care and emotional nurturance of others," a respite from "the physical exhaustion and the emotional depletion brought about by the fact that no one within the patriarchal family is charged with *their* care."[48]

And finally, to return to the social circumstances of the later Middle Ages, marriage to an old man soon gave some women adult autonomy and the sure social position of widows with control over property. The central role of the Virgin Mary in representations of Pentecost, an older woman to whom younger men defer, suggests something of that authority. In the English N-Town play of Mary's Assumption, God, at Mary's behest, gathered the apostles from the "dyveris contreys" in which they were preaching because Mary wanted them at her bedside when she died.[49] The interweaving of ideas of widowhood, power, and devotion to the Virgin Mary found expression in the imagery on the seal used by Margaret, Lady Hungerford and Botreaux, from 1462 until she died in 1478 (Fig.

Figure 8. Seal of Margaret, Lady Hungerford and Botreaux (d. 1478)
(London, British Library, seal XCII.23)

8).[50] The kneeling woman with open book is framed by the arms of her father and of her husband, who died in 1459, signaling that she draws her power from them but wields it in her own right. Carol M. Meale notes the resemblances to representations of the Virgin Mary, whom Margaret especially venerated. Meale cites the Virgin of Humility and the Virgin in the Annunciation as visual parallels, but I also call attention to the many other representations in which Mary is shown reading, including those that present her as an older woman and an authority figure for the apostles in the years before her death.

Meale suggests the possibility that the seal was "perhaps designed as a pious gloss on the public assertiveness of Margaret's political role."[51] This was a role she had only as widow of a powerful older man.

Our understanding of the piety of late medieval women has centered on various responses to the incarnate Christ, whether that of the female mystic who sees herself as mother to the infant Jesus,[52] or the nun's affective identification with the Passion. Sarah Beckwith, who characterizes this as a "very material mysticism," acknowledges that much of the literature stimulating this kind of piety was written for nuns or recluses.[53] That is not to deny that some laywomen, notably Margery Kempe, pursued such practices. But perhaps more accessible to lay women whose social situation paralleled that of Radway's romance readers were exemplars like St. Anne and the Virgin Mary, whose lives, as represented in the realistic detail of late medieval art, seemed to mirror their own.[54]

In this paper I have taken cultural representations as documents that reveal the contested nature of ideology, in an attempt to uncover some of the reasons that medieval women participated in patriarchy, to understand its appeal, rather than to condemn it as a monolithically negative institution. Although the romance of God the Father and the Virgin Mary forwarded the interests of patriarchy, it may also have created for medieval women, as romance reading did for the women in Radway's study, "a feeling of hope, provid[ing] emotional sustenance and produc[ing] a fully visceral sense of well-being."[55] Thus the representations of God the Father providing "care and emotional nurturance" to the Virgin Mary answer my opening question (can men mother?) in the qualified affirmative: women need to believe that a man can mother and, for a variety of reasons, cultural representations of older men respond to that need.[56]

NOTES

    1. Evelyn Nakano Glenn, "Social Constructions of Mothering: A Thematic Overview," in *Mothering: Ideology, Experience, and Agency*, eds. Evelyn Nakano Glenn, Grace Chang, and Linda Rennie Forcey (New York and London, 1994), p. 3 (citing Alison M. Jagger, *Feminist Politics and Human Nature* [Totowa, NJ, 1983], p. 256).

    2. Caroline Walker Bynum, "Jesus as Mother and Abbot as Mother: Some Themes in Twelfth-Century Cistercian Writing," in *Jesus as Mother:*

Studies in the Spirituality of the High Middle Ages (Berkeley, 1982) pp. 110–69. Publications on this subject since Bynum include Charles Cummings, "The Motherhood of God According to Julian of Norwich," in *Medieval Religious Women,* vol. 2, *Peaceweavers,* eds. Lillian Thomas Shank and John A. Nichols (Kalamazoo, 1987) pp. 305–14; Gertrud Jaron Lewis, "Christus als Frau: Eine Vision Elisabeths von Schönau," *Jahrbuch für internationale Germanistik* 15 (1983), 70–80.

3. For an insightful analysis of Julian's writing, see Denise Nowakowski Baker, *Julian of Norwich's Showings: From Vision to Book* (Princeton, 1994). On p. 123 she discusses the passage in Julian that I summarize here.

4. Baker, *Julian,* pp. 119, 120.

5. Baker, *Julian,* p. 123.

6. Baker, *Julian,* p. 123.

7. Baker, *Julian,* p. 133.

8. Baker, *Julian,* p. 187. She cites Caroline Walker Bynum's essay "The Body of Christ in the Later Middle Ages: A Reply to Leo Steinberg," in *Body in Medieval Religion* (New York, 1991), pp. 79–117 in support of this point.

9. Quoted in Baker, *Julian,* p. 108.

10. I made this argument in a paper read at the Robert Branner Forum for Medieval Art on April 28, 1994, entitled "Gendering the Godhead: The Masculinization of God the Father in Later Medieval Art." I do not reject Caroline Walker Bynum's observation that "Pictures of the Holy Family are themselves theological statements," but I would argue that they are embodiments of social ideology as well ("The Body of Christ in the Later Middle Ages: A Reply to Leo Steinberg," in *Fragmentation and Redemption: Essays on Gender and the Human Body in Medieval Religion* (New York, 1991) p. 80.

11. This scene is illustrated in Codex Vindob. 2670, fol. 73. See Uta Schwab, "Sigune, Kreimhilt, Maria und der geliebte Tode," in *Zwei Frauen vor dem Tode,* Verhandelingen van de Koninklijke Academie voor Wetenschappen, Letteren en Schone Kunsten van België, Klasse der Letteren, Jahrgang 51, 1989, Nr. 82, and figure 36.

12. Pamela Sheingorn, "The Bosom of Abraham Trinity: A Late Medieval All Saints Image," in *England in the Fifteenth Century: Proceedings of the 1986 Harlaxton Symposium,* ed. Daniel Williams (Woodbridge, 1987), pp. 273–95.

13. See, for example, the Annunciation illustrating the opening of Matins for the Hours of the Virgin on fol. 45 of the *Rohan Hours* (Paris, BN MS lat 9471; 1419–27).

14. For an example of God the Father at the Nativity, see the illustration to Prime of the Hours of the Virgin on fol. 52v of a Book of Hours by the Master of the Munich Golden Legend (Baltimore, Walters

Art Gallery W 288; 1425–30). On this manuscript, see Roger S. Wieck, *Time Sanctified: The Book of Hours in Medieval Art and Life* (New York, 1988) cat. 34; for a color plate of fol. 52v, see Pl. 3.

15. *The Bedford Hours* (London, BL MS Add. 18850) was made ca. 1412. For a color plate of the Crucifixion, which is on fol. 144r, see Ruth Mellinkoff, *Outcasts: Signs of Otherness in Northern European Art of the Late Middle Ages* (Berkeley and Los Angeles, 1993) vol. 2, Pl. IX.25.

16. See, for example, the *Grande Pietà ronde* of ca. 1400 by Jean Malouel, illustrated on p. 43 of *Les fastes du gothique: le siècle de Charles V* (Paris, 1981).

17. For examples see the Assumption of the Virgin, fol. 88 of the *Belles Heures of Jean, Duc de Berry*, dated 1404–08, and the "Coronation of the Virgin by God the Father," a panel painting on oak attributed to a west German artist and dated about 1460 (Wallraf–Richartz Museum, WRM 112). For an illustration see *Christus und Maria: Westdeutsche Kunstwerke der Gotik* (Cologne, 1956), cat. no. 100.

18. The Transportation of the Holy House of Loreto is catalogue no. 276 in Richard S. Field, *Fifteenth Century Woodcuts and Metalcuts from the National Gallery of Art* (Washington, D.C., n.d.).

19. See Pamela Sheingorn, "The Holy Kinship: The Ascendancy of Matriliny in Sacred Genealogy of the Fifteenth Century," *Thought: Fordham University Quarterly* 64 (Sept. 1989), 268–86.

20. Nancy Chodorow, *The Reproduction of Mothering: Psychoanalysis and the Sociology of Gender* (Berkeley, 1978), as quoted by E. Ann Kaplan, *Motherhood and Representation: The Mother in Popular Culture and Melodrama* (London and New York, 1992) p. 32.

> What is important about Chodorow's work is its challenge to Freud's phallocentrism, its attention to the *girl's* pre-Oedipal and Oedipal struggles, its positing of a specificity in itself to the feminine (however encumbered that notion might be by essentialism, it has a rhetorical force that is important and provoking); its suggestion that female identity is less rigid than men's because of the girl's *double* identification (pre-Oedipally with the mother—an identification that continues post-Oedipally with the Father); and finally its hopeful suggestion that the exclusivity of the reproduction of mothering to the female child is not inevitable or unchangeable (Kaplan, p. 33).

However, Kaplan goes on to note that Chodorow's solution is "problematic because [she] confuses the social and psychic mothers" (p. 33).

21. Janice Radway, *Reading the Romance: Women, Patriarchy, and Popular Literature* (1984; Chapel Hill, 1991, with a new introduction by the author).

22. Radway, *Reading the Romance*, p. 13.

23. Radway, *Reading the Romance*, pp. 13–14.

24. Radway, *Reading the Romance*, p. 14.

25. The relevant portion of this mid-second-century text is reproduced as an appendix to the introduction in *Interpreting Cultural Symbols; Saint Anne in Late Medieval Society,* eds. Kathleen Ashley and Pamela Sheingorn (Athens, GA, 1990) pp. 53–57.

26. Mellinkoff, *Outcasts*, vol. 1, p. 79.

27. Field, *Fifteenth Century Woodcuts*, p. 156.

28. Radway, *Reading the Romance*, p. 14.

29. Radway, *Reading the Romance*, pp. 59–60.

30. Judith Butler, *Bodies that Matter: On the Discursive Limits of "Sex"* (New York and London, 1993), p. 2.

31. Radway, *Reading the Romance*, p. 14.

32. I have learned much from the following two essays: Claire Johnston, "The Subject of Feminist Film Theory/Practice," and Annette Kuhn, "Women's Genres," both published in *The Sexual Subject: A Screen Reader in Sexuality* (London and New York, 1992).

33. Radway, *Reading the Romance*, p. 56.

34. Radway, *Reading the Romance*, p. 16.

35. Radway, *Reading the Romance*, p. 57.

36. Radway, *Reading the Romance*, p. 14.

37. *Primer of Claude of France, 1505–1510*, Cambridge, Fitzwilliam Museum, MS 159, p. 1. For a description of this manuscript, see M.R. James, *A Descriptive Catalogue of the Manuscripts in the Fitzwilliam Museum* (Cambridge, 1895) no. 159, pp. 356–59. For the historical material I relate here, see John Harthan, *The Book of Hours* (New York, 1982), pp. 136–37. For a discussion of this manuscript in relation to the issue of female literacy, see Pamela Sheingorn, "The Wise Mother: The Image of Saint Anne Teaching the Virgin Mary," *Gesta* 32.1 (1993), pp. 69–80.

38. Harthan, *The Book of Hours*, p. 136.

39. Harthan, *The Book of Hours*, p. 137.

40. Madeline H. Caviness, "Patron or Matron? A Capetian Bride and a Vade Mecum for Her Marriage Bed," in *Studying Medieval Women*, ed. Nancy F. Partner (Cambridge, MA, 1993), p. 41. For an illustration of fols. 15v–16r, see plate 2.

41. Valerie Walkerdine, "Some Day My Prince Will Come: Young Girls and the Preparation for Adolescent Sexuality," in *Schoolgirl Fictions* (London, 1990), pp. 87–88.

42. Linda Brownrigg, "The Taymouth Hours and the Romance of *Beves of Hampton*," in *English Manuscript Studies 1100–1700*, vol. 1, ed. Peter Beal and Jeremy Griffiths (Oxford, 1989), p. 238. *The Taymouth Hours*, an English Book of Hours in the British Library (Yates Thompson MS 13), is dated 1330–1340.

43. See Roger S. Loomis, "A Phantom Tale of Female Ingratitude," *Modern Philology* 14 (1916–17) 751–55.

44. Valerie Wayne, "Introduction," in Edmund Tilney, ed., *The Flower of Friendship: A Renaissance Dialogue Contesting Marriage* (Ithaca, 1992), p. 3.

45. Wayne, p. 2, citing Raymond Williams, *Marxism and Literature* (Oxford, 1977), pp. 113, 119.

46. This quotation is taken from the portion of Christine's "Letter to the God of Love" translated by Marcelle Thiébaux in *The Writings of Medieval Women: An Anthology*. 2nd ed. (New York, 1994), p. 432.

47. Radway, *Reading the Romance*, p. 54.

48. Radway, *Reading the Romance*, p. 12.

49. *The N-Town Play. Cotton MS Vespasian D. 8*, ed. Stephen Spector, 2 vols. E.E.T.S. Supplementary Series, 11 (Oxford, 1991).

50. Carole M. Meale, "'...alle the bokes that I haue of latyn, englisch, and frensch': Laywomen and Their Books in Late Medieval England," in *Women and Literature in Britain 1150–1500*, ed. Carol M. Meale (Cambridge, 1993), pp. 128–58; seal illustrated Plate I, p. 129.

51. Meale, "Laywomen and Their Books," p. 129.

52. See, for examples, Rosemary Hale, "*Imitatio Mariae*: Motherhood Motifs in Devotional Memoirs," *Mystics Quarterly* 16.4 (1990), 193–203; Ulinka Rublack, "Female Spirituality and the Infant Jesus in Late Medieval Dominican Convents," *Gender and History* 6.1 (April 1994), 37–57.

53. Sarah Beckwith, "A Very Material Mysticism: The Medieval Mysticism of Margery Kempe," in *Medieval Literature: Criticism, Ideology and History*, ed. David Aers (New York, 1986), pp. 34–57.

54. Another body of material worth considering here would be Middle English romances. Jennifer Fellowes observes that in these texts the "mothers of Romance heroines are conspicuous by their absence," (p. 54), suggesting that the heroine's search for a fitting partner may be intensified by the absence of the nurturing mother. See Jennifer Fellowes, "Mothers in Middle English Romance," in *Women and Literature in Britain, 1150–1500*, ed. Carole M. Meale (Cambridge, 1993), pp. 41–60.

55. Radway, *Reading the Romance*, p. 12.

56. This essay was originally presented at the 1994 Barnard College Medieval-Renaissance Conference; I wish to thank Antonella Ansani and Catharine Randall Coats for including the session sponsored by the Medieval Feminist Art History Project. I also wish to thank Sharon Kraus and Carol Weisbrod, from whose comments and editorial advice this work has benefitted greatly.

JOSEPH AS MOTHER:

ADAPTATION AND APPROPRIATION IN THE

CONSTRUCTION OF MALE VIRTUE

Rosemary Drage Hale

An examination of the appropriation and redeployment of Marian images in the construction of the late medieval cult of St. Joseph, including representations of Joseph in the "madonna pose" and the use of the lily as an emblem of purity.

It is hardly contested that the discipline of history—the manner of dealing with the written text and the record of events—has undergone a paradigm shift in recent years, and among the most striking aspects of this new historical discourse is the importance of gender. As Caroline Walker Bynum remarks, "it is no longer possible to study religious practice or religious symbols without taking gender—that is the cultural experience of being male or female—into account."[1] In the same vein, Joan Wallach Scott asserts that "history is no longer about the things that have happened to women and men and how they have reacted to them; instead it is about how the subjective and collective meanings of women and men as categories of identity have been constructed."[2]

Such is the theoretical point of departure for my research on the cult of St. Joseph. As well, the study is imbedded in a larger question concerned with the interaction of religious symbols and culturally constructed images of gender in late medieval Europe. The ecclesiastical transformation of the cult of St. Joseph in the early fifteenth century, and its concomitant adaptations and appropriations through the seventeenth century, are profoundly important elements in an examination of particular aspects of lay masculinities in late medieval and early modern Europe. Two models of Joseph precede the fifteenth-century transformation. In "popular" drama and ritual, he is depicted as a doddering old cuckold—a feeble man. But he is also seen iconographically, or in sermon and treatise, in the image of an ancient wizened Church Father, the "bread of heaven"'s servile protector. He is transformed to mirror the image of the mature, productive layman, advancing from peasant to bourgeois and rising from servitude to authority and dignity. If we look closely at this process, however, there is a curious and somewhat unexpected feature. While the emergence of the Joseph cult aligns with socially constructed paradigms of behavior for married laymen, attributes and elements from the powerful Marian cult are selectively appropriated and woven into the fabric of this holy male figure. Not only is Joseph widely depicted in the "Madonna pose," standing alone embracing the Christ Child; he is depicted with the lily, an emblem of purity. He is said to have been sanctified in the womb, and sermons describe his heart pierced by the sword of sorrow. Like the image of Mary enfolding worshippers in her mantle, Joseph came to represent the locus of guardianship for the Church. Just as tradition held that Christ and Mary were bodily assumed into Heaven, many argued that Joseph at death also rose bodily into Heaven; Mary was held to have been crowned in Heaven, and Joseph is often represented wearing a crown.

The Oxford English Dictionary defines "appropriation" as "the making of a thing private property."[3] The use and manipulation of signs, a process we might think of in terms of a "sociology of representation," is certainly a political matter. Appropriation touches on power; it is an activity invested with authority. The appropriator acts on the power and authority to take, borrow, and use. Joseph is not the appropriator in the history of his representation; he is a constructed saint. As Pierre Delooze has said, "all saints are more or less constructed in that, being necessarily saints for other people, they are remodeled in the collective representation which is made of them."[4] This is especially important as regards the late medieval construction of St. Joseph to mirror and act as paradigmatic for lay male virtue, a reflection of and a model for masculinity. Yet this model appropriated and adapted elements and features associated with a cult of the feminine maternal, that of the cult of Mary as mother of Jesus.

Before examining the selective appropriations from the cult of Mary, it will be useful to look briefly at Joseph's image prior to the fifteenth-century transformation. David Herlihy asserts that Joseph is all but invisible in early medieval writings and that the index to the *Patrologia Latina* provides not one reference to Joseph.[5] True, but misleading, for the index is faulty; many passages in the *Patrilogia* explicitly and directly concern and focus on Joseph. And while it is also true that the Joseph cult did not begin to flourish until the fifteenth century, theological questions about Joseph were significant to the Church Fathers and to many prominent medieval authors. Origen, Jerome, Augustine, Ambrose, Tertullian, Clement of Alexandria, Maxim of Tours, Bede, Rupert of Deutz, Bernard, Peter Comestor, Bonaventure, all make use of widely held notions and images of Joseph.

Josephine themes emerge time and again in the works of early ecclesiastical leaders and theologians: his Davidic descent, his virtue, and his role as foster-father of the Child. All are concerned with his virtue, particularly that of justice. Matthew 1:10 identifies Joseph as a "just" man, and many Church Fathers and medieval commentators drew on this passage when discussing Joseph. Both Origen and Jerome, for example, argued that justice as exemplified by Joseph encompassed all other virtues. As Jerome put it: "The spouse of Mary was just, it is said. He had faith and charity, but justice is the harmonious assemblage of all virtues."[6] Not surprisingly, ideas about Joseph articulated by Augustine and Bernard of Clairvaux (1090–1153) are prominent in late medieval sermons. Augustine's interest in Joseph was twofold: his perpetual virginity and a theology of adoptive fatherhood. Bernard's interest, on the other hand, was more devotional in nature. In a homily praising Mary, he said that "one need not doubt that Joseph was a faithful and good man to whom the mother of our Savior was betrothed. He was a loyal servant, a prudent man, whom the Lord chose as protector for his mother and nourisher and caretaker of his flesh. And finally, he was Mary's only and most faithful assistant in the Lord's grand purpose on earth."[7] Bernard considered Joseph's virtue suited him to carry, embrace, and foster the Child. The notion of fatherhood as guardianship was the vital aspect of Bernard's representation of Joseph, and one expressed by later medieval preachers; in an oft-quoted phrase, Bernard says that "Joseph received the guardianship of the living bread from Heaven for himself and the whole world."[8] While these images may suggest a process of appropriation, they are primarily exploited as theological reference points.

Rupert of Deutz (1075–1135) drew on a Nativity sermon by Augustine to call Joseph "the highest rung of the ladder on which the Lord rested. This was the blessed Joseph, husband of Mary— resting on him as a child born into the world without a father."[9] When God rested on Jacob's ladder, he made use of Joseph's loving fatherhood and tender carrying into safety. For Bonaventure, Joseph offered a model of devotion toward Mary and the Child. In a sermon on the Vigil of the Nativity, he advocated imitating Joseph as a complete model of humility, piety, justice and charity.[10] He repeated this suggestion in a Christmas sermon, saying that Joseph's profound reverence and abundant justice were there for listeners to discover as models of virtue. It was in that era of affective devotional literature that Joseph emerged as an exemplar, and it is significant that at the same time the cult of Mary was markedly strong. Such imagery was the foundation upon which the early modern interpretation of Joseph as a strong protector of the Church could be constructed beside culturally fixed maternal images of the tender nourisher.[11]

Images fostered by ecclesiastical *auctoritas* were by no means the only portrayal of Joseph prior to the emergence of his cult; the "popular" image of Joseph before the fifteenth century is significantly more complex, and troubling for the historian. The most fruitful evidence comes from nativity dramas which date to the fifteenth century, though there is ample proof of a long performance history.[12] Theo Meier observes that "the longing of medieval people to understand divine symbols and the living image is especially drawn out at Christmas because here the divine is revealed in its most human form, namely the child."[13] A keen interest in dramatizing human realism is thus evident in these vernacular medieval cradle-rocking rituals and plays, and their imagery focuses on Mary's human maternity and Joseph's human qualities of fatherhood.[14] These paraliturgical cradle plays and rituals (*Kindelwiegenspiele* and *Christkindelwiegenfeier*), performed during Christmas festivals, brought Incarnation theology into the context of the laity's everyday life; they also offer evidence for Joseph's imitation of Mary's maternal role.

In each of the three extant cradle play texts—*Kindelwiegenspiele*, from Hesse, Sterzing and Erlau—a living infant or *figur* (effigy) is ritually swaddled, placed in a cradle and rocked by Joseph at Mary's request:[15]

> Joseph (carrying the cradle): "Mary, I have considered it well and brought you a cradle in which we can lay the little child...."[16]
> Mary (sings): "Joseph, dear husband mine, help me rock the little one."
> Joseph responds: "Happily, my dear little wife, I'll help you rock the little child."
> Mary says: "Take the cradle in your hands and allow my child to be known and rock him nicely so that he doesn't cry."[17]

Variants of this song were used in all three cradle-plays and were associated with a cradle-rocking ritual as well. It was so beloved in Germany that well into the sixteenth century preachers in reformed areas used the song as a source for Christmas sermons and women adapted the melody for lullabies.[18] In the cradle-rocking ceremonies and plays, music and singing accompanied the ritual rocking of the cradle, contributing to the elevated mood of celebration. Most important, the hymn's lyrics identify the function of *imitatio Mariae*: Mary asks Joseph to help rock the Child and as he does, his performance exhorts others to "rock the cradle" privately and venerate the Child publicly and communally. The performative behavior is, of course, fundamentally maternal.

The cradle-rocking rituals, the *Christkindelwiegenfeier*, are similar to the plays.[19] While we cannot accurately date the first performances of the cradle-rocking ritual, we can rest assured that the rituals predate the plays.[20] Regardless of its origins, evidence for ritual performance at home survives, significantly long after church performances disappear. It was popular in Tirol into the twentieth century, adapted to a home-centered ceremony and maintained even in reformed areas of Germany.[21]

One particular image associated with the vernacular Nativity plays and cradle rituals became a locus for comic behavior. The popular and profane scenes of Joseph preparing the Child's food or bath have profound bearing on discussions of maternal aspects of the Joseph cult.[22] The feeding scene in the cradle plays and rituals put Joseph centerstage as the locus of merriment. The ground of the levity is his inept imitation of maternal behavior; humor arises from the out-of-place, with the husband rocking, bathing, or feeding the Child. Though he is played for laughs, it is most significant that

Joseph is depicted in the role of "nutritor." One city chronicle demonstrates how this scene reflected the popular image of Joseph. As a feeble old man he is pushed into lighting a fire and making porridge for the Child. The Child begins to cry and Mary asks Joseph to feed him; but the Child spits out the food because it is too hot. The Child will not stop crying and soon the two, Joseph and the Child, end up in a fistfight. The Child easily wins against the feeble old man.[23]

These images were reproduced on altar paintings; the popular iconographic motif of Joseph cooking for the Child or preparing his bath began to appear around 1350 and virtually disappeared around 1450.[24] One art historian characterized such fourteenth-century images of Joseph as "submissive, nurturing, and unmanly," and claimed they were deliberately contrasted to the grandeur of the Incarnation.[25] The image lost its appeal as Joseph was transformed from aged, bumbling cuckold to robust provider and intercessor for the Church. But while he did not altogether lose the maternal attributes, his cult abandons humorous elements and, as we will see, adopts current features from the Marian cult and appropriates new ones as well.

Joseph's *imitatio Mariae* is an essential element in the cradle-rocking plays and rituals. His performance's relation to the plays' reflective image of the family is critical to our understanding of the ordinary worshipper's *imitatio Mariae*. Mary was primarily responsible for the Child's nourishment; Joseph could not nurse Him. Hence he is depicted preparing food, rocking Him, warming the bath—all manifestations of a paternal *imitatio Mariae*. The cradle play was a ritualized presentation of the Incarnation carrying with it the image of Christ's childhood with two parents: it portrayed a family that was holy, but human. Even behind the humorous abuse of Joseph there was thus an admonition to imitate Mary. Joseph's behavior taught the male worshipper that he was obligated to care for and nurture the infant in imitation of Mary. Like John lamenting with Mary beneath the Cross, Joseph's rocking and cooking provided men access to an identification with what was regarded as the maternal role—in one case, care and nurturance of the Child; in the other, sorrow as profound as that of the mother for her Son. The stereotype of incompetence may have been the source of merriment and humor, but the comic scenes were thoroughly based on an imitation of Mary's maternal behavior.

The cradle-rocking plays and rituals offer several elements of interest to historians of medieval popular religion, most notably the collective performance aspect. The dramatizations were performed by and for the community. The audience was collectively called to silence. The language was vernacular, the visual element clothed in attributes from home and family. The importance of Joseph's character was new at this time, and corresponded to the burgeoning Joseph cult in the late Middle Ages. The didactic lesson of celebration at the birth of the divine Child was communicated to the viewers in terms of a real family—mother, father and son.

But the early fifteenth-century Joseph cult, a creation of such churchmen as Pierre d'Ailly, Jean Gerson, Bernardino da Siena, Bernardino de Feltre and Isidore Isolanis, intentionally created a distance from these profane images. The Josephine virtues these men zealously promoted were purity, wisdom, justice, economic prudence and virility, and tenderness. They also made it clear that he was in the prime of manhood, a laborer, a tradesman, and in no way aged, feeble, or cuckolded. The new Joseph was constructed to resemble members of an emerging burgher class of merchants, artisans, and tradesmen now more actively involved in the economic and devotional life of the Church. Interestingly, however, the aggregate of virtues and symbols with which he comes to be represented draws from the cults of Mary and her mother Anne.

Jean Gerson (1363–1429) was among the first to work for an official feast day honoring Joseph. In 1413, after appealing to Rome for a feast day honoring the marriage of Joseph and Mary, he asked the Duke of Berry to use his influence for the institution of such an office at Notre Dame. In 1479, the feast day was added to the Roman calendar by Sixtus IV, who officially sanctioned March 19 as St. Joseph's feast day. Gerson's writings leave no doubt of his interest in encouraging public devotion to Joseph, with predominantly male lay involvement. The inventory relevant to Gerson's Josephology includes Latin and vernacular sermons, a lengthy French treatise titled *Considérations sur saint Joseph*,[26] and a 120-verse Latin poem, *Josephina*. Most important for understanding Gerson's revised Joseph are three sermons he preached at the Council of Constance between 1416 and 1418. Two recurring motifs in these works bear on the appropriation of Marian imagery. First, Gerson repeatedly presents the marriage of Mary and Joseph as paradigmatic for the union of Christ and His Church. Second, he focuses frequently on Joseph's age, making several arguments against the accuracy of an elderly Joseph.

Like the ecclesiastical leaders who preceded him, Gerson characterizes Joseph as a symbol of guardianship: as "lord" of the household, he is responsible for protecting and guarding the Child and his mother. Gerson recasts responsibility for the well-being of the Church, and Josephine imagery is the chief building block for his attempts to mend the ecclesiastical fractures of the Great Schism: the Church, in need of protection and unity, should champion the symbolism inherent in the character of Joseph. Gerson opens one sermon to the Council by identifying Joseph's supreme worthiness: "O Joseph, you are sublime. O you, with incomparable dignity. Even the mother of God, the mistress of the world, did not think you unworthy to call you lord."[27] It is noteworthy that this sermon was delivered on the feast of *Mary*'s Nativity and employs for Joseph appellations normally accorded to Mary. Gerson also exploits earlier imagery of Joseph as *nutritor Christi*, elevating it from a position of mockery to one of paradigmatic virtue. As nutritor, Joseph was responsible for providing food, education, and protection. In the same sermon he says, "Let us consider again who nourished the infant Jesus, led him into Egypt, disciplined him paternally. This was Joseph, his father. We must say, in short, that he accomplished all the necessary care of a good and loyal father. Even Jesus having been made by God honored Joseph as his father, his nourisher, his guide, his defender, his teacher and instructor."[28]

In constructing, or rather reconstructing, Joseph in the late medieval period, one of the most significant challenges confronting the Church leaders involved altering his image from that of an old and feeble man, supported by official and popular images, to that of a middle-aged, physically fit tradesman. Prior to the early fifteenth century, the question of Joseph's age when he married, when Christ was born, when they fled to Egypt, is not an issue. But for Gerson, d'Ailly, Bernardine of Siena, Isolanis and others it takes on great significance. Gerson inaugurates the debate in one of the sermons he delivered to the Church leaders at Constance. Regarding Joseph's age, he said:

To confirm the perpetual virginity of Mary and to preserve the idea of a most chaste and modest cohabitation, it is not necessary to believe Joseph feeble [the word "frigid" is used here] when he married Mary, she being an adolescent at the time. It was, moreover, possible for the Holy Spirit to preserve his chastity through the repression or extinction of original desire whether he was a very old man or a mature man. Now it seems to me that everyone knows an aged man— some 70 or 80 years old—who perished pursuing vile and base pleasures through shameful designs....After all, he who feels the virtue of grace knows that he cannot continue to exist unless it is willed by God. Thus, I think, Joseph to have been young just as Isidore places the end of youth at the twenty-eighth year when adolescence ends, up to the age of fifty when old age begins. Hence Joseph was first betrothed when he was under the age of fifty."[29]

Gerson then argues that since the Protevangelium of James (which does indicate an elderly Joseph) has been condemned by canon law, it should not be used to oppose this view. He then outlines his rationale for an un-aged Joseph. First, he claims that Joseph would have to have been a certain age (*perfectam aetatem*) in order to have been able to care properly for Mary and the Child; a broken and impotent man would have been inappropriate, and an aged man would have required ministrations rather than be able to offer them. Second, he states that a younger Joseph would be better able to preserve Mary's reputation: for people to believe Joseph to be the father, physical fatherhood had to have been regarded as possible. Isidore Isolanis in the early sixteenth century refers to the best choice for Joseph's age as *aetatem virilem*, a virile age. Gerson, Bernardine of Siena, and Bernard of Luxembourg all claim that Isaiah 62:5: "A young man will marry a virgin," applies to Joseph.

This is not the image of Joseph those listening to these sermons would have seen around them, and like others arguing for a younger Joseph, Gerson explicitly addresses the problematic of available iconographic images. "Why was Joseph painted old—with a flowing beard?" he asks.[30] Gerson, Geiler von Keysersberg and Pierre d'Ailly rationalized that painting Joseph as an old man in the early Church had enabled the mystery of Mary's perpetual virginity to take root. They reasoned that depicting her beside a young man would have inspired carnality in the beholders' minds. They also turned to Wisdom 4:8–9: "Old age is not to be honored for the length of time nor measured by numbers of years, rather understanding is gray hair.

For an old man a blameless life is ripe old age." Thus they maintained that while Joseph was in reality a young man, he was represented as an old man because the white hair and age represented early churchmen's notion of wisdom and understanding.

Concern about Joseph's age provides an essential clue to an idealized image of late medieval masculinity. The paradigm shift in the characterization of Joseph reflects to some degree a shift in attitudes toward the value of youth over age, and of competent productivity over assumed weakness in old age. It indicates that the highest valence went to mature economic vigor, not to the wisdom of gray hair. But while Joseph receives a remarkable face lift, he was not made over into a youth corresponding to Mary's adolescence; he was reconstructed as a man between the age of thirty and fifty. Notwithstanding the profane world of cycle dramas as well as a fair degree of local variation, Joseph came to be characterized as a full-grown adult, not aged, and fit enough to provide physically for, and to protect, Mary and the Child. Given this idealized image, guilds and confraternities dedicated to St. Joseph depicted him as an effective household manager, a good husband and loving father—all likely reflective of self-image.

The rapid growth of brotherhoods and confraternities dedicated to Joseph offers further evidence of how the Church involved a male middle-aged laity in the construction of a new image of Joseph. A case in point: in 1487 Bernardine de Feltre was sent to Perugia to settle discord between rival families, and there, like Gerson, he used Joseph as a rallying point for unity and reconciliation. His sermon for Joseph's feast day inspired the feuding male laity to form a confraternity dedicated to St. Joseph as protector of the Church, and to erect a new chapel to house a Josephine relic, the marriage ring.[31] Bernardine insisted that such a confraternity would unite the feuding merchant class under one goal of assuming guardianship of the local church and protection of a sacred relic. And from this there developed one of the many confraternities dedicated to St. Joseph and the protection of the Church. Perugian city chronicles indicate that brotherhoods dedicated to Joseph participated in Corpus Christi processions carrying signs of their affinity and devotion to Joseph: a small wooden cradle, or carpentry or wheelwright tools. A painting commemorating such a procession was commissioned from Raphael in 1504; in the background, he depicted the chapel built to house the ring and, in the foreground, a betrothal scene in which all figures aside from the officiating priest (Joseph, Mary and the witnesses), are shown as young representatives of the merchant class.

Church leaders and theologians explicitly used the betrothal or marriage contract to justify an array of visual and textual associations about Joseph. Betrothal imagery functions as more than a symbolic point of reference engaging Joseph and Mary as paradigms of ecclesiastical and social unity, and is critical to the notion of appropriated imagery. It represented Joseph's *right* to appropriation— his lordship, ownership, and authority over the household and the family.

We can do little more than speculate what impact the new interpretation of Joseph had on the cult of Mary. In her work on medieval spiritual marriage, however, Dyan Eliott argues that as the Joseph cult was encouraged by the ecclesiastical hierarchy, there was a corresponding decline in the image of a powerful Mary.[32] As the image of Joseph as head or lord of the household gained prominence, Mary was rendered as meeker, humbler, more submissive than in the texts and iconography of the twelfth to fourteenth centuries. Her role as coredemptrix was challenged at the Council of Trent and devotional images such as the popular Shrine Madonna, which implied Mary's existence prior to that of the Trinity, were thenceforth forbidden. Devotion to the Holy Family and veneration of Joseph as an intercessor and protector did not replace or displace Mary as intercessor, but most likely diminished the near-goddess cult of the late Middle Ages. The new accent was on family: the Holy Household of Joseph, Mary and the Child as the paradigm of an idealized family. This reality gave greater power and authority to the character of Joseph; but while his virtues of justice and dignity in conjunction with physical vigor were now related to images of authority and responsibility, they also used and adapted attributes and characteristic features belonging to Mary.

There are many visual examples of image appropriations in the construction of the Joseph cult. The figure of Mary standing or sitting embracing the Child is universal in Marian iconography from the sixth century onward; with the humanization of Christ in the twelfth century and the spread of Franciscan spirituality in the thirteenth, such images came to reflect a lifelike tenderness between Mary and her Child. But as the imaged and textualized portrayal of Jesus' childhood and Mary's maternal role received greater attention, an equally significant effect on the portrayal of Joseph followed. One of the most striking images which appears after the emergence of the cult of Joseph is that of the Madonna stance: images of Joseph standing or sitting, holding the Child. Joseph is no longer the isolated figure in the Nativity scene, sleeping or hosting visitors; no longer the feebled cuckold. He is invested with a visibly maternal role which parallels and assumes Mary's symbolic representation of *ecclesia*.

Along with the realistically human images of mother and child ubiquitous in the early fourteenth century is that of Mary (or another woman saint) holding the Child's hand, often walking in a pastoral scene. The image of Joseph walking with the Child was nowhere to be found before the early fifteenth century, but it was popular in the early sixteenth, and by the seventeenth it virtually displaced the production of parallel Marian images. For example, the "Master of the Holy Kinship" painted in 1590 a young Joseph and older Peter taking the Child for a walk. In profoundly significant ways this image echoes the popular late medieval iconography of Anne, Mary, and the Child, in which Anne often carried a book and held or sat near her daughter and grandchild. Here, Peter, placed symbolically in Anne's position, carries a book, and Joseph takes the Child's hand.

Lilies as traditional symbols of Mary's purity were also appropriated symbolically, to represent Joseph's virginity. By the early seventeenth century, Joseph was widely depicted holding the Child and receiving a crown in Heaven—imagery reminiscent of one of the most popular medieval Marian images, her coronation in Heaven. In one such image, painted by Luc Sibreque in 1605 in Krakow for a Joseph confraternity, Mary is marginalized in the lower right corner of the painting and does not wear a crown. The image of the solitary Joseph with the Child was imported into the New World by Spanish and Dutch missionaries. Seventeenth- and eighteenth-century retablos, oil painted on tin, frequently represented Joseph in full or half-standing madonna poses wearing a regal crown.[33]

Late medieval images of Mary and Joseph were constituted in terms of socially-constructed notions of marriage.[34] The images of Joseph walking with the Child, caressing Him, reading to Him or teaching Him his trade did not replace or negate his presence in Nativity imagery. Joseph was represented as the location of authority within the household, the *pater familias*. The Holy Family came to be seen as an earthly Trinity, in which Joseph's role paralleled that of God the Father. If the human husband/ father had right of possession over all earthly goods in return for his guardianship, protection, and provision, it was not surprising that the "master" of the Holy Family had rights of ownership over his wife's holiness and virtue. The Holy Household under Joseph's lordship became a microcosm for the Church and for political order. Hence, the constellation of images which figured in the Joseph cult could be appropriated from that of Mary, his spouse, because by right of marriage they were Joseph's as well. Whatever Mary had, possessed, owned—her virtues, her attributes, her child—belonged also to Joseph.

We may never be able to reconstruct accurately what moved preachers like Gerson, d'Ailly, the Bernardines, and others to cast Joseph in a new light, but I think it likely that the construction drew from and influenced the status of men in late medieval European culture. That such a construction appropriates features predominantly maternal is profoundly significant. As we examine texts and visual images associated with the rise and spread of the Joseph cult, we are faced with a number of vexing questions—about agency and intent, about the multiplicity of social meanings in the use and manipulation of images, about the theoretically troubling distance between public discourse and private practice and between ideological paradigms and daily life. How do we historicize representational activity juggling both theory and context? How do we disentangle our ethnocentric ideas about gender constructions from those which might well have been fundamental aspects of the medieval habitus? What does seem clear is that masculinist paradigms of the "just man," the "true man," images of Joseph who protects, nourishes, and guides his son, provide us with data. They not only reflect particularities about family life in late medieval and early modern Europe; they offer images of idealized marriage and paradigmatic fatherhood. They illuminate the ways in which men in medieval Christianity conceived of and experienced "manhood," and how ecclesiastical authority exploited maternal Marian images and metaphors to sustain notions of power and privilege.

114   MEDIEVAL MOTHERING

NOTES

1. Caroline Walker Bynum, Stevan Harrell, and Paula Richman, eds., *Gender and Religion: On the Complexity of Symbols* (Boston, 1986), p. 1.

2. Joan Wallach Scott, *Gender and the Politics of History* (New York, 1988), p. 6.

3. *OED*, 2nd edn., 1:587.

4. Pierre Delooze, "Towards a Sociological Study of Canonized Sainthood in the Catholic Church," in *Saints and Their Cults*, ed. Stephen Wilson (Cambridge, 1983), p. 195. The same point is made by Edith Wyschogrod in *Saints and Postmodernism* (Chicago, 1990), pp. 6–9.

5. David Herlihy, *Medieval Households* (Cambridge, MA, 1985), p. 127.

6. *PL*, 23:203.

7. *PL*, 183:69–70.

8. *PL*, 183:69.

9. Francis L. Filas notes that Joseph champions the "fatherly" care of Jesus in "Introduction to the Theology of Saint Joseph," *Cahiers de Joséphologie* 2 (1954), 207.

10. "Joseph sancti devota pietas, quia esset justus et nollet eam traducere." See Blaine Burkey, "The Feast of St. Joseph: A Franciscan Bequest," in *Cahiers de Joséphologie* 19 (1971), 649–50.

11. The term "maternal" does not denote an argument for a socio-biological interpretation. I regard as culturally determined the maternal aspects of Mary's relationship to the Christ Child or the appropriation of maternal aspects of Mary's relationship.

12. On the dating of texts and reference to earlier performance, *The Ludus incunabilis Christi*, ed. K. F. Kummer, *Erlauer Spiele* (Vienna, 1882), p. 5; Konrad Ameln, "Resonet in Laudibus—Joseph, lieber Joseph mein," *Jahrbuch für Liturgik und Hymnologie*, 15 (1971), 74; Richard Froning, ed., *Das Drama des Mittelalters* (Wissenschaftliche Buchgesellschaft, 1964), pp. 902–39, and Walter Lipphardt, "Die Weihnachtsgeschichte," in *Convivium symbolicum. Abendländsiches Leben in Bild, Ton, Wort*, eds. E. Lutze and K. Blum, 2 vols. (Bremen, 1958), vol. 2, pp. 29–448. Most scholars would agree that religious plays "achieved their essential development between the tenth and thirteenth centuries" (Karl Young, *The Drama of the Medieval Church*, 2 vols. [Oxford, 1933], 2:397). For vernacular drama in Germany, Eckehard Simon suggests that the period 1450–1525 was the most significant for the production of MSS (*The Dictionary of the Middle Ages*, 4:266). This does not, however, preclude earlier performance of vernacular religious drama or ritual. Louise Berthold, "Die Kindelwiegenspiele," in *Beiträge zur Gestichte der deutschen Sprache und Litertur* 56 (1932), 210, argues that the cradle plays would have had a prior performance history, perhaps as early as the fourteenth century. Jansjürgen Linke, "Germany and German-Speaking Central Europe," in Eckehard Simon, ed., *The Theatre of Medieval*

Europe (Cambridge, 1991), p. 208, identifies 162 religious plays written in medieval Germany and shows that religious plays were recorded as early as 1250.

13. Theo Meier, *Die Gestalt Marias im geistlichen Schauspiel des deutschen Mittelalters* (Berlin, 1959), p. 134.

14. Young, *Drama of the Medieval Church*, 2:423, claims that increased use of vernacular for devotional purposes had an impact on religious drama and its appeal to the ordinary worshipper. His point is that as religious drama "relinquished its close association with established worship," it abandoned the Latin liturgy.

15. The Hesse text is ed. Walter Lipphardt, *Die Weinachtsgeschichte* (*Convivium Symbolicum*, 2:29–48), also ed. in Froning, *Drama des Mittelalters*, pp. 904–39. The Sterzing text is ed. R. Jordan, "Das Sterzinger Weinachtsspiel vom jahre 1511 und das Hess. Weihnachtsspiele," *Jahrbuch des k. k. Staatsobergymnasiums in Krumau* 29 (1901–02), 1–27. The Erlau text is ed. K. P. Kummer, *Erlauer Spiele* (Hildesheim, 1977), pp. 5–9.

16. A MS identifying participants in the Bozen Corpus Christi procession (1543) indicates that the *Tischler* (carpenter) played the part of Joseph and walked beside Mary carrying a cradle. That Joseph here hands Mary the cradle suggests that the carpenters' guild sponsored the Hesse play. See Bernd Neumann, *Geistliches Schauspiel im Zeugnis der Zeit: Zur Aufführung mittelalterlicher religiöser Dramen im deutschen Sprachgebiet*, 2 vols. (Munich, 1987), 2:234.

17. From *Ludus de nativitate domini*, ll. 151–206.

18. Martin Rössler, *Bibliographie der deutschen Liedpredigt* (Nieukoop, 1976), identifies over 30 such sermons in the sixteenth century.

19. On the distinction between *Spiele* and *Feier*, Clifford Flanigan, "Medieval Latin Music-Drama," in Simon, *Theatre of Medieval Europe* (Cambridge, 1991), pp. 32–36, identifies *feier* as liturgical celebration or ceremony, and *spiel* as a play, arguing that what makes a performance a ritual, a play, or both lies with the performers and the audience and the use they make of the "text." It is a question of intent.

20. Konrad Ameln, "Resonet in laudibus," p. 73, claims the church cradle-rocking ritual preceded the plays.

21. Karl Weinhold, *Weihnachtsspiele und-lieder aus Süddeutschland* (Graz, 1885), p. 49; for the home ritual, Robert Scribner, "The Impact of Reformation on Daily Life," in *Mensch und Objekt in Mittelalter und in der frühen Neuzeit: Leben-Alltag-Kultur* (Vienna, 1990), p. 322. Evidence for its continued popularity comes from reformers outraged by the practice.

22. A useful discussion of the motif is Leopold Schmidt's "Sankt Josef kocht ein Müselein: zur Kindelbreiszene in der Weihnachtkunst des Mittelalters," *Europäische Sachkultur des Mittelalters* (Vienna, 1980), pp. 143–67.

23. This unique evidence for the Joseph scene comes from Georg Wickram's Cologne Chronicle (c. 1557). See Neumann, *Geistliches Schauspiele*, 2:922 [no. 3764].

24. Marjory Bolgar Foster, *The Iconography of St. Joseph in Netherlandish Art, 1400–1550* (Ph.D. diss., University of Kansas, 1978), p. 49.

25. Henk van Os, *The Art of Devotion in the Late Middle Ages in Europe 1300–1500* (Princeton, NJ, 1994), p. 140.

26. *Considérations sur saint Joseph* was written in 1413 as part of a celebration of Joseph at Notre Dame cathedral.

27. Jean Gerson, *Opera omnia*, 7 vols., ed. Louis Ellies du Pin (Hildesheim, 1987) vol. 3, p. 1356.

28. *Opera omnia*, 3.66.

29. *Opera omnia*, 5:352.

30. *Opera omnia*, 7:72.

31. For the ring as relic, F. Ciatti, *Ristretto dell'istoria del sacro anello di Maria Vergine che si conserva nella chiesa cattedrale di Perugia* (1649); discussed in Ludovic de Besse, *Le bienheureux Bernardin de Feltre et son oeuvre* (Tours, 1902), pp. 205–07.

32. Dyan Elliott, *Spiritual Marriage: Sexual Abstinence in Medieval Wedlock* (Princeton, NJ, 1993), p. 100.

33. Joseph Chorpenning, ed., *Patron of the New World: Spanish American Colonial Images of St. Joseph* (Philadelphia, 1992), and idem, ed., *Mexican Devotional Retablos from the Peters Collection* (Philadelphia, 1994).

34. Cynthia Hahn, "'Joseph will perfect, Mary enlighten and Jesus save thee': The Holy Family as Marriage in the Merode Triptych," *Art Bulletin* 68 (1986), 54–66, discusses the simultaneously mundane and sacral roles of Mary and Joseph, emphasizing their marriage's intimate unity as emblematic of its message for the beholder. She claims the triptych can best be understood in "light of the sacrament and practice of marriage."

IS MOTHER SUPERIOR?

TOWARDS A HISTORY OF FEMININE
*Amtscharisma**

Felice Lifshitz

> *No studies have yet explored the authority and office of female monastic*
> *superiors, nor have the latter been taken into account in studies of male*
> *monastic authority. Various sources, particularly monastic rules and*
> *conciliar legislation, are used to open the issue.*

Amtscharisma: IS MOTHER SUPERIOR?

Many studies have explored the authority and office of male superiors of male monastic communities, particularly within the framework of Benedictine monasticism,[1] that form of communal regular life that was founded by Benedict of Monte Cassino (480–c. 560), and whose generalized enforcement—through the reformations of Boniface, then of Benedict of Aniane—became a central feature of Carolingian policy from the mid-eighth century.[2] Monasticism could never have become a mass institution had it not been possible to set up monasteries wherever there was a market for the regulated lifestyle, irrespective of the presence of a charismatic leader. The rule of St. Benedict very much facilitated the institutionalization of masculine religious lordship. Indeed, the widespread acceptance of a monastic rule in and of itself, as a constitutional principle, enabled male individuals not personally possessed of spiritual charisma to control male religious communities by virtue of their occupation of an office. It was the office of the Benedictine abbot itself that came, legally, to possess *Amtscharisma*, that is, the charisma necessary for rulership. *Amtscharisma* was also a necessary prerequisite for religious communities to acquire permanence.

Benedict of Nursia was able to articulate traditional monastic formulae in ways that were concrete and clear without sacrificing flexibility. Central to his rule was the authority of the male abbot to command, paired with the obligation of the male monks to obey.[3] The authority of the Benedictine male abbot was bolstered both by his position as vicar of Christ, and by the associative resonances between the paternal figure of the male *abbas*, "father," and the male *pater-familias*. However, Benedict also insisted on the paternal(istic) care the abbot must feel for his sons; such solicitude tempered the patriarchal aspects of the abbatial figure.

No studies have been made of the authority and office of female superiors of female monastic communities, nor have female superiors been taken into account in any of the hundreds of studies of male monastic authority. Female monastic authority and feminine *Amtscharisma* cannot be assumed to be identical to male monastic authority and masculine *Amtscharisma*;[4] certainly there is no shortage of material through which to open the matter for discussion.

Penelope Johnson's observation that "cultural blinders have created an entire corpus of literature about monasticism that defines the institution as male" is even more apt when applied to studies of superiors of female monastic communities than when applied to members of those communities.[5] The issue of gender specificity in monastic governance is by no means simple and clear-cut. Sometimes the very developments which have fostered the tendency to define the institution of monasticism as male are themselves evidence of a noteworthy degree of egalitarian gender blindness on the part of monastic legislators. Benedict of Nursia's rule was never intended by him to have any application to women.[6] Whereas Augustine of Hippo, Caesarius of Arles, Aurelian of Arles, and other monastic legislators had written for or at least tacitly permitted their work to be used by both male and female communities, Benedict produced only one version of his rule, a version whose gender pronouns, titles, etc., were exclusively masculine.[7] Therefore, despite the availability in the eighth century of feminine rules, it was a rule intended solely for masculine use that was selected by reformers for universal gender-blind application. A similar gender fluidity marks the major text which was responsible for spreading the Benedictine observance in the Frankish world. Benedict of Aniane's florilegium, the *Concordia regularum*, arranged extracts from other rules around related chapters of the Benedictine rule itself in order to demonstrate that the entire monastic tradition was in accord concerning the observances which he wished to make universal.[8] Not only did Benedict adopt as his universal model a rule gendered as male, but he also gendered as male all extracts from other rules, even those which were drawn from rules for female religious.[9] Thus, while Benedict effectively demonstrated that the entire monastic tradition harmoniously *defined monasticism itself* as a male experience, his procedure seems to indicate that he considered female monastic experience the equivalent of male monastic experience.[10] The various ninth-century commentaries on the Benedictine rule and on Benedictine monastic life, which were designed to facilitate the real-life introduction of Benedictinism into Francia, also resolutely defined the monastic experience as male, without a single reference to female religious.[11]

The Carolingian tradition of gendering even female monasticism as masculine has reinforced the tendency of scholars to ignore women by facilitating the fantasy that, having discussed the role of the male religious superior, one has effectively also discussed the role of the female religious superior. Yet, the moment one poses the specific question of how females governed religious communities in the era of institutionalized—as opposed to charismatic—monasticism, one has to wonder how similar feminine *Amtscharisma* can have been to masculine *Amtscharisma*. The source of the authority of the abbatial office in Benedict's rule is made absolutely clear: the abbot is called a father because he is the representative of the Father of all, Jesus Christ, and therefore partakes in Christ's paternal authority.[12] The *office* of the abbot, *abbatia*, was defined as *paternity*.[13] If women could not legally be priestly representatives of Christ in the hierarchical, official church, if women could not be fathers, how did they exercise institutionalized authority in religious communities?

To assert that female religious superiors based their authority instead on maternality would be problematic. Although many scholars have considered mothers to have been responsible, during the period covered by the present essay, for the moral and religious upbringing of their children, even the strongest scholarly statement of the *maternal responsibility to nurture* does not assert any *maternal authority to command*.[14] When scholars have discerned in some cultural value system during this same period, the fifth through the eleventh centuries, something which they see fit to call a maternal office, *officium matris*, they have described that office in terms of "maternal cares" and "maternal piety": duties and obligations towards the poor, the weak, the sick, etc., with no reference to power or authority, only to burdens.[15] Meanwhile, specialists in later periods have read the use of feminized language and particularly of maternal imagery in connection with normatively male authority figures— abbots, for instance—as signs of ambivalence, even anxiety, over rulership and of a desire to soften that masculine authority. Gendered stereotypes of power, at least in the twelfth century, held that Father Jesus rules with authority, while Mother Jesus loves and nurtures.[16]

I make no attempt in the present essay to provide a universal or theoretical model of feminine *Amtscharisma* or to generalize about the "nature" of women, or authority, or women and authority. Instead, I raise some preliminary points concerning abbesses based on a series of monastic rules—Benedictine and otherwise—the obvious starting point for a study of the authority of female religious superiors. However, it is not possible simply to extrapolate from theoretical models of power, as embodied in constitutions, to the actual exercise of authority over people. The reading of printed "editions" of texts can be a starting point for historians, but ought never to constitute the entire evidentiary base of any study, although it too often does. Monastic rules therefore represent only a starting point for the study of how authority was in fact constituted and exercised by women over women in religious communities. In the final section of the essay, I try to understand the actual workings of authority in a particular community, Niedermünster of Regensburg, based on some relevant manuscript remains of that house.

HONORARY PATERNITY: WITHIN THE ENCLOSURE, WITHOUT THE HIERARCHY

Early in the fifth century, Bishop Augustine of Hippo was faced with a rebellion of the female religious in an unnamed monastery over which his sister ruled as *praeposita*. The gendered nature of the north African rebellion is particularly striking: while the female religious addressed by Augustine seem willing, even eager, to be ruled by their male *praepositus*, they consider it acceptable to throw off the authority of their female *praeposita*.[17] The terms in which Augustine urges the community to retain its *praeposita* are likewise significant. Augustine appeals to a certain filial piety for the woman under whom, like a spiritual mother, the members of the community had been educated and veiled. The gratitude and loyalty which the female religious are urged to feel as a result are never, however, couched in terms of obedience.

Spiritual maternity was not a sufficient guarantor of authority over a female monastic community in the fifth century. Where in Roman or barbarian or canon law were the superiority and authority of the *mater-familias*, as opposed to those of the father of the family, assured?[18] Of course, broad social forces encouraged the rejection of *all* parental authority in late antiquity. Until the seventh century, a monastic lifestyle could often be achieved by both men and women only by rebellion against the wishes of biological or socioconventional parents.[19] How was it possible to encourage individuals, who had already rebelled against a social institution as crucial and powerful as the family, to become obedient? Theoretically, the issues facing proponents of male and female monasticism should have been identical in this regard; yet it seems clear from the very small number of female houses that were established before 600 A.D. compared with the number of male houses in operation, that the female stream of monasticism suffered more from the problematics of authority during the heroic age of monasticism than did the male stream.

The strong anti-parental-authority current in late ancient and early medieval culture was more corrosive of potential maternal claims to authority than it was to paternal ones, in that the former were not upheld by explicit legal codes and a whole series of semi-conscious social expectations. Instead of reinforcing maternal authority, popular culture celebrated the rebelliousness of daughters against their mothers. One of the most famous romances of the late ancient world, well-known and influential in both Greek and Latin monastic circles by the fourth century, was the *Acts of Paul and Thecla*.[20] The dramatic centerpiece of Thekla's life was the scene in which her own mother, shrilly but ultimately without success, sought to have her daughter killed for refusing to marry.[21]

The biological and civil-legal family was replaced, for those in the monastic movement, by an eschatological family.[22] All the earliest known uses of the word *abba*—"father"—in the context of an eschatological family connote a charismatic *pater pneumatikos*; likewise, charismatic women such as Makrina were described by their biographers and followers as *amma*—"mother"—as a function of their pneumatic, personal leadership.[23] Yet, when a noncharismatic figure such as Augustine's sister sought to control a group of female religious, Augustine's rhetoric of her maternity may have tended more to invite rebellion against her than to encourage obedience to her. Indeed, matern(al)ity was so far from being considered a source of authority that most female claims to status and power on the level of men in late Roman and early medieval culture are understood by scholars to have been based precisely on the repudiation of wife- and motherhood, and the embracing, instead, of virginal asceticism.[24]

Under the circumstances, a maternal strategy was not particularly suited to the development of a feminine *Amtscharisma*. It is against such a cultural background that the work of Caesarius of Arles should be understood. Bishop Caesarius of Arles (470–542) was the first person to compose a rule of communal life intended specifically for female religious, namely for the virgins of his sister Caesaria's monastery of Saint-Jean of Arles.[25] The series of writings which Caesarius produced for and about female religious throughout the first half of the sixth century are striking for two divergent rhetorical tendencies. On the one hand, Caesarius never was able to decide what to call a female religious. He vacillated among *soror* (sister), *virgo* (virgin), and *filia* (daughter) for nearly half a century. He was certain only that a female religious was not the precise equivalent of a male religious, and he never once used the term *monacha* (monk). On the other hand, he did become increasingly convinced about what to call the head of a community of female religious. In the course of time the title *abbatissa* edged out *prior*, *senior* and *mater* (mother) until it became the only word ever used by Caesarius to describe the leader of the community.[26]

An *abbatissa*, or abbess, is *not* a mother; an *abbatissa* is a female father. The etymology of the title is the masculine title of paternal authority *abba* (father); there is not even the slightest resonance either of *amma* or of *mater*. Caesarius stood absolutely on the cutting edge of monastic history: the earliest dateable evidence for the use of the word *abbatissa* comes from the gravestone of Abbess Serena, buried in Rome in 514.[27] Therefore, one aspect of the first specific solution proposed for the problem of feminine *Amtscharisma* was honorary fatherhood. But there was more that Caesarius considered specific to the governance of female religious.

A striking and original feature of Caesarius' rule was to assure the *abbatissa* formal independence from her bishop.[28] Unfortunately, this Caesarian sheltering of female abbesses from the ecclesiastical hierarchy ultimately prevented the establishment of a feminine *Amtscharisma* by weakening the position of the Caesarian abbess. Here is the great paradox of abbatial authority: one of the best ways to guarantee to a noncharismatic superior the ability to control religious subordinates is to enmesh that superior within a broader chain of command which will reinforce his or her position; in other words, to subject him or her to a superior. The fundamental piece of canonical legislation governing male monasteries in Merovingian Gaul, as formulated at the first national council of Orléans in 511 and thereafter cited in all chronological and systematic canonical collections for the next four centuries, betrays the complex dynamics of authority structures; a single canon, canon nineteen, asserted *both* that abbots should be under the power of the bishops (and be corrected by their bishops in case of error) *and* that monks should be subjected to their abbots. Abbatial subjection to bishops and abbatial authority over monks were often two sides of the same coin.

The section of the Caesarian rule which most clearly betrays the fragility of the office of an abbess who is not subjected to/reinforced by episcopal authority is the following: the abbess was not allowed to alienate by sale or gift any property of the monastery or to institute anything contrary to the rule; were she to attempt any such thing, the Caesarian rule explicitly urged the sisters of the monastery to prevent her from carrying out her intentions.[29] In other words, rebellion, disobedience and the taking of the law into their own hands was permitted to the female inhabitants of Saint-Jean of Arles. Without the judicial superiority of the bishop, what other recourse could there be? In contrast, the Rhône valley Council of Epaon had long since required abbots to keep records of their sales and bequests so that the local bishop could watch over the temporalities of the monastery.[30]

The Caesarian abbess was not only weakened by the loss of episcopal or hierarchical reinforcement to her office, she was also diminished in stature by means of the feature intended by Caesarius to compensate, from his episcopal perspective, for the loss of hierarchical control over the head of the religious community of Saint-Jean. The exemption of the Caesarian abbess from episcopal authority necessitated her strict subjection, instead, to perpetual claustration. Claustration of the members of the community, as a disciplinary technique in support of the superior's *Amtscharisma*—

enclosure itself being an innovative feature of the Caesarian rule—
would not have been a surprising suggestion in and of itself. It is
only in terms of force, acrimony, and even violence that Wemple
characterizes relations between mothers and daughters in sixth- and
seventh-century Gaul.[31] The harshness of strict, life-long claustration
was not at all out of keeping with the Merovingian mother-daughter
relationship.[32] But Caesarius imposed enclosure on the superior as
well, thereby robbing her of one aspect of official superiority over
her flock.[33] The *Abbatissa* Caesaria's decades of success at Saint-Jean
of Arles probably resulted from the force of her own erudite *doctrina*[34]
and not from any *Amtscharisma* inherent in the Caesarian abbess.

At least one other charismatic woman is known to have used the
Caesarian rule with success. St Radegund (c. 518–587) seems to have
chosen the Caesarian rule for her foundation at Poitiers[35] precisely
because of that rule's guarantee of exemption from episcopal control.
According to Gregory of Tours, she reformed her own monastery
through changing the dedication of the house—from the Virgin
Mary to the Holy Cross—and by introducing the Caesarian rule,
both while in the very midst of an altercation with, and against the
wishes of, the bishop of Poitiers.[36] After the charismatic saint's own
death, however, that very lack of episcopal control over the abbess
of Holy Cross resulted in a rebellion of the *puellae* of the monastery
against their *abbatissa*.

Within two years of Radegund's death, Bishop Gregory of Tours
received an unexpected visit from forty of the *puellae* of Holy Cross.
The members of the rebellious group had bound themselves by an
oath to have their new *Abbatissa* Leubovera ejected from the
monastery, on the grounds that she humiliated them and now wished
to enlist Bishop Gregory's help for their cause.[37] Bishop Gregory's
presentation of the scandal at Holy Cross of Poitiers minimizes the
importance of how the abbess treated her subordinates—it was
immaterial to him as long as she did not act contrary to the rule of
the monastery[38]—and foregrounds instead the fact of historical
nonalliance between the *abbatissa* and the bishop of Poitiers as the
material cause of the rebellion. The rebel *puellae* continued for almost
two years to reject the authority of Leubovera, accusing her of a
number of crimes and, on one occasion, causing her to be physically
attacked.[39] Abbess Leubovera herself, recognizing the weakness of

her position and unwilling to trust in any Caesarian *Amtscharisma*, put herself under the power of the bishop of Poitiers.[40]

The spectre of the rebellious *puella* who had scorned her family's wishes only to join a religious community haunted the eschatological family in the heroic of monasticism; in 589 and 590, at Holy Cross of Poitiers, that spectre took on flesh. The Caesarian solution to feminine *Amtscharisma*, namely a female father independent of the male hierarchy but subjected to the physical cloister, was a failure.

THE EFFLORESCENCE OF FEMALE MONASTICISM IN THE SEVENTH AND EIGHTH CENTURIES: CHARISMA OR *Amtscharisma*?

From the end of the sixth century, the conventional family was rehabilitated in male monastic circles. Prospective monks tended less often to be men who had begun their professional lives through an act of individualistic rebellion against the wishes of their parents.[41] Indeed, parents were increasingly likely themselves to place their young sons in monasteries, assuring for those boys a completely monastic formation and strong ties of loyalty with the eschatological family.[42] Yet, in an era when fewer males had to rebel against the authority of their parents in order to take up a monastic vocation, a significant proportion of female religious still began their professional lives through an act of disobedience to parental authority.[43] The female monasteries of Gaul were therefore filled, almost by definition, by self-willed individualists when, in the seventh and early eighth centuries, large numbers of female monasteries were founded.[44]

Does the transformation of female monasticism into a mass movement mean that a successful solution to the problem of feminine *Amtscharisma* had been developed? Not necessarily. The majority of the many female houses founded in Gaul and Italy during the period of expansion were ephemeral, implying that their existence was dependent on the presence of charismatic leaders; the office of the superior itself could not guarantee institutional continuity. The throngs of enthusiastic, rebellious *puellae* of Gaul had little difficulty finding charismatic leaders. Although only 8 percent of sixth-century saints had been female, by the early eighth century, 23.5 percent of saints were female, the highest percentage ever attained by women.[45]

Several attempts were made during the late Merovingian period to provide a constitution for female monastic communities. Despite Benedict of Nursia's framing of his rule with only males in mind, these late Merovingian feminine rules are all primarily drawn from the Benedictine rule (albeit as part of an eclectic mix of monastic traditions) and indeed provide the very earliest evidence of the influence of benedictinism anywhere in the Frankish world![46] Two late-Merovingian female rules survive in their entirety. The earlier of the two establishes a religious superior who is officially so weak that only a charismatic saint could hope to succeed in the position; the later rule, on the other hand, seems to provide a fullfledged example of practicable feminine *Amtscharisma* and may indeed stem from a milieu in which such a thing was in fact a reality during the period in question. The rule composed c. 650 by Bishop Donatus of Besançon for Jussa Moutier in Besançon combines with extracts from the Benedictine rule numerous excerpts from the rule of Caesarius and a number of original features, with a few citations from a penal code attributed to Columbanus.[47] The Benedictine rule is likewise the primary source of an anonymous rule written in Gaul during the late seventh or early eighth century, again along with excerpts from the Caesarian rule and a few citations to the "Columbanian" penal code but also making liberal use of the rule of Donatus itself.[48] The latter rule is called in its only manuscript source—Benedict of Aniane's *Codex regularum*—and by its editor, the *Regula cuiusdam patris ad virgines*; however, in view of the likelihood of female authorship of works preserved anonymously but known to have come from a female monastic milieu,[49] I would suggest a designator that is more descriptive of the text and gender neutral concerning authorship, such as "the rule of the abbess."

The rule of Donatus and the "rule of the abbess" are similar in length, subject matter and sources and yet completely opposed to each other in spirit. The "rule of the abbess" hardly ever refers to the leader of the community by any title other than *abbatissa*, and that title itself appears most of the time in combination with words of authority, judgment, or command; on the other hand, Donatus uses *mater* almost as frequently as he does *abbatissa*.[50] The *abbatissa* of Donatus' rule[51] is the cloistered Caesarian abbess; indeed, Donatus elaborated on Caesarius' rules for the enclosure of female religious, while retaining the Caesarian permission for the community to resist, even rebel against, its abbess. Even in comparison with the Caesarian rule, the role of the abbess in the *regula Donati* is so attenuated that she is almost effaced. She is overshadowed, instead, by a *mater* modelled upon the loving Benedictine male abbot of Chapter 64 of the Benedictine rule, the parent who bears the heavy burden of caring for children; yet Donatus' *mater* possesses little of the authoritarian patriarchal qualities of the Benedictine male superior. Donatus replaces the Benedictine obligation to obey the community's father with the exhortation to love its mother. In order to compensate for the Donatian *mater's* constitutional incapacity to discipline her subordinates—the Benedictine penal code, in which the abbot's decisions are paramount, having been severely truncated—Donatus inserts a series of specific corporal punishments which take discipline out of the purview of the *mater* and builds it into the rule itself.

Bishop Donatus evidently believed that the monastic experience and monastic governance were completely gender specific; he avoids translating Benedict's *abbas* as *abbatissa*, preferring *mater*, and he never calls the female religious *monachae* but rather *ancillae Christi* (nursemaids of Christ) or *sorores*. But the most distinct feature of Donatus' rule for female religious is the complete lack of *Amtscharisma* it offered to any potential religious ruler. Nothing could be farther from the institutional utility possessed by the "rule of the abbess," whose practical applicability and consonance with the authoritarian Benedictine rule was recognized by no less a person than Benedict of Aniane, who used almost the entire rule for his *Concordia regularum.*[52] There is little in the "rule of the abbess" to indicate that its author considered the female monastic experience to differ in any way from that of men. This monastic legislator's abbess is the authoritarian Benedictine abbot reinforced by anything in the traditions of Caesarius, Donatus, or Columbanus that could increase her power over her subordinates, such as the requirement that the *monachae* confess to the abbess or her deputies.[53]

The "rule of the abbess" establishes the complete authority of the abbess in Chapter 1, then proceeds down a hierarchy of monastic offices, all strictly subordinated to the abbess, in Chapters 2 through 4; a long chapter—22—later establishes that the hierarchical principle must rule all relations in the community. Biblical citations are used to analogize the abbess with paternal and pastoral figures; when the abbess is "mater," it is in the guise of a mother who rules and coerces. Normally, however, she is *abbatissa*, and the disciplinary life of the community officially depends entirely on her judgment. There is no sign of any attempt at cloistering the abbess or even the *monachae*, as the female religious are consistently called.

Although the "rule of the abbess" has always been connected with Gallic—or Frankish—monasticism, and seems to have been written down on the continent, its spirit hardly matches what is known of early medieval female communities in what is now France. Instead, its provisions, particularly those concerning the *Amtscharisma* of the female monastic superior, seem very much in keeping with the venerable female monastic superior who has been discerned in the writings and attitudes of eighth- and ninth-century Anglo-Saxons, both in the British Isles and in continental Saxony. Schneider and Atkinson both cite repeatedly, and exclusively, Bede, Boniface, Rudolf of Fulda, and Alcuin to demonstrate that there existed in early medieval Europe an *officium abbatissae* and a respect for spiritual maternity.[54] The "rule of the abbess," which survives only through Benedict of Aniane's *Codex regularum*, could well have originated in Anglo-Saxon monastic circles on the continent, particularly given that Benedict found the female rules that he included in his collection in a now-lost manuscript of Fulda.[55]

Although we do not now know whether the rules of Donatus or "of the abbess" were actually used during the seventh- and eighth-century effloresence of female monasticism, we can see in the two rules attestations to the diversity of the possible solutions which were advocated during that era in order to provide a constitution for female religious.

A CASE STUDY IN DISTORTED BENEDICTINISM: THE ABBESS OF NIEDERMÜNSTER HAS NO STAFF

From the middle of the eighth century, the Benedictine rule was imposed from above on female monasteries just as it was on male monasteries. However, supplementary Frankish conciliar and capitular legislation attempted to distort the Benedictinism practiced in female communities by imposing obligations of cloister drawn from the Caesarian tradition.[56] The legal terminology surrounding the office of abbess also differed from that surrounding the office of abbot.[57] Even under the full-fledged Benedictine regime which came to dominate Latin Europe during the tenth and eleventh centuries, the problematics of authority were never fully resolved in female communities. It is perhaps significant that the most important female saint of the Benedictine order, Benedict's sister Scholastica, has been celebrated since the twelfth century at the earliest as a paradigm of *disobedience,* a characteristic antithetical to everything Benedictinism seeks to inculcate in its communities.[58]

Other practices and institutions that grew up around the Benedictine rule likewise worked so as to distort the Benedictinism of female communities, particularly where the authority of the abbess was concerned. The Benedictine rule did not itself provide any guidance for the ceremonial installation of the head of the community. The liturgies which were developed in order to fulfill this perceived void were themselves gendered in such a way as to withhold the full force of Benedictine *Amtscharisma* from female occupants of the abbatial office. The so-called *Romano-Germanic Pontifical,* compiled c. 950, was in common use throughout the Holy Roman Empire by the end of the tenth century.[59] The *ordines* which were used for the ordinations of abbots and abbesses, respectively, differed in significant ways. When a bishop ordained a male abbot, he invested that abbot with a *baculum pastoralitatis*, a pastoral staff, the symbol of ruling power carried by bishops and by kings as well as by abbots and gave the new abbot a copy of the monastic rule.[60] The female abbess, on the other hand, received no *baculum* and therefore was never invested with *personal* authority in connection with her office, although she did benefit—unlike the Caesarian abbess—from a broad institutional backing to her position through her hierarchical relationship with the bishop; instead of a staff, the Benedictine abbess received, ceremoniously, only a copy of the monastic rule which she was supposed to enforce.[61]

We are fortunate in possessing, for at least one female monastic community, specific manuscript evidence of how the abbesses of the house sought to compensate for the relative weakness of their office compared with that of their male abbatial colleagues. One strategy, so elegant in its simplicity as to be almost breathtaking, was to draw on the Carolingian tradition of gender fluidity in monastic legislation, and to appropriate, to the fullest possible extent, the resonances of paternal authority implicit in the feminized male title *abbatissa*. Two abbesses of Niedermünster of Regensburg, first Abbess Uota in the late tenth century, then Abbess Eilika in the mid-eleventh century, had copies made of the Benedictine rule in which they claimed the plenitude of abbatial-paternal authority through changing nothing from Benedict's original besides *abbas* to *abbatissa*, *monachus* to *monacha*, and so forth.[62] The *abbatissae* of Niedermünster claimed to be fathers, pastors, and vicars of Christ, just as was any male superior of a religious community. *Abbates* and *abbatissae* are fathers who must be obeyed.

In the case of the eleventh-century codex, produced c. 1040–1044 under Abbess Eilika, it is much more than the Benedictine rule itself that bolsters the authority of the abbess.[63] The eleventh-century copy of the rule is part of a larger, formerly independent *libellus*— comprising folios 51r–119v of Berlin, Staatsbibliothek zu Berlin Preußischer Kulturbesitz MS theol. lat. qu. 199—whose overall structure and artistic program make brilliant use of every possible means to reinforce the authority of the abbess. On fols. 51r–54r, there is a computus. However, the computus runs almost imperceptibly into a text of the liturgy for the ordination of an abbess and then for the consecration of a virgin, both according to the Romano-Germanic Pontifical (fols. 54v–57v and fols. 57v–66r, respectively). The computus is encased within an architectural framework and arranged on the page first according to the multi-lobed form of canon tables, then according to the two-lobed conventional iconography of the Ten Commandments of Sinai; both the architectural framework and the layout of text as though it were on the two tablets of the Mosaic Law continue to be used for the two *ordines*. The official positions of the abbess and of her virgin subordinates are shown to be a solid part of the very architecture of the church, as important as the computus through which one calculates the date of Easter.

The Benedictine abbess had what the Caesarian abbess did not: a dramatic liturgical moment which put her in relation to the ecclesiastical hierarchy; the artistic program of the Niedermünster *libellus* is specifically designed to milk every possible drop of authoritative resonance out of that particular ceremonial moment and to enmesh the abbess within a cosmic scheme of sacred history and sacred typology. Moreover, the artistic program of the codex works to reinforce the centrality of the abbess in ways that defy any simplistic, monolithic attempt to understand the authority of the *abbatissa* exclusively as honorary masculine paternity. When, during the abbess' ordination ceremony, the bishop gives her a copy of the Benedictine rule, he says to the abbess-elect:

> Suppliant, we beseech you, Lord God omnipotent,
> who caused Mary, sister of Moses, to go out ahead
> joyfully among the watery waves, with tympana and
> choruses, with the rest of the women, to the shore
> of the sea, for the sake of your faithful servant
> N. who is today established in the maternal throne
> as abbess over all those women subjected to her.[64]

Under an architectural framework of the tablets of the law as given by God to Moses on Sinai, the bishop gives the law to the new abbess, who is assimilated to Moses' sister Mary, said to be the leader of the women of Israel. Through this ordination ceremony, the abbess-elect is installed *materna in cathedra* (in the maternal throne). There soon follows a visual depiction of the maternal throne: an illumination of Mary, mother of God, enthroned on her maternal seat, with Jesus—a miniature adult—on her lap.[65] On the reverse of that folio, an enthroned St. Benedict *pater et pastor*, holding a pastoral staff and giving a copy of his rule to an abbess, replays once again the law-giving moment.[66] The law may be given by fathers, by Moses, by the bishop of Regensburg, by St. Benedict, but women are led by mothers: by Moses' sister Mary, by Jesus' Mother Mary, who was the patron saint of Niedermünster, by the abbess of the house.

The gender of the Benedictine abbot is a simple thing: he is male and, when he parents his flock in the monastery, he is a father. But what can one say that is simple about the gender of the Benedictine abbess, or rather about the gender of the *office* of the Benedictine abbess and about the guise in which she parents her female flock? By virtue of the etymology of her title, she is a female father; by virtue of the stipulations of the rule itself she is a female father who stands in the stead of Christ; by virtue of her ordination ceremony she is a castrated father, or at least a deformed one, for she bears no staff; finally, also by virtue of her ordination ceremony, she occupies a maternal throne. How female abbesses actually managed to impose their authority on the women subordinated to them and how they were perceived by those women, whether as mothers or as fathers or as a combination of both, would be worth investigating farther. If the situation at Niedermünster in the eleventh century is at all representative of female religious communities, "Mother Superior" is a singularly incomplete and misleading translation of the title *abbatissa*.

NOTES

*This essay is dedicated to Suzanne Fonay Wemple and Robert Somerville, the dominant figures in my undergraduate education; the essay represents a synthesis of their training in the study of female religious and of legislative sources, respectively.

1. All future studies must begin with the comprehensive study of masculine monastic *Amtscharisma* by Franz Felten, "Herrschaft des Abtes," in *Herrschaft und Kirche: Beiträge zur Entstehung und Wirkungsweise episkopaler und monastischer Organisationsformen* ed. Friedrich Prinz, Monographien zur Geschichte des Mittelalters 33 (Stuttgart, 1988), pp. 147–296. Also see Karl Blume, *Abbatia. Ein Beitrag zur Geschichte der kirchlichen Rechtssprache*, Kirchenrechtliche Abhandlungen 83 (Stuttgart, 1914; reprt. Amsterdam, 1965); Adalbert de Vogüé, *La communauté et l'abbé dans la règle de saint Benoît* (Bruges, 1961), pp. 121–40; Karl Bosl, "Die *Familia* als Grundstruktur der mittelalterlichen Gesellschaft," *Zeitschrift für Bayerische Landesgeschichte* 38 (1975), 403–24; Giles Constable, "The Authority of Superiors in Religious Communities," in *La notion d'autorité au moyen âge. Islam, Byzance, Occident* (Colloques internationaux de La Napoule Organisés par George Makdisi, Dominique Sourdel and Janine Sourdel-Thomine, 1978; Paris, 1982), pp. 189–210.

2. Rosamond McKitterick, *The Frankish Church and the Carolingian Reforms* (Cambridge, England, 1975); Josef Semmler, "Benedictus II: Una regula–una consuetudo," in *Benedictine Culture, 750–1050*, eds. W. Loudaux and D. Verhelst, Mediaevalia Lovaniensia-Studia 1. 11 (Leuven, 1983), pp. 1–49; Réginald Grégoire, "Il Monachesimo Carolingia dopo Benedicto d'Aniane (†821)" *Studia monastica* s. 3, 24 (1982), 349–88.

3. Benedict of Nursia, *Benedicti regula (editio altera emendata)*, ed. Rudolf Hanslik, CSEL 75, 2nd ed. (Vienna, 1977). Chapter 2 of Benedict's regula, the treatise on abbatial directorship, was one of the two most often cited extracts from the text. See Réginald Grégoire, "Enquête sur les citations de la règle de saint Benoît dans l'hagiographie latine mediévale," *Studia monastica* s. 3, 16 (1975), 747–62.

4. There is little warrant for making such assumptions concerning any historical phenomena since Joan Kelly posed her famous question "Did Women Have a Renaissance?," in *Becoming Visible: Women in European History*, eds. Renate Bridenthal and Claudia Koontz (Boston, 1977), pp. 137–64; reprinted in Joan Kelly, *Women, History and Theory. The Essays of Joan Kelly*, Women in Culture and Society (Chicago, 1987).

5. Penelope Johnson, *Equal in Monastic Profession: Religious Women in Medieval France* (Chicago, 1991), p. 3. Only a single entry appeared under the category "abbesses" in Oliver Leonard Kapsner, *A Benedictine Bibliography* (Collegeville, Minnesota, 1982), and that was a seventeenth-century controversial tract: Ascanio Tamburini de Marradio, *De iure abbatissarum et monialium; sive Praxis gubernandi moniales* (Lyons, 1668).

For an example of the continued tendency to ignore female religious, see Ludo J.R. Milis, *Angelic Monks and Earthly Men. Monasticism and Its Meaning to Medieval Society* (Woodbridge, 1992), p. xii; against Milis' misguided rationale, see Stephanus Hilpisch, *Geschichte der Benediktinerinnen*, Benediktinisches Geistesleben. Zeugnisse und Abhandlungen aus dem Gebiet des Askese und Mystik 3 (St. Ottilien, 1951), pp. 55–58.

6. Hilpisch, *Benediktinerinnen*, p. 17; Philibert Schmitz, *Histoire de l'ordre de Saint Benoît*, 7 vols. (Maredsous, 1956), 7:9–11.

7. The vast majority of the extant manuscript copies of Benedict's rule and all of the earliest copies are gendered throughout as masculine (Benedict, *Regula,* ed. Hanslik, pp. xxii–xlvii).

8. Benedict of Aniane, *Concordia regularum*, PL 103: 717–1380; Adalbert de Vogüé, *Les règles monastiques anciennes* (400–700), Typologie des sources du moyen âge Occidental 46 (Turnhout, 1985), pp. 42, 44–45; Semmler, "Benedictus II," pp. 27–28.

9. Hope Mayo, "Three Merovingian Rules for Nuns," 2 vols. (Ph.D. diss., Harvard University, 1974), 1:55, 60–62 catalogues those excerpts.

10. Although Benedict also preserved earlier feminine rules in the female gender in his *Codex regularum* (Mayo, 1: 44–46, 62), it was the *Concordia regularum* which was frequently copied and which became an influential text; in any case, Benedict of Aniane's life work turned all rules besides that of Benedict of Nursia into museum pieces.

11. Smaragdus, *Diadema monachorum*, PL 102:593–690; Smaragdus, *Commentaria in regulam sancti Benedicti*, PL 102:689–932; Mayke de Jong, "Growing up in a Carolingian Monastery: Magister Hildemar and His Oblates," *Journal of Medieval History* 9 (1983), 99–128.

12. Benedict, *Regula* 2, lines 1–3, ed. Hanslik.

13. "...abbatia, quae paternitas latino nomine dicitur" (Council of Meaux-Paris (845–846) canon 10 in MGH Leges Sectio 2: Capitularia Regum Francorum, 2.2, ed. A. Werminghoff (Hannover, 1893), p. 400.

14. Clarissa W. Atkinson, *The Oldest Vocation: Christian Motherhood in the Middle Ages* (Ithaca, NY, 1991), pp. 90–99; Suzanne Fonay Wemple, *Women in Frankish Society. Marriage and the Cloister, 500–900* (Philadelphia, 1981), pp. 59–60.

15. Maria Stoeckle, "Studien über Ideale in Frauenviten des 7. bis 10. Jahrhunderts" (Ph.D. dissertation, Munich, 1957), pp. 64–74; Dagmar Beate Schneider, "Anglo-Saxon Women in the Religious Life. A Study of the Status and Position of Women in an Early Medieval Society" (Ph.D. diss., Cambridge University, 1985), pp. 109–29; Atkinson, *Oldest Vocation,* pp. 67–95. Schneider does sometimes depart from the stereotype of burdened, sacrificial maternity; see above, p. 12.

16. Caroline Walker Bynum, "Jesus as Mother and Abbot as Mother: Some Themes in Twelfth-Century Cistercian Writing," in *Jesus as Mother. Studies in the Spirituality of the High Middle Ages*, Publications of the Center for Medieval and Renaissance Studies 16 (Berkeley, 1982), pp. 110–69.

17. Augustine of Hippo, *Obiurgatio*, in *La règle de saint Augustin*, ed. Luc Verheijen, 2 vols. (Paris, 1967), 1:105–7.

18. David Herlihy, *Medieval Households, Studies in Cultural History* (Cambridge, MA, 1985), pp. 2–50 summarizes the relevant patriarchal legislation. However, for evidence of matrilineal/matriarchal practices and maternal "heads of household," see Wemple, pp. 31, 49, 59–61, 64–65, 232 note 61; M.-P. Deroux, "Les origines de l'oblature bénédictine," *Revue Mabillon* 17 (1927), 1–16, 81–113, 193–217, 305–51 at pp. 92–94; Atkinson, pp. 90–91; and Carl I. Hammer Jr., "Family and *Familia* in Early-Medieval Bavaria," in *Family Forms in Historic Europe*, eds. Richard Wall, Jean Robin and others (Cambridge, England, 1983), pp. 217–48 (to which, compare Wemple, pp. 70–74 and Herlihy, pp. 57–67). Nevertheless, the thrust of most legislation is clearly patriarchal.

19. Alessandro Barbero, *Un santo in famiglia. Vocazione religiosa e resistenze sociali nell'agiografia latina medievale* (Turin, 1991), pp. 7–40; Atkinson, pp. 16–22; Wemple, pp. 149–58; Frantisek Graus, *Volk, Herrscher und Heiliger im Reich der Merowinger. Studien zur Hagiographie der Merowingerzeit* (Prague, 1965), pp. 468–76; Katharina Weber, "Kulturgeschichtliche Probleme der Merowingerzeit im Spiegel frühmittelalterlicher Heiligenleben," *Studien und Mitteilungen zur Geschichte des benediktiner Ordens und seiner Zweige* 48 (1930), 349–403.

20. Ruth Albrecht, *Das Leben der heiligen Makrina auf dem Hintergrund der Thekla-Traditionen. Studien zu den Ursprüngen des weiblichen Mönchtums im 4. Jahrhundert in Kleinasien*, Forschungen zur Kirchen-und Dogmengeschichte 38 (Göttingen, 1986), pp. 239–320.

21. Albrecht, *Makrina*, p. 250.

22. Atkinson, *Oldest Vocation*, pp. 14–16.

23. Albrecht, *Makrina*, pp. 138–41.

24. Rosemary Radford Reuther, "Mothers of the Church: Ascetic Women in the Late Patristic Age," in *Female Leadership*, eds. R. Reuther and E. McLaughlin (New York, 1979), pp. 71–98; Jo Ann McNamara, *A New Song: Celibate Women in the First Three Christian Centuries*, Women and History 6/7 (New York, 1983); Susanna Elm, *Virgins of God: The Making of Asceticism in Late Antiquity* (Oxford, 1994).

25. Caesarius of Arles, *Regula ad virgines*, ed. and trans. Adalbert de Vogüé and Joël Courreau, *Oeuvres monastiques*, vol. 1, *Oeuvres pour les moniales*, Sources Chrétiennes 345 (Paris, 1988). Caesarius' rule was composed in stages between 512 and 534. The first known written rule, composed by Pachomius (286–346), had applied both to male and female communities (Albrecht, *Makrina*, pp. 111–21). Augustine of Hippo was content to see his *praeceptum*, originally written for the brothers of his entourage, be transposed into the feminine gender by members of a female community (Verheijen, *Règle de Saint Augustin*, 2:197–203). The only other early feminine rule, that by Bishop Aurelian of Arles, was almost identical

to that same bishop's rule for male religious from which it was adapted; both Aurelian rules were composed c. 550 (Mayo, 1:68–119, 2:3–69).

26. De Vogüé and Courreau in Caesarius, *Oeuvres monastiques*, 1:88–92.

27. Albrecht, *Makrina*, p. 143; Schmitz, *Ordre de Saint Benoît*, 7:213.

28. De Vogüé and Courreau in Caesarius, *Oeuvres monastiques*, 1:50; Caesarius, *Regula ad uirgines* 64, 1–3, ed. de Vogüé and Courreau; Mayo, 1:22–23. It may be that the Caesarian rule positively guaranteed something which was already *de facto* true in any case. The canons of the various early fifth-century Gallic councils which worked for the subjection of male abbots to bishops never mentioned female houses, and the widespread assumption that the canons applied to female religious superiors may not be warranted. For the conciliar legislation, see *Concilia Galliae anno 511–anno 695*, ed. Charles de Clercq, CCSL 148A (Turnhout, 1963), or *Les canons des conciles mérovingiens* (VIe–VIIe siècles) ed., notes and trans. Jean Gaudemet and Bernard Basdevant, Sources Chrétiennes 353/354 (Paris, 1989): Orléans I (511) canons 19, 22; Epaon (517) canons 8, 9, 10, 19; Orléans II (533) canon 21. For attempts to control (male) monasteries, see Leo Ueding, *Geschichte der Klostergründungen der frühen Merowingerzeit*, Historische Studien 261 (Berlin, 1935), pp. 32–46.

29. Caesarius, *Oeuvres monastiques*, 1 ed., de Vogüé and Courreau, chapter 64.

30. Canon 8, Council of Epaon (517).

31. Wemple, *Women in Frankish Society*, pp. 60–63.

32. However, before putting too much weight on the harshness of the rule of life-long claustration for female religious, we should also pause to consider the fact that large numbers of women—professed virgins or avowed widows—lived as lay *conversae* either in their own homes or in very small, nonregulated communities (Jean-Marie Guillaume, "Les abbayes de femmes en pays franc, des origines à la fin du VIIe siècle," in *Remiremont. L'Abbaye et la ville,* ed. Michel Parisse (Actes des journées d'études vosgiennes, Remiremont, avril 1980; Nancy, 1980), pp. 29–46; Wemple, pp. 155–57; Henry Neff Waldron, "Expressions of Religious Conversion among Laymen Remaining within Secular Society in Gaul: 400–800 A.D." (Ph.D. diss., Ohio State University, 1976). Perhaps women who actually chose to join a community, rather than just changing their vestments and lifestyle, were actively seeking such a level of segregation from the world.

33. Jane Tibbetts Schulenberg, "Strict Active Enclosure and Its Effects on the Female Monastic Experience (c. 500–1100)," *Medieval Religious Women 1: Distant Echoes*, Cistercian Studies 71 (Kalamazoo, 1984), pp. 51–86 discusses the potentially detrimental effects of Caesarius' theories of enclosure of the abbess on female monasticism in general.

34. In a long letter to two Frankish women who wished to adopt her rule, Caesaria II (Caesarius' niece) made almost no reference to the rule

itself as a support or even guide for her leadership strategies; instead, she
repeatedly recommended practices inspired directly by scriptural
injunctions, and encouraged the constant study of scripture itself by all the
women religious (Caesaria of Saint-Jean, *Epistle* to Richild and Radegund,
ed. de Vogüé and Courreau in Caesarius, *Oeuvres monastiques,* 1:476–95).

35. Wemple, pp. 154–58; Guillaume, "Les abbayes de femmes," pp.
34–37.

36. Gregory of Tours, *Libri decem historiarum* 9. 40, ed. Bruno
Krusch, MGH SRM 1.1, 2nd ed. (Hannover, 1951), pp. 464–65. Radegund
was not, of course, herself abbess of Holy Cross, but her charisma would
have reinforced the authority of the Abbess Agnes, the saint's protegée.

37. Gregory, *Libri decem historiarum* 9. 39, ed. Krusch, p. 460.

38. Throughout his account of the rather drawn-out rebellion,
Gregory grounds all legal proceedings on the notion of enforcement of the
Caesarian rule, a technicality which provides further evidence of the fact
that monasteries under the rule of Caesarius were independent of episcopal
control per se. Gregory includes in his narrative a copy of a letter sent by
the Council of Tours (567) to St. Radegund, through which letter the
bishops of the region gave the saint permission to gather under the rule of
Caesarius women from their various dioceses; the bishops then went on
to emphasize how, according to the Caesarian rule, women who voluntarily
entered the monastery would then be subject to excommunication for the
breaking of cloister (Gregory 9. 59, ed. Krusch, pp. 460–63). The same
bishops legislated as part of the canons of the council of Tours for
excommunication of males who either took vows in monasteries or declared
their intention to do so and then broke cloister or married a woman (canon
16 [15]). Three other canons of the council of Tours also legislated explicitly
for the inhabitants and abbots of male monastic houses (canons 7, 17 [16]
and 18 [17]). All this is also in keeping with the implications of the
distinction which had been drawn at the provincial council of Arles in 554
concerning the monastic houses of the region. According to canons 2 and
3, the discipline of male monasteries, male monks, and male abbots
pertained to the bishop in whose diocese the houses were located; in
contrast, canon 5 gave bishops the limited role of assuring that abbesses of
female monasteries did not contravene the rule but put the bishops in no
direct relation with the *puellae* or the *abbatissa* except as mediated by the
rule. For references, see above note 28.

39. Gregory's extended account can be found in *Libri decem
historiarum* 9. 39–43 and 10. 15–17, 20, ed. Krusch, pp. 460–75, 501–9, 513.

40. Gregory 9. 40, p. 465.

41. Barbero, *Un Santo in famiglia,* pp. 41–52, 59–76.

42. De Jong, "Growing Up"; Deroux, "Oblature," pp. 81–91.

43. Barbero, *Un Santo in famiglia,* pp. 53–55, 77, 89–124; Stoeckle,
pp. 35–41.

44. Lina Eckenstein, *Woman Under Monasticism. Chapters on Saint-lore and Convent Life Between AD 500 and AD 1500* (Cambridge, England, 1896), pp. 51–78; also see Guillaume, "Abbayes de femmes" pp. 38–42; Wemple, pp. 158–65; Dorothy de Ferranti Abrahamse, "Byzantine Asceticism and Women's Monasteries in Early Medieval Italy," in *Distant Echoes,* eds. Nichols and Shank, pp. 31–49.

45. Jane Tibbetts Schulenberg, "Sexism and the Celestial Gynaeceum," *Journal of Medieval History* 4 (1978), 117–34.

46. Grégoire, "Citations de la Règle," p. 747; de Vogüé, *Règles monastiques,* p. 59; Francois Masai, "Fragment en onciale d'une règle monastique inconnue démarquant celle de saint Benoît (Bruxelles II 7538)," *Scriptorium* 2 (1948), 215–20, plates 26–7; Schmitz, *Ordre de Saint Benoît* 7:12; *Benedicti Regula,* ed. Hanslik, p. xlvii (for Gaul) and p. xlviii (for the Iberian peninsula); Lazare de Seilhac, "La règle de saint Benoît dans la tradition au féminin" in *Regula Benedicti studia. Annuarium internationale,* ed. Makarios Hebler (Sechster International Regula-Benedicti-Kongreß, Bruges, 1986; St. Ottilien, 1989), pp. 57–68.

47. Adalbert de Vogüé, "La Règle de Donat pour l'Abbesse Gauthstrude" in *Benedictina* 25 (1978), 219–313.

48. Mayo, "Three Merovingian Rules for Nuns," pp. 189, 214–17.

49. Rosamund McKitterick, "Frauen und Schriftlichkeit in Frühen Mittelalter," in *Weibliche Lebensgestaltung im frühen Mittelalter,* ed. Hans-Werner Goetz (Cologne, 1991), pp. 65–118, especially p. 107.

50. See J.-M. Clément, *Lexique des anciennes règles monastiques Occidentales, Instrumenta Patristica* 7A, 2 vols. (Steenbrugis, 1978), 1:6–8 and 705–6.

51. I summarize below the relevant findings of de Vogüé's detailed analysis of the rule in *Règle de Donat,* especially pp. 231–32.

52. Mayo, "Three Merovingian Rules for Nuns," 1:184.

53. For the text of the rule, see Mayo, "Three Merovingian Rules for Nuns," 2:142–213.

54. Schneider, "Anglo-Saxon Women," pp. 109–29; Atkinson, *Oldest Vocation,* pp. 67–95.

55. De Vogüé and Courreau in Caesarius, *Oeuvres monastiques* 1:137.

56. Suzanne Fonay Wemple, "Les traditions Romaine, Germanique et Chrétienne," in *Histoire des femmes en Occident,* dir. Georges Duby and Michelle Perrot, vol. 2, *Le Moyen age,* dir. Christiane Klapisch-Zuber (no place of publication, 1991), pp. 185–216, especially pp. 205–07; Schulenberg, "Enclosure," pp. 56–62, 70–78, which should be read in conjunction with Grégoire, "Monachesimo Carolingio."

57. When Benedictine monasticism was institutionalized, the use of the title *abbas* was legally restricted to male heads of regular abbeys and forbidden to those who headed communities of canons; on the other hand, all female monastic superiors held the title *abbatissa* (Blume, *Abbatia,* p. 60; Schmitz, *Ordre de Saint Benoît,* 7:40).

58. Jane Morrissey, "Scholastica and Benedict: A Picnic, A Paradigm" and Gerard Farrell, "Saints Benedict and Scholastica: The Liturgical Music," in *Equally in God's Image: Women in the Middle Ages,* eds. Julia Bolton Holloway, Constance S. Wright, and Joan Bechtold (New York, 1990), pp. 251–57 and 258–59; also see the comments of the editors on p. 217.

59. Cyrille Vogel and Reinhard Elze, *Le pontifical romano-germanique du xe siècle,* 3 vols., Studi e Testi 226/227/269 (Vatican City, 1963–1972).

60. *Pontifical,* ed. Vogel and Elze, 1:62–69.

61. *Pontifical,* ed. Vogel and Elze, 1:76–82. Other potentially significant differences between the male and female *ordines* include the bishop's address concerning paternity (which begins the male *ordo* only and which precedes the *Pater noster,* evoking divine parallelism) and the failure of the bishop to prostrate himself along with the abbess-elect (although he does do so along with the abbot-elect).

62. Bamberg, MS Lit. 142 (tenth century, Niedermünster), fols. 6r–57v; Berlin, Staatsbibliothek zu Berlin-Preußischer Kulturbesitz MS theol. lat. qu. 199 (eleventh century, Niedermünster), fols. 68r–119r. The only change in these feminized versions of the Benedictine rule compared with the original is that the chapters dealing with priests resident in the monastery are moved to the end of the rule, almost as an appendix, because of their obvious inappropriateness; it is worth emphasizing that regulations concerning guests, religious who are artisans, religious on pilgrimage, and the like are neither shifted nor excised. For the place of the Niedermünster versions in the typology of Benedictine rule copies, see the section on the rule entitled "de vulgo recepto" in Hanslik, ed. *Benedicti regula,* pp. lv–lxiv. A copy of the rule of Caesarius was appended to the Benedictine rule in Bamberg, MS Lit. 142, fols. 62r–83v, a copy which significantly altered Caesarius' rule, often so as to increase the power of the abbess (de Vogüé and Courreau in Caesarius, *Oeuvres monastiques* 1:129–34).

63. That the abbess of Niedermünster felt particular concern about issues of authority may be indicated by the marginal notes—all reading *proba*—made, by a hand contemporary with the rest of the *libellus,* throughout the text of the Benedictine rule, next to every section of the rule specifically relevant to the *officium* of the superior of the community.

64. "Domine Deus omnipotens qui sororem Moysi Mariam preeuntem cum ceteris mulieribus inter aequoreas undas cum tympanis et choris laetam adlitus maris venire fecisti, te supplices deprecamur pro fideli famula N. que hodie materna in cathedra super universas subditas sibi abbatissa constituitur." (I cite the *ordo* from Berlin MS theol. lat. qu. 199 fol. 56v).

65. Berlin MS theol. lat. qu., fol. 67r.

66. For the illuminations see *Regensburger Buchmalerei. Von frühkarolingischer Zeit bis zum Ausgang des Mittelalters,* Bayerisches Staatsbibliothek München/Ausstellungkataloge 39 (Munich, 1987), catalogue #21, pp. 35–36, plates 17, 101.

MATERNITY IN AELRED OF RIEVAULX'S LETTER TO HIS SISTER

Susanna Greer Fein

In De institutione inclusarum, *a work addressed to his recluse sister, Aelred of Rievaulx provides spiritual insight through a womb-centered imagery of sexual arousal, pregnancy, childbirth, and maternal pathos that analogizes anchoritic cell to female body.*

Affective metaphors of physical maternity became, for many early Cistercian writers, a standard way to define God's devotion for men and the male writers' own Christian devotion to the needs of others. To see an abbot's role as analogous to that of a mother with her children—as authority supplemented with love—apparently fit well the spiritual ideals cultivated in their communities of men.[1] Caroline Walker Bynum views the Cistercian material primarily and logically as an *oeuvre* composed by men (almost always abbots) for an audience of men (almost always monks), not as reflective of attitudes toward women.[2] Bynum maintains a careful distinction between the terms *feminine* (as in maternal imagery) and *female* (as in flesh-and-blood women), advising readers that

> We cannot assume that twelfth-century monks associated the feminine with the female to the extent that we do or that they associated certain physical or affective responses with sexuality in the way that we do.[3]

Bynum's sensible caution is less useful when some subjects are not male. Barbara Newman, for example, suggests that when medieval male writers gave advice to religious women, certain topics, such as chastity and community, were apt to be treated in gender-specific ways.[4] The purpose of this essay is to examine how one Cistercian abbot handled the subject of maternity in a work addressed to a woman who was his own sister.

Early Cistercians were not neutral on the subject of women. Their hostility is well documented: the order excluded nunneries, even those with strong ties to Cistercian houses, from official recognition until sometime in the thirteenth century.[5] While actively avoiding women, the abbots could not have entirely avoided the dual-gendered world inhabited by their natural families, their former acquaintances, and their patrons outside the monastery walls.[6] A French priory founded at Jully apparently "to accommodate the wives and dependents of the monks at Cîteaux," had as its first prioress Bernard of Clairvaux's sister-in-law (the wife of his eldest brother); Bernard's own sister Humbeline later became prioress.[7] Such women were literate, devout, and intimately familiar with the Cistercian movement. One influential treatise, written by Aelred, third abbot (1147-67) of Rievaulx Abbey in Yorkshire (one of England's first Cistercian houses), demonstrates that a Cistercian writer's address to a female could inspire a gender-specific exposition. *De institutione inclusarum* was written explicitly for Aelred's sister "by birth and in spirit" (*carne et spiritu*)[8] in response to her repeated request that he compose a book of guidelines for the anchoritic life she had adopted, that is, a book to serve as a spiritual aid for herself and other women for whom she served as mentor.

No Cistercian father excelled Aelred in fashioning a life lived within a maternal sensibility. Aelred frequently traveled outside the cloister on "a constant round of visits to his relatives and peers"[9] and both in the cloister and outside it, Aelred cared about the cultivation of friendships and of family bonds. The son of an old and distinguished Saxon line of married priests, Aelred entered Rievaulx as a novice in 1134. He advanced rapidly, becoming novice master in 1142, abbot of a daughter house, Revesby, in 1143, and finally abbot of Rievaulx itself in 1147. Walter Daniel, disciple and biographer of Aelred, reports that the abbot's dying words to his monks were: "I love you all... as earnestly as a mother after her sons."[10] Walter Daniel further describes how the gentle Aelred, in his last years of painful, arthritic infirmity, "never crushed the spontaneity of his young men" as he allowed them to gather round his bed twenty or thirty at a time; he compares their eager flocking round their abbot to the easy familiarity a prattling child feels towards its mother.[11] The same conceit exists in another writer's dedication of a book to Aelred. In his life of St. Cuthbert, Reginald of Durham offers a compliment to

Aelred's maternal instincts, writing that "We have often drunk the milk of refreshment and consolation from the breasts of your maternal compassion."[12] A nurturing spirit pervades Aelred's own writings, which reveal a personality marked, as Knowles says, by "personal love and sympathy and...wise direction of souls."[13]

In his capacity as "wise director," Aelred wrote many works of monastic theology. At the command of Bernard of Clairvaux, who noted Aelred's fervor and intelligence when they met in 1142, the young monk wrote the *Speculum caritatis*, on the virtue of charity, before he was made an abbot. This work was followed by other writings upon saints, sermons on Isaiah, a famous tract on spiritual friendship, and an unfinished theology of the soul, *De anima*. If Walter Daniel's chronology can be trusted—and scholars do not doubt it—at about the same time that Aelred composed *De spirituali amicitia* he wrote another influential treatise, the letter to his anchorite sister where he lays out the rules for a solitary, religious life.[14] As author of this treatise Aelred secured a permanent place in the history of English literature: his letter partly inspired later works such as the *Ancrene Wisse*, and his Latin was translated at least twice into Middle English.[15]

Aelred and his sister exemplify one of several instances in English history of a close spiritual relationship between a prominent man and a devout woman. In an earlier generation Goscelin, chaplain of Wilton Abbey, had guided Eve, a woman consecrated to the royal abbey at a very young age; his letter to her about her enclosed life in France reveals a man deeply bound to his former charge and mourning their separation.[16] Throughout Aelred's lifetime, that is, for a remarkable span of sixty years, the hermit Godric of Finchale lived in the Yorkshire wilderness and near him for several of these years, in an enclosed cell, lived his sister Burcwen, described as a virgin "from her mother's womb."[17] Like his friend Aelred, Godric oversaw—both as brother and as well-practiced ascetic—the spiritual discipline of his sister. Richard Rolle's vocation as itinerant hermit and counselor to women is a later example of a similar situation. While the composition of several Rolle works is tied to his relationship with the young recluse Margaret Kirkby, it is Rolle's unnamed sister who figures in the story of how he first became a hermit. She aided him in his flight from his family by secretly meeting him in the forest and supplying him some odd garments with which he could begin his ascetic life: their father's raincloak and two of her own tunics—one white and one gray—which he donned "so that in some measure, he might present a confused likeness to a hermit."[18]

These analogous relationships help to place Aelred's letter to his sister in a larger context that includes the longstanding tradition of spiritual instruction written by men for women. Ann K. Warren groups *De institutione inclusarum* with Goscelin's *Liber confortatorius*, the *Ancrene Wisse*, Rolle's *Form of Living*, and Walter Hilton's *Scale of Perfection*: These "major works...were created for specific women with whom the writers had previous relationships"and they "carry the meanings of those relationships forward" in tones that are "personal, individual, and often loving."[19] Aelred's treatise does indeed glow with the stimulus of personal engagement, but it casts a light somewhat different from these other works. Because Aelred's contemporary monastic "family" consisted of his brothers, who are often termed his "sons," his sisterly audience here is both foreign to him (a woman) and yet innately familial. It is the reality of Aelred's separation from women that led Aelred's modern biographer, Aelred Squire, to remark upon the abbot's "feeling of timidity and inexperience in dealing with the problems of women."[20] At the same time, Squire notes that Aelred's deep sense of connectedness to an audience is his rhetorical strength: "where the note of intimacy is struck, the effective stimulus reveals itself as the personal claim of others."[21]

The intimate tone used by Aelred throughout the treatise bespeaks a close relationship with his sister (whom he addresses as *soror* and *virgo*), but there are several indications that Aelred imagined a wider audience, one composed of more women and also of men.[22] The letter nonetheless remains quite personalized: Aelred remarks his sister's literacy, her habitually small appetite, her former chastising of him for youthful lapses, and her virginity in comparison to his failure.[23] In these human details one glimpses the secret sharings of a joint childhood. Aelred modestly ascribes his delay in fulfilling his sister's request to his unworthiness, but he may also have been reluctant to involve himself in the spiritual guidance of women.[24] One modern reader has posited that Aelred's address to *soror* is a conventional fiction masking Aelred's desire to write a work of advice to women recluses.[25] There is, however, no compelling reason to doubt Aelred's own words that he and his epistolary object are related *carne*, "by birth," that is, true siblings. It was his habit as a writer, seemingly here as elsewhere, to address or depict actual persons, as he does in the revealing dialogue with "Walter" (that is, Walter Daniel) in *De spirituali amicitia*.[26]

Nevertheless, lacking the sister's own words, history, and even name, we cannot hope to examine the effect of the treatise upon her life as a recluse.[27] We may not ascertain that she read it or received it or even that its circulation in Aelred's day reached other women readers. Because of these historical silences, the only approach to "knowing" the sister is to consider the rhetorical presence constructed by Aelred in the text of *De institutione inclusarum*. What emerges from the abbot's epistolary discourse is a presence made specific by a few personalized details and yet critically defined as a woman potentially filling several gendered roles. Aelred positions the recipient not only as sororal and virginal but also as filial in reference to his higher maternal wisdom and as physiologically female in her womb-centered means for understanding outer behaviors and inner spiritualities. In sum, Aelred's discourse embodies the subject as female.

When Aelred employs figures of sexual arousal, pregnancy, childbirth, and effusive maternal pathos, his purpose is to evoke in his sisterly reader a response inherent in her body in order to guide her to spiritual insight. The fusion of body and spirit occurs both in Aelred's statement of a personal tie to his reader ("by birth and in spirit I am your brother and unable to refuse any request you make") and in the method he says he will use ("I shall,...wherever it seems helpful, blend the spiritual with the corporal").[28] Gender difference guides Aelred's handling of sexualized material throughout the treatise. When Aelred writes elsewhere about sexual temptation—to a male novice—his language is cautious and coy as if by being too explicit he may corrupt a young man's innocence.[29] Not so when he writes to a woman, even one physically and spiritually a virgin. Aelred's feminine imagery, based in the subject's body, takes for granted a transvalued spiritual response. The treatise thus represents a pedagogical act of both tenderness and audacity, directed toward someone with whom the author feels a close physical connection.

Recognizing this rhetorical method allows us to examine anew Aelred's attitude toward women.[30] In outlining for his recluse sister behavioral regulations (for the "outer man") and spiritual meditations (for the "inner man"), Aelred expects the diligent attention of a devout and intelligent sensibility. He satirizes the weaknesses of some recluses, but he does not talk down to his sister. The corporal appeal is not to a carnal stupidity thought to belong to women; rather, it is to a spiritual asset immanent in her womanly anatomy. Bypassing innate, experiential knowledge of her own body, Aelred's sister is to depend on her brother's extra-feminine guidance in an affective, often womb-centered mode of meditation. Aelred will show his carnal sister how to be the woman *he* is—one not of flesh but of spirit.[31] For Aelred, who believed in the natural equality of men and women, feelings of love, respect, and friendship would seem to have motivated this gesture.[32]

What seems to matter most to Aelred as he formulates his rhetorical subject is that she is *akin to him in flesh*, and yet—unlike him—she is *female*, having a womb. Aelred states how they share the same origin: "Up to this point, sister, we have run the same course, we were alike in everything: the same father begot us, the same womb bore us and gave us birth."[33] A womb metynomically venerates their mother. Aelred's sister has been blessed, too, with a womb and with God's grace as a sanctified virgin. Aelred, spiritual mother of souls, possesses the wisdom to explain the holy keeping of these blessings. The subject's gender thus inspires much of the feminine imagery. By the same token, the meditations are for men, too, and indeed for Aelred himself. They are aids for a devout meditant to experience vicariously the hallowed sensations of Mary as Mother of God or of Jesus as Mother.[34] But the stimulus for his writing them down would seem to be the female bodily understanding of his immediate audience.

In Aelred's treatment the anchoritic ideal reflects the miracle that took place in the Virgin's womb. The life of solitude may lead to "fruitfulness,"[35] the cell becoming a metaphor for the womb. As a fruit ripening within the womb/cell, the anchoress as woman possesses (and must guard) the physical center for contemplative spirituality, the womb of her own body. Aelred advises that an anchoress must never admit a man into her cell—lest she be "drawn forth pregnant from her cell," or an infant betray "its birth by its wailing."[36] In warning that a man admitted may result in a baby emitted, Aelred equates cell and female body (to be exact, vagina/womb). The equation is apparent again when Aelred specifies the dangers in allowing the cell's walls and windows to be violated with wayward chatter and outside visitors:

> Now they speak without reserve, their purpose no longer being to arouse desire but to gratify it.... The opening of the cell must somehow be enlarged to allow her to pass through or her paramour to enter; what was a cell has now become a brothel.[37]

The invaded cell denotes lost female chastity. In contrast, in the silence of the private cell the virgin will experience the constant presence of Christ, who is irresistibly attracted to her virginity,[38] and in seclusion with her spiritual Spouse, the danger is reversed: she will emulate St. Agnes, who spurned the advances of a wicked man and "turned a brothel into an oratory."[39] Even as a symbol for Christ's tomb, the cell serves as spiritual womb: buried with Christ, the anchoress is, paradoxically, in a state of new birth, having undergone purification from the natural, earthly birth everyone suffers through a mortal mother.[40] Thus, "dead and buried to the world," the anchoress lives the contemplative life of Mary (as opposed to her sister Martha): "She just sat at Jesus' feet and listened to what he had to say."[41]

Virginity dominates the virtues espoused in *De institutione inclusarum*,[42] and physical motherhood is an experience Aelred's sister cannot expect to know. But while Aelred forbids her this role, he fashions his own identity as spiritual counselor in ways perhaps more maternal than fraternal. For Aelred the spiritual essence of maternity resides in the wise guidance and governance of other souls, a meaning that arises, for example, from his account of the nun of Watton. There, in discussing the case of a pregnant nun where he was called in to adjudicate, Aelred puts forth an ideal of nurturing authority (exhibited by the "wiser mothers," *matronae sapientiores*) in pointed contrast to the scandal of an actual pregnancy.[43] Among persons devoted to God, spiritual motherhood fosters the religious community; physical pregnancy, however, is deformity. As recluse, the sister must spurn motherhood of all kinds except in an interiorized emulation of the Virgin and Jesus. Moreover, Aelred's rhetoric of instruction positions her not as mother but instead as a daughter ready to accept the counsel of "abbot as mother." Since this counsel is also from a sibling of opposite gender, the subject of maternity becomes nuanced further with thoughts of bodily difference, relatedness, and shared family heritage, for which lack of offspring would have had some import.

The topic of motherhood often enters the latently charged context of *De institutione inclusarum*, where it is shaded in ways ranging from condemnation of sinful pregnancy to full-blown meditation upon God's incarnation in Mary. As one would expect, when Aelred advises his sister on external behaviors, the sentiments that prevail are anti-maternal. The rules, for example, prohibit Aelred's sister from ever establishing a school for girls, for teaching children may lead to misplaced affections:

> Swayed by their childish dispositions, [the recluse] is angry one minute and smiling the next, now threatening, now flattering, kissing one child and smacking another. When she sees one of them crying after being smacked she calls her close, strokes her cheek, puts her arms around her neck and holds her tight, calling her: "My own baby girl, my own pet." There before her very eyes, even though she may not yield to them, the recluse has worldly and sensual temptations, and amid them all what becomes of her continual remembrance of God?[44]

Later, in a typical rhetorical move, Aelred inverts this "outer" proscription against mothering children in one of the meditative exercises. Indulgence in vicarious maternal feelings can be healthful to the soul if one passionately identifies with the Virgin as mother of the child Jesus. The meditation offers an affective, lingering enactment of Mary's joy upon giving birth: "Embrace that sweet crib, let love overcome your reluctance, affection drive out fear." It is soon followed by a call to feel Mary's anguish as she hunts for her twelve-year-old boy in Jerusalem: "Join his Mother in looking for him during those three days."[45] As in Aelred's account of the nun of Watton, maternal feelings may be cultivated in spiritual matters but are to be scrupulously avoided in mundane facts of the flesh, where they distract one from God.

Aelred's advice to his sister springs from an inquisitiveness about female physiology, specifically, the possession of a womb and the ability to bear a child. To echo Warren's observation, the imagery of *Ancrene Wisse* tends to be anal, whereas in Aelred it is invariably genital,[46] and—I would add—reproductively female. It is not extraordinary for Aelred to ask the meditant to "enter" a hallowed womb, or even two, as he does in calling for contemplation and glorification of the wombs made sacred by their occupants, those of

Mary and Elizabeth.[47] Another meditative regimen elicits his sister's affective participation in the conception of God in the Virgin's womb:

> First enter the room of blessed Mary and with her read the books which prophesy the virginal birth and the coming of Christ....O sweet Lady [Mary], ... with what a fire of love you were inflamed, when you felt in your mind and in your womb the presence of majesty....All this was on your account, virgin [sister], in order that you might diligently contemplate the Virgin whom you have resolved to imitate and the Virgin's Son to whom you are betrothed.[48]

A caring brother asks his sister to imagine the Virgin's uterine union with God, sensually evoking the pleasure aroused by the Child/Bridegroom's presence within Mary's body. The actions blend male and female sexual experience: one enters "the room" and reads the books, acts of penetration that enable one to affect the Virgin's experience; one becomes vicariously "inflamed" as the Virgin's womb is filled with the godhead; and finally the sister lives this experience as her own, because she, too, is both virgin and eager bride. In this meditational exercise Aelred plays the role of go-between for God and virgin, stimulating in his sister a maternal-erotic sensation of impregnation.[49] Aelred's spiritualized rhetoric strives to capitalize upon his sister's fleshly response.

In an especially rich meditation upon Scripture, Aelred interweaves opportunities for his sister to identify with the three Marys (Contemplative, Virgin, and Magdalene).[50] Always the meditant woman is asked to focus upon the faces of the central participants—the Marys and Christ—and to engage deeply in their emotions. Aelred's three Marys conform to familial paradigms: Mary the Contemplative as daughter of Christ, Mary the Virgin as mother, Mary Magdalene as wife. Theologically, of course, the Virgin also embodies all three roles in herself, in her filial/maternal/spousal relationship to Father, Son, and Holy Ghost. Beyond these feminine models, however, Aelred's preeminent vision of the maternal essence resides in his perception of Jesus as divine Mother, an attitude expressed with special fervency through the image of Savior on the Cross—"his outspread arms will invite you to embrace him, his naked breasts will feed you with the milk of sweetness to console you"[51]—an image that positions the meditant no longer as a mother herself but as a sucking, purely sensate infant. Christ's outstretched arms of nurturing, protective redemption inspire Aelred's corresponding vision of how the Christian needs to respond to the world's suffering:

> What is more humane than pity? Let this be your alms. So embrace the whole world with the arms of your love and in that act at once consider and congratulate the good, contemplate and mourn over the wicked. In that act look upon the afflicted and the oppressed and feel compassion for them. In that act call to mind the wretchedness of the poor, the groans of orphans, the abandonment of widows, the gloom of the sorrowful, the needs of travellers, the prayers of virgins, the perils of those at sea, the temptations of monks, the responsibilities of prelates, the labors of those waging war. In your love take them all to your heart, weep over them, offer your prayers for them.[52]

Separated from the world and "dead" to it, the sister is, nonetheless, to speak for the worldly afflicted in her prayers. This passage offers a summation of Aelred's sense of Christian duty; his solicitous tone for his sister's spiritual welfare invites one to hear in it his own Christ-like love for her. Composing this treatise is an act of "motherly" concern for her and for other recluses.

Aelred's view of his sister and her procreative potential—indeed, of women generally—is influenced by his Cistercian environment and colored strongly by his personality. Uncompromising Cistercian belief in chaste asceticism could turn easily to misogyny and reprobation of one's own uncloistered female family members. It is said that Bernard of Clairvaux refused even to look upon his worldly married sister—who had betrayed their mother's wish that she be consecrated—and another brother called her a "dressed-up dunghill."[53] In a letter Bernard approvingly quotes Jerome's dictum:

> If your mother should lie prostrate at the door, if she should bare her breasts, the breasts that gave you suck, … yet with dry eyes fixed upon the cross go ahead and tread over your prostrate mother and father.[54]

Aelred found a way to soften this policy in *Speculum caritatis*,[55] yet an element of it surfaces in *De institutione inclusarum* when he condemns the parental acts that engendered him and his sister. Calling them "evil," Aelred asserts that "they shall nonetheless result in good through the virtues of the two ascetic offspring."[56] Aelred further regards his sister as his feminine other half, the virginal vessel who balances out his own early failures in chastity:

With my wretchedness then in the loss of my chastity compare your
own happiness in the protection accorded to your virginity by God's
grace....So you exult in these riches which God's grace has preserved
for you, while I have the utmost difficulty in repairing what has been
broken, recovering what has been lost, mending what has been torn.
Yet in this respect I would have you emulate me. How you would
have to blush if after all my sins I were found equal to you in the next
life. The glory of virginity is often tarnished by vices which make
their way later on, while the reformation of a man's life and the
replacement of vices by virtues can cancel the infamy of his former
behavior.[57]

Aelred's reasoning here is subtle. Although his sister has maintained
virginity, her virtue may have deluded her into an insidious tolerance
of idle sins; Aelred, acutely aware of his fall, may by his diligence
ultimately reach a sanctity equal to hers. This argument suggests a
kind of balance achieved by sister and now-chaste brother, the virgin
and the reformed chaste.

In his relationship with his sister, Aelred seems to envision a
spiritual good greater than natural marriage or parenthood,[58] that is,
an intimate merging of two parallel individuals of opposite gender
in spiritual union with God's oneness. Their union reflects the
mystical relationship between the Virgin Mary and John the
Evangelist, two virgins joined by Christ. From His maternal pose
(arms outstretched on the Cross), Jesus brought Mary and John
together, newly born as "mother and son," and as virgins coequal
before God.[59] The acts of Aelred's parents reach fruition, then, in the
realization of human spirituality at its fullest—male chaste and female
virgin formed in the same womb returning to their Creator in an act
of wholeness, a spiritual rebirthing taking place through cloister and
cell.

Aelred's position in relation to his sister is, throughout the letter
and increasingly in the three meditations at the end, a mix of spiritual
solicitude and strict behavioral proscription informed by metaphors
of human intimacy, sexuality, impregnation. Such metaphors,
directed at a woman who has minimal contact with the outside world,
are charged with calculated contrast. Spiritualized maternity remains
carefully distinguished from the cares, pleasures, and fleshly burden
of physical motherhood, to the point even of warning against
transferred feelings for a schoolchild. In advocating sympathy for
the orphaned and widowed, Aelred prohibits the anchorite sister

from face-to-face contact with those for whom she might abstractly and through prayer show sympathy. At the same time, a language of rapturous, affective metaphor suffuses each of Aelred's attempts to describe the anchoress's virginal state of marriage to the Holy Bridegroom and Mother Mary's feminine experiences at Annunciation, Nativity, and Crucifixion—events to be vicariously, sexually, maternally experienced by the meditant (female reader, male writer, larger audience).

In the end the mystery of the Virgin's multiple relationship to the triune God—daughter, wife, and mother—comes to be a cosmic reflection of the complex spiritual relationship Aelred forges with his sister: brother/sister, mother/daughter, even, in Aelred's final metaphors, virginal husband/wife:

> These, sister, are some seeds of spiritual meditation which I have made it my business to sow for you... to the end that from them a rich crop of the love of God may spring up and grow to maturity. Meditation will arouse the affections, the affections will give birth to desire, desire will stir up tears, so that your tears may be bread for you day and night until you appear in his sight and say to him what is written in the Song of Songs: "My Beloved is mine and I am his" [2.16].[60]

In *De institutione inclusarum* Aelred exalted the womb, the locus of Mary's holy maternity, as he wrote to his sister, because she had a womb and a virginal life of solitude that placed her metaphorically inside of one. In her he finds a fleshly counterpart to himself, different only in gender and in degree of chastity—ways in which he sees them each complementing the other. The seeds planted in Aelred's sister by a wise and loving brother will lead her to a spiritual "birthing" of desire for the love of God, who is to be her (and her motherly abbot brother's) one true Spouse.

NOTES

1. Caroline Walker Bynum, "Jesus as Mother and Abbot as Mother: Some Themes in Twelfth-Century Cistercian Writing," in her *Jesus as Mother: Studies in the Spirituality of the High Middle Ages* (Berkeley, CA, 1982), pp. 110–69, esp. p. 155.

2. "The Cistercian conception of Jesus as mother and abbot as mother reveals not an attitude toward women but a sense (not without ambivalence) of a need and obligation to nurture other men, a need and

obligation to achieve intimate dependence on God" (Bynum, "Jesus as Mother," p. 168; see also pp. 139–40, 167).

3. Bynum, "Jesus as Mother," p. 162.

4. Barbara Newman, *From Virile Woman to WomanChrist: Studies in Medieval Religion and Literature* (Philadelphia, 1995), pp. 19–45.

5. See Sally Thompson, "The Problem of the Cistercian Nuns in the Twelfth and Early Thirteenth Centuries," in *Medieval Women: Essays Edited and Presented to R.M.T. Hill*, ed. Derek Baker, Studies in Church History Subsidia 1 (Oxford, 1978), pp. 227–52; Janet Burton, *Monastic and Religious Orders in Britain, 1000–1300* (Cambridge, 1994), pp. 101–06; Louis J. Lekai, *The Cistercians: Ideals and Reality* (Kent, OH, 1977), pp. 347–63; Penelope D. Johnson, *Equal in Monastic Profession: Religious Women in Medieval France* (Chicago, 1991), pp. 251–52; and references gathered by Bynum, "Jesus as Mother," p. 168, n. 182.

6. For examples of women patrons of English Cistercians, see Bennett D. Hill, *English Cistercian Monasteries and Their Patrons in the Twelfth Century* (Urbana, IL, 1968), pp. 68–70. Bernard advised nuns (Newman, *Virile Woman*, pp. 36, 313) and corresponded with laypersons, including married couples (John R. Sommerfeldt, "The Social Theory of Bernard of Clairvaux" in *Studies in Medieval Cistercian History*, CS 13 [Spencer, MA, 1971], pp. 40–46). On connections between monasteries and families in France, see Johnson, *Equal in Monastic Profession*, pp. 248–57.

7. Thompson, "Problem of the Cistercian Nuns," pp. 229–30; Lekai, *The Cistercians*, p. 347. For Bernard's sister Humbeline, see Watkin Williams, *Saint Bernard of Clairvaux* (Westminster, MD, 1952), pp. 29–30; and James Cotter Morison, *The Life and Times of Saint Bernard* (London, 1868), pp. 322–23.

8. The English translation is by Mary Paul Macpherson: Aelred of Rievaulx, *Treatises; The Pastoral Prayer*, intro. David Knowles, CF 2 (Spencer, MA, 1971), pp. 43–102 (hereafter "Aelred Treatises"; the phrase appears on p. 43). For the Latin original see Aelred of Rievaulx, *De institutione inclusarum (De inst. incl.)*, ed. C.H. Talbot in *Aelredi Rievallensis opera omnia*, vol. 1: *Opera ascetica*, ed. A. Hoste and C.H. Talbot, CCCM 1 (Turnhout, 1971), pp. 637–82 (the phrase appears on p. 637).

9. Douglas Roby, "Chimaera of the North: The Active Life of Aelred of Rievaulx," in *Cistercian Ideals and Reality*, ed. John R. Sommerfeldt, CS 60 (Kalamazoo, MI, 1978), p. 164. See also Marsha Dutton, "Introduction to Walter's *Vita Aelredi*," in *Walter Daniel: The Life of Aelred of Rievaulx & The Letter to Maurice*, trans. F.M. Powicke, CF 57 (Kalamazoo, MI, 1994), pp. 31–36; and David Knowles, *The Monastic Order in England*, 2nd ed. (Cambridge, 1966), pp. 62–63.

10. *The Life of Ailred of Rievaulx* (hereafter *Life*), trans. F.M. Powicke (1950; repr. London, 1963), p. 58.

11. Aelred Squire, *Aelred of Rievaulx: A Study,* CS 50 (Kalamazoo, MI, 1981), pp. 129–30; for the young monks gathering at Aelred's bed, see Walter Daniel, *Life,* p. 40. On Aelred's behavior, see Brian Patrick McGuire, *Friendship and Community: The Monastic Experience 350–1250,* CS 95 (Kalamazoo, MI, 1988), pp. 334–48.

12. Squire, *Aelred,* p. 130, translating Reginald of Durham, *Libellus de admirandis beati Cuthberti virtutibus,* Surtees Society 1 (London, 1835), p. 1.

13. Aelred, *Treatises,* p. xi. See esp. *Life,* pp. 5, 17. On Aelred's personality, see also Amédée Hallier, *The Monastic Theology of Aelred of Rievaulx: An Experiential Theology,* trans. Columban Heaney, CS 2 (Shannon, 1969), pp. 168-69; Aelred Watkin, "St. Aelred of Rievaulx," in *Pre-Reformation English Spirituality,* ed. James Walsh (Bronx, NY, 1966), pp. 56–66; and McGuire, *Friendship and Community,* pp. 296–38.

14. Squire, *Aelred,* dates *De inst. incl.* 1163–64, between *De spirituali amicitia* and *Vita Edwardi* (p. 119). Following the same chronology, Powicke however dates it c. 1160–62 (*Life,* pp. xcvii, 41).

15. See John Ayto and Alexandra Barratt, eds., *Aelred of Rievaulx's De institutione inclusarum: Two English Versions,* EETS OS 287 (London, 1984); Anne Savage and Nicholas Watson, trans., *Anchoritic Spirituality: "Ancrene Wisse" and Associated Works* (New York, 1991), pp. 183, 444.

16. Sharon K. Elkins, *Holy Women of Twelfth-Century England* (Chapel Hill, NC, 1988), pp. 21–27. See also C.H. Talbot, "Godric of Finchale and Christina of Markyate," in Walsh, *Pre-Reformation English Spirituality,* pp. 46-49.

17. Elkins, *Holy Women,* p. 39, translating Reginald of Durham, *Libellus de vita et miraculis s. Godrici heremitae de finchale,* ed. Joseph Stevenson, Surtees Society 20 (London, 1847), pp. 23, 139–44 (esp. p. 140). See also Squire, *Aelred,* p. 119; and Rotha Mary Clay, *The Hermits and Anchorites of England* (London, 1914), p. 134. Aelred visited Godric in 1159 (Roby, "Chimaera of the North," pp. 157–58), a few years before he composed the treatise to his sister.

18. Clay, *Hermits and Anchorites,* p. 106. See also Hope Emily Allen, *Writings Ascribed to Richard Rolle, Hermit of Hampole* (London, 1927), p. 56; and Frances Beer, *Women and Mystical Experience in the Middle Ages* (Woodbridge, 1992), p. 111.

19. Ann K. Warren, *Anchorites and Their Patrons in Medieval England* (Berkeley, CA, 1985), p. 103. For a list of works of instruction dated 1075–1225, many specifically to women, see Newman, *Virile Woman,* pp. 314–16.

20. Squire, *Aelred,* p. 127.

21. Squire, *Aelred,* p. 151.

22. Aelred, *Treatises,* p. 52 (*De inst. incl.,* p. 642), mentions a readership of several more women. Elsewhere, the sense of audience widens—sometimes in digressions—to include literate and illiterate (p. 56),

strong and weak (p. 61), whoever has chosen a life of solitude (p. 62), virgins of both genders (p. 64), men who need to remember to keep their chastity (pp. 66-8), monks (p. 76), and, finally, "anyone" (p. 102; *De inst. incl.*, p. 682). See also Squire, *Aelred*, p. 119; and Elkins, *Holy Women*, p. 214, n. 31.

23. Aelred, *Treatises*, pp. 56, 59, 93–94.

24. Thompson, "Problem of the Cistercian Nuns," 239; Lekai, *The Cistercians*, p. 347.

25. Marsha Dutton, "The Conversion and Vocation of Aelred of Rievaulx: A Historical Hypothesis," in *England in the Twelfth Century*, Proceedings of the 1988 Harlaxton Symposium, ed. Daniel Williams (Woodbridge, 1990), p. 32, n. 3; see also Squire, *Aelred*, p. 118.

26. Dutton, "Introduction," pp. 13–16.

27. The names of Aelred's great-grandfather, grandfather, father, and two brothers have been preserved, but the names of his female relations are lost to history. On Aelred's family, see Squire, *Aelred*, pp. 7–12; Powicke, *Life*, pp. xxxiv–vi; Dutton, "Introduction," pp. 19–22. Except for Aelred's treatise, a sister's existence is not recorded. Speculation has placed her cell "between Hexham and Durham" (Squire, *Aelred*, p. 119) and made her older than Aelred (Talbot, "Godric," p. 54). On the lives of medieval recluses, see Jean Leclerq, "Solitude and Solidarity: Medieval Women Recluses," and Patricia J.F. Rosof, "The Anchoress in the Twelfth and Thirteenth Centuries," both in *Peaceweavers*, vol. 2 of *Medieval Religious Women*, CS 72 (Kalamazoo, MI, 1987), respectively, pp. 67–83 and 123–44.

28. Aelred, *Treatises*, pp. 43–44; *De. inst. incl.*, p. 637.

29. Aelred of Rievaulx, *The Mirror of Charity*, trans. Elizabeth Connor, CF 17 (Kalamazoo, MI, 1990), p. 131; *Speculum c[h]aritatis, PL* 195:529–30). See also McGuire, *Friendship and Community*, p. 306.

30. Locating in Aelred a naive unfamiliarity with women (Squire, *Aelred*, p. 127), a purported indifference toward women (McGuire, *Friendship and Community*, pp. 300, 332), or a concern for female "fragility" (Watkin, "St. Aelred," p. 64) does not readily account for the generous spiritual offering the letter to his sister represents. It has also been argued (with male bias) that Aelred's affective style occurs because a woman's "intellectual interests would be less developed than her feminine feelings" (*De inst. incl.*, p. viii). The general argument that "male authors who wrote to edify women were deeply and self-consciously concerned with gender" is, however, well borne out in Aelred's treatise (Newman, *Virile Woman*, pp. 28–30; see also Caroline Walker Bynum, "'... And Woman His Humanity': Female Imagery in the Religious Writing of the Later Middle Ages," in *Fragmentation and Redemption: Essays on Gender and the Human Body in Medieval Religion* [New York, 1991], pp. 151–79).

31. For a further perspective on male religious appropriation of femaleness, see Bynum, "'... And Woman His Humanity'," p. 166.

32. Aelred states elsewhere that the genders are "equal and, as it were, collateral, and that there is in human affairs neither a superior nor an inferior, a characteristic of true friendship" (Aelred of Rievaulx, *Spiritual Friendship*, trans. Mary Eugenia Laker, CF 5 [Kalamazoo, MI, 1977], p. 63; *De spirituali amicitia, PL* 195:667). On the gender-neutral ideal of the religious life, see Newman, *Virile Woman*, pp. 20–21.

33. Aelred, *Treatises*, p. 93; *De inst. incl.*, pp. 673–74.

34. Aelred used the term *meditatio* to mean affective rumination and visualization of holy circumstances, not mystical contemplation; see John R. Sommerfeldt, "The Vocabulary of Contemplation in Aelred of Rievaulx' *On Jesus at the Age of Twelve, A Rule of Life for a Recluse*, and *On Spiritual Friendship*," in *Heaven on Earth*, ed. E. Rozanne Elder, CS 68 (Kalamazoo, MI, 1983), pp. 72–89.

35. Aelred, *Treatises*, p. 45; *De inst. incl.*, p. 637. See also Aelred's discussion of how silence brings the recluse "great peace and abundant fruit" (p. 50; *De inst. incl.*, p. 641).

36. The full context is an assertion that too many anchoresses are comfortable with minimal standards of behavior (Aelred, *Treatises*, p. 51; *De inst. incl.*, p. 642). Here Aelred is not speaking about his sister personally, for he notes her habitual circumspection in avoiding contact with men (Aelred, *Treatises*, p. 52; *De inst. incl.*, p. 642).

37. Aelred, *Treatises*, p. 47; *De inst. incl.*, p. 638. See also Squire, *Aelred*, p. 121.

38. Aelred, *Treatises*, p. 63; *De inst. incl.*, p. 650. See also Aelred, *Treatises*, pp. 51, 121.

39. Aelred, *Treatises*, p. 65; *De inst. incl.*, p. 652.

40. Aelred, *Treatises*, pp. 72–73; *De inst. incl.*, p. 658. The metaphors occur within an analogy to the processing of linen from flax. See also Squire, *Aelred*, pp. 123–25.

41. Aelred, *Treatises*, p. 75; *De inst. incl.*, p. 660.

42. Walter Daniel describes her solely by her virginity and her anchoritic condition (*Life*, p. 41).

43. *PL* 195:789–96. For a summary, see Elkins, *Holy Women*, pp. 106–17; and Giles Constable, "Aelred of Rievaulx and the Nun of Watton: An Episode in the Early History of the Gilbertine Order," in Baker, *Medieval Women*, pp. 205–26. Roby, "Chimaera of the North," p. 158, dates the incident c. 1160.

44. Aelred, *Treatises*, pp. 49–50; *De inst. incl.*, pp. 640–41. See also Newman, *Virile Woman*, p. 39.

45. Aelred, *Treatises*, pp. 81–82; *De inst. incl.*, pp. 663–64.

46. Warren, *Anchorites*, p. 109.

47. In a meditation upon the occupants of their wombs (based upon Luke 1.39–44), Aelred minimizes the mothers and emphasizes the agency

of Christ and John the Baptist. He asks his virginal sister to "enter" each womb that bore these two (Aelred, *Treatises*, p. 81; *De inst. incl.*, p. 663).

48. Aelred, *Treatises*, pp. 80–81; *De inst. incl.*, pp. 662–63. See also Talbot, "Godric," p. 50.

49. Aelred's imagery is indebted, in part, to the mystical tradition expressing divine love as an erotic union of Bridegroom Christ and female soul; see Bernard McGinn, "The Language of Love in Christian and Jewish Mysticism," in *Mysticism and Language,* ed. Steven T. Katz (New York and Oxford, 1992), pp. 202–35. Such imagery appears widely in English works of the next generation (influenced by Cistercian and Franciscan thought); see Savage and Watson, *Anchoritic Spirituality*, p. 24, and John Bugge, *Virginitas: An Essay in the History of a Medieval Ideal* (The Hague, 1975). The stimulation of a female reader by a male writer is, of course, rather different from maternal-erotic experiences detailed by women mystics, as, for example, when Christina of Markyate (a contemporary of Aelred) envisioned an erotic mothering of the infant Christ (*The Life of Christina of Markyate, A Twelfth Century Recluse*, ed. and trans. C.H. Talbot [Oxford, 1959], pp. 118–19). For other women mystics having maternal-erotic visions of Christ, see Bynum, "'… And Woman His Humanity'," pp. 168–75.

50. *De inst. incl.*, chap. 31 (Aelred, *Treatises*, pp. 82–92).

51. Aelred, *Treatises*, p. 73; *De inst. incl.*, p. 658. The notion of Christ's milk, repeated elsewhere by Aelred (pp. 87, 90), was much used by Bernard (Bynum, "Jesus as Mother," pp. 115–18). On the image of the feminine Christ, see also Giles Constable, "Twelfth-Century Spirituality and the Late Middle Ages," *Medieval and Renaissance Studies*, 5 (1971), 45–46.

52. Aelred, *Treatises*, pp. 77–78; *De inst. incl.*, pp. 661–62. See also Squire, *Aelred,* p. 126.

53. The story is told by Jacobus de Voragine, *The Golden Legend, Readings on the Saints*, trans. William Granger Ryan, 2 vols. (Princeton, 1993), 2:102. On the sister's subsequent renunciation of the world, see n. 7 above.

54. Letter 322 (*PL* 182:527), trans. Bynum, "Jesus as Mother," pp. 145–46.

55. Aelred, *Mirror of Charity*, pp. 261–65 (*PL* 195:598-600); McGuire, *Friendship and Community,* p. 313; and Roby, "Chimaera of the North,", p. 164.

56. Aelred, *Treatises*, pp. 92–93; *De inst. incl.*, p. 673. On the contemporary notion that chaste relationships between men and women led to a higher good, see Constable, "Aelred," pp. 220–21.

57. Aelred, *Treatises*, pp. 93, 95-96; *De inst. incl.*, pp. 674–76. See also Marsha Dutton-Stuckey, "A Prodigal Writes Home: Aelred of Rievaulx' *De institutione inclusarum*," in Elder, *Heaven on Earth*, pp. 35–42; Newman, *Virile Woman*, p. 30; and Elkins, *Holy Women*, p. 215, n. 47.

58. It is tempting to compare Aelred's thought here to Gregory of Nyssa's fourth-century attitude about his consecrated sister Macrina's virginity. See Peter Brown, *The Body and Society: Men, Women, and Sexual Renunciation in Early Christianity* (New York, 1988), pp. 277–79, 298–99.

59. Aelred, *Treatises*, pp. 73–74; *De inst. incl.*, pp. 658–59. Clay, *Hermits and Anchorites*, p. 80, notes that an ancient "anchoridge" within Durham Cathedral—described in the sixteenth century—conformed to guidelines set down by Aelred: crucifix, white cloth, images of Mary and John. On this passage, see also Bynum, "Jesus as Mother," pp. 164–65. On special devotion to Mary and John, see Constable, "Spirituality," p. 46; Elkins, *Holy Women*, p. 215, n. 43.

60. Aelred, *Treatises*, p. 102; *De inst. incl.*, p. 681.

In the Meydens Womb: JULIAN OF NORWICH AND THE POETICS OF ENCLOSURE

Maud Burnett McInerney

The concept of Jesus as mother of the human soul is most fully elaborated in the work of Julian of Norwich. Gestation and labor are essential images for the female anchorite's relationship to Christ, for complex connections between Christ, Mary, and the Christian soul, and for Julian's relationship to her own text.

> For the almyghty truth of the trynyte is oure fader, for he made us and kepyth us in hym. And the depe wysdome of þe trynyte is our moder, in whom we be closyd. And the hye goodnesse of the trynyte is our lord and in hym we be closyd and he in us. We be closyd in the fader, and we be closyd in the son, and we are closyd in the holy gost. And the fader is beclosyd in us, and the holy gost is beclosyd in us... (LT 54:563)[1]

In Julian of Norwich's *Revelation of Love*, the Trinity's reciprocal presence within the Christian soul and the soul's within the Trinity express the integral unity which binds the two, the crucial *onyng* of mystical theology. In the passage quoted above, the almost mesmeric repetition of the words *closyd* and *beclosyd* demands attention. The Middle English verb *closen*, with its variants *beclosen* and *enclosen*, has a wider range of meaning than its modern descendant. It can be glossed as to close or to shut; to block an entrance or passageway; to fortify; to entomb or bury. Julian's contemporary Wycliffe asks: "what cursed spirit stirith prestis to close hem in stonys or wallis for al here life?"[2] In 1489, William Brown of Stamford left 20s. to each recluse at Stamford "if any be closid there."[3] *Closyd* thus does not simply describe a relationship between container and contained; it also evokes the tradition of anchoritism, of which Julian is the most famous example.

That Julian was an anchorite is not a mere biographical footnote to the *Revelation*. Writings for and about anchorites imply an intimate relationship between enclosure and the representation of the female body. Not only was anchoritism always more popular among women than men;[4] the anchorhold was perceived as miming the womb. Potentially chaste, it was still vulnerable (inclined, for some writers) to violation by outside influences and inherent female sinfulness. In marked contrast to writings which strove to render the female recluse voiceless, so her words might not seduce herself or others, Julian's Long Text establishes the anchoritic voice as authoritative not in spite of but because of its femininity. Confronted with an experience and an understanding which overflow traditional structures of signification, painfully aware of the limitations of language and of the restrictions imposed upon feminine speech, Julian develops the concept of enclosure into an imagistic system which plays upon the related images of anchorhold and womb, developing a discursive strategy that links the apophatic and the maternal.

What we know about Julian, apart from a few indications in contemporary wills, derives from her own writing and from the scribal introduction to the Short Text's single manuscript, which describes it as a "visionn schewed be the goodenes of god to a devoute womann, and hir name es Julyan, that is recluse atte Norwyche and ʒitt ys on lyfe" (ST 1:201). This statement guarantees the provenance of the text, represented as indistinguishable from Julian's *visionn*; that the visionary herself is still alive, and a recluse, are given as though they provide evidence of textual veracity. The *Revelation* is thus grounded in the person and the personal visionary authority of a single anchorite. The Long Text's language often seems to confirm this scribal opinion of anchoritism's importance to the text; through metaphor, allusion, and temporal complication, it evokes a particular mode of thought and language founded upon ideas of enclosure.

Is it plausible to assume, however, that Julian was already enclosed and therefore thinking like an anchorite when she composed the Long Text? Colledge and Walsh argue that she was not. As they imagine her life, Julian was a nun when she experienced her visions in 1373; fifteen years later, she received a secondary illumination. She remained in her convent for a further five years, until "twenty yere after the tyme of the shewyng saue thre monthys" (LT 51:520). Then she wrote the Long Text and entered the anchorhold. This chronology is unconvincing. It is partly based on a reference to a "Julian anakorite" in the will of Roger Reed, dated 1393–4. This at best provides a *terminus ante quem*, for Julian must have been enclosed for some little time before it was made. That the first bequest to Julian should so precisely coincide with the proposed date of her enclosure seems too great a coincidence. Nothing, of course, proves that Reed's bequest was really the first made to Julian as a recluse; it is merely the earliest *surviving* bequest.

What if Julian entered the anchorhold before her 1393 illumination? She claims to have spent almost twenty years contemplating the significance of her visions; where better to do so than in an anchorite's cell? Colledge and Walsh assume that it was impossible or unlikely that she composed the Long Text in the anchorhold,[5] but their own arguments for Julian's advanced educational formation equally support an early entry into the anchorhold. "The variety and modernity of her vocabulary indicate that she was not limited, in contacts and conversation, before she completed the Long Text, in the way in which one might expect an anchoress to be if she took her vocation seriously."[6] The vocabulary to which they refer is an intellectual one, which they indicate as originating in such works as *Ancrene Riwle* or Hilton's *Scale of Perfection*, written specifically for recluses and thus likely furnishings for an anchorite's cell. The very modernity of thought which Colledge and Walsh see as incompatible with Julian's enclosure during the composition of the Long Text may equally well be taken as evidence *for* enclosure.

Colledge and Walsh seem aware that Julian wrote like an anchorite even while they deny she wrote *while* an anchorite; they note the "congruity between Julian's modes of self-expression and those of the *Ancrene Riwle*."[7] Their desire to see Julian as an anchorite only after the Long Text's composition seems based upon their reading of a single sentence of hers than upon any hard evidence. According to them, Julian had fulfilled God's will

> when she was able to write, in the last chapter of her long text: "This book is begun by God's gift and his grace; but it is not yet performed, as I see it." Then, we believe, she retired to the anchorhold for its performance, through a yet more intenstified form of contemplative living.[8]

I see no evidence that the "performance" of the book must refer to
Julian's devotion to a stricter form of the contemplative life. The
sentence following the one the editors quote, in fact, suggests an
altogether different meaning. What Julian actually says is this:

> This boke is begonne by goddys gyfte and his grace, but it is nott
> yett performyd, as to my sight. For charyte, pray we alle togedyr
> with goddes wurkyng, thankyng, trustyng, enjoyeng....For truly I
> saw and understode in oure lordes menyng that he shewde it for he
> will haue it knowyn more than it is. (LT 86:731–2)

This book will be "performed," according to God's command, when
the most essential of the revelations He made to Julian is "knowyn
more than it is."[9] This can happen only when, after reading Julian's
book, all people can pray "togedyr with goddes wurkyng, thankyng,
trustyng, enjoyeing." The editors' insistence that Julian became an
anchorite only after completing the Long Text seems based on an
idealized vision of the anchorhold as a place of pure and total
withdrawal from the world and of Julian as a writer who was not
only orthodox but possessed of a "sober piety" (not the
"extravagances" of Richard Rolle) and "indifferent to her fame."[10] It
is an open question whether Julian was enclosed when she wrote the
Long Text, but she was certainly thinking like an anchorite.

The most influential rules for female anchorites, Aelred's *De
institutis inclusarum* and the anonymous *Ancrene Wisse*, imagine an
intimate connection between the enclosed life and the anchoress'
physical nature. Both reflect misogynistic assumptions about women,
religion, and feminine speech more clearly than the actual female
experience of anchoritism, but their popularity suggests they
conditioned that experience, determining how women like Julian
might understand their own devotional practices and experiences.
Aelred's letter, composed for his enclosed sister, repeatedly emphasizes
that the anchoress may be walled away from the world but cannot
be cut off from its temptations. The temptations with which he
most concerns himself are that classic feminine duo, loquacity and
sexuality, which he connects implicitly in a passage that echoes
through later rules for women:

> Nowadays you can hardly find a recluse before whose window there
> is no garrulous and rumour-mongering old woman, who wastes her
> time with stories, feeding her on rumours and slander... she may
> slip in something improper, depicting the lust of young widows ...
> Meanwhile [the recluse's] mouth is slack with laughter and cacklings,

and poison absorbed along with pleasure is poured into her limbs and vitals. And so when time obliges them to take their leave, the recluse withdraws laden with sensual delights and the old woman with food.[11]

This passage links speech inextricably to sex. The pleasure the anchorite takes in the old woman's gossip is voyeuristic; beyond this, Aelred's vocabulary suggests that conversation between the two women perverts, or substitutes for, the sexual act. When the old woman "slips in something improper," the verb (*interserat*) is the same Ovid uses when Venus sneaks kisses from Adonis between words.[12] "Improper" is too timid a translation for *illecebrosa*, which suggests something seductive, sexy, even lewd. The image of the anchoress convulsed with laughter, her mouth open while the old woman pours words into her, suggests orgasm, and sensual satisfaction is underlined by the exchange: pleasure fills the anchorite and she burdens the old woman with food.

Aelred is less anxious about his sister's susceptibility to physical lust than about her vulnerability to the more insidious seduction of words. He advises his sister that she must reflect always upon her body, "sanctified by God, incorporated with Christ, dedicated to the Holy Spirit":[13] the virgin must be especially careful of her chastity, not for her own sake but for the sake of the One who inhabits her virgin body. She must beware of any shadow on the serenity of her chastity,[14] not only physical contact but the equally dangerous verbal contact permitted by the anchorite's single window. The verbal threat is figured as a parody of the immaculate conception: the Virgin became pregnant by the Word of God and was often imagined to have conceived through the ear. Words are thus imagined as potentially fertilizing, and human words may prove as potent, if less wholesome, to the anchorite as the divine words were to Mary. The anchorite must therefore maintain a silence as complete as her physical separation from the world; without it, that separation is hypocritical.

Ancrene Wisse further develops Aelred's implication about the temptations of speech to the enclosed woman and the image of the anchorite's body as a womb-like refuge for Christ. The conjunction of verbal and sexual misconduct is indicated in the contrast between Eve, who had a long chat with the serpent in Eden, and Mary, whose conversation with the angel was brief and pointed.[15] The *Wisse* author finds unflattering comparisons for the talkative anchorite, a cackling hen or a grindstone grinding chaff rather than wheat. In the most extended metaphor, her face, especially the mouth from which speech issues, becomes the pit of hell:

> The Pit is her fair face, and her white neck, and her light eye, and her hand if she holds it out before his eyes; and further, her speech is a pit, if it is not controlled, and all other things whatsoever that belong to her through which sinful love may be aroused. All this our Lord calls a pit.[16]

Woman's physical nature (face and voice, standing in for another, unmentionable, "pit") is depicted as repulsively attractive to men. Her body sins even involuntarily by arousing sin in others, whether by letting her voice be heard or her body seen. Since she may sin actively by speaking, or passively by being spoken to (Aelred's gossip reappears in the *Wisse*), it is no surprise to find St. Paul's prohibition on preaching applied with special force to female recluses.[17] Enclosure makes a woman no less dangerous to the male of the species, for the danger is located in her physical being.

The solution to this predicament is not to eliminate female sexual nature, an impossibility evident to the *Wisse* author, but to transform it. Throughout the work, Mary balances Eve's baleful influence. In Mary, the body itself is transformed: Eve's womb brought forth the first children of original sin, conceived in lust, but Mary's brings forth the Child without sin, conceived without lust or fleshly agency. In the long central meditation on birds, the anchorite is encouraged to make herself and her anchorhold a refuge for Christ, just as Mary's womb once was. Anchorite and cell are compared to nests, "hard on the outside, with thorns that prick, and... on the inside soft and yielding....Place [Christ] in your nest, that is, in your heart."[18]

By a precise inversion typical of the *Wisse*, the only way the anchorite can make her body a receptacle worthy of Christ is by entering his body: "'My dove,' He says, 'come and hide thyself in the holes in my limbs, in the hole in my side.'"[19] The image of the dove is revived and the movement of body into body reversed when the *Wisse* author instructs the anchorite that "the mildness of a dove and other like virtues are beautiful in God's eyes.... Make of them His arbor within yourselves, for it is His delight to dwell there."[20]

Even if Julian could read and write only English (allegations of her total illiteracy have dried up in the last generation), she was probably familiar with the much-copied *Wisse*, intended for just such an audience as she. Without ever mentioning the anchorhold, her

Revelation shows the same emphasis on reversible or permeable boundaries, along with similar movements of one body into or through another. It shows an equally pervasive awareness of the female body as an enclosure which, like the anchorhold, functions at different times as prison and as refuge. Julian comes to appreciate and represent the female body differently from Aelred or the *Wisse* author. She emphasizes not inalienable sexuality as inherited from Eve but inalienable capacity for maternity as modeled on that of the Virgin.

Julian appears to react against *Wisse*'s reiteration of the Pauline prohibition on female preaching when she writes:

> Botte god forbede that ye shulde saye or take it so that I am a techere, for I meene nought soo, no I mente nevere so; for I am a womann, leued, febille and freylle. Botte I wate wele, this that I saye, I hafe it of the schewynge of hym that es souerayne techare... .Botte for I am a womann, shulde I therefore leve that I shulde noght telle yowe the goodenes of god, syne that I sawe in that same tyme that is his wille, that it be knawenn? (ST 6: 40–52)

Significantly, the Long Text contains no such disclaimer on the grounds of Julian's sex. Colledge and Walsh suggest that this passage was perhaps "deleted as likely to antagonize male readers; but, on the other hand, the notably more tranquil tone of the Long Text at this point could suggest that in later years Julian had gained assurance."[21] How is Julian's description of herself as *leued, feybille and freylle* more antagonistic to a male reader than her tacit refusal to apologize for her gender? Her Long Text presents her visions and her exegesis of them more authoritatively than the Short Text. To suggest that she has simply "gained assurance" does not go far enough toward defining that assurance. After all, a general denial of superiority over her fellow Christians is retained in the Long Text (LT 321:2–8).

The insistence on God's position as teacher, rather than on the anchorite's role in teaching, is also retained in the Long Text, which adapts "And I am sekere that he that behaldes it thus, he schalle be trwely taught and myghttelye comforthtede, if hym nede comfort" (ST 6:38–39) into "And I hope by *the grace of god* he that behold it thus shalle be truly taught and myghtly comfortyd, yf him nedyth comfort" (LT 322:7–19; my emphasis). The shift in the agent of teaching and comfort from the impersonal to the divine is inconspicuous but clear. The Long Text again emphasizes God's instructive capacity: "But I trust in our lord god almightie that he shall of his godness and for our love make yow to take it more ghostely and more sweetly than I can or may tell it" (LT 9:32–34). To authorize the lesson she undeniably teaches, Julian represents herself as the agent of the divine teacher, not as a teacher in her own right.

The omission of the disclaimer based on the unworthiness of her sex suggests that Julian's increased assurance may be located precisely in a redefinition of the value of her gender. The anchoritic writings discussed above define and evaluate the female body along very particular lines; in the years between the composition of the Short and the Long Texts, Julian clearly developed familiarity with the didactic and imagistic tendencies of such writings. But to suggest that this familiarity made her "the inheritor of a tradition almost three centuries old, of writing for women about the experiences and reality of a life of prayer"[22] and thus accounts for the "maturity" of her style is to assume that writing *for* women, or even *about* women, automatically provides an acceptable model for a woman writing *as* a woman. Given the anchoritic corpus's misogyny, Julian's familiarity with it may have increased her personal dilemma: it placed her within an ascetic tradition that prejudged women's spiritual capacities according to assumed physical incapacities or weaknesses.

Julian's version of anchoritic spirituality builds upon the paradoxical inversions and reversals of the enclosed life. Entombed in her cell, the anchorite is simultaneously dead and alive and hopes through her death from this world to ensure life in the next. More fundamental even than the paradox of dying to live is the paradox of being enclosed in a narrow place to gain access to the limitless unplace which is Heaven: "'My cell is so narrow,' you may say, but oh, how wide is the sky!" the Benedictine Goscelin wrote to his friend Eve in one of the earliest English rules for anchorites.[23] The outside world is the true prison cell, and the cell the world, as Julian acknowledges: "this place is pryson, this lyfe is pennannce" (LT 77:693). In the world of the anchorite's imagination, all things are turned inside out. The infinite exists within the finite just as the spirit exists within the flesh. Julian expresses relationships between divine and human, body and soul, in terms of paradoxical enclosures. She constructs, as it were, an Escherian *matrushka*: the body of the last, smallest, and most interior doll opens to reveal the first and the largest. In such a universe, boundaries (the walls of the anchorhold, the womb of the Blessed Virgin) become permeable by strange influences.[24]

Julian is often considered the most theological, the most logocentric, the least apophatic of medieval woman mystics; Colledge and Walsh's entire commentary seeks to prove how systematic and rational her method is, how much an heir she is of the tradition of the Church Fathers, even of Scholasticism. Attempts to validate Julian's theology often coincide with efforts to distance her from the tradition of female mysticism, characterized as affective, emotive, and irrational. Thus Riehle observes that her "words reveal a maturity quite remarkable in a lay-person and especially in a woman,"[25] dissociating Julian from what is, to him, the distasteful emotionality and "immaturity" of mystics such as Kempe, with her "sick, neurotic psyche."[26] Such efforts then attempt to promote Julian to the rank of honorary man, thereby legitimizing her access to theological truth. As Ward notes, this is patronizing: "There is a kind of presumption in supposing that she could not possible have thought for herself, that the little lady would need male instruction and had to have books to read."[27]

None of this implies Julian's proto-feminism. She is not as indebted to paternal and patristic authority as her editors would have her; neither does she attack such authority or its chosen modes of discourse. She does not question Christianity's logocentrism—rather, she uses patriarchal logic in a very idiosyncratic way to gesture toward the doubly unrepresentable: mystical understanding and feminine experience.

Julian's vision of all creation reduced to the size of a hazelnut serves as a starting point from which to observe the subtlety and complexity of her use of feminine images:

> And in this he schewed me a lytille thynge, the qwantite of a haselle nutte, lyggande in the palme of my hande, and to my undyrstandynge that, it was as rownde as any balle. I lokede þer opon and thought: whate maye this be? And I was annswerde generaly thus: It is alle that ys made. (ST 6:212–213)

Colledge and Walsh see marked similarities of both "thought and language"[28] between this passage and Wisdom 11.23–26: "Indeed, before you the whole universe is as a grain from a balance, or a drop of morning dew come down upon the earth...."[29] Like William Blake, who saw infinity in a grain of sand and eternity in an hour, Julian was no doubt familiar with the biblical text that Colledge and Walsh indicate as the "source" of her vision. That Blake's imagery is closer to that of the Bible highlights Julian's deviance from it, making such deviance more rather than less significant by a sort of metaphorical *lectio difficilior*. With an obvious simile available, she chooses an original one: the hazelnut is not only small, it is a container like the anchorhold or the womb, as a hard shell contains the meat of the nut, its living essence.[30]

Julian moves directly from the image of the hazelnut to a vision of the Virgin, a "sympille maydene and a meeke, yonge of age, in the stature that scho was when scho conceyvede."[31] Mary's intact yet fruitful body reproduces in human form the sealed container of the hazelnut. And, like the "lytille thynge," it is filled with God's love in the form of the Son of Man. It contains, in the form of the Christ child, a whole new world for mankind. Julian is clear that she sees the Virgin at the time (if not the very moment) of conception, when her pregnancy is still invisible, latent, known only to Mary herself— and to Julian. The emphasis is not therefore on the visible pregnancy but on the experience of wonder and joy at the conception of Christ, which at this moment unites Julian and Mary in secret knowledge. The close relationship of the hazelnut image to the vision of the Virgin thus expands its significance beyond that of the source-passage in Wisdom, allowing it to include the mystery of the Incarnation.

The layering of image upon image is equally multivalent in Julian's description of the blood that flows from beneath the crown of thorns as

> lyke to the droppes of water that falle of the evesyng of an howse after a grete shower of reyne, that falle so thycke that no man may nomber them with no bodely wyt. And for the rondnesse, they were lyke to the scale of heryng in the spredyng of the forhede. (LT 22–26)

The qualities emphasized are quantity—the "thycke" raindrops, the "rondnesse" of the fish's scales (like that of the *lyttel thynge*, or a pregnant belly). These images appeal to the experience of everyday life in a damp climate, where herring was a common winter food. Each expands and reinforces, even permeates the other. The scales are silvery and round; raindrops are round as well as silvery as they drop from the eaves; fish come from the water, rain is water. Both thus resonate with the moisture-related imagery so important to

Julian. The ordinariness of such images is extraordinary in its application to something doubly extraordinary: the Savior's mystical blood and Julian's vision of this blood in such quantities that it seems to her it must soak her bed. The effect of such *hamly* description applied to such an unfamiliar event is nothing short of *unheimlich*.

Julian's use of similes of fluidity or liquidness is one of the hallmarks of her imagistic style. It makes possible the development of the theme of the motherhood of God. Fluids, tears, blood, milk, were all intimately related in medieval thinking; they marked the experience of women and also of Christ. Aristotle characterized men as hot and dry, women as cold and moist and disadvantaged by that cold moisture. Yet this physical fluidity allowed the identification of the female body with the body of Christ and, conversely, the body of Christ with the female body.[32] The mechanics of the *Revelation* is a mechanics of fluids. As Irigaray says:

> It is already getting around—at what rate? in what contexts? in spite of what resistances?—that women diffuse themselves according to modalities scarcely compatible with the framework of the ruling symbolics. Which doesn't happen without causing some turbulence, we might even say some whirlwinds, that ought to be reconfined within solid walls of principle, to keep them from spreading to infinity.[33]

Irigaray might have been writing for or about Julian, whose "modalities" were so incompatible with the patriarchal symbolics of her time that her book was rarely copied. One scribe felt driven to justify her orthodoxy in a postscript.[34] Julian transgresses boundaries we take for granted, not only those between male and female but those between real and figurative, between "bodily" and "ghostly" sight, between "sensuality" and "substance." Her language and thought thus "spread to infinity," imagining a future unity of the human and the divine in which *alle shalle be wele, and alle shalle be wele, and alle maner of thynge shalle be welle* (LT 27:405).

When Julian speaks of God as our Mother in the theological climax of her book, she is not making an identification which would have outraged her contemporaries. Indeed, Bernard of Clairvaux, William of SaintThierry, St. Anselm, Aelred of Rievaulx, and the *Ancrene Wisse* author represent Christ as a mother. Julian's evocation of Christ as our Mother, however, differs significantly from that of the

Cistercian authors claimed as her models, for her feminization of divinity goes well beyond the use of feminine epithets for God.

According to Bynum, when Bernard of Clairvaux uses maternal imagery to describe Christ or other male figures, "the maternal image is almost without exception elaborated not as giving birth or even as conceiving or sheltering in a womb but as nurturing, particularly suckling."[35] Similarly, Aelred focuses on Christ's breasts and images of nursing in *De Institutis Inclusarum*, recommending that the anchorite be satisfied with one image of the crucified Christ in her cell, which will console her "with milk from his naked breasts."[36] St. Anselm also invokes Christ as a mother in his prayer to St Paul:

> Are you not a mother who like a chicken collect your chicks beneath your wings? Truly, lord, you are also a mother. For what others conceived and brought forth, they received from you. First you died laboring to bring them forth, and that which they themselves have borne, and then you gave birth to them in dying. For if you had not so labored, you would not have died. And had you not died, you would not have brought them forth...[37]

The motherhood of God is employed by these writers as an image to make a particular point about the obligations of priests (Bernard), anchorites (Aelred), or the apostle Paul (Anselm). They emphasize feminine attributes, rather than a female or feminized body. Both Bernard and Aelred focus on breasts, the most visible, external mark of motherhood and femininity, as metaphors for divine nourishment. Even Anselm, who uses the vocabulary of childbearing, does so abstractly; he does not imagine the processes of labor and birth in a physical body or through particular organs. His laboring Christ does not bleed, sweat, or manifest physical symptoms of childbirth. Instead, the concrete image Anselm elaborates is that of the hen protecting its chicks. This "feminine" behavior is easily appropriated by the male; as Ruddick reminds us, "although most mothers have been and are female, mothering is potentially work for males and females."[38]

In most iconographic representations of a "lactating" Christ, the Savior offers the wound in his breast to a worshipper with the same gesture used by the nursing Virgin, but His breast is not engorged or feminized. The feminization of the male body of Christ remains partial, and His is not, in any case, the body of everyman. We do not imagine Bernard's or Aelred's bodies undergoing a miraculous physical change when they speak of themselves as "mothers" to their monks; their language is understood as metaphorical. They co-opt positive feminine characteristics such as nourishing, without adopting negatively valued female attributes. Christ's body is sexed male even as it adopts characteristics normally associated with the female. This feminization of function does not include an actual movement from one sex to the other but allows the Cistercian writers to see in the (male) body of Christ the image of their own (male) bodies. The body of the Son of Man and the bodies of the men who follow Him are reassuringly similar; invested with feminine abilities or not, the bodies themselves are resolutely male, superior to the female. Cistercian efforts to adopt for Christ certain desirable feminine functions without corresponding physical femaleness and to imagine him giving birth without the benefit of a female body recall Ruddick's warning in *Maternal Thinking*:

> ...so long as we fear and deny the distinctly female character of birth, we risk losing the symbolic, emotional, and ultimately political significance of birth itself. There is a philosophical tradition that honors mind over body, idea over matter, the word over the bloody, shitty mortal flesh—a tradition that feeds off fear and contempt for female procreative bodies.[39]

Cistercian maternal imagery functions to dissociate motherhood from the "female procreative body"; it does not so much blur boundaries between genders as create a distinction between anatomical sex and gender. Only a female body can lactate, but the nourishing function, once separated from that female body, is as accessible to men as to women and need not affect the sex of the body which performs it. The abbot can thus continue to be a man, even while loving his monks like a mother. The ambivalent figure of the lactating Christ is the bridge which allows this process to occur.

A fourteenth-century woman thinking or writing about Christ's body and her relationship to it does not enjoy gendered identity with that body. The process of projection must, of necessity, be different for her. St. Bernard imagines the male body of Christ in his own body, then maps onto it certain feminine characteristics. In contrast, Julian imagines her female body mapped onto that of God and makes the body of Christ participate in female, rather than feminine, functions. He not only possesses such feminine abilities as nurturing and nourishing but he actually conceives, gestates, and

labors with all the marks of the "bloody, shitty mortal flesh" that
Cistercians controlled and denied by ascribing them to the female
Other. As Heimmel puts it, "to Julian, God is never simply 'like' a
mother. For her, He is a mother and the most ultimate of mothers."[40]
In the imagery and narrative structure of the *Revelation*, Julian reveals
a fascination with the most inalienably female aspect of motherhood:
the act of giving birth.

Julian links Christ's humanity to His pain, that inheritance from
His human mother experienced most fully on the Cross:

> For the godhed sterte from þe fader into þe maydyns wombe, fallyng
> into the takyng of our kynde, and in this fallyng he toke grete soore.
> The soore that he toke was oure flesshe, in whych as sone he had
> felyng of dedely paynes. (LT 51: 540)

The emphasis on Christ's pain, the representation of the Passion as
labor, of Christ's body as capable of female functions, not just
feminine behavior, and the relative scarcity of images of lactation,
all mark Julian's *Revelation* as profoundly different from the works
that may have influenced her. Such elements, all intensified in the
Long Text, also suggest that Julian stopped doubting herself on the
grounds of her sex, as the Short Text's disclaimer suggests. She came
rather to see being a woman as a particularly powerful route to
understanding Christianity's central mystery: the Incarnation.[41] This
understanding of the relationship between human being and Savior
is also profoundly indebted to an understanding of the relationship
between Christ and the anchorite within the physical context of the
anchorhold. Christ enters Mary's womb as the anchorite enters the
anchorhold, exiling Himself from the wider spaces of His divine
origins; from that womb, He is born to give birth to Christianity.

Two births take place in the *Revelation*. Christ labors on the Cross
to give birth to mankind (the image is not original to Julian, though
she develops it in original ways); the text itself mimics the process of
labor to give birth to meaning—the final, long-delayed
understanding of the visions—for Julian herself, and for her *evynn
cristene*.

Julian's vision of Christ on the Cross graphically emphasizes His
physical pain; she sees floods of blood, nails stretching the wounds
in hands and feet, flesh pulling away from bone and *saggyng
downwarde* (LT 17:362). The worst aspect of His pain is the "drying"

He suffers after pouring forth His blood and the terrible thirst which accompanies it:

> I saw iiij maner of dryeng. The furst was blodlesse, the secunde payne folowyng after, the thurde is that he was hangyng uppe in the eyer as men hang a cloth for to drye, the fowyrth that the bodely kynde asked lycoure, and there was no maner of comfort mynystryd to him. A, hard and grevous was that payne; but much more harder and grevous it was when þe moystur fayled, and all began to drye, thus clyngyng. (LT 17: 364)

Julian does not at first relate Christ's suffering on the Cross to the pain of labor; only in Chapter 63 does she say that "in the takyng of oure kynd he quyckyd vs, and in his blessyd dyeng upon the crosse he bare vs to endlesse lyfe" (LT 63:616). Yet it is worth noting that loss of fluid and extreme thirst are part of any birth-labor. Marguerite d'Oignt's account of the Crucifixion, like Julian's, emphasizes the loss of moisture and the pain that accompanies it:

> The mother who bore me labored for perhaps a day to give me birth, or for a night, while you, lovely, sweet lord, suffered pain because of me not for a night or a day, but rather were in labor for more than thirty years. Ah, lovely, sweet lord, how you must have suffered, your labor was so painful that your holy sweat was like drops of blood which ran over your body and down to the ground.[42]

Here, unlike Anselm's almost philosophical evocation of conception and birth, Christ is represented as suffering labor pains in physical, even realistic ways, marked by flowing blood and sweat. This is no abstract metaphor but represents an activity often perceived, especially but not exclusively by men, as "savage, barbaric, primitive, or loathsome."[43] The emphasis on physical bodily suffering, extraordinary pain, and the flow of blood and water (suggesting amniotic fluid as well as sweat) makes Christ's body immediately apprehensible as female, and it is pain, not nourishing or bringing forth souls, which makes Christ a mother:

> For the flode of mercy that is his deerworthy bloode and precious water is plentuous to make us feyer and clene. The blessed woundes of oure sauiour be opyn and enjoye to hele us. The swete gracious hands of oure moder be redy and diligent about us.(LT 608:64–67)

Julian's vision further indicates the relationship between Christ's death and giving birth by juxtaposing His pains with the Virgin's suffering at the foot of the Cross, when "Crist and she was so onyd in love that the grettnes of her loue was cause of the grettnes of her peyne..." (LT 18:366). Mary was believed to have borne Christ without labor pains, remaining virgin *in partu* and *post partum*. Her pain is postponed from the moment of her son's birth to his death; as Mater Dolorosa, she embodies the pain of all mothers. Christ speaks to Julian as a mother in Chapter 24, saying, "And now is my bitter payne and alle my harde traveyle turnyd to evyrlasting joy and blysse to me and to the."

At other moments in the *Revelation*, the Virgin and Christ are almost identified as one, as when Julian states:

> Thus oure lady is oure moder, in whome we be all beclosyd and of hyr borne in Crist, for she that is moder of oure savyoure is mother of all þat ben savyd in our sauyour; and oure savyoure is oure very moder, in whome we be endlesly borne and nevyr shall come out of hym. (LT 57: 580)

This passage also illustrates a paradox implicit in Julian's use of childbearing imagery. In one sense Christ's labor on the Cross, to give birth to the saved, is temporal, occurring at a single, supercharged moment in history; in another, his pregnancy with humanity is eternal—we *nevyr shall come out of hym*. Time is both linear and circular, like Julian's narrative itself, in which a second labor takes place that both parallels and traverses Christ's.

The Long Text resists efforts to force it into conformation with linear schematics such as Augustine's corporeal, imaginative, and intellective vision.[44] Despite Julian's status as most (theo)logical of women mystics, despite her professions of orthodoxy and her reputation as resolutely logocentric, the meaning of her text overflows the language in which it is conveyed. The text's development is not purely logical or intellectual; it is organic, combining logic and intuition as Julian's theology deftly combines *substance* and *sensuallite, grace,* and *kynde.* It reflects to an astonishing degree the physical experience of childbirth, so that Julian's book reproduces for her readers the experiences of both Christ and visionary as it labors to give birth to understanding.

Julian's visions and her meditation on them proceed in orderly fashion (simultaneous in the Long Text, though the visions preceded exegesis in actual experience). Confronted with the divine, her intellect functions clearly, dissociated from the suffering body whose eyes remain fixed on the crucifix. There are moments of apophasis in the vanishing drops of blood which flow in the First Revelation, marking timeless time as Julian beholds them with the Virgin "in the same tyme" (LT 7:310), but she retains control of her narrative: from the vision of the Crown of Thorns she extracts and precisely enumerates six "understandings" (LT 8:317). Some things are harder to represent than others—the Third Revelation, for instance, when she sees "god in a poynte" (LT 11:336)—but Julian proceeds from one argument to another, dissecting her understanding for our benefit. In the earlier stages of labor, pain is not absent, but it is manageable. The tendency is to think one can remain in control; Julian succeeds in controlling the representation of her revelations up to a point.

The crux in the *Revelation* which eventually causes a breakdown in Julian's linear, logical representation of her experience is the question of sin, first raised in the Third Revelation: "I merveyled in that syght with a softe drede, and thought, What is synne?" (LT 11:336). She answers almost immediately: "alle thynges that is done is welle done, for our lord god doth all" (LT 11:338), but the issue is not resolved, and haunts the rest of the text. For the moment, Julian moves on, through a series of revelations, to Christ's death. His extraordinary pain causes the visionary and her text to suffer extraordinarily in sympathy, as though experiencing labor's "transitional" phase when systems for managing pain, fear, and confusion are likely to give way. Julian's material begins to slip out of control; lists stretch and shatter under the pressure of experience and the effort to bring forth meaning from it: "it is gods wylle, as to my understandyng, that we haue iij maner of beholdyng of his blessyd passion," she writes at the end of Chapter 20. "The furst is the harde payne that he sufferyd with a contriccion and compassion" (LT 20:377–78). For the moment, she cannot finish the list; the next two elements are delayed until LT 22:386 and LT 23:389, respectively. Understanding of the Passion is spread across three chapters and two separate revelations, the Eighth and Ninth. Linear time, like the linear narrative, is being pulled out of shape.

The Thirteenth and Fourteenth Revelations—that *alle shalle be wele* and that God is *grownd of our beseking*—are the densest and most difficult for Julian and for her readers. This can be seen schematically in the space each requires for exegesis. Previous revelations occupy frequently only one and at most four or five chapters, but Revelation Thirteen runs from Chapters 27–40, and Fourteen from 41–63. The narrative's shape is thus swollen—pregnant as it were; to explain this, Julian writes theology rather than replicating a straightforward visionary experience. Furthermore, as Watson demonstrates, it becomes evident to the reader that the experience of these revelations extends beyond the period of Julian's illness at the age of thirty.[45] The text's distortion is not only quantitative in that some revelations are longer than others; it is temporal, in the complete breakdown of distinction between experience and narrative in these central chapters. Distinction itself is no longer a possibility. The physical or intellectual pain suffered by Savior, visionary, and reader unites them all in a textual space outside the limitations of time or linear thought.

Like an intimation of things to come, the question of sin provoked the first fissure in Julian's narrative; in the Thirteenth Revelation it returns in full strength. "*Synne is behovely, but alle shalle be wele and alle shalle be wele, and alle maner of thynge shalle be wele*" may be Julian's only immediately quotable passage, but it is neither simple, self-explanatory nor comforting, demanding absolute faith in God's compassion and goodness, and in His ability to resolve the paradox of the existence of evil. For a mind less logical than Julian's, acceptance would have been easier. Her experience of and in the text parallels childbirth: at the moment of greatest pain she must not resist nor act at all but become completely passive and trust in an unimaginable outcome, since "we mey nott have thys in fulhed whyle we be here" [i.e., in this world] (LT 40:456).

Julian's labor overlaps Christ's, his to bring forth Christianity, hers to bring forth understanding of one of its essential paradoxes. The language of Revelation Thirteen is full of openings and enclosures, movements of one body into or through another. Thus at LT 31:418: "we be enclosyd in rest and in pees," like *Ancrene Wisse*'s dove hiding in Christ's wounds, inevitably recalls the anchorhold's quiet, identifying it with the peace within Christ's womb. Secrets, *prevytes*, are opened by Christ, like his wounds, and entered into by the visionary: "And therfore hath he grett reuth, and therfore he wylle make them opyn to vs hym selfe, wher by we may knowe hym and loue hym and cleue to hym" (LT 34:430–31).

No sooner is the Thirteenth Revelation resolved (insofar as it can be in this life) than that of the Fourteenth bears down upon Julian; initially, it does not appear acute. Here, however, she is confronted with the "example" of master and servant, most mysterious of the revelations, which she apprehends "full mystely" (LT 51:513), and which for twenty years defies her attempts to bring forth its meaning (LT 51:519). In birth labor, contractions at transition seem interminable; so, too, in Julian's spiritual labor. The understanding she finally gains of the parable of lord and servant leads her directly into the theology of God's motherhood, in Chapters 51 to 63, where images of pregnancy and childbirth define the relationship of human and God.

The presence of a divine womb, in which the human soul is formed and shaped and from which it is born, is here powerfully and explicitly evoked:

> For in that same tyme that god knytt hym to oure body in the meydens wombe, he toke oure sensuall soule, in whych takyng, he us all havyng beclosyd in hym, he onyd it to oure substance. (LT 57:579–80)

The word *knytt* occurs as early as 1400 to describe the formation of fruits on a tree, and by the early seventeenth century it is used for the formation of a fetus. I understand the term here in the same sense, since Julian is describing a process within the Virgin's womb. The soul's formation in Christ is then imaged as a child's formation within its mother's body, when Julian claims (following Aristotelian ideas on conception and gestation) that our *beyng* originates in God our Father, while in God our Mother "we have oure reformyng and our restoring, in whome oure partys be onyd..." (LT 58:587). The following passage echoes contemporary scientific knowledge of reproduction:

> The moder may geve her chylde sucke hyr mylke, but oure precyous moder Jhesu, he may fede us wyth hym selfe, and doth full curteisly and full tendyrly with the blessyd sacrament, that is precyous fode of very lyfe....The moder may ley hyr chylde tenderly to hyr brest, but oure tender mother Jhesu, he may homely lede us in to his blessyd brest by his swet open syde...(LT 596–98. 29–41)

The gift of milk from mother to child is contrasted with Christ's gift of His own *selfe*, His flesh and blood in the form of the Sacrament. The contrast is less strong than it initially appears; breast milk was understood to be merely transformed menstrual blood, which migrated upwards after nourishing and forming the fetus in the womb.[46] When Christ nourishes the soul with His sacramental flesh and blood, within His body and through a form of lactation, He performs a more explicit version of a natural maternal and female function. It is as though His body were transparent, revealing processes which in a human mother are occult and mysterious. This transparency of Christ's body is alluded to as early as the Tenth Revelation, when He looks into His side and shows Julian

> a feyer and delectable place, and large enow for alle mankynde that shalle be savyd and rest in pees and in loue. And ther with he brought to mynde hys dereworthy blode and hys precious water whych he lett poure out for love ... (LT10: 394–95)

Salvation is made possible by the permeable, female nature of Christ's body, which exudes cleansing and nourishing blood and water and can be entered, becoming a refuge like *Ancrene Wisse*'s nest. The process of salvation cannot, however, be described as consisting simply of the soul's entry into the womb–like space of the Sacred Heart or of the rebirth of humanity's collective soul in Christ's suffering on the Cross. For Julian, the process is an infinitely more involved series of reflections and inversions, of bodies engendered and gestating within other bodies. To become our mother, Christ first had to enter His mother's body:

> And that shewde he in the furst, where he brughte þat meke meydyn before the eye of my understondyng, in þe sympyll stature as she was whan she conceyved; that is to sey oure god, the souereyn wysdom of all, in this lowe place he arayed hym and dyght hym all redy in oure poure flessch, hym selfe to do the servce and the officie of moderhode in alle thyng. (LT 60:594–95)

This initial entry into the Virgin's womb clothes the divine spirit in flesh and makes possible all future identification of human flesh with that of the Savior. It also demands a transformation of humanity, so that having entered into Mary, Christ may enter into us:

> A hye understandyng it is inwardly to se and to know that god, whych is oure maker, dwellyth in oure soule, and a hygher understandyng it is and more, inwardly to se and to know oure soule that is made dwellyth in god in substance, of whych substance by god we be that we be. (LT 54:561–62)

Like the *Wisse* author, Julian sees soul and body as intrinsically, inseparably linked; the intermingling of the two is what she defines as *sensualite*.

Julian's text reproduces in a very different tone the double movement of the anchorite into Christ's wounds and Christ into the anchorite's heart or womb, already familiar from *Ancrene Wisse*. The anchorhold's presence, so physical and immediate as to be claustrophobic in the *Wisse*, is more impressionistically evoked by Julian, most memorably in the passage quoted at the beginning of this essay. The paradoxical relationship, which allows the infinite and eternal qualities of *almyghty truth, depe wysdome*, and *hye goodnesse* simultaneously to contain and be contained by the human receptacle, recalls the anchorhold's severely limited space in Goscelin's *Liber confortatorius* and *Wisse*, encapsulated in the wider world of the flesh, yet containing the widest world of the spirit.

This series of reflections and reversals, of movement into and out of Christ's and the visionary's bodies, this fluid intermingling of states of being, transforms and even subverts the *Wisse*'s expectations. In Julian's text, the anchorhold itself is not the tomb of the living dead whose hands would be ruined by digging her own grave;[47] it represents the fruitful hollowness of three bodies—that of the Virgin, that of Christ's body which was contained therein, and that of Julian herself, the lover of Christ who both contains and is contained by Him. The anchorhold represents the body of God and the body of the anchorite, containing the spiritual all to the exclusion of the worldly nothing. The motherhood of God, which transforms the sexual and sinful female body into a generative and holy one, is the central image that allows this refiguration of the *Wisse*'s world from one in which the pit of Hell is always present into one in which Julian can ask for "som syȝt of hel and of purgatory" (LT 33:427) and be denied it. The anchorhold itself continues to figure its occupant's body but also figures Christ's maternal body into which the anchorite has entered. Its power of enclosure becomes redemptive; it is no longer the martyr's prison cell but the hazelnut in the palm of the anchorite herself, containing all things, evoking the Virgin's womb.

In Julian's contention that we must know God if we are to know our own souls and know our own souls if we are to know God, there is a paradox similar to that of the body which is at once enclosed and enclosure.

> That wurschypfull cytte þat oure lorde Jhesu syttyth in, it is oure
> sensualyte, in whych he is enclosyd; and oure kyndly substance is
> beclosyd in Jhesu, with þe blessyd soule of Crist syttyng in rest in þe
> godhed. And I saw full suerly that it behouyth nedys to be that we
> shulde be in longyng and in pennance into þe tyme that we be led so
> depe in to god that we verely and trewly know oure owne soule ...
> (LT 56:572–73)

Here Christ becomes the receptacle, womb, or anchorhold, in which
the human soul is contained. Simultaneously, He Himself is
contained within another entity, the city (in the Middle Ages enclosed
by walls), which proves to be that of human *sensualite*, the quality
He took on in His human mother's womb. In contrast to the
extraordinary moment when Christ gave birth to humanity on the
Cross, Julian now represents an infinite gestation, an eternity of
security in Christ's womb: "Plentuously, fully and swetely was this
shewde; and it is spoken of in the furst, where it seyde we val in hym
beclosyd, and he is beclosyd in us" (LT 57:580). Finally, the Fourteenth
Revelation closes with a recapitulation of the Thirteenth's *alle shalle
be wele* (LT 64:618).

The concise Fifteenth Revelation, in contrast to the two which
precede it, is full of language suggesting the moment of birth itself.
The visionary resumes control of her narrative, as a woman in the
final stages of labor may regain control of her body. "Afore this tyme
I had grete longyng and desyer of goddys gyfte to be delyuerde of
this worlde and of this lyfe," Julian says at the beginning of the
chapter (LT 64:619). Instead, she is delivered of an understanding of
joy, a moment represented as an actual birth:

> And in thys tyme I sawe a body lyeng on þe erth, whych body shewde
> heuy and feerfulle and with oute shape and forme, as it were a swylge
> stynkyng myrre; and sodeynly oute of this body sprong a fulle feyer
> creature, a littylle chylld, full shapyn and formyd, swyft and lyfly
> and whytter than the lylye, whych sharpely glydyd vppe in to hevyn.
> (LT 64:622–23)

Julian explains this vision: the grotesquely swollen body is the
"wretchednysse of oure dedely flessch," the same that Christ took
on in the Virgin's womb, while the child is the immortal soul. The
maternal body's ugliness in this image does not signal revulsion from
the female nor from the process of birth. This ugliness goes beyond
the human realm into that of the sacred; it is the product of a pain

which is in no way negative but rather the positive marker of the Christian as the product of Christ's labor on the Cross.

In the Fifteenth Revelation, Julian distinguishes also between movement out of the womb of our "mother," Christ, and back into it. The first of these mimics the biological process of birth; she describes it as according to nature, or *kynd*, while the second is according to supernatural *grace*: "Thus I understode that all his blessyd chyldren which be come out of hym by kynd shulde be brougt agayne in to hym by grace" (LT 64:619). Christ's female body is evidently capable of actions beyond those of human women, reversing the process of birth and returning the child to its original refuge, the womb.

In the "real time" of Julian's illness, there is a breathing space between the Fifteenth Revelation and the final one the next night, as "conclusyon and confirmation to all the xv," a sort of afterbirth. The Sixteenth Revelation differs from the previous fifteen in several ways. Throughout it, other people (a priest, friends, attendants) appear briefly; slowly, the normal world replaces the supernatural. The bulk of the revelation is less an independent shewing than a revelation about the method of the earlier revelations. After an initial moment of doubt followed by a dream of the devil, Julian has a vision of the infinite space of her own soul, with Christ seated in glory therein "in pees and rest" (LT 68:640). Her last visual experience of the divine offers a kind of closure to what has gone before, marking a return to the human world: "And sone all was close, and I saw no more afftyr this" (LT 68:647). This is succeeded by a last temptation by the devil (manifested as a *stynch* [LT 69:648]), whom Julian defeats by again turning to the crucifix which first precipitated the revelations. Here she finds proof that her visions were real, that her faith is strong enough to preserve her. It is thus a sort of metavision, validating the rest.

From Chapter 70 to the book's end, Julian reflects upon and clarifies what has gone before—a process which overflows the Sixteenth Revelation, since it includes reference to her long-delayed understanding of the parable of lord and servant (LT 82:717). She regains control of the text and of her understanding of it; she lists things again, explaining, for example, the method of the visions "by bodely syght, and by worde formyd in myne understondyng, and by gostely sight" (LT 73:666). The labor of the text is over; these are the motions of tidying up the newborn, wrapping it, presenting it to the world.

The first words of the Short Text of the *Revelation* describe Julian as a recluse. The last of the Long Text include a prayer for her soul: *Explicit liber revelacionum Julyane ana(c)orite Norwyche, cuius anime propicietur deus* (LT 86:734). The two texts are thus framed, enclosed by the anchorhold. Within this scribal container, an account of Julian's revelations develops from the linked images of anchorhold and womb and into a theology and a language that depend upon and derive from female experience. Philosophical and logocentric on one level—the "masculine" level which has seduced so many male and clerical readers—Julian's *Revelation of Love* has its roots in apophatic paradox, in a biological imaginary which overflows the prescribed boundaries of narrative and language. For Julian, woman's body is not divided and divisive but the ultimate agent of union. All paradox, all conflict, between mystical and nonmystical experience, between modes of perceiving and modes of speaking perception, between human and divine, is resolved metaphorically through the physical functions of the female body, albeit a body which transcends earthly flesh. The Trinity itself, as well as the created world, is enclosed in the body of Christ our Mother:

> Thus in oure fader god almyghty we haue oure beyng, and in oure moder of mercy we haue our reformyng and oure restoryng, in whom oure partys be onyd and all made perfyte man, and by yeldyng and gevyng in grace of the holy gost we be fulfyllde. And our substannce is in oure fader god almyghty, and oure substannce is in oure moder god all wysdom, and oure substannce is in oure lorde god the holy gost all goodnes, for oure substannce is hole in ech person of the trynyte, whych is one god. And oure sensuallyte is only in the seconde person, Crist Jhesu, in whom is the fader and þe holy gost. (LT 58: 587–88)

NOTES

1. Edmund Colledge and James Walsh, *A Book of Showings to the Anchoress Julian of Norwich*, 2 vols. (Toronto, 1978). Long and Short Texts are indicated as LT and ST. The numeral before the colon indicates the chapter, the numeral after it the page number according to this edition.

2. Hans Kurath et al., eds., *Middle English Dictionary* (Ann Arbor, 1952 ff.).

3. Ann K. Warren, *Anchorites and Their Patrons in Medieval England* (Berkeley, 1985), p. 258.

4. Warren, p. 20.

5. See Nicholas Watson, "The Composition of Julian of Norwich's *Revelation of Love,*" *Speculum* 68 (July 1993), p. 675, n. 89. As far as I can see, the *only* reason for Colledge and Walsh's insistence that Julian was not enclosed until 1393 is their belief that her book must have been written outside the anchorhold.

6. Colledge and Walsh, "Editing Julian of Norwich's *Revelations,*" *Mediaeval Studies* 38 (1976), p. 416.

7. Colledge and Walsh, "Editing Julian," p. 411.

8. Colledge and Walsh, "Editing Julian," p. 418.

9. Grace M. Jantzen, *Julian of Norwich, Mystic and Theologian* (London, 1987), p. 21.

10. See Colledge and Walsh, *Showings,* pp. 196–97; I am indebted to Nicholas Watson for this insight.

11. Aelred of Rievaulx, *De institutis inclusarum* II, pp. 20–34. Translations mine.

12. See *Meta.* X, p. 559.

13. *De inst. incl.* XV, pp. 494–95.

14. *De inst. incl.* XV, pp. 508–10.

15. *Ancrene Wisse,* J.R.R. Tolkien, ed., EETS 246, p. 35. All translations from *Ancrene Wisse* are those of M.B. Salu, *The Ancrene Riwle* (London, 1955).

16. *Ancrene Riwle,* Mabel Day, ed., EETS o.s. 225, p. 25. Translation from Salu.

17. *AW,* p. 38.

18. *AW,* p. 71.

19. *AW,* p. 151.

20. *AW,* p. 173.

21. Colledge and Walsh, *Showings* , p. 222, n. 40.

22. A.M. Allchin, "Julian of Norwich and the Continuity of Tradition," *The Medieval Mystical Tradition in England: The Exeter Symposium,* ed. Marion Glasscoe (Exeter, 1980), p. 74.

23. Goscelin of St. Bertin, *Liber confortatorius,* ed. C.H. Talbot, *Analecta monastica: Studia Anselmiana* xxxvii (Rome, 1955), p. 77: 8. Translation mine.

24. Caroline Walker Bynum argues that the female body is, by definition, a permeable body. See "The Female Body and Religious Practice" in *Fragmentation and Redemption* (New York, 1991), pp. 186–87. While Julian's illness was free of paranormal phenomena, Bynum says, at least so far as we know, her text nevertheless builds on images of a similarly permeable female body .

25. Wolfgang Riehle, *The Middle English Mystics,* tr. Bernard Standring (London, 1981), p. 30.

26. Riehle, p. 96.

27. Benedicta Ward, "Julian the Solitary" in *Julian Reconsidered*, ed. Kenneth Leech and Ward (Oxford, 1988), pp. 25–26.

28. Colledge and Walsh, *Showings*, p. 213, n. 11.

29. *New American Bible*, St. Joseph edition (New York, 1992).

30. Nicholas Watson, "The Trinitarian Hermeneutic in Julian of Norwich's Revelation of Love," *The Medieval Mystical Tradition in England: Exeter Symposium V*, ed. Marion Glasscoe (Oxford, 1992), p. 88.

31. In the Long Text (end of Chapter 4, beginning of Chapter 5), the movement is in the opposite direction, from the Virgin to the hazelnut, but the two remain contiguous as well as associatively linked.

32. This is Bynum's argument in *Fragmentation and Redemption*, esp. pp. 100–14. See also *Holy Feast and Holy Fast*, p. 269 ff.

33. Luce Irigaray, *This Sex Which Is Not One*, tr. Catherine Porter (Ithaca, NY, 1985), p. 106.

34. Colledge and Walsh, *Showings*, p. 734, n. 23.

35. Bynum, *Jesus as Mother*, p. 115.

36. *De inst. incl.*, p. 26.

37. Anselm, *Oratorio ad Sanctum Paulum*, Schmitt, v. 3, pp. 40–41. Translation mine.

38. Sara Ruddick, *Maternal Thinking: Towards a Politics of Peace* (London, 1990), p. 40.

39. Ruddick, p. 49. The tradition according to which Mary gave birth without any of the normal physiological symptoms is another example of birth being "rescued" from the realm of the female.

40. Jennifer P. Heimmel, *"God is our Mother": Julian of Norwich and the Medieval Image of Christian Feminine Divinity* (Salzburg, 1982), p. 51.

41. "Religious women in the later Middle Ages saw in their own female bodies not only a symbol of the humanness of both genders but also a symbol of—and a means of approach to—the humanity of God." Bynum, *Holy Feast and Holy Fast*, p. 296.

42. Marguerite d'Oignt, *Oeuvres*, eds. Antonin Duraffour, P. Gardette, P. Durdilly (Paris, 1965), pp. 77–78. Translation mine.

43. Carol H. Poston, "Childbirth in Literature," *Feminist Studies* 4:18–31, quoted in Marta Weigle, *Creation and Procreation: Feminist Reflections on Mythologies of Cosmogony and Parturition* (Philadelphia, 1989), p. 130.

44. Watson, "Trinitarian Hermeneutic," p. 87.

45. Watson, "Trinitarian Hermeneutic," p. 98.

46. Isidore, *Etymologiarum*, 11.1.77, quoted in Thomas Laqueur, *Making Sex: Body and Gender from the Greeks to Freud* (Cambridge, MA, 1990), p. 36.

47. *AW*, p. 62.

THE INVERTED METAPHOR:
EARTHLY MOTHERING AS *Figura* OF DIVINE LOVE IN JULIAN OF NORWICH'S *Book of Showings*

Andrew Sprung

> *The child-before-the-mother stance was a late medieval strategy to establish a safe field for inquiry into the nature of human desire, will, and perception. For Julian, this field is literally the body of Mother Jesus; since God is "verily" our mother, an earthly mother's teaching, protection, and suffering are imperfect figura of God's absolute nurturance.*

The theme of God's motherhood," writes Caroline Bynum, "is a minor one in all writers of the high Middle Ages except Julian of Norwich."[1] Yet this "minor" theme is part of a network of images, stances, and constructed relationships central to medieval spirituality and epistemology. It is true that Julian alone substantiates or essentializes the idea of *God* as mother—and in no uncertain terms: "As verily as God is our father, as verily is God our mother; and that showed he in all."[2] At the same time, Julian adopts a widespread strategy of spiritual inquiry and self-definition when she declares, "I understood none higher stature in this life than childhood in feebleness and failing of might and of wit in to the time that our gracious mother hath brought us up to our father's bliss" (LT 63, p. 617). This stance of child-before-the-mother is used by major religious and secular writers alike to establish a safe field, overseen by a numinous guarantor, for inquiry into the nature of human desire, will, and perception.

While the emotional keynote of the child-before-the-mother stance is reassurance, the intellectual thrust is toward education, the spiritual growth of the individual. In Julian's understanding of the human condition, falling is, first, a necessary means to knowledge, and second, a lesson that takes place in a kind of baby-proofed spiritual nursery:

> for it needeth us to fall, and it needeth us to see it; for if we fell not, we should not know how feeble and how wretched we be of our self, nor also we should not so fulsomely know the marvelous love of our maker. . . and by the assay of this falling we shall have an high and a marvelous knowing of love in God without end. . . .The mother may suffer the child to fall some time and be diseased in diverse manner, for its own profit, but she may never suffer that any manner of peril come to her child for love (LT 61, pp. 603–04).

The sequence of "showings" that make up Julian's revelation constitutes a safe space into which Julian may retreat at will: she is enjoined to "take it, and learn it, and keep thee therein, and comfort thee therwith, and trust thereto, and thou shalt not be overcome" (LT 70, p. 573). The need to establish such a safe space and the imperative to dramatize an educative process founded, as Julian's is, upon error and correction give shape to major literary forms of the Late Middle Ages: the poem of consolation or confession, the dream vision, the debate. In these framed dialogues, a numinous interlocutor often serves as a kind of special education teacher addressing questions or illustrations toward the particular learning disability of the disordered soul. As Julian puts it, "our good Lord answered to all the questions and doubts that I might make" (LT 31, p. 417).[3]

Julian's motherly teacher works through three modes: " by bodily sight, and by word formed in my understanding, and by ghostly sight" (LT 9, p. 323). Salvific knowledge comes to Julian, that is to say, through gazing upon the mother (all bodily sights are of face and body of Christ), through the voice of the mother, and through a trans-sensual mode, "ghostly sight" that Julian "cannot full tell" but which she represents as sight within sight, face within face, voice within voice. Ghostly sight is represented as "the inward chere" of every showing (LT 19, 52, 55, 71) or as what the Lord said "in his meaning." These modes of working—introjection of both the face and voice of the mother—at once invite psychoanalytic reading and call into question, as Sarah Stanbury has recently done, unmodified application of "the ahistorical assumptions of an ego psychology based on the castration complex."[4]

Stanbury suggests that what she calls a "feminist masterplot" of contemporary criticism, in which a male protagonist defines himself through projection of lack onto a first fetishized and then denigrated female figure, does not fully account for what is being sought in the numerous medieval texts that hinge upon a protagonist's gaze upon a numinous other. Seeing more in such a gaze than a fascinated projection and disavowal of the threat of castration, Stanbury invokes Nancy Chodorow to suggest that castration anxiety screens an earlier "loss of union with the mother"[5] and asserts, "the desire for union with an often metaphoric feminine is in fact central to medieval Christian imagery." In the exchange of gazing between the grieving Pearl-poet and the authoritative Pearl-maiden and in the gaze of the narrator upon the wounded but all-powerful lamb, Stanbury sees neither abjection nor projection of loss but a complex exchange of woundedness, compassion, power and joy.[6]

Julian's double vision of the double *chere* of Christ also entails an exchange of joy and pain, power and lack. Her conjoining of the divine father and mother complicates the Lacanian algebra that, in Stanbury's words, "assumes culture is instituted in Lacan's third term, the Law of the Father or paternal prohibition of mother/son incest."[7] Julian's vision of union with the mother does not violate the incest taboo nor circumvent it but *pre-empts* it in a union that is pre- or trans-sexual: "our saviour is our very mother, in whom we be endlessly born and never shall come out of Him" (LT 57, p. 580).

Perhaps the most difficult aspect of Julian's thought for a twentieth century mind to grasp is her inversion of the "Jesus-as-mother" metaphor. In Julianic assertions such as "our savior is our very mother" and "verily is God our mother," God is tenor, not vehicle. Earthly motherhood, Julian is at pains to demonstrate, is an imperfect *figura* of divine motherhood. Earthly life's *prelude* to individuation, location within the body of the mother, is the promised *end* of ghostly life. Limitations and prohibitions to union with the earthly mother do not apply to "the uniting between God and man's soul" (LT 1, p. 281). Indeed, the aspect of Julian's revelation that she herself finds most troubling, because apparently heretical, might be stated quite plainly in psychoanalytic terms: *there is no Law of the Father.* God "may not forgive, for he may not be wroth"; he may not be wroth because "we worketh ever more his will and his worship duringly without stinting." Nothing "lets" union but sin, but "sin is no-deed" —in some fundamental sense, it *cannot be done*, it does not proceed from or damage the "Godly will that never assenteth to sin" that is present in souls of each of the saved (LT 49, p. 505; LT 44, p. 483; LT 37, p. 443).

At the same time, Julian experiences union in this life as partial and intermittent, suffused with the pain of separation. Julian accords herself the narrator's, the subject's, the hero's privilege of painful progress: her final chapter asserts that "this book. . . is not yet performed" and concludes with a divine exhortation to continued struggle coupled with a promise of ever-increasing knowledge: "hold thee therein, and thou shalt witten and knowen more in the same" (LT 86, p. 733). For Julian, to "hold thee therein" is to locate herself in the alternating current of union and separation. The life cycle of sin and penance, exemplified by Julian's erring struggle to see her revelation as God sees it, describes a perforated line which defines the individual soul without separating her from the mother in whom she is endlessly born.

The core of Julian's vision is of a division: the "blessed heart cloven in two" (LT 24, p. 395). The revelation of this cloven heart follows in the wake of Julian's vision of Christ's "double chere": she enters his side after experiencing the changing of his *chere* from pain to joy. The cloven heart is not simply an emblem of Christ's martyrdom but of his eternal doubleness as "very god and very man," grounded sufferer and joyous overseer. It is this clovenness at the very core of union that gives union an eternal impulse, allowing eternal progress inward. The two *cheres* of God (the *chere* of pain or pity and the *chere* of joy), eternally *oned*, are also eternally cloven, eternally interfacing. This doubleness, redoubled within the person of each of the saved, is literally at the heart of both the divine essence and the human soul in perpetual union with that essence (indeed, this union is what makes the essence double, the heart cloven).[8]

Julian's systaltic movement into and out of God's presence instances a mode of subjectivity in which both lack and plenitude are internalized: God is always here/not here, there/not there, me/not me. In fact Julian projects lack as well as plenitude onto Christ himself—a lack that is figured through the offices and modes of working of Motherhood. For Julian, humanity and divinity suffer reciprocal need, offer mutual fulfillment, and ultimately engender— give birth to—one another. God's motherhood is predicated upon his birth within the souls of the saved: "When Adam fell God's son fell ... into the slade of the maiden's womb" (LT 51, pp. 533–34). This

falling, the Incarnation, is the act through which Christ becomes a
mother: "[because] he would all wholly become our mother in all
thing, he took the ground of his work full low and full mildly in the
maiden's womb" (LT 60, p. 594). The sixteenth showing situates this
enclosure within the souls of the saved: "That worshipful city that
our Lorde Jhesu sitteth in, it is our sensuality, in which he is enclosed"
(LT 56, p. 572). Christ gives birth to us by being born within us.[9]

Both ends of this unitary, reciprocal birthing work through the
gaze, the *oneing* of *cheres*. Stanbury has analyzed the participatory
power of Mary's gaze in those late medieval lyrics that place her in
dialogue with her crucified son, describing, again, an exchange both
of pain and of salvific power.[10] Julian, enacting Mary's experience,
first of Christ's pain, then of his joy, does so through fixing her eyes
upon the crucifix. The focal point of her bodily vision is the *chere* of
Christ; the fulcrum of her ghostly sight is the changing of that *chere*;
and finally, the process of complete union of which the revelation is
a preview is imaged essentially as an act of gazing:

> Glad and merry and sweet is the blessedfull lovely chere of our Lord
> to our souls, for he beheld us ever living in love longing, and he will
> our soul be in glad chere to him, to yield him his mead. And thus I
> hope with his grace he hath and more shall draw the outer chere to
> the inner, and make us all at one with him, and each of us with other
> in true lasting joy that is Jhesu (LT 71, p. 656).

Like Julian's systaltic movement into and out of Christ's body, this
focus on the blissful *chere* of a loving mother can be illuminated by
British psychoanalyst D.W. Winnicott's recasting of the Lacanian
mirror stage as an interaction between mother and infant. Winnicott's
account of this interaction, and of its replay in cultural experience,
provides a striking analogy to Julian's account of her visual and verbal
interaction with God. Winnicott's almost exclusive focus on mother–
child relations may help us to see more clearly medieval strategies
for negotiating desire and loss that differ markedly from our more
worldly, achievement-oriented models.

According to Winnicott, the mother enables her infant's ego
development by fostering the infant's gradual awareness that its
mother is external to itself. The infant begins life totally "oned" to
the mother in its own perception as if the services provided by the
mother are an extension of itself or of its wishes. The mother must
first provide this illusion and then gradually wean the child off of it

by a gradated failure to respond totally to the infant's needs: "The mother's eventual task is gradually to disillusion the infant." [11] Julian's account of the Lord's rapid-fire alternation of absence and presence in the seventh showing provides an analogue and condensed image of this process. After filling Julian with "everlasting sureness, mightily fastened without any painful dread," God leaves her "to my self in heaviness and weariness of my life and irkeness of my self," and then repeats both experiences, "now that one and now that other, diverse times, I suppose about twenty times." Like Winnicott's mother, Julian's God would have his "child" know simultaneously that "he keepeth us ever in like sure, in woe and in weal" and that "for profit of man's soul a man is sometime left to him self" (LT 15, p. 354–55). [12]

Winnicott names *play* as the process by which both infants and adults negotiate the boundary between the self and the external world. This negotiation is a perpetual strain. We begin in and long for union; we must endure separation; we develop autonomy by playing in a "potential space" between internal and external reality. Infants play by adopting "transitional objects," objects which substitute for the mother in her absence and which the infant regards simultaneously as "me/not me." The transitional object, a token at once of the infant's autonomy and of the mother's benevolent oversight, enables the progressive introjection of the maternal presence. In infancy, the object in question is one with which the infant comforts herself bodily: a bit of blanket, her own thumb. Since no human being ever completes the play process—ever succeeds, that is, in regarding anything or anyone external to the self as wholly "not me"—all subsequent object relations replay the original boundary negotiations between self and (m)other. To play is alternately to project power onto such objects and to withdraw it—to construct and deconstruct fictions. In this play at the boundary we simultaneously or alternately regard the external world as within our omnipotent control—fully present—and recognize that it is beyond such control, existent in its own right, and therefore, intermittently at least, absent to us. "The essential feature in the concept of transitional objects and phenomena…is *the paradox, and the acceptance of the paradox*: the baby creates the object, but the object was there waiting to be created and to become a cathected object." [13]

The Shakespearean critic C.L. Barber, translating Winnicott into literary terms, calls the infant's transitional object a "synecdoche" for the mother.[14] The scrap of blanket, substituting for the mother's presence, is like a scrap of the "symbiotic all" of which the mother herself is representative—herself a synecdoche. This formulation is congruent with Julian's repeated reminders that she is seeing, knowing, *oneing* with God *in part*. Julian's images of God, her showings, are figured as synecdoches for the God-mother whom she will see and know in full after death. In this life, we cannot see God's blessed *chere* fully; we cannot *one* without also knowing our separation—that we are "letted" from full union by sin (LT 27, p. 404).

In this condition of imperfect union, the pain of separation is perpetual: the Lord "seeth all our living here to be penance. For kind longing in us to him is a lasting penance in us" (LT 81, p. 715). The showings, as a personal, interior ground of faith, serve as transitional objects, tokens of God's continuing presence that remind Julian simultaneously that she is partly separated from God and that this separation is temporary and in one sense illusory: "Peace and love is ever in us, being and working, but we be not ever in peace and in love" (LT 39, p. 453). Like the faith of which they are both a source and an effect, the showings are something to hold on to, to contemplate, to be renewed by— even to refashion in the light of new understanding. The Lord explictly enjoins Julian to *play* with the revelation—to take "space and tyme to beholde it," "to take hede to all the propertes and the condescions that were shewed" —and also to use it to sustain herself in his (partial or apparent) absence: "take it, and learn it, and kepe thee therein, and comfort thee there with, and trust thereto, and thou shalt not be overcome" (LT 8, p. 318; LT 51, pp. 522–23; LT 70, p. 653).

In one key sense, this object of supreme trust is an opposite rather than an analogue of Winnicott's transitional object, of which Winnicott writes, "its not being the breast (or the mother), although real, is as important as the fact that it stands for the breast (or the mother)."[15] In this world, we are not born *into* our mothers; the transitional object enables a provisional autonomy that Julian does not seek. In short, the object is *not* the mother, whereas for Julian, the showing in a real sense *is* Christ, our "very mother." Yet this opposition is not absolute. While the transitional object is not the mother, it is a token, means, representation of the self's autonomy, of an ability to interact with external reality—an ability engendered by an introjection of the mother's nurturing powers. Julian's Mother Jesus, "ever in us," seated in the soul, hypostatizes this introjected mother and in turn projects "him" outward as an all-encompassing presence, "our clothing, that for love wrappeth us and windeth us." (LT 53, p. 299).

Freud reduces doctrines and images of paradise to reminiscences of prenatal and early infantile experiences of oneness with the world-as-mother's-body. Julian inverts the Freudian analogy: the mother's womb, arms, breast, the playspace she oversees (wherein the child is suffered to fall), are imperfect *figurae* of the "fair blessyd place" at the cloven core of the God-mother's body. Julian plays consciously on the difference between the finite maternal nurturance that is our earliest earthly experience and the infinite provision of divine nurturance that stretches from without-beginning to without-end. Indeed, those few chapters in which Julian explicitly develops a theology of divine motherhood are built rhetorically on a sustained contrast between the earthly and heavenly mother:

> We wit that all our mothers bear us to pain and to dying.
> A, what is that? But our very mother Jehsu, he alone
> beareth us to joy and to endless living (LT 60, p. 595).

> The mother may give her child suck her milk, but our
> precious mother Jhesu, he may feed us with him self, and
> doth full courteously and full tenderly with the blessed
> sacrament, that is precious food of very life (LT 60, p.
> 597).

> The mother may lay her child tenderly to her breast, but
> our tender mother Jhesu, he may homely lead us in to his
> blessed breast by his sweet open side, and show us there
> in part of the Godhead and the joys of heaven, with ghostly
> sureness of endless bliss (LT 60, p. 598).

> The mother may suffer the child to fall some time and be
> diseased in diverse manner, for its own profit, but she
> may never suffer that any manner of peril come to her
> child for love. And though our earthly mother may suffer
> her child to perish, our heavenly mother Jhesu may never
> suffer us that be his children to perish, for he is almighty
> (LT 61, p. 605).

This extended comparison reflects Julian's intense awareness of the limitations of earthly nurturance. Nourishment is not total; union at the breast is not total; protective oversight may fail; even birth-giving itself is provisional. The divine compensation is adjectivally underscored: in contrast to the unmodified or "earthly" mother, Jesus is our "very mother," our "precious mother," our "tender mother," our "heavenly mother."

For Julian as for Winnicott, the process of differentiation from the mother's encompassing presence is necessary on the one hand, painful and dangerous on the other. For Julian, the "singular self" carves an eternal identity by overcoming particular sins and temptations: in heaven, "the token of sin is turned to worship" (LT 38, p. 447). These tokens are individuated: as "diverse sins" are punished with "diverse pains," so are the saved sinners rewarded with "diverse joys" (LT 38, p. 445). Sin is the formative element, marking off self from other and leading to self-knowledge and knowledge of God's love. For Winnicott, aggression plays a very similar role, leading to recognition of the mother's otherness: "it is the destruction of the object that places the object outside the area of the subject's omnipotent control."[16] This impulse is world formative: "it is the destructive drive that creates the quality of externality ... The destructiveness, plus the object's survival of the destruction, places the object outside the area of objects set up by the subject's projective mental mechanisms."[17] The infant accordingly "destroys" the mother "in fantasy" in the instant it recognizes the mother's externality. By "surviving" this attack of fantasy, the mother empowers her child to recognize the externality of objects outside the self. To "survive" is to refrain from retaliating—that is, not "to suffer change in quality, in attitude" in response to the infant's destructive fantasy.[18] For Julian, sin, in light of the ghostly will that never assents to sin, appears as just such a fantasy, or "no-deed." Julian's core insight—potentially heretical but unshakeable—is precisely that God does *not* retaliate. As we have seen, he "may not forgive, for he may not be wroth" (LT 49, p. 505).

In Julian's dialectic, moreover, difference must be posited for union to be experienced. It is God who wills the flow of diversities; it is response to sin that diversifies the community of perfect wills; it is Julian's error that brings on further revelation. Julian spells out a dialectic movement, turn and counter-turn, away from God and back toward him:

He loveth us endlessly, and we sin customably, and he showeth it us full mildly. And then we sorrow and mourn discreetly, turning us in to the beholding of his mercy, cleaving to his love and to his goodness, seeing that he is our medicine, witting that we do but sin (LT 82, p. 718).

Winnicott describes a similar movement at a crucial stage of mother-infant relations that he dubs "the use of an object":

The subject says to the object: "I destroyed you," and the object is there [that is, undestroyed in reality] to receive the communication. From now on the subject says: "Hullo object!" "I destroyed you." "I love you." "You have value for me because of your survival of my destruction of you." "While I am loving you I am all the time destroying you in (unconscious) *fantasy*."[19]

This process, moreover, is the foundation of creative life and once enabled, never ends: it continues "from now on," as does Julian's cycle of "customeable" sin and repentence.

To "survive" an attack of fantasy is to refrain from retaliating—that is, to maintain a loving gaze. The mother's maintenance of what Julian calls a "blessedful lovely chere" is essential, in Winnicott's scenario, because the mother's face is "the precursor of the mirror"—that is, of the provisional self-image of the developing ego. When the mother looks at the infant, "what she looks like is related to what she sees there"; if the mother's face reflects love and acceptance, the infant will develop the ego strength to perform the leap of imagination by which we recognize the existence of objects beyond our omnipotent control.[20] *Chere*, which can mean the face itself, the facial expression, or a person's overall manner,[21] is a more suggestive word in this context than any modern counterpart.[22]

A crucial component of Julian's theology, we have noted, is that God does not have a wrathful *chere*. God's wrath is a projection of our own destructive impulse. God does not "accuse" us; we accuse ourselves. The reality of this projection is "saved" only by God's willing it upon us, as a gesture that will turn us back to him:

For it longeth to man meekly to accuse him self, and it longeth to the proper goodness of our Lord God courteously to excuse man. And these be two parts that were showed in the double chere in which the lord beheld the falling of his loved servant .... Thus will our good Lord that we accuse our self wilfully, and truly see and know...his everlasting love...to see and know both together is the meek accusing that our good Lord asketh of us (LT 52, p. 553).

Given this writing-out of divine wrath, the only remaining element of potential threat or "change" in God's *chere* is its expression of pain—which Julian witnesses and shares in excruciating detail. Crucial to Julian's experience of this pain, and of its transition to bliss, is a recognition that God's *chere* of pain does *not* represent a temporal change—"a change in quality, in attitude." Rather, God's *chere* of pain, like his *chere* of pity, is eternally ex-scribed as the outward *chere*, an eternal part of God, eternally subordinated to the inward:

> That other chere was showed inward, and that was more highly and all one; for the life and the virtue that we have in the lower part [the outward chere] is of the higher, and it cometh down to us of the kind love of the self by grace. Between that one and that other is right nought, for it is all one love, which one blessed love hath now in us double working; for in the lower part be pains and passions, ruths and pities, mercies and forgiveness and such other, which be profitable. But in the higher part be none of these, but all one high love and marvelous joy, in which marvelous joy all pains be wholly destroyed (LT 52, p. 553).

The inward *chere* is always present, always unchanged. The movement from one *chere* to the other, the changeover, takes place within the human subject: we are drawn from the outward *chere* into the inner.

The "double chere," within Christ and within Julian, suggests a divided identity, a split self—precisely the effect, according to Lacan, of the mirror stage of ego formation. According to Lacan, identification with an imago—conscious self-conceptualization—is always alienated, always a "desire of the other." [23] This is certainly the case for Julian, who is "learned to know my self" in contemplating Mary's virtues as well as in her image of Christ-as-Adam. But Julian's self-image is *consciously* split, permanently split. And for Julian, it is the alienation, not the image, that is delusional.

In the Lacanian scenario of ego-genesis, an infant or toddler, "held tightly by some support, human or artificial" receives from the mirror a first image of self as an integrated figure, presumably akin to the more powerful figures surrounding him. The keynote in the process is *anticipation*: the subject is aware, from the start, of a gap between his "turbulent" experience of self and the more integrated image:

> The fact is that the total form of the body by which the subject anticipates in a mirage the maturation of his power is given to him only as *Gestalt*, that is to say, in an exteriority in which this form is

certainly more constituent than constituted, but in which it appears
to him above all in a contrasting size that fixes it and in a symmetry
that inverts it, in contrast with the turbulent movements that the
subject feels are animating him.[24]

In the gap between the "turbulent" self and the "symmetric" imago
with which the child wishfully identifies, there enters a lifelong chain
of identifications, through which the ego undergoes "social
determination, in a fictional direction." With this entry into fictional
conceptualization, a certain preconscious unity with the external
world-as-mother is lost. As Kaja Silverman puts it, "the child makes
its self-discovery through a process of subtraction—through the
understanding that it is what is left when a familiar object (such as
the mother) has been removed...it could almost be said that to the
degree that the object has been lost, the subject has been found."[25]
To find the externality of the object is to posit the autonomous self.
The mother, as numinous guarantor of the questing subject's play, is
the figure of wholeness out of which the subject's identity must be
cut. Yet this cut, for Lacan, establishes a "mirage," an alienated image,
an empty self.

Winnicott pushes this process back into infancy: from the
beginning, there is the mother's specular gaze. Thus, from the
beginning, self-perception is enmeshed with perception of the
(m)other.[26] If the mother's face is the first mirror, its internalized
image could also be called the first transitional object, enabling "the
beginning of a significant exchange with the world, a two-way process
in which self-enrichment alternates with the discovery of meaning
in the world of seen things."[27]

It is just this merging within a mirror image that Julian figures in
the lord-servant parable. In the figure of the servant, Julian's image
of herself-in-Adam is enmeshed with her image of Christ. The
"double" aspect of the image, moreover, bridges the gap between
the experienced self and the projected, ideal self. Julian's fallen servant,
lying in his "slade," is like a comfortless infant, unable to avail himself
of the mother's presence: "he groaneth and moaneth and walloweth
and wryeth, but he may not rise nor help him self by no manner of
way. And of all this the most mischief that I saw him in was failing
of comfort, for he could not turn his face to look up on his loving
lord" (LT 51, p. 515). His bodily experience resembles that of Lacan's
infant, "sunk in motor incapacity," subjected to "turbulent
movements" and a "fragmented body image" : he wallows and

writhes; he may not rise or help himself. The "seven great pains" he suffers include feebleness and blindness, pain and heaviness, and—"most marvelous" to Julian—the perception "that he lay alone" (LT 51, p. 516). The fall, in sum, induces a complete regression precisely because the sustaining *chere* of the lord-mother is hidden: "This man was hurt in his might and made full feeble, and he was [a]stonied in his understanding, for he was turned from the beholding of his lord" (LT 51, p. 522).

Yet this fallen figure is one with the figure of the glorified Christ. Julian pointedly contrasts the outer and inner "sight" of the servant: the simply clad laborer, who cannot stand "even right" before his lord, in his "white kirtle, single, old and all defaulted, dyed with sweat as it should soon be worn up, ready to be ragged and rent" is also the son who "standeth before the father even right richly clothed in blissful largeness, with a crown upon his head of precious richness" (LT 51, pp. 527–28; LT 51, p. 544).

The glorified figure, object of Julian's desire, subject of her self-definition, is in Lacanian terms delusional, alienated: socially determined by "holy church," it contrasts with the real, the known or felt present reality, the "turbulent movements" which could stand as a figure for the workings of the psyche throughout this life. For Julian, these are precisely the grounds for considering this life, in which "we do but sin," the delusion, alienating us from our own ghostly will. From this perspective, the glorified Christ only *appears* alienated: "peace and love is ever in us, being and working, but we be not ever in peace and in love" (LT 39, p. 453). She lays claim to another experiential source, one not fragmented or turbulent: the sight and feeling of the Christ within, of the mother within.[28]

For Julian, moreover, whereas Christ is "ground and head of this fair [human] kind," Christ, the "perfect man," is in turn grounded in, seated in, incarnated in, Adam. The ideal does not cancel out the this-worldly "real" : the ragged, rent kirtle remains a part of the God-man in whom Julian knows herself. The self-image is split: both figures are a part of it. Julian's whole struggle is "to see and know both together."

In this struggle, Julian refuses both self-negation and projection of lack upon a particular group: though she pays lip service to the dogma of the damned, her universe kept by a wrathless God has no real place for them, as they have no place in her vision.[29] Julian deals with lack by standing in the cleft, as it were, of Christ's heart and seeing, on either side of her, a split image: the servant as Adam and the servant as Christ. "The virtue and the goodness that we have is of Jesu Christ, the febleness and blindness that we have is of Adam, which two were showed in the servant" (LT 51, p. 534). This split is in turn mirrored in Julian's ghostly visions of Mary: "Right as I had seen her before, little and simple, right so he showed her then, high and noble and glorious" (LT 25, p. 400). Both images, mirror images of each other, are mirror images for Julian as well: she, as one of the saved, is the Adam who is Christ, and the church who is Mary.[30] For Julian, the splitting of the ego opens up a space for blissful pain, profitable penance, unity-in-division. For this life, Julian's stance is in the breach, where she strives continually to "see and know both together," to know simultaneously the fracture and the unity between both halves of her double vision of a figure who is herself, and all humanity, and God.

In developing the idea of Christ as mother, Julian paradoxically degenders this idea, breaking the binary code of gender upon which our ordinary understanding of "motherhood" is founded.   Rachel Jacoff has noted that Julian does not define God's fatherhood and motherhood oppositionally:

> Since Julian's idea of God does not include a wrathful or finally even a judgmental dimension, she does not need to set the maternal nature of God in opposition to that of the paternal. For her the paternal and maternal are complementary aspects, both protective, loving, and salvific. The fluidity of Julian's language thus both suggests and undercuts traditional gender distinctions.[31]

We might further inquire: when *judgment* is all but factored out, introjected as a shadow of that shadow, sin, what "paternal" element is left to "complement" the "maternal"? In fact, Julian uses no ordinarily gendered imagery at all to figure God: he feeds us from his breast, not his breasts; he leads us into his side, not his womb: his motherhood, insistently crossed with the male pronoun, is neither male nor female.

When the Trinity is reconfigured as father, mother, and holy spirit that is "the even love which is in them both" (LT 51, p. 533), all anthropomorphic imagery takes on equal status as metaphor that offers essential, if partial, correspondence to the divine reality. To posit a double-gendered God is a way to override the binary oppositions of male and female, God and man, to locate both lack and plenitude in both parties and thus to refuse to limit, define, control either party. Such inscription of difference allows for eternal escape, alternately from difference and from nondifferentiation, through the wounded side, in the cloven heart.

NOTES

Many thanks to Tom Hahn, who has read this argument in multiple forms and countless drafts, renewing it with "lightings and touchings" at every stage.

1. Caroline Walker Bynum, *Jesus as Mother: Studies in the Spirituality of the High Middle Ages* (Berkeley, CA, 1982), p. 168.

2. Edmund Colledge and James Walsh, eds., *A Book of Showings to the Anchoress Julian of Norwich*, 2 vols. (Toronto, 1978), 2 (Long Text) 59, p. 590. All passages from Julian's text are cited from this edition, vol. 2, the Long Text (LT), by chapter and page number. I have modernized the spelling and made occasional syntactic adjustments. All emphases in passages cited from Julian's *Book* are mine.

3. John Anthony Burrows notes in *Ricardian Poetry: Chaucer, Gower, Langland and the "Gawain" Poet* (London, 1971), p. 106, the propensity of late fourteenth-century English writers to create narrative personae that "confront the reader with a knowledge of human weakness formed in the confessional." Russell Peck draws an analogy between psychoanalysis and the confessional therapy dramatized in medieval poems of consolation in the introduction of his edition of John Gower's *Confessio Amantis* (New York, 1968), pp. xi–xiv.

4. Sarah Stanbury, "Feminist Masterplots: The Gaze on the Body of *Pearl*'s Dead Girl," in *Feminist Approaches to the Body in Medieval Literature*, eds. Linda Lomperis and Sarah Stanbury (Philadelphia, 1993), p. 105.

5. According to Nancy Chodorow, women do not repress or disavow the desire for maternal union as thoroughly as men do (*The Reproduction of Mothering: Psychoanalysis and the Sociology of Gender* [Berkeley, CA, 1978], Chaps. 7–8, 19).

6. Stanbury, "Masterplots," p. 107.

7. Stanbury, p. 105.

8. Cf. Walter Hilton, *The Goad of Love*, ed. Clare Kirchberger (London, 1952), Chap. 1, p. 49: "at the opening in his side may our heart enter and be joined to his."

9. For discussion of the reciprocity and reversibility that permeate Julian's account of the God/human relationship, see Maud Burnett McInerney's essay in this volume.

10. Sarah Stanbury, "The Virgin's Gaze: Spectacle and Transgression in Middle English Lyrics of the Passion," *Publications of the Modern Language Association*, 106.5 (1991), 1083–93.

11. *Playing and Reality* (New York, 1989), pp. 10–11.

12. Bernard of Clairvaux, *On the Song of Songs II*, trans. Kilian Walsh, vol. 3 (1976) of *The Works of Bernard of Clairvaux*, 7 vols. (Kalamazoo, MI, 1970–80) Sermon 32.2, p. 135, describes a similar rhythm of presence and absence in the visitations of God-as-bridegroom.

13. Donald Woods Winnicott, *Playing and Reality*, p. 89, author's emphasis.

14. C. L. Barber, review of Stephen Booth's *Shakespeare's Sonnets*, *New York Review of Books*, 25 (6 April 1978), p. 36.

15. Winnicott, *Playing*, p. 6.

16. Winnicott, *Playing*, p. 90.

17. Winnicott, *Playing*, pp. 93–94.

18. Winnicott, *Playing*, p. 93.

19. Winnicott, *Playing*, p. 90.

20. Winnicott, *Playing*, pp. 111–12.

21. Hans Kurath and Sherman H. Kuhn, eds., *Middle English Dictionary* (Ann Arbor, 1959).

22. The unchanging *chere* of a maternal figure is a frequent focus of late medieval secular and religious works alike. See the steady, blinding "gladande glory" of the Pearl-maiden's face when she is first glimpsed in the dream-vision (169–84); the obsessive focus in Chaucer's *Clerk's Tale* on Grisilde's "sad visage" and "glade chiere" (Frag. IV, 693, 1045); and the focus on Mary's gaze in a number of lyrics, including no. 182 in Maxwell Luria and Richard L. Hoffman, eds., *Middle English Lyrics* (New York, 1974).

23. Jacques Lacan, *Ecrits. A Selection*, trans. Alan Sheridan (New York, 1977), p. 5.

24. Lacan, *Ecrits*, p. 2.

25. Kaja Silverman, *The Acoustic Mirror. The Female Voice in Psychoanalysis and Cinema* (Bloomington, IN, 1988), p. 7.

26. Jacqueline Rose, in "Introduction—II," *Feminine Sexuality: Jacques Lacan and the Ecôle freudienne*, trans. Juliet Mitchell and J. Rose (New York, 1982), pp. 27–57, criticizes Winnicott for reifying the mirror-image provided by the mother. But Winnicott himself stresses repeatedly the fictional, illusional nature of transitional phenomena (e.g., *The Spontaneous Gesture: Selected Letters of D. W. Winnicott*, ed. F. Robert Rodman [Cambridge, 1987], 43 [to Roger Money-Kyrle, November 27, 1952]). Winnicott, unlike Lacan, regards imagos as playthings, illusions, the fictional nature of which is to be recognized and maintained as paradox, rather than as delusions that must be either overinvested in or deconstructed.

27. Winnicott, *Playing*, p. 113.

28. Freud would equate this experience of presence with the "oceanic feeling," a feeling that he cannot discover in himself and which he reduces to a nostalgic fantasy of infantile or prenatal union with "the external world as a whole." There are, however, no empirical grounds for such a reduction;

see Sigmund Freud, *Civilization and Its Discontents*, trans. James Strachey (New York, 1961), pp. 11–12.

29. It would be worthwhile to trace various strategies employed by religious women for effacing the division between the saved and damned. The thirteenth-century Hadewijch of Brabant seems, in her visions, to suggest a continuity between Hellish, Purgatorial, and Heavenly experience, as if these three "places" are different positions, occupied at some point by every soul (Columba Hart, ed., *Hadewijch: The Complete Works* [New York, 1980], Visions 5 and 6, pp. 276–80, and Vision 11, p. 292). See also Peter Dronke, *Women Writers of the Middle Ages* (Cambridge, 1984), p. 209, for an account of the beliefs of unlettered twelfth-century Provençal women in a damnation-free ultimate existence.

30. Julian explicitly equates "oure moder holy church," traditionally equated with Mary, with Christ himself (LT 61, p. 607), implying that the community of the saved *is* the savior.

Simon Tugwell, in "Julian of Norwich as a Speculative Theologian," *English Mystics Newsletter* 9.4 (1983), 199–209, notes that Julian's virtual equation of Christ's suffering and human sin similarly suggests a Christ who serves as a kind of figure for a composite human identity.

31. Rachel Jacoff, "God as Mother: Julian of Norwich's Theology of Love," *Denver Quarterly* 18.4 (1984), 137. See also Caroline Bynum's claim that women mystics tended less than their male counterparts to oppose the fatherly and motherly aspects of God in "'… And Woman His Humanity': Female Imagery in the Religious Writing of the Later Middle Ages," *Gender and Religion: On the Complexity of Symbols,* eds., Caroline Walker Bynum, Stevan Harrell, and Paula Richman (Boston, 1986), pp. 257–88.

OLD NORSE MOTHERHOOD

Jenny Jochens

The scarcity of affective motherhood in the Old Norse world as evidenced in family sagas and the laws is explained by the phenomena of infanticide, fostering, and illegitimacy. Following a woman's biological career, the evidence is analyzed according to the sex of the offspring, and the question is asked whether affective motherhood was introduced by Christianity.

One morning in the spring of 1011 Ásdís Bárðardóttir accompanies her son Grettir as he leaves home in northern Iceland. Among her four children Ásdís had always "loved Grettir greatly." His father, Ásmundr, however, "did not care much for him." Grettir, now aged fifteen, has been sentenced to three years of exile for manslaughter. Ásmundr has arranged his son's ship passage but provided only meager supplies and no weapons; the two men "separated with little love." Ásdís is embarrassed over Grettir's poor outfitting and gives him a beautiful sword which she has hidden in her clothing. Receiving his thanks, Ásdís wishes him well and returns home. Settling down on board ship, Grettir recites a stanza in which he tells his shipmates that he has been equipped rather shabbily by his father but that Ásdís's gift confirms the "old proverb" (*orðskvið...fornan*), that "the mother is best for the child" (*bezt er barni...móðir*). The captain agrees that it is obvious "that she cared for him the most."[1]

A modern reader might readily understand the mutual love and devotion in the mother-son relationship revealed here, one of several such scenes between Ásdís and Grettir.[2] Since poetry is generally considered to be older than prose, the inclusion of maternal affection in Grettir's stanza and its reinforcement by an "old proverb" suggest that bonding between mother and child was well defined and well articulated in the Norse world by the early eleventh century. This conclusion would probably be premature. Written around 1300 or perhaps a little later, *Grettis saga*, in which this vignette is found, is one of the youngest among the sagas of Icelanders (also known as the family sagas). As in many of these narratives, numerous stanzas are embedded in the prose, more than half (forty-seven) of which are assigned to Grettir. The age of the poetry is always vexing, however, and scholars are of the opinion that *Grettis saga* contains few original stanzas, and the one that the protagonist allegedly recites after having received the sword from his mother is not among them.[3] The prose author not only composed this stanza but incorporated the "ancient proverb" to add credence to its age. At best, mother love as exemplified in this vignette may have been familiar to a fourteenth-century public or perhaps was merely advanced by the author.

This conjecture is based on the observation that Ásdís and Grettir represent a rare case in the Old Norse corpus of a devoted mother and son in the manner of, for example, Augustine, the church father, and his mother Monica. In fact, motherhood and mothers' relations with their children are subjects that receive scant attention in the sagas. It is easier, for example, to demonstrate paternal pride in children and fathers' grief over their loss.[4] When mothers are included in the narratives, they are more likely to be callous or indifferent, an attitude I shall illustrate by an episode in an older text that occurred allegedly a generation earlier and about thirty miles from where Ásdís gave Grettir the sword.

About 980 Þuríðr takes her one-year-old daughter Gróa out of bed in the middle of the night and sails with her and a few men to an island where her husband, Geirmundr, is becalmed, waiting for winds to carry him back to his native Norway. Two weeks earlier, Geirmundr had abandoned Þuríðr, his wife of three years, refusing to leave funds for her and their daughter. Þuríðr orders her men to render Geirmundr's dingy unseaworthy and boards his ship while all are asleep. Finding her husband in a hammock, she places their daughter next to him, removes his sword, and departs. When the girl starts to cry, Geirmundr wakes up, reaches for his sword, and orders his men to pursue in the dingy, an attempt which Þuríðr's forethought foils. Calling out to his wife, Geirmundr at first offers both daughter and money in return for the sword, but when Þuríðr refuses, he places a curse on it which will haunt her family for generations. Geirmundr, Gróa, and the entire crew, however, perish on their way to Norway.[5]

The paucity of Old Norse evidence on motherhood, the frequency of callous attitudes such as Þuríðr's, and the scarcity of acts of devotion like Ásdís's square with the conclusion reached by recent scholarship, that love and self-sacrifice (beyond the demands imposed by biology) are not universal and "essential" features of maternal behavior; rather, motherhood is a social construct varying with culture and time.

It can be argued that Christianity became the most potent force in shaping western attitudes of motherhood, but a full appreciation of the new religion's role on this issue as on so many others is possible only if its influence can be contrasted with that of the previous pagan culture.[6] Although the Norse texts that depict paganism were not inscribed until the thirteenth century and thus were exposed to unavoidable Christian mediation by authors and scribes, they nonetheless present the fullest evidence of the pre-Christian culture. Because of affinities among the entire Germanic peoples, conclusions reached about the Norse may perhaps be applied to the Anglo-Saxons and continental Germanic tribes as well, among whom pre-Christian evidence is even more scarce.

It is, of course, impossible to determine whether the paucity of information on affective Norse motherhood reflects deficiency of mothers' feelings, inability of women to articulate their emotions, or, equally plausible, the disinterest by male authors to include maternal expressions in their narratives. Before examining in greater detail the evidence available concerning Norse motherhood, I shall nonetheless face this absence and try to account for it or its lack of articulation.

It deserves remembering that Germanic religion—best known from Norse sources—contains no exemplary model of a loving mother-child couple such as the Christian Mary and Jesus or the oriental Isis and Horus.[7] Among human women, furthermore, Germanic myth preserves the image of a mother (Guðrún) who personally killed or at least was responsible for the death of her young son or sons, a deed committed in order to convince her husband that his own subsequent death at her hand would not be avenged.[8] Most important, pagan society contained three features that—if not unique to the north—were at least more pronounced and ingrained than elsewhere in Europe and which may have restrained or deferred the mother-child bonding which the modern world finds natural. They include infanticide, fostering, and illegitimacy.

INFANTICIDE

In the Norse world, mere birth was not enough to guarantee an individual's life.[9] Of equal importance was the father's acceptance of the infant. The Norwegian laws state categorically that "every child must have a father."[10] Immediately after birth the baby "was carried" (*borinn*) to the man in a formal ceremony that determined its fate.[11] A child not yet presented in this way was "un-carried" (*úborinn*), a condition fraught with serious legal consequences. Examining the infant, the father looked for family resemblances; if he liked what he saw, he accepted paternity, gave the child a name chosen from notable but deceased members of the family on either side, sprinkled it with water, and allowed it be returned to the mother for its first feeding.[12] If the man did not accept the child it "was carried out" (*út borinn*), that is, it was exposed out of doors and left to die in the harsh climate. In other words, at the broad level of free people, not even a married woman who had carried her pregnancy to term was assured that she could keep her child. More difficult was the situation of mistresses who were numerous in Norse society in both pagan and Christian times. If a man already possessed healthy heirs by his wife, he might not be willing to accept these spurious offspring. A first requisite for a mistress was to be near the putative father when her term arrived, even when he was constantly on the move, as was occasionally reported in the narratives.[13] A female slave might at times be allowed to keep her child, especially if she had been impregnated by her master, but doubtlessly most such offspring were exposed.[14]

Although it is self-evident, the point needs to be made that infanticide is of particular concern to women. Nine months' pregnancy—involving discomfort, nausea, and restricted movement under the best of circumstances and culminating in a painful, prolonged, and at times dangerous delivery—increased the mother's involvement in the baby over the father's. In the pagan world, however, a woman could not be certain of keeping her child. Furthermore, if the infant was exposed, she would have to recover faster after parturition than if she had kept it, since the intermittent respite provided by nursing was replaced by an immediate return to full-time work despite her aching, bleeding, and lactating body. That exposure was most often inflicted on infants of the mother's own sex may have exacerbated her pain. The sagas of Icelanders report six cases of exposure of infants, three of which were decided by the husband, two by brothers, and one by the wife for the child of her husband's mistress. Depicting the Nordic context, the kings' sagas and the heroic sagas each contain a single incident. In all eight occurrences the child was found and saved, a fact which doubtlessly caused the story to be recorded.[15] That fatal exposure of children was linked with pagan observance is clear, however, from another narrative in which it was suggested that "children be exposed and old people killed" in order to improve the weather.[16]

The clearest evidence of pagan infanticide emerges from the historical accounts that record the peaceful acceptance of Christianity by the *althing* in Iceland in the year 1000. Among them the oldest and most trustworthy is the historian Ari Þorgilsson's written about 1125. Relying on reports from people whose close relatives had been present at the event, Ari stated:

> It became established in law that everybody should be Christian and undergo baptism. . . . but concerning child exposure (*barnaútbuðr*) and the eating of horse meat (*hrossakjǫtsát*) the old law should remain valid. People could sacrifice (*blóta*) in secret if they wished . . . . But after a few years this heathenism was abolished like the rest.[17]

Clearly, infanticide was abolished under the influence of Christianity. In Iceland the process was accomplished with relative ease. Sometime during the decade 1122–33 the so-called Christian law was appended as a preamble to the secular law which had been committed to writing in 1117, and the combined result became known as *Grágás* (Grey Goose). Its two existing versions open with a declaration of faith followed by the statement that "every child that is born is to be brought for baptism at the first opportunity, however deformed it may be."[18] If observed, this clause would assure the conversion of the entire population in one generation and preclude infanticide as well.

The process was slower and more difficult in Norway, however, where laws continued to bristle with prohibitions throughout the medieval period, suggesting that infanticide persisted.[19] In pagan times the decision to expose a newborn had been a paternal privilege. Accompanying the ecclesiastical efforts to abolish exposure, however, the practice was transformed into a female crime. Churchmen were the first to accuse women of killing infants. A late twelfth-century law enacted a procedure for the bishop's official to follow if a woman had exposed (*sleget utt*) her child. Only an oath from the parturient woman's helper that the child was stillborn would save her from a fine.[20] Another law is more explicit:

> If the child has died when people return to her [the mother] and they can determine by marks, by hands or by bands, that the child has been strangled or suffocated, and if she is conscious, then she is the murderer of her child. She is to forfeit her property and peace in the country as well as her chattel. She must go to a pagan country and never live where Christian people are. The murder of a pagan is worse than the murder of a Christian because the soul of a person who dies a pagan is lost.[21]

Churchmen themselves may have been responsible for bringing about conditions that caused women to act in this way. Obvious to any mother, the first bonding with the child occurs during pregnancy. In the Old Norse world, however, the father's preponderant role in the newborn's fate, in particular the distinct possibility that he might order its exposure, may have inhibited women from emotional attachment to their children during pregnancy; furthermore, the experience of having had one infant killed may have rendered bonding with subsequent children more difficult.

FOSTERING

Even when a woman was allowed to keep her child, the period of mother-child bonding was often cut short because of the institution of fostering. I am not concerned here with the fostering arranged in cases of parental death or poverty which was part of Iceland's remarkable system of social welfare. In addition, the Norse peoples created another system of fosterage—perhaps Irish in inspiration— not prompted by economic necessity but by the wish to provide the child with social networks outside its biological kin, similar to the Christian system of god-parentage.[22] Fosterage was found mainly among royalty and other well-to-do parents. In these circles fathers frequently accepted offers from men belonging to a lower social class to foster their children, a service for which remuneration was established by law.[23] Fostering was so common that the remark that "all the children grew up at home" was offered as an unusual occurrence.[24] Childless couples could also make the foster child their heir. Normally a child lived with the foster family between the age of eight and sixteen, but occasionally infants as young as one year were sent away from home, as in the case of Halldórr Óláfsson who was fostered by the old Bersi at this age and to whom I shall return.[25]

I shall limit myself to those features of fostering that involve bonding between mother and child. To the modern reader, the most surprising cases may be those in which "for her comfort" (*til hugganar*) a well-off young widow was offered—and accepted—a proposal of fostering her infant; thus Guðrún welcomed a proposition to have her son fostered immediately after his birth shortly after her husband's death, and Hrefna gave up her baby boy of a few months after her husband was killed.[26] In addition to economic security, fosterage also provided ties as binding as blood relations. In this way the sons obtained new networks of kin relations, but bonding with the mother was most often precluded, and—most surprising to the modern reader—she did not seem to have desired her son's company. It is plausible that the customary waiting for and uncertainty about the father's acceptance had conditioned mothers to abandon their infants willingly under other circumstances as well. A new attitude is discernible, however, in the grieving widow Dalla in a late text who asks for (and is given) her husband's six-year-old cousin to foster, because—as she explains—she will receive comfort from living with someone related to her husband.[27]

One may wonder whether the constant option that a child be sent away for fostering prevented the development of what modern society considers normal mother-child bonding. Invariably, the father made decisions of fosterage and little is known of the mother's wishes. As a rare exception, Hǫskuldr proposes to his former mistress, Melkorka, that their seven-year-old son, Óláfr, be sent to the "old and childless" Þórðr whose wife has just left him. Melkorka's displeasure, however, is not affective but social, since she does not consider Þórðr of sufficiently high standing for her son. She acquiesces, nonetheless, when Hǫskuldr holds out the likelihood that Þórðr will pass his fortune on to Óláfr. Þórðr lives nearby, and Hǫskuldr also consoles her that she will be able to visit the boy whenever she wants.[28] In this case Melkorka remains close to her son, but other mothers were less fortunate because their young children were taken far away from home. Thus, in 1181 the father of

the three-year-old Snorri Sturluson brings the boy from the parental
home, Hvammur, in northern Iceland to Oddi in the southern part
where he is placed in fosterage with Jón Loptsson. Snorri may not
have seen his mother until his wedding sixteen years later.[29] Since
Jón lived at Oddi with both his wife and a mistress, the young boy
may have received loving female attention assumed necessary for a
child's normal development in modern society, but other children
were less lucky in this regard. The old and childless Hróar offers to
foster Geitir's six-year-old son Þiðrandi, promising the father that
the boy will become his heir and Geitir will thus be able to reserve
his own inheritance for his older son. One may wonder about
Þiðrandi's feelings when he leaves home and his adjustment at Hróar's
place, but the author assures his readers that after he has been there
for a while "it was clear to everybody that Hróar loved him very
much."[30]

The pervasive male focus of saga authors is undoubtedly the reason
that more boys than girls are reported as being fostered away from
home. A few cases indicate, however, that it also happened to girls.[31]
Nonetheless, it was more common that a foster mother (fóstra) or—
occasionally—a foster father (fóstri) were brought to the farm and
given responsibility for a girl. Likewise, boys who remained at home
were also raised by a fóstra or fóstri. A life-long bonding often
developed between the foster father or mother and his or her charge.[32]
Again, the authorial male focus attributes greater importance to foster
fathers than foster mothers, but nonetheless, foster mothers are also
in evidence. The mutual devotion between the twelve-year-old Egill
and his foster mother, Þorgerðr, is thus obvious when she, trying to
divert his father's anger from him, sacrifices her life and he in return
kills his father's favorite workman.[33] Occasionally a woman would
bring her own fóstra with her in her marriage and have the older
woman raise her own children in due course.[34]

These scattered vignettes suggest that a foster mother was often
emotionally closer to the child she was raising than the mother herself,
even when both women were present on the farm. If women
frequently shared their own children with foster mothers, they also
received foster children to care for. When foster parents lacked
children of their own, they allowed their charges to assume the
affective role of biological children. It is difficult to find a more
loving parental relationship than the one between Gísli and his wife,

Auðr, and their two foster children, Geirmundr and Guðríðr, whom they are raising because the children lack others to care for them (they are *úmegð*). The girl (Guðríðr) stays with Gísli and Auðr until Gísli is killed. She and her brother go with Auðr to Norway where they eventually marry.[35] When mothers kept their own children at home, they seemed to have accepted foster children with love: when Óláfr offers to foster Bolli, his half-brother's three-year-old son, his wife "Þorgerðr received him well. . . and they (Óláfr and Þorgerðr) loved him no less than their own children."[36] The reality or possibility of having children sent away for fostering at a tender age and/or the sharing with hired foster parents the affection of those children who remained at home may, therefore, have caused mothers to develop weak maternal bonding. On the other hand, women who received foster children themselves on their farms or who were hired to care for the children of others, often developed life-long affective attachments to people to whom they were not related.[37]

ILLEGITIMACY

Although pagan society had institutionalized monogamy and privileged legitimate over illegitimate heirs long before the arrival of Christianity, Nordic men engaged in extramarital affairs with slaves and servants whose offspring were often disposed of through infanticide. Slaves eventually disappeared and churchmen preached marital fidelity, but men continued their ingrained sexual habits into the Christian era as they lived openly with mistresses, at times ignoring marriage altogether, and procreating with servants.[38] Since the Christian prohibition against infanticide was generally accepted, it became impossible to dispose of illegitimate children through exposure, thus mandating their accommodation in law and social practice.

The persistence of illegitimate births had as a result that the man's recognition of paternity remained essential into the Christian period, because the father was economically responsible for the child until age sixteen. If he refused paternity, the child became the responsibility of the mother and her family. The concern was therefore not only the woman's but also that of her own native family. In Iceland, the law obligated a pregnant unmarried woman to identify the impregnator to her father or other guardian. If she refused, her guardian was required to return with five neighbors and together they were to "torture her," without leaving wounds or blue marks, until she revealed the name.[39] In Norway law makers exploited the woman's vulnerability during labor. Her guardian was to stand in the door to her room at the commencement of labor and order her to disclose the name of the child's father.[40]

Frustrated in their efforts to impose monogamy and fidelity, churchmen began to place the burden for sexual transgressions on the most accessible and visible object, a pregnant unmarried woman. In ecclesiastical legislation and fulminations from the pulpit, women were assigned responsibility for male transgressions of the Christian sexual code. In contrast to the pagan tradition, women were now assumed to be initiators of sexual relations, even seducing churchmen into breaking their vows of chastity. Unmarried women were not granted the lighted candle with which a new mother was honored when she was readmitted to church after her confinement. When a mistress fell ill, she was refused the last sacrament.[41] It is no wonder, perhaps, that a few mothers did away with their illegitimate children as suggested by the Norwegian law mentioned earlier. Fear of childbirth itself, mounting attacks from priests against illegitimacy, and perhaps, as a last resort, wishful thinking find touching expression in stories of miracles in which the Virgin Mary or one of the Icelandic saints offered help to unmarried women in difficult births, at times removing the child or even disposing of the mother's soiled clothing.[42]

Among the three problems I have examined, fosterage remained unchanged from pagan into Christian times, and it may have discouraged maternal bonding with children. Churchmen succeeded in abolishing pagan infanticide, thus eliminating another reason for women's apprehension about motherhood. Ironically, however, the persistance of extramarital relations—despite churchmen's promotion of marital fidelity—resulted in illegitimacy becoming a more visible and serious problem in Christian times than it had been during paganism. It may have increased the anxiety of unmarried pregnant women and perhaps prompted some of them to do away with newborns. In other words, throughout pagan and Christian times, serious obstacles inhibited the easy and spontaneous growth of maternal bonding in the north.

OLD NORSE MOTHERS

Having examined reasons that might explain the paucity of information about Old Norse motherhood, I now turn to the scanty evidence. As far as possible I shall attempt to proceed according to the biological framework and follow a mother from the stage of pregnancy through old age.[43] The condition of a woman being pregnant is most often signaled by the term that "she was not well" or "she was not alone."[44] It is rare to find as detailed a description as the one the unmarried Friðgerðr offered of herself to her employer: "As you know I have demonstrated here that I can work hard, but now it has become more difficult for me because I am growing larger and I have trouble walking. I have not needed help from others before, but now I seem to be needing assistance the way things are going, because I am pregnant."[45] Despite Friðgerðr's protestations, women appear to have worked up to the last minute before giving birth and their condition did not prevent travel.[46] The birth itself was expressed by the term that the woman "became lighter." What little is revealed about the birth process itself suggests that delivery techniques were universal and changed little over time. Only women were present. The normal position was for the woman to kneel on the floor, with helpers ready at her knees or supporting her arms. As the birth progressed, she would shift to a knee-elbow position, and the child would be received from behind.

Although evidence is scarce, it seems clear that women in ancient and medieval Iceland nursed their babies.[47] Churchmen appear to have understood women's special dietary needs and exempted pregnant women and nursing mothers from fasting during the first Lent after delivery; if they nursed for two more Lenten periods, they were expected to fast.[48] These rules suggest a nursing period of two to two-and-a-half years, and, in fact, a late narrative reports that a mother weaned her two-year-old daughter before undertaking a long journey.[49] Tacitus had already praised Germanic mothers for nursing their babies. For children to receive their first nourishment from lactating women—mothers and wet-nurses—has been the norm in all traditional societies until modern technology provided other options. At some point during the late Middle Ages, however, Icelandic mothers came to consider their own milk inferior and ceased to nurse. Instead they fed their infants cows' milk and even cream and gave them meat and fish, pre-chewed and thinned with melted butter from the third or fourth month. The result was an extremely high infant mortality which received international attention in the seventeenth century when it was described by foreign visitors who quickly identified malnutrition as the cause.[50]

I wish to return to ancient and medieval Iceland and examine mothers' relations with children as these grew up. The observation about Þórólfr, Skalla-Grímr and Bera's first son who survived after "many children had died in infancy," that "both father and mother loved him dearly" is unusual.[51] As illustrated by Grettir's example, parents usually paired off with their children as mothers felt closer to boys and fathers to girls.[52] In the following I shall therefore divide the evidence from the saga narratives by the gender of the children.

MOTHERS AND DAUGHTERS

Information about mothers and daughters—not to speak about a loving relationship—is extremely rare. As an apparent exception, it is worth noticing the brief acquaintance between Jófríðr and her infant daughter. Before his departure, Þorsteinn orders his pregnant wife to expose their child if it is a girl. Immediately after the birth of an unusually beautiful girl, Jófríðr remarks that "I look with such love at this child that I cannot bear to have it exposed."[53] Defying her husband, she has the girl brought to her sister-in-law who names her Helga, raises her, and reveals her identity to Þorsteinn six years later. Although he accepts his daughter and brings her back home, no further evidence of Jófríðr's relationship with Helga has survived. The story seems to have been prompted by the girl's exceptional beauty.[54] *Egils saga* contains a vignette that reveals at least a brusque kind of intimacy between a mother and her ten-year-old daughter. Entertaining Egill and his party, a Swedish host pretends to have nothing but the ubiquitous curds (*skyr*) to serve. While the guests are eating, the daughter is playing on the floor. The mother summons her and in a whisper orders her to tell Egill that better fare is available. The father becomes annoyed and slaps the girl but orders better food and drink to be brought out. The result is one of the worst drunken brawls in saga literature; the next day mother and daughter are obliged to persuade Egill not to kill their husband and father.[55] *Víglundar saga*, a late text, contains the arresting story of the relationship between a mother and her daughter which fits my opening example of Þuríðr and Gróa. Þorbjǫrg cares so little for her daughter Ketilríðr that she even refuses to teach her needlework. Her husband lets the girl be fostered at the neighboring farm where she not only learns the skill but also falls in love with the son. When her mother becomes aware of this, she orders her to return and tries to force the girl to marry older suitors of her choice.[56]

These examples represent the available evidence of mothers' affections for daughters among the numerous families recorded in the vast saga literature. Even less evidence has surfaced of daughters' love for mothers; at best the texts occasionally mention grown women's fondness for their old foster mothers. Leaving this meager harvest of mother-daughter relations, I shall turn to evidence of mothers and sons.

MOTHERS AND SONS

In the patriarchal tenor of the sagas, boys were more valued than girls. It is not surprising, therefore, that daughters are absent and more information survives on mothers and sons. Grettir was not the only son to be loved better by his mother than by his father. A similar statement is made about Þorsteinn Egilsson.[57] The common authorial remark that a father "did not care much for his son" induces the reader to expect a positive statement about the mother's love.[58] Even when such feelings were not articulated, however, authors were able to show the differences between paternal and maternal feelings. Egill's father was critical toward him throughout his life, but his mother showed him her affection. When Egill has killed a man—at the age of six—his father is far from pleased, but his mother declares that he is "viking-material" and will soon be ready for a ship.[59] Perhaps the most touching mother-son relationship is the story of the Irish slave Melkorka and her son Óláfr. Of royal origin, Melkorka copes with her enslavement by pretending to be mute. Having given birth to her master's son, she secretly teaches him to speak Irish. When he eventually is fostered nearby they retain a close relationship.[60]

A group of mothers went to great pains to protect their sons from death and persecution during infancy and youth. They include women who had produced royal sons but whose husbands or lovers had died. Ástríðr gives birth to Óláfr Tryggvason in secret after her husband's death, and she keeps the child hidden during his first three years. Ásta is pregnant with Óláfr *helgi* (St. Óláfr) when her husband leaves her for another woman, and she gives birth after his death (both mid-tenth century).[61] Among the women in the sagas of Icelanders, Helga saves her four- and eight-year- old sons by helping them swim across a sizeable sound.[62] Although it may be presumed that these women loved their sons, the stories were undoubtedly preserved to prepare for the men's future glory. Too much intimacy with a mother and female affairs was not recommended, as seen in the story of a young man who is being chided for having wasted his time discussing cooking with his mother.[63]

Since saga women were portrayed with particular prominence in the two areas of magic and inciting, it is not surprising that mothers engaged with their sons in these activities.[64] If knowledgeable in magic, mothers (and foster mothers) instructed their sons in the art and used their expertise directly by protecting them in battle with magical clothing or by stroking their bodies.[65] Female magic, however, was not as common as female inciting. Among the ubiquitous inciting women found in the sagas of Icelanders I shall single out the sizeable group of mothers who goaded their sons, both as young boys and grown men.[66] In the first group the most famous case involved Guðrún's inciting of her two sons aged twelve and sixteen. Having preserved for twelve years the blood-drenched clothes in which her husband Bolli has been killed, Guðrún finally spreads them out on the ground, summons her sons, and urges them to avenge their father. In a swift action they comply, killing the man who has given their father his death blow.[67] More common is the situation where a mother urged grown sons to take action. One woman not only used words but also slaps one of her sons, serves a symbolic meal of enormous pieces of meat and stones as a reminder of the need for revenge, and insists on joining the band herself.[68] Although in this case the sons are able to prevent the mother from witnessing the action, in another, a mother—Þorgerðr who has encouraged revenge on Bolli for his share in the murder of her son Kjartan—accompanies her four remaining sons on the journey, enters the hut where they are attacking Bolli, and urges them to finish the task.[69]

This story contains features of interest to my subject. The leader of the brothers is Halldórr, the boy who has been sent away to be fostered at the age of one.[70] From another narrative it is known that he later names his own son Bersi after his foster father, suggesting their good relationship.[71] Halldórr returns home during his youth, and after his father's death he takes over the paternal farm where his mother continues to live. Like his father, Halldórr is a peace-loving man, but he is unable to resist his mother's repeated whetting concerning Kjartan. In other words, although Halldórr had lived with his foster father long enough to form a close relationship, his absence from home had not obstructed the usual bonding between mother and son that allowed her to incite him as an adult. It will also be recalled that the object of Þorgerðr's anger is the same Bolli whom she thirty years earlier "received well...and loved no less than [her] other children."[72] Þorgerðr's whetting is not caused by grief over Kjartan's loss, however, and the scene does not illustrate the victory of biological motherhood over attachment to a foster child but rather a preoccupation with honor and its reparation in revenge to which authors attributed a specifically female signature in their narratives. Þorgerðr knew the price she might have to pay for inciting her remaining sons. Bolli's sons in turn seek revenge, as mentioned, and after they have killed the man most responsible for their father's slaying, they are ready to move against Þorgerðr's remaining sons. Only a negotiated settlement and heavy fines prevent further bloodshed, which could have eliminated Þorgerðr's family.[73]

These consequences are demonstrated with remarkable clarity in *Brennu-Njáls saga*, the most splendid of the sagas of Icelanders, which has received numerous interpretations. For my purpose here it is of interest to note that the saga can be read as the disastrous consequences of the brusque way Bergþóra, Njálls wife, treats Hallgerðr, an invited guest, when she asks her to cede her place at the dinner table for Bergþóra's daughter-in-law who arrives late.[74] Hallgerðr and Bergþóra first trade insults and then proceed to engineer three sets of stylized killings in each other's households. When Bergþóra's side has suffered the third killing and Hallgerðr has added verbal insults, Bergþóra whets her sons to revenge. As the feud escalates, she incites them on two more occasions.[75] The victims slain in return for the killings provoked by Bergþóra's whetting include Hǫskuldr, Njálls illegitimate son. In the end—when the enemies of Bergþóra's sons burn their farm—Bergþóra and Njáll, their three sons, and only grandson perish in the fire together with many members of the household. The entire reproductive efforts of Bergþóra and Njáll thus came to naught as a result of her goading.[76]

Undoubtedly, mothers maintained close—if not loving—relations with their sons. A man's debt to his mother was acknowledged in law as he was made responsible for maintaining her if she needed it, even by going into debt if necessary. Although a mother was only fifth in line to inherit from her offspring, her reproductive efforts were rewarded, as the law secured her maintenance by her children if she became destitute.[77] A short narrative confirms this stipulation by relating that before departing from Iceland, a man leaves his mother enough money to support her for three years; when the time expires, he returns—despite tempting offers from kings—to prevent her from becoming a beggar.[78]

To sum up, the Norse material which most faithfully preserves the pagan tradition reveals a certain distance and coolness between mothers and children. That this attitude is an original and purduring feature of motherhood in the Norse world is suggested by the continued existence of Grýla, an ancient figure from folklore representing an ugly, ravenous mother. Coming down from the mountains every year at Christmas time, Grýla terrorizes Icelandic children under the age of six as she searches for badly behaved children, bundling them into her sack and abducting them.[79] In late saga narratives, however, a few features suggest more familiar aspects of mother-child bonding: the devoted relationship between Ásdís and Grettir, a mother grieving over the loss of children, and a widow who found comfort in the company of a child related to her husband.[80]

In conclusion I need to call attention to another body of Norse literature explicitly shaped by Christianity: the lives of Icelandic bishops and collections of miracles which they allegedly performed. The material is not large, but these texts reveal brief glimpses of mothers who were devoted to their children. The mother of the future Bishop Þorlákr, for example, taught him history and genealogy. Ordinary mothers (and fathers) showed concern for their children, took care of them in illness, prayed for them, and grieved over them when they disappeared or died. If space permitted a close analysis, it would reveal Christian attitudes well known from the continent. The interpretation of this new Christian evidence, however, is extremely problematic. It might be argued, on the one hand, that the everyday life portrayed in these miracle stories had not changed greatly over time and that the maternal bonding portrayed in these texts applied not only to medieval but also to pagan times. Passed over in silence by the relentlessly patriarchal bias of the saga authors, mother love might have been present in the saga age but unarticulated in the texts. An alternate explanation could suggest that the parental affection, modeled on Mary and Jesus, which is found in the miracle stories was new and sponsored by the Christian clergy. Eventually this attitude made inroads on some of the later narratives that portrayed ancient times, as witnessed in the initial story of Ásdís and Grettir. Whereas the surviving evidence seems to favor the latter explanation, it remains plausible that both trends were present.

NOTES

1. *Grettis saga Ásmundarsonar*, ed. Guðni Jónsson, *Íslenzk fornrit* 7 (Reykjavík, 1936), pp. 36, 49–50. On proverbs, see Hermann Pálsson, *Úr hugmyndaheimi Hrafnkels sögu og Grettlu*. Studia Islandica 39 (Reykjavík, 1981). Hermann does not discuss this proverb.

2. For further illustrations, see *Grettis saga*, pp. 38, 41, 153, 155–56, 209–10.

3. *Grettis saga* might be included among the so-called skalds' sagas; see Laurence de Looze, "The Outlaw Poet, the Poetic Outlaw: Self-Consciousness in *Grettis saga Ásmundarsonar*," *Arkiv for nordisk filologi* 106 (1991), 85–103.

4. A rare exception is found in a late narrative; when Ragnheiðr's two young sons (age three and five) have been killed, she is inconsolable, takes to her bed, and dies of grief: see *Finnboga saga* in *Kjalnesinga saga*, ed. Jóhannes Halldórsson, *Íslenzk fornrit* 14 (Reykjavík, 1959), pp. 299–300.

5. *Laxdæla saga*, ed. Einar Ól. Sveinsson, *Íslenzk fornrit* 5 (Reykjavík, 1934), pp. 80–83.

6. For an analysis of western motherhood, see Clarissa W. Atkinson, *The Oldest Vocation: Christian Motherhood in the Middle Ages* (Ithaca, NY, 1991).

7. The only evidence of maternal love is Frigg's relations with her grown son Baldr; see Snorri Sturluson, *Gylfaginning*, ed. Anthony Faulkes (Oxford, 1982), pp. 45–46.

8. In the various versions of the Nibelung story the woman is named Guðrún (Eddic poetry), Grímhildr (*Þiðreks saga*), or Kriemhilt (*Nibelungenlied*).

9. For a longer version of this section, see Jenny Jochens, *Women in Old Norse Society* (Ithaca, 1995), chap. 3. Used with permission of the publisher, Cornell University Press.

10. See, for example, *Norges gamle love*, 5 vols., ed. R. Keyser, P.A. Munch (Christiania [Oslo] 1846–95), 1:130.

11. On the importance of the ceremony, see Vilhelm Grönbech, *The Culture of the Teutons*, 2 vols., trans. W. Worster (London, 1931), 1:291–300.

12. Among many illustrations, see *Vatnsdœla saga*, ed. Einar Ól. Sveinsson, *Íslenzk fornrit* 8 (Reykjavík, 1939), pp. 36–37.

13. For illustrations, see Jochens, *Women*, chap. 3.

14. See the exceptional case of the slave Melkorka; her prominent master accepted their son because of his good looks; *Laxdœla saga*, p. 27. Occasionally a child born by a servant to a widower would be accepted by his new wife but the mother would be sent away; see *Fljótsdœla saga*, in *Austfirðinga sǫgur*, ed. Jón Jóhannesson, *Íslenzk fornrit* 11 (Reykjavík, 1950), pp. 237–40.

15. See the discussion between John Boswell and Carol Clover as reported in the latter's "The Politics of Scarcity: Notes on the Sex Ratio in Old Norse Society," *Scandinavian Studies* 60 (1988), 147–88, esp. 150–59. The cases are identified in this article.

16. *Reykdœla saga*, in *Ljósvetninga saga*, ed Björn Sigfússon, *Íslenzk fornrit* 10 (Reykjavík, 1940), pp. 169–70.

17. *Íslendingabók. Landnámabók*, ed. Jakob Benediktsson, *Íslenzk fornrit* 1 (Reykjavík, 1968) p. 17.

18. *Gragas: Lagasafn islenska þjóðveldisins*, eds. Gunnar Karlsson, Kristján Sveinsson, Mörður Árnason (Reykjavík, 1992), p. 1. Translation in *Laws of Early Iceland* 1, trans. Andrew Dennis, Peter Foote, Richard Perkins (Winnipeg, 1980), p. 23.

19. For illustrations and a possible explanation for the difference, see Jochens, *Women*, chap. 3.

20. *Norges gamle love*, 1:303.

21. *Norges gamle love*, 1:340.

22. For possible Irish influence, see Gerd Kreutzer, *Kindheit und Jugend in der altnordischen Literatur. Teil 1. Schwangerschaft, Geburt und früheste Kindheit* (Münster, 1987), pp. 221–34. On god-parentage, see Joseph H. Lynch, *Godparents and Kinship in Early Medieval Europe* (Princeton, NJ, 1986).

23. The principle of the foster parents being from a lower social class than the biological parents is stated several places; see, for example, *Laxdœla saga*, p. 75. On the legal aspects, see *Grágás*, pp. 227, 233. The remuneration was known as the *auðæfi*.

24. Among many examples, see *Gísla saga*, in *Vestfirðinga sǫgur*, eds. Björn K. Þórolfsson and Guðni Jónsson, *Íslenzk fornrit* 6 (Reykjavík 1953), p. 7.

25. *Laxdœla saga*, pp. 75–76. From another text it appeared that Bersi's wife was against the arrangement and he had to entrust the child to another woman living on his farm (see *Kormáks saga* in *Vatnsdœla saga*, pp. 259-60). In her old age, Guðrún fosters her granddaughter from the age of one; see *Laxdœla saga*, p. 212.

26. See *Laxdœla saga*, pp. 100, 158.

27. This vignette is found in the young *Finnboga saga* (*Kjalnesinga saga*, p. 314); see note 4 for another new emotion in this text.

28. *Laxdœla saga*, pp. 37–38.

29. On Snorri's relationship with his mother and other women, see Jenny Jochens, "Wealth and Women in Snorri's Life," *Sagnaþing helgað Jónasi Kristjánssyni*, 2 vols., ed. Gísli Sigurðson, Guðrún Kvaran, Sigurgeir Steingrímsson (Reykjavík, 1994), 1:445–63.

30. *Fljótsdœla saga*, in *Austfirðinga sǫgur*, pp. 221–22.

31. See, for example, Steingerð r (*Kormáks saga*, in *Vatnsdœla saga*, p. 206) and Guðríð r (*Eiríks saga rauða*, in *Eyrbyggja saga*, eds. Einar Ól. Sveinsson, Matthías Þórðarson, *Íslenzk fornrit* 4 [Reykjavík, 1935], p. 203), and Þórkatla (*Reykdœla saga*, in *Ljósvetninga saga*, pp. 160, 164).

32. The foster parents were often addressed affectionately as *fóstri minn* or *fóstra mín*; see, for example, *Grettis saga*, pp. 104, 245.

33. *Egils saga Skalla-Grímssonar*, ed. Sigurður Nordal, *Íslenzk fornrit* 1 (Reykjavík, 1933) pp. 101–02.

34. See Syrpa who fostered both Þorgerð r and—with a little deception—her son Finnbogi; *Finnboga saga* in *Kjalnesinga saga*, pp. 255–56. When Melkorka sends her son Óláfr to visit her father who is king in Ireland, her first concern is for her old *fóstra*, and she refuses to understand why he does not bring her back with him; *Laxdœla saga*, pp. 51, 58–61.

35. *Gísla saga*, in *Vestfirðinga sǫgur*, pp. 35, 41, 44–45, 51, 64, 78, 99–100, 109–12, 117–18.

36. *Laxdœla saga*, p. 75. See note 25 for the case of a wife who refused her husband's wish to foster a young child.

37. Else Mundal suggests that fosterage gave children a double dose of parental love, but the evidence is too meager to warrant this conclusion; see Else Mundal, "Forholdet mellom born og foreldre i det norrøne kjeldematerialet," *Collegium medievale* 1 (1988), 9–26, esp. 22.

38. On these problems, see Jenny Jochens, "The Illicit Love Visit: An Archaeology of Old Norse Sexuality," *Journal of the History of Sexuality* 1 (1991), 357–92.

39. *Grágás*, p. 129.

40. *Norges gamle love*, 1:358, 367, 419.

41. See Jochens, *Women*, chap. 2.

42. See, for example, *Biskupa sögur*, 2 vols. (Copenhagen, 1858–78), 2:167, 169; *Maríu saga*, ed. C. R. Unger (Christiania [Oslo], 1871), pp. 156–57. This is a common topos in continental literature, especially concerning pregnant nuns; see John Eastburn Boswell, *Kindness to Strangers: The Abandonment of Children in Western Europe from Late Antiquity to the Renaissance* (New York, 1988), pp. 372–73.

43. For more details on pregnancy and birth, see Jochens, *Women*, chap. 3.

44. Examples are conveniently collected in Wolfgang Krause, *Die Frau in der Sprache der altisländischen Familiegeschichten* (Göttingen, 1926), pp. 229–30.

45. *Ljósvetninga saga*, p. 65.

46. For illustrations, see *Svarfdœla saga* (*Eyfirðinga sǫgur*, ed. Jónas Kristjánsson, *Íslenzk fornrit* 9 [Reykjavík, 1946]), p. 153 and *Vatnsdœla saga*, p. 41.

47. For the pagan setting, see *Flóamanna saga* (in *Harðar saga*, ed. Þórhallur Vilmundarson and Bjarni Vilhjálmsson, *Íslenzk fornrit* 13 [Reykjavík, 1991]), pp. 288–89. For a medieval illustration, see *Sturlunga saga*, 2 vols., ed. Jón Jóhannessson, Magnús Finnbogason and Kristján Eldjarn (Reykjavík, 1946), 1:221.

48. *Grágás*, p. 33. The stipulation is found in the Christian Law section. The Norwegian Christian law admonished parents—father and mother—to protect children under seven from all dangers except illness (*Norges gamle love*, 2:328).

49. *Fljótsdœla saga*, in *Austfirðinga sǫgur*, pp. 238–39. Grieving over the death of his grown son whom he miraculously had fed as an infant by cutting his own nipples, a man acknowledged the special bonding resulting from nursing when he stated that "he could feel compassion for women when they loved 'breast children' more than other people"; *Flóamanna saga*, in *Harðar saga*, p. 312.

50. See Helgi Þorláksson, "Óvelkomin börn?" *Saga* 24 (1986), 79–120. Since mothers did nurse their children throughout the medieval period, I shall not enter into the discussion of why the change occurred.

51. *Egils saga*, p. 80.

52. In case of men and girls, it is also found in foster relations; see the case of Gísli and his foster daughter; *Gísla saga* in *Vestfirðinga sǫgur*, pp. 44–45, 99–100.

53. *Gunnlaugs saga ormstungu* (in *Borgfirðinga sǫgur*, ed. Sigurður Nordal and Guðni Jónsson, *Íslenzk fornrit* 3 [Reykjavík, 1938], pp. 55–56.

54. Known as Helga the Beautiful, she was said to be the most beautiful woman who had ever lived in Iceland. Jófríðr had another daughter from a previous marriage and ten children with Þorsteinn.

55. *Egils saga*, pp. 224–28. A mother in Norway does not go to a party with her husband but remains home with her sick grown daughter; *Grettis saga*, p. 62. A mother wants to bring her young daughter with her to Christmas mass in a church and expresses fear for her safety when Grettir carries them both across a river; *Grettis saga*, pp. 210–11.

56. In *Kjalnesinga saga*, pp. 75–76, 81–82, 85–87, 95, 97, 103.

57. *Egils saga*, p. 274. See also Orens Þáttr, in *Harðar saga*, p. 399.

58. See *Bandamanna saga* (in *Grettis saga*), pp. 294–95 where the mother's feelings are not mentioned.

59. *Egils saga*, pp. 99–100.

60. *Laxdœla saga*, pp. 22–28, 49–51.

61. After her royal lover's sudden death in 1204, Inga Varteig gives birth in secret to the future Hákon Hákonarson. For references to these and other examples, see Jenny Jochens, "The Politics of Reproduction: Medieval Norwegian Kingship," *The American Historical Review* 92 (1987), 327–49. esp. 342–43.

62. *Harðar saga*, p. 89.

63. *Víga-Glums saga* (in *Eyfirðinga sǫgur*), p. 62.

64. On magic, see Jenny Jochens, "Magie et répartition entre hommes et femmes dans les mythes et la société germanico-nordiques à travers les sagas et les lois scandinaves," *Cahiers de civilisation médiévale* 36 (1993), 375–89. On inciting, see her "The Female Inciter in the Kings' Sagas," *Arkiv för nordisk filologi* 102 (1987), 100–19. See also her *Old Norse Images of Women* (Philadelphia, 1996), in press, chaps. 5 and 8.

65. See Ljótr and her son Hrolleifr (*Vatnsdœla saga*, pp. 50–55, 64–70). For magical clothing, see the shirt made by Katla for her son Oddr (*Eyrbyggja saga*, p. 34). Among many examples of foster mothers stroking their sons' bodies, see Hrói's foster mother (*Reykdœla saga* [in *Ljósvetninga saga*], p. 167).

66. Space does not allow an analysis of the maternal inciting discourse. While the full goading chorus included references to men's mental and physical deficiencies in courage and deeds as well as in physical strength and sexual potency, mothers avoided accusations of sexual passivity; as an exception, see Þórdís in *Hávarðar saga Ísfirðings* (in *Vestfirðinga sǫgur*), p. 306.

67. *Laxdœla saga*, pp. 176–81, 186–93. See also Droplaug and her two young sons; *Droplaugarsona saga* (in *Austfirðinga sǫgur*), pp. 145–46.

68. Þuríðr (in *Heiðarvíga saga* [*Borgfirðinga saga*], pp. 254, 276–79.

69. *Laxdœla saga*, pp. 161–63, 165–68.

70. See above and note 25.

71. The man was known as Kerru-Bersi; see *Eyrbyggja saga*, p. 181.

72. Þorgerðr herself remarked that Bolli had "cruelly repaid his fosterage" (*Laxdœla saga*, p. 159).

73. See *Laxdœla saga*, pp. 208–11, 218–21.

74. *Brennu-Njáls saga*, ed. Einar Ól. Sveinsson, *Íslenzk fornrit* 12 (Reykjavík, 1954), p. 91.

75. *Brennu-Njáls saga*, pp. 114, 229, 252.

76. Only three granddaughters (through a daughter)—about whom nothing is known—carry Bergþóra's and Njáll's genes in the third generation; see *Brennu-Njáls saga*, p. 463. To the debate among saga scholars concerning the historicity of the frequency of the inciting woman, sociobiologists might point out that the reproductive devastation illustrated in Bergþóra's case would suggest that the whetting woman was more of a literary topos than a social and historical phenomenon.

77. *Grágás*, p. 75. For certain groups the rule applied to both men and women; for details, see Jenny Jochens, "Gender Symmetry in Law: The Case of Medieval Iceland," *Arkiv för nordisk filologi* 108 (1993), 46–67, esp. 64–65.

78. See *Auðunar þáttr vestfirzka, Vestfirðinga sǫgur*, pp. 361, 366.

79. See Terry Gunnell, *The Origins of Drama in Scandinavia* (Rochester, NY, 1995), pp. 160–78.

80. See above and note 4.

THE VIKING'S MOTHER:

RELATIONS BETWEEN MOTHERS AND THEIR

GROWN SONS IN ICELANDIC SAGAS

Stephan Grundy

The mother-son relationship in Icelandic sagas is a close one, especially when the mother appears as a witch who protects or promotes her son. Contrasted with her legal and physical powerlessness, the witch-mother's social and personal power intensified the relationship; her actions reinforce the social norm and call attention to its boundaries.

The popular image of the men on whose deeds the Icelandic sagas were based is a fierce and self-reliant one—indeed, the very epitome of self-sufficient manhood. One does not often imagine the ferocious Viking or legendary hero (or villain) going home to his mother for help against his foes or acting as her agent in the masculine spheres of law and war. Nevertheless, this is the usual pattern followed in the sagas. From the prosaic deeds of the Icelanders to the fantastic doings of ancient kings, the relationship between mother or adoptive maternal figure and grown son stands out as a one of unusual closeness, in which the mother's ability to affect the world for her son's benefit, and dedication to doing so, is remarkable for its power in both the supernatural and social spheres. This relationship is particularly noticeable when the mother is a witch wielding her abilities largely for the benefit of her adult son, as supernatural action is one of the most direct forms of power available to women in the world of the sagas, but the maternal witch also acts as counsellor, strategist, and mediator in more ordinary social situations on her son's behalf.

As a literary motif, the malignant maternal witch shows up strongly in the Vǫlsung/Niflung legends, in which the three chief heroes, Sigmundr, Sigurðr, and Gúnnarr, each confront the mother of their primary antagonists, Siggeirr, the Gjúking brothers, and Atli. The first and the last are more peripheral to the plot, with the maternal element an embellishment. In the *Vǫlsunga saga*, Sigmundr is bound in stocks with his brothers; a she-wolf comes to eat one of them every night, but Sigmundr is able to overcome her. The saga-man explains the antagonism of the she-wolf to the Vǫlsungs with the simple statement, "And it is said by some men that the she-wolf was Siggeirr' s mother, and she had taken on this likeness through trollcraft and sorcery."[1] A similar situation appears in *Oddrúnargrátr* 32, where Gunnarr's death in the snake-pit is described: Gunnarr, as according to Norse tradition, has charmed the snakes by playing the harp with his feet, but "Then Atli's wretched mother came darting out—may she wither away!—and dug into Gunnarr's heart."[2] Although this poem appears to be a later and more literary construction than most of the Vǫlsung/Niflung lays,[3] the identification of the fatal snake as Atli's mother provides a striking parallel with the identification of the she-wolf as Siggeirr's mother: if the *Oddrúnargrátr* poet were not directly influenced by some form of the Sigmundr legend, the two would have to be independent duplications of the witch-mother motif. In both cases, a supernatural element is introduced to the hero's detriment. McMahon argues convincingly that "People listening to the story of Gunnar' s death had no difficulty in accepting the possibility that Atli' s mother could turn into a snake and commit a murder,"[4] which can only be properly motivated by explaining the unnatural beast as the mother of the hero's antagonist.

The third maternal witch in the Vǫlsung legends, Grímhildr, is central to the plot. She is constantly brewing magical drinks and manipulating the course of action. In Chapter 28, Grímhildr gives Sigurðr a horn of ale that causes him to forget Brynhildr even as he agrees to swear loyalty to the Gjúkings; in Chapter 29, in order to win Brynhildr for Gunnarr, "The two exchanged shapes, as Grímhildr had taught them, Sigurðr and Gunnarr";[5] in Chapter 34 (based on *Guðrúnarkviða* II, 21–24, partially quoted in the saga's text), in order to convince Guðrún to trust her brothers again and marry Atli, "Grímhildr brought Guðrún an evil drink. And she had to take it, and must forget her grievances afterwards."[6] Although Grímhildr appears as the dominant figure throughout her section of the saga, and is characterized as generally malignant, the sole purpose of her

activities seems to be to help her sons, in particular Gunnarr. It is
worth noting here that a similar closeness does not appear, either in
the Vǫlsung/Niflung materials or elsewhere, between mother and
daughter: Guðrún is specifically sacrificed by her mother for the
sake of her brothers.

It might be hypothesized that Grímhildr had in some way
influenced the other two witch-mothers of the legend. However,
similar figures appear not only in the legendary sagas (*fornaldarsǫgur*)
but in the family sagas as well. Though in rare instances a witch can
be hired to do something, as when Þóroddr hires Þorgríma galdrakinn
to raise a tempest against Bjǫrn, [7] or is forced to act on her own
behalf, as discussed later, whenever her magical activities appear as a
significant element of the plot, she is almost inevitably working for
the sake of her children or foster children. In *Eyrbyggja saga*, we have
the unpleasant mother-son pair, Katla and Oddr Kǫtluson: when
Oddr is being chased by his foes, Arnkell and Þórarinn, Katla disguises
him three times as ordinary household items or creatures (a spindle,
a goat, a boar). It is not until Þórarinn calls on the help of his own
mother, Geirríðr, that they are able to defeat Katla's magic: Katla
says, "Troll-Geirríðr is coming there, and then no twistings of sight
will be effective." [8] The situation is a magical duel between two
mothers, not for personal power or pleasure (though the two are
rivals with reason to dislike each other) but, ultimately, on behalf of
their sons. A similar magical duel, which ends in the death of the
two women, is that between Þorbjǫrg katla and Þorgríma smíðkona,
over the ring Sótanaut that each wants for her children. [9] *Vatnsdœla
saga* describes how the woman Ljót first prepares a sacrifice for her
son Hrolleifr, then, when he has been slain, looks at his slayers with
her head between her legs for the purpose of enchanting them. [10] In
Landnámabók, the men defend themselves against her gaze by hewing
off her son's head and throwing it in her face. [11] In *Vatnsdœla saga*,
Ljót ends by commenting that their "luck" has overcome her; in
Landnámabók, she says that the earth is turning before her eyes, but
they would have suffered all madness (if she had been successful). A
similar example of a protective and magical mother (or, in this case,
foster-mother) presented in a bad light is Þuríðr, the foster mother
of Þorbjǫrn ǫngull in *Grettis saga*, who insists on accompanying her
foster son to meet Grettir and curses the hero on behalf of her son,
which leads to her carving and enchanting the malignant runes that

bring about Grettir's death. [12] In *Gísla saga*, when Þorsteinn has been wounded, his mother, Auðbjǫrg, binds his wounds, then goes outside and circles the house widdershins, looking towards the eight directions and pointing up her nose. An avalanche promptly strikes the house of the wounder, killing twelve men. [13]

Until the very latest and most dubious sagic romances, the chief saga examples of apparently magical women who do not have a maternal role (or indeed, any family-related role at all) are the *vǫlvur*, or prophetesses, who appear in *Eiríks saga rauða*, the romantic *Ǫrvar-Odds saga*, *Hrólfs saga kraka*, and *Norna-Gests þáttr*. These women, interestingly, are always positive figures, even when Þórbjǫrg litilvǫlva performs the act of divinatory mediumship described as *seiðr* (here she is summoning, placating, and interrogating spirits rather than speaking with her own gift of inspired foresight [*spá*]), she is never referred to as *seiðkona*, which apparently had considerable negative connotations due to the general usage of *seiðr* as meaning to affect consciousness in a detrimental manner. [14] The *vǫlvur* are almost never seen using magic in an operant manner. For instance, Þórbjǫrg litilvǫlva does not heal or curse; the Heiðr of *Hrólfs saga kraka* can see through a mundane disguise but is not, even for good payment, capable of creating a magical one, only of pretending that she can see no more; [15] the "norns" of *Norna-Gests þáttr* can determine the infant Gestr's fate by speaking it in a prophetic context, but the offended youngest "norn" is not able to set a plague of boils on the rowdies who jostled her off her chair, [16] nor can the *vǫlva* of *Ǫrvar-Odds saga* avenge rude and rough treatment. [17] The one saga exception to this rule, Þórdís spákona, acts magically only to bring about a judgement that she has made, using her powers to enforce her word in the same way that a man would use legal or physical influence, [18] in a manner very comparable to that of Þórdís in *Gunnars saga keldugnúpsfífls* (discussed below)—this falls into a very different category of magical action.

To what degree the Norse prophetesses (in literature or society) retained the holy character of figures such as the seeress/priestess Veleda mentioned by Tacitus is another problem. Jochens' contention that the equality of men in "what had been primarily a female profession (magic) during the pagan period" was a clerical attempt to "domesticate pagan magic" [19] is only arguable if *seiðr*, prophecy, and other forms of magic are identified as a single complex.

Divination (*spá*), however, is almost always presented in a positive light, often as a highly active social function. Gísli Pálsson comments that "Significantly, some saga accounts suggest divination was used to discover free-loaders, to detect the abuse of the rule of reciprocity. In *Þorvaldar þáttur víðförla* (Chapter 2), Thordis 'the diviner' reveals the source of Kodrans' s (sic) money. She accuses him of earning his money 'with force and power as awards for settlements,' collecting it 'by greed in debt and rent beyond fairness.'" [20] Miller also discusses the public consultation of a diviner as a social control mechanism to, for instance, deal with a suspected theft. [21] Nor is there evidence for magic in general as a female preserve, as shown, for instance, by the dominance of masculine names in runic inscriptions of the Iron Age, including those which appear to be operant. While one need not accept the Erulian-*Männerbünde* theory of runic development and dissemination that Flowers promotes, these inscriptions do seem to show a significant male presence in the realm of "magic." [22] Norse supernatural activity, indeed, appears to have had many forms and degrees, as suggested by the rich number of words for such activity and those who engaged in it [23] and it is reasonably safe to set women who were presented as exclusively or chiefly diviners in a separate category from that of Katla, Gerríðr, Ljót, Þuríðr, and Grímhildr.

What was it about medieval Icelandic society that so strongly emphasized the maternal function as one of the chief motivations for supernatural activity? One component of the answer has, in my opinion, been furnished already by R.C. Ellison's article on seventeenth-century Icelandic witch trials. This article points out the striking gender discrepancy between the witch persecutions in Iceland and those on the continent: although several hundred persons were burned in Iceland, only a handful of them were female. The author poses the theory that this was due to Icelandic social organization: because old women were not marginalized or forced to live in a separate dwelling at the fringes of the village but continued to live in the house of their son's family where their actions were visible to all, it was not possible for the suspicion of witchcraft to arise. [24] A similar situation applied in the age of the sagas: for an older, single woman to be a witch in medieval Iceland, she would have to practice her craft with the approval of her son and would, therefore, presumably be exercising it chiefly for his benefit.

Other components, however, may come to light when the general role of females in Icelandic society, and particularly that of older mothers, is examined. Women appear as the prime movers in most Icelandic sagas: a general overview of some characteristic examples is given by Judith Jesch. [25] Jesch argues that "Although the sagas present an alternative to the legal process, a way in which women could participate in public life, there is no evidence that this alternative existed outside literature. The female inciters of the sagas are literary clichés." [26] The reality of this role is, however, supported by skaldic poetry. Jesch cites the verses of Þjóðólfr Arnórsson describing the admiration of the women watching the departure of Haraldr harðráði's fleet, quoting Haraldr's own statement that "Necklace-bearer once bade me / hold high my helmet-support / in the weapon-din where / war-icicles met skulls." She also comments that, "Having urged men into battle, women become the arbiters of how well they perform there": Skúli Þorsteinsson worries that a woman (Valkyrie of the drinking vessel) won't have seen him fighting; Liðamannaflokkr mentions a woman watching Knútr' s capture of London (1016) and includes a stanza of boasting about battle deeds, directed at a woman. [27]

The poetry preserved in *Egils saga* also shows the importance of a woman's judgement of a man's battle worth: when Egill wishes to sit beside the daughter of Arnfiðr jarl and drink with her in the evening (the saga explains that it was customary for male-female pairs to drink together), she asks,

> What are you doing in my seat, young man?
> You have seldom given
> warm meat to the wolf.
> I would rather be by myself.
> You did not set the raven in harvest-time
> screaming over blood,
> You were never at work
> when hard-biting edges came together. [28]

Egill answers by saying,

> I have fared with bloodied brand,
> so that the wound-partridge (raven) followed me,
> and screaming spears;
> Hard was the way a-viking,
> we battled from wrath,

fire ran around the dwellings of men,
we let bloodied bodies
sleep in the gateways.

"Then they drank together in the evening and were
altogether cheerful." [29]

Although direct information is lacking for the intervening centuries,
the conduct of Norsewomen in regards to their warriors is remarkably
similar to that described by Tacitus for Germanic women of the first
century:

close at hand, too, are their dearest...here are the witnesses who are
in each man's eyes most precious; here the praise he covets most:
they take their wounds to mother and wife, who do not shrink from
counting the hurts or demanding a sight of them: they minister to
the combatants food and exhortation. Tradition relates that some
lost or losing battles have been restored by the women, by the
incessance of their prayers and by opposing their breast...[30]

The female function of encouraging, witnessing, and judging the
men in battle appears to be something intrinsic in the culture rather
than simply a literary theme of antiquarians looking back on the
past. The skaldic texts, as well as the sagas, demonstrate the social
importance of women in this manner, and, hence, their power. In
the sagas, women frequently shame their men into action. While
the taunts of men could be ignored or met with other taunts and, if
necessary, weapons, the shame laid on a man by a woman could
only be dealt with by direct action in the matter that she had brought
up to him.

There are also other significant indications that women may have
enjoyed considerable power in Norse, and especially Icelandic, society.
Jón Haukur Ingimundarson observes that

Bridewealth and dowry were legally the personal property of the
wife....These provisions suggest to us that by marrying off a woman
her guardian and her kin group were able to invest livestock, land, or
other property or resources with other kingroups, with the objective
consequences of maintaining a broad base for subsistence and market
production and operationalizing trade enterprises. I would therefore
in one way analyze the literary figure of the household mistress, who
is often depicted as strong-willed and independent, with considerable
rights to property...and as an overseer of the production of homespun
cloth...in terms of a woman's negotiation power and relative

autonomy, for articulating the interest of her husband, in-laws, children, and other kin. [31]

The precise degree of economic and social freedom and power which Norsewomen enjoyed has been much debated[32] and is beyond the scope of this essay. However, it may be generally observed that the contradictory evidence of the law codes and the sagas, for instance, might indicate an often tense dichotomy between women's legal rights and their social influence: a dichotomy that the various presentations of "witchcraft" could, at times, serve to resolve.

The relationship between females, social power, and supernatural activity is complex. As with the later witch trials, magic may be identified as a means by which the socially powerless gain power. However, as Gísli Pálsson observes,

> The women arrested for witchcraft are…likely to be 'marginal' in the sense that they are heads of their own household.…Of the 38 women labelled as witches 10 are identified as widows or heads of a household. In at least three cases the saga-writer makes specific references to the woman's property: 'Thordis…was wealthy' (*Gunnars saga keldugnúpsfífls* chap. 1); 'Thorgrima…became rich and powerful' (*Harðar saga og Hólmverja* chap. 3); 'Esja was…a widow and very rich' (*Kjalnesinga saga* chap.2)" [33]

He also notes that men of high position were equally susceptible to accusations of magic, and that in many cases concerning both genders—25 out of 39 men, 38 women, and one case of unspecified gender, the accused were not reported to use their powers:[34] the mention of magic may be as stylized a characterization as the usual description of notable men of being tall and well built, for instance. Barþi Guðmundsson, too, comments on the link between farmsteads bearing women's names, the frequency of matronymics, and the accusation of female farmholders or women whose sons bear matronymics (one may compare the previously mentioned Oddr Kǫtluson) of witchcraft. [35] While some of Gudmundsson's theories about the links between skaldcraft, magic, and the social power of women may be overstated, as when he confidently states that "among the women practicing witchcraft the custom arose of naming children after their mother,"[36] he is able to establish a relatively solid correlation between prominent women and witchcraft accusations.

The maternal role as supernatural guide and protector of a grown son may also be partially explained by this link between unusual social power and accusations of witchcraft: Miller observes that the"women who were formally accused…as witches tended to be widows independently established on their own farms. It is also noteworthy that the sorcery of these widowed householders often consisted of no more than making their sons or slaves weapon proof. Did such accusations reflect a horror of households that were well protected by males, but directed by women?" [37] In *Barðar saga snæfellsáss*, we see such an example: Hildigunnr is accused of witchcraft and summoned and, to avenge herself, tells her son Einarr of this and gives him a new kirtle; he then goes forth and kills the accuser, Lon-Einarr. The fatal blow is struck when Lon-Einarr's breech-string breaks, which might, to the audience of the day, have implied Hildigunnr's magical interference in the fight. [38] In the *Hauksbók* version of the *Landnámabók* account of the same story, it is stated that "no iron would bite Einarr's kirtle" [39]—a typical protective magic for a mother to weave for her son, as seen, for instance, in *Hamðismál*. It is not clear whether "horror" is the emotion the sagaman intends to evoke, but the pattern is certainly characteristic of the phenomenon Miller describes.

It is only when a woman lacks a son, husband, or brother to represent her and must act directly in the legal field where she has no recognised personal power that she is reduced to achieving by magic what a man would achieve by legal action and force of arms. One instance of this, the use of magic by Þórdís spákona in *Eyrbyggja saga* to enforce her judgement, has already been cited. Another, and even clearer, example appears in *Gunnars saga keldugnúpsfífls*: when Þórdís' brother is slain, "she made a great magic against Gunnarr, so that he could not sit comfortably, neither at home nor in any other stead," [40] finally bringing him to such a state of desperation that he is willing to pay her the due weregild. These two sagas stand out as marked exceptions to the usual pattern, more clearly underscoring how seldom Icelandic women needed to use magic to further their ends rather than relying on more mundane forms of influence over their menfolk and, thus, emphasizing the degree of power actually possessed by women in the social field. The contrast also offers one compelling reason for the mother to use all the powers at her disposal to protect her son: he is her effective arm in matters of money and judgement.

The role of the witch mother, indeed, seems to be an intensification of the normal maternal role in the sagas. Typically, a mother (or foster mother) is expected to advise her son, to arrange things on his behalf, to protect him when necessary and, when problems between father and son cause the family unit to disintegrate, to provide the son with the means to seek his own way. The expectation that an older mother will be a leader and adviser to her sons produces the great matriarchs such as Unnr djúphugaða who, after the death of her husband and son, gathers her clan and people together and leads them from Scotland to Iceland. Choosing her grandson Óláfr feilan as her son's replacement, Unnr, in her old age, arranges a great banquet at which she announces that Óláfr shall inherit from her, then cheerfully says that she must go to sleep. Her work done, she is found dead early the next day, and "Now all was drunken together: Óláfr' s wedding and Unnr' s arvel." [41] The intensity of the mother-son relationship is particularly obvious when the son is characterized as strong-willed and cross-grained, as is the case with Egill Skalla-Grímsson, Grettir Ásmundarson, and the *fornaldarsaga* character Heiðrekr the Wise. Grettir's constant clashing with his father causes Ásmundr to send him off with nothing but a bag of oats and a little woven cloth; when Grettir asks for weapons, Ásmundr answers, "You have never listened to me, and I do not know how you shall win those weapons which are needful; I shall not give them to you," but his mother takes him aside and, in secret, gives him the sword of her grandfather. [42] A similar, if more extreme, situation occurs in *Hervarar saga ok Heiðreks*: when Heiðrekr has slain his brother, his father wishes to have him hanged, but Hervǫr convinces her husband to give Heiðrekr wise advice, then follows her son to slip the youth gold and her father's sword Tyrfingr. [43] The two accounts are similar enough that, if one did not exert direct influence on the other, it may well be suspected that both fit into the pattern of a literary motif. Yet motifs of this type are likely to some degree to reflect social ideals.

Egils saga shows a less extreme but similar pattern. When the young Egill has killed a playmate and thus started a battle between the Myramen and Borgarmen, "Skalla-Grímr was little pleased, but Bera said Egill to be of viking-stuff and said that it must be certain that he would have a warship when he was full-grown." [44] A few years later, when Egill is twelve, his father goes berserk during a ballgame and attacks him; Egill's foster-mother, Þorgerðr brak (who is described in this passage as a sorceress but never shown practising magic), manages to turn the fit against herself instead. Skalla-Grímr kills her, but Egill's life is saved. [45]

Very few older women appear in the sagas who are not either mothers or foster mothers, and when such a woman stands out as an important part of the story, her presence brings about a certain degree of social disruption. The most blatant example of this is Þórgunna from *Eyrbyggja saga*. She is a rich immigrant to Iceland with enviable treasures, tall and physically powerful, with black eyebrows that meet over her nose: though vigorous, she is thought to be in her fifties. Perhaps surprisingly, she is not accused of witchcraft, though she falls out with Þorgríma galdrakinn, who is most certainly a witch; she also seems to appear later as a ghostly seal, [46] but to what degree this is a sign hinting at personal magical powers, as opposed to a normal (for Icelandic literature) manifestation of her unusually strong personality, may be debated. [47] It is clear, however, that her presence brings disruption and quarrels, and is the start of a host of strange events. The most salient aspect of her strangeness and disruptive character, however, is her relationship with the young Kjartan. "Kjartan, the farmer's son, was there thus among men, that Þórgunna wished most to be with him, and she loved him greatly, but he would rather have little to do with her, and she was often irritable about that. Kjartan was then thirteen or fourteen winters." [48] Here the normal relationship between a maternal figure and her son or foster son is altered, as is everything else about Þórgunna, to something peculiar. This ironic relationship reversal is capped by the happenings after Þórgunna's death, when the seal, presumably Þórgunna, comes up through the floor and stares eagerly at Þórgunna's precious bed-hangings, which she had ordered be burnt: only Kjartan is able to beat it back down into the ground, [49] the "son" directly counteracting the supernatural activity of the "mother."

The unusual nature of Þórgunna's tale strongly underscores the importance of the maternal role to the older woman. Without that role, fulfilled either in regard to a son/young kinsman or a fosterling, the woman is a strange figure indeed, outside the pale even for a witch, and her existence can only bode disintegration and disaster, although Þórgunna is presented as a dedicated Christian who does no harm to any.

Given the above examples, which demonstrate both the basic paradigm of the mother-son relationship and the peculiarly unsettling effect of its alteration, the frequent identification of the witch as a mother working with and for her sons or foster sons is no longer surprising. On the one hand, she is largely constrained by practical considerations: if she wishes to be secure in her legal rights and protected against physical attack, she must have a son who is willing and able to act for her as effectively as possible. On the other, whether she deals well or badly with people outside her family, her primary loyalty as a mother is expected to be towards her son; her chief social duty is to guide him and work for his benefit as well as she can. The combination of a woman' s implicit social and personal power and explicit legal and physical powerlessness intensifies the mother-son relationship: it also defines the character and functions of the

NOTES

1. *En þat er sǫgn sumra manna, at su hin sama ylgr veri modir Siggeirs konungs, ok hafe hun brugdit a sik þessu like fyrir trollskapar sakir ok fiolkyngi.* Vǫlsunga saga ok Ragnars saga loðbrókar, ed. Magnus Olsen (Copenhagen, 1906–08), p. 12.

2. *Þá kom in arma   út scævandi*
    móðir Atla   hon scyli morna!
    Oc Gunnari   gróf til hiarta
Edda: Die Lieder des Codex Regius nebst verwandten Denkmäler, 3rd ed., ed. Gustav Neckel, rev. Hans Kuhn (Heidelberg, 1962), p. 239.

3. *The Poetic Edda,* ed. Lee Hollander, 2nd ed. (Austin, TX, 1962, reprt. 1986), p. 279.

4. James V. McMahon, "Valkyries, Midwives, Weavers, and Shape-Changers: Atli's Mother the Snake," *Scandanavian Studies* 66.4 (1994), 475–87.

5. *Skipta nu litum, sem Grimhilldr kende þeim Sigurdi ok Gunnare.* Vǫlsunga saga, p. 67.

6. *Siþan ferde Grimhilldr henne meinsamligan dryck. ok vard hun vid at taka ok munde siþan einghar sakar. Vǫlsunga saga,* p. 87.

7. *Eyrbyggja saga,* eds. Einar Ól. Sveinsson and Matthías Þórðarson, *Íslenzk fornrit* 4 (Reykjavík, 1935), p. 109.

8. *Mun Geirríðr trollit þar komin, ok mun þá eigi sjónhverfingum einum mega vid koma. Eyrbyggja saga,* p. 53.

9. *Harðar saga,* eds. Þórhallur Vilmundarsson and Bjarni Vilhjálmsson, *Íslenzk fornrit* 13 (Reykjavík, 1991), p. 95.

10. *Vatnsdœla saga*, ed. Einar Ól. Sveinsson, *Íslenzk fornrit* 8 (Reykjavík, 1939), pp. 68–70.

11. *Landnámabók*, ed. Jakob Benediktsson, *Íslenzk fornrit* 1 (Reykjavík, 1986), p. 222.

12. *Grettis saga Ásmundarsonar*, ed. Guðni Jónsson, *Íslenzk fornrit* 7 (Reykjavík, 1936), pp. 245–50.

13. *Gísla saga Súrssonar*, eds. Björn K. Þórólfsson and Guðni Jónsson, *Íslenzk fornrit* 6 (Reykjavík, 1943), pp. 59–60.

14. *Eiríks saga rauða*, eds. Einar Ól. Sveinsson and Matthías Þórdarson, *Íslenzk fornrit* 4 (Reykjavík, 1935), pp. 206–08.

15. *Hrólfs saga kraka ok Bjarkarímur*, ed. Finnur Jónsson (Copenhagen, 1904), p. 11.

16. *Flateyjarbók*, 3 vols.(P.T. Malling: Christiania, 1860–68), vol. 1, p. 358.

17. *Ǫrvar-Odds saga*, ed. R.C. Boer (1888), p. 11, cited by Dag Strömbäck, *Sejd* (Lund, 1935), p. 96.

18. *Vatnsdœla saga*, pp. 120–21.

19. "Old Norse Magic and Gender: Þáttr Þorvalds ens víðförlan," *Scandinavian Studies* 63 (1991), 305–37, p. 308.

20. Gísli Pálsson, "The Name of the Witch: Sagas, Sorcery, and Social Context," *Social Approaches to Viking Studies*, ed. Ross Samson (Glasgow, 1991), pp. 157–68, p. 166.

21. William Ian Miller, "Dreams, Prophecy, and Sorcery," *Scandinavian Studies* 58 (1986), pp. 101–23, pp. 108–09.

22. Stephen E. Flowers, *Runes and Magic* (New York, 1986), pp. 90–92.

23. For instance: *spákona/spámaðr*="prophetess/prophet"; *fjǫlkunningr*="much-knowing"; *seiðkona/seidmaðr*=practitioner of *seiðr; vǫlva* = "prophetess/female magician"; *vitki*=lit. "a wise man," but used only for "wizard." Also *trollskapr, trolldómr*="magic"; *galdr*="a vocal charm"; *gandr*=roughly "an enchanted item or being."

24. R.C. Ellison, "The Kirkjuból Affair: A Seventeenth-Century Icelandic Witchcraft Case Analyzed," *The Seventeenth Century* 8 (1993), 217–243.

25. Judith Jesch, *Women in the Viking Age* (Woodbridge, 1991), pp. 182–87.

26. Jesch, *Women in the Viking Age*, p. 190.

27. Jesch, *Women in the Viking Age*, pp. 152–55.

28. *Hvat skaltu, sveinn, í sess minn?*
þvít þú sjaldan hefr gefnar
vargi varmar bráðir,
vesa vilk ein of mína;
sáttaðu hrafn í hausti
of hræsolli gjalla,

vastaðu at, þars eggjar
á skelþunnar runnusk.
Egils saga Skalla-Grímssonar, ed. Sigurdur Nordal (Reykjavík, 1933),
p. 121.

29. *Farit hefk blóðgum brandi,*
    svát mér benþiðurr fylgdi,
    ok gjallanda geiri;
    gangr vas harðr af víkingum;
    gerðum reiðir róstu,
    rann eldr of sjǫt manna,
    létum blóðga búka
    í borghliðum sœfask.
Þá drukku þau saman um kveldit ok váru allkát. (*Egils saga*, p. 121.)

30. *et in proximo pignora...hi cuique sanctissimi testes, hi maximi laudatores: ad matres, ad coniuges vulnera ferunt: nec illae numerare aut exigere plagas pavent, cibosque et hortamina pugnantibus gestant.*
    Memoriae proditur quasdam acies inclinatas iam et lagantes a feminis restutas constantia precum et obiectu pectorum....
Tacitus, *Germania*, ed. and trans. M. Hutton, rev. E.H. Warmington, The Loeb Classical Library (reprt., Cambridge, MA and London, 1980), 1 edn. 1970, pp. 142–43.

31. Jón Haukur Ingimundarson, "Spinning Goods and Tales: Market, Subsistence, and Literary Productions," *From Sagas to Society*, ed. Gísli Pálsson (Middlesex, 1992), pp. 217–30, p. 229.

32. Some of the chief arguments for the autonomy of women are presented by Anne Stalsberg in "Women as Actors in North European Viking Age Trade," *Social Approaches to Viking Studies*, ed. Ross Samson (Glasgow, 1991), pp. 75–86; Nanna Damsholt in "The Role of Icelandic Women in the Sagas and in the Production of Homespun Cloth," *Scandinavian Journal of History* 9 (1984), 75–90; and Carol Clover in "The Politics of Scarcity: Notes on the Sex Ratio in Early Scandinavia," *Scandinavian Studies* 60 (1988), 147–88. The counter-argument, that these views appear to be based on a one-sided and inferential interpretation of the available data and are strongly contradicted by the lack of legal rights suffered by Scandinavian women, is presented by Gunnar Karlsson in "Kenningin um fornt kvenfrelsi á Íslandi," *Saga* 24, 45–77.

33. Gísli Pálsson, "The Name of the Witch," p. 93.

34. Gísli Pálsson, "The Name of the Witch," pp. 160–61.

35. Barþi Guðmundsson, *The Origin of the Icelanders*, trans. Lee Hollander (Lincoln, NE, 1967), pp. 30–35.

36. Barþi Guðmundsson, *Origin*, p. 31.

37. William Ian Miller, "Dreams, Prophecy, and Sorcery," *Scandinavian Studies* 58 (1986), 101–23, p. 115.

38. *Barðar saga snæfellsáss*, eds. Þórhallur Vilmundarson and Bjarni Vilhjálmsson, *Íslenzk fornrit* 13 (Reykjavík, 1991), pp. 120–21.
39. *en kyrtil Einars bitu eigi járn. Landnámabók*, p. 109.
40. *Gunnars saga keldugnúpsfífls*, ed. Jóhannes Halldórsson, *Íslenzk fornrit* 14 (Reykjavík, 1959), p. 377.
41. *Var nú drukkit allt saman, brullaup Óláfs ok erfi Unnar. Laxdæla saga*, pp. 11–13.
42. "*Eigi hefir þú mér hlýðinn verit; veit ek ok eigi, hvat þú munir þat með vápnum vinna, er þarft er; mun ek ok þau eigi til láta.*" *Grettis saga Ásmundarson*, ed. Guðni Jónsson, *Íslenzk fornrit* 7 (Reykjavík, 1936), p. 49.
43. *Hervarar saga ok Heiðreks*, ed G. Turville-Petre, 2nd edn. (London, 1976), pp. 24–26.
44. ...*lét Skalla-Grímr sér fátt um finnask, en Bera kvað Egil vera víkingsefni ok kvað þat mundu fyrir liggja, þegar hann hefði aldr til, at honum væri fengin herskip. Egils saga Skalla-Grímssonar*, p. 100.
45. *Egils saga Skalla-Grímssonar*, pp. 101–02.
46. *Eyrbyggja saga*, p. 147.
47. Knut Odner's argument that "Þórgunna's appearance as a seal is part and parcel of a role as mediator between several worlds, culminating in the statement that 'Þórgunna's knowledge belongs to the vertical model; it is fate. The norns, to whom Þórgunna is related, sit under the tree Yggdrasill and spin the destinies of men," is, to put it kindly, strained. "Þórgunna's Testament: A Myth for Moral Contemplation and Social Apathy," in *Sagas to Society*, ed. Gísli Pálsson (Glasgow, 1991), pp. 125–46, p. 139.
48. *Kjartan, sonr bonda, var þar svá manna, at Þórgunna vildi flest við eiga, ok elskaði hon hann mjǫk, en hann var heldr fár við hana, ok var√ hon opt af því skapstygg. Kjartan var þá þrettán vetra eða fjórtán ok var bædi mikill vexti ok skǫruligr at sjá. Eyrbyggja saga*, chap. 50, p. 139.
49. *Eyrbyggja saga*, chap. 53, p. 147.

FEMALE NETWORKS FOR FOSTERING
LADY LISLE'S DAUGHTERS

Barbara A. Hanawalt

The Lisle Letters *contradict the view that the fostering of medieval noble children was a patriarchal act that deprived children of parental affection. They illustrate instead warm relations between foster parent and child, the importance of female networks in placing children, and fostering's potential benefits for children.*

Stepparents and foster parents have received surprisingly little attention from historians, given that three very strong traditions condemn these relationships. Our fairy tales, dating from the sixteenth century and earlier, give vivid pictures of wicked stepmothers; as we are raised with these stories, one would think we would all be seeking the prototype of Cinderella's stepfamily. Furthermore, historians have long known that high mortality in the pre-modern world meant that stepparents were common, affecting perhaps a third of all children.[1] The second myth, posited by modern historians, is based on the account of an Italian merchant visiting England in the fifteenth century, who claimed that English parents did not love their children because they fostered them at an early age: "the want of affection in the English is strongly manifested toward their children," who were put at seven or eight "to hard service in the houses of other people" where they performed the "most menial offices."[2] Though his English informants told him they sent their children to other houses for training and discipline because they loved them so much, many historians side with the Italian visitor, claiming the children were deprived of sentimental bonds with biological parents.[3] The third myth originates in arguments which emphasize patriarchy's omnipresent role in determining the fates of women and children, regarded by those who advance such arguments as mere puppets in the paternal game.[4]

Rather than a foreign visitor or modern historians, all of whom had, or have, their own childrearing myths, we must listen to the voices of those who lived at the time. I have elsewhere investigated the care of parents and friends in selecting service and apprenticeship positions for children in medieval London and the continued protection they provided if these arrangements failed; in the countryside, care was manifested in complicated family strategies to provide enough resources for all children to marry or make a living.[5] The sources of information for these two environments, however, do not allow a thorough investigation of women's role in rearing the children in their care—matriarchs as opposed to patriarchs or surrogates to biological parents. Patriarchy was only one side of arranging fostering for children, whose nurturing was perceived to be the responsibility of both parents; husbands' testaments, for example, explicitly named wives as guardians of their children.

For evidence on more intimate aspects of mother/daughter, mother/stepdaughter, and fostering relations I have turned to letters concerning one woman, Honor Grenville Basset, Lady Lisle. While Honor also made intricate arrangements for her sons, the evidence for her daughters is particularly interesting because of the known importance of female networks.[6] A brief introduction to the family and their letters provides a context for looking at a woman who acted as mother, stepmother, and matriarch. The Lisle letters include official, personal, and business correspondence of the household of Arthur Plantagenet, Viscount Lisle, between 1533 and 1540. Arthur was the sole surviving (illegitimate) child of King Edward IV. He weathered the Tudor purge by serving first his half-sister Elizabeth, Henry VII's wife, and then his nephew Henry VIII. In 1533 Henry appointed Arthur governor of Calais, a position requiring diplomatic and managerial skills. Calais was the last English possession in France and through it went diplomatic missions, merchants of the Staple, soldiers, sailors, religious dissidents, and other rogues. The political situation required agility; these were the years of Henry's divorce from Katherine of Aragon, his remarriage and later the fall of Anne Boleyn, his break with the Roman Church, and the rise of his minister, Thomas Cromwell. Aging and increasingly impoverished as governor of Calais, Lord Lisle managed (literally) to keep his head through these changes, but when his Pole relatives came under suspicion for Catholicism, he, too, was suspected of treason. In 1540, he was taken to the Tower of London; Crown commissioners searched his house at Calais and impounded all correspondence. The letters for these years were thus preserved as a remarkably rich collection. Muriel St. Clare Byrne assembled the letters in an exemplary edition with an informative narrative of events noted in the correspondence.[7] The main figures who appear in the letters, political ones apart, are Arthur Lisle and his second wife, Honor Grenville Basset; their business factor, John Husee; their children and their sponsors; and a variety of relatives, friends, clients, functionaries, envoys, members of the Calais community, servants, tutors, and so on. Arthur and Honor did not produce children together, but such gentry marriages typically combined the children of earlier marriages to make a numerous family. From his first marriage Arthur had three daughters: Elizabeth, Frances, and Bridget. Honor was the second wife of John Basset, a West Country knight whose daughters from his first marriage, Jane and Thomasine, became Honor's charges. Honor and John Basset had had seven surviving children: John, George, James, Philippa, Katherine, Anne, and Mary (*LL*, 1:313–14).[8] Honor thus had a crowd of children and stepchildren to educate, foster, and marry off.

Much rested on adolescent children's placement. It was in those formative years that parents had to think ahead to the formation of advantageous marriages, perpetuation of the lineage, and establishment of careers or sufficient landed property. Well-born parents also wanted their children trained in life skills: manners, languages, ease in social discourse, dress, demeanor, and physical attractiveness were essential to a successful young courtier, male or female.[9] Influential social connections acquired during fostering were also useful. Parents thus spent money and time searching for households suitable to train their children when they were at least seven or eight, though more likely in their teens. They preferred a household whose head was of higher social status than their own; children could thus form contacts to further careers or marriages. The desirable fostering arrangement also assured training in necessary social skills. If literacy was valued, the household must have a tutor; if needlework was important, the lady of the house must be skilled; if the young person was designated for a court career, languages and fine manners were essential. Parents might also be concerned that sponsors or foster parents would be congenial surrogates, so the children would not be unduly miserable.

The Lisle letters are used here to investigate three key themes. First, fostering was not necessarily a loveless arrangement even if it was meant to provide children with training to better their station in life. Second, mothers or stepmothers were more instrumental in making these latently powerful social and political arrangements than has been assumed. Third, the Lisle letters correct the impression created by some social commentators, such as Sir Thomas Elyot (quoted in *LL*, 3:217), that daughters were seen as a burden. The family could benefit from connections made by an attractive and accomplished daughter; practical parents saw their daughters as part of family strategies for social advancement and invested money not only in dowries, but also in placing their daughters.[10]

PHASE ONE: FOSTERING IN CHILDHOOD

Honor and Arthur Lisle seemingly preferred to see to their children's and stepchildren's early training at home (*LL*, 2:246). The move to Calais, however, dispersed the children, who spent little time there but appear to have been in environments where they were well cared for and often loved. The Basset boys were placed in English households; the two eldest Basset daughters stayed with married siblings, and the other girls went to Calais, except for Arthur's youngest. The experiences of this seven- or eight-year-old, "Little Mistress Bridget," were probably typical of the "professional child care" nunneries and monasteries provided for well-born children: religious instruction, reading and writing (probably English), needlework, and manners (*LL*, 3:78–79).[11] At the dissolution in 1542, St. Mary's in Winchester housed twenty-six children, with Bridget heading the list as most prestigious, and the abbess' matter-of-fact letters suggest a woman accustomed to a childrearing role. In response to repeated inquiries, she kept Honor informed of Bridget's expenses for a year and thirty-three months and receipt of 70s. toward her board (about a shilling a week): "Also, Madame, I have laid out for her, for mending of her gowns and for ij matins books, iiij pair of hosen, and iiij pair of shoes, and other small things, iijs. vd." (*LL*, 3: no. 539). The only luxury was an ermine bonnet Honor sent for Bridget, perhaps never delivered. The impression is that Bridget wore out her clothing or grew out of it and always seemed short of appropriate attire (*LL*, 3: nos. 533, 535, 539, and 5: nos. 1224, 1226). The letters indicate that affectionate concern was part of the younger children's care. All in response to inquiries from Honor and sometimes Lord Lisle, the letters show the parents as concerned about the health and welfare of Bridget and the three Basset boys as about their education. Bridget is called "little Lady Bridget," (*LL*, 3: no. 533), and their French tutor wrote of George and James as children (*enfant*; *LL*, 3: nos. 545, 548). James' tender years evoked particular comment; at seven, too young to dress himself, he was called "child," "our little man," and even "that sweet babe"(*LL*, 3: nos. 552, 552a, 553, 554, 557, 559). Such terms vanished as the children reached adolescence; correspondents now referred to them as "Mrs. Anne" or "Mr. John." The transition to the teen years, then, represented a conscious change of status for the children as well as in the surrogate care and education they would need.[12]

PHASE TWO: FOSTERING AND "FINISHING" ARRANGEMENTS

Far-sighted parents were sensitive to political and cultural drifts in the volatile early sixteenth century. French was replacing Latin as the language of diplomacy and continental court style influenced the English; Thomas Boleyn, for example, made great efforts on behalf of his daughters and placed his daughter Anne with Margaret of Austria at the Burgundian court. Like Boleyn, Lisle saw that opportunities at Henry VIII's court required a French education, and he and Honor used the French connections they made in Calais to foster and educate the younger Basset children (*LL*, 1: 25).[13] Anne and Mary were apparently more beautiful than their older sisters and still young enough to profit from the changed circumstances resulting from Honor's remarriage. The older girls stayed in Calais; Anne and Mary were placed with noble French families known to Lord Lisle. At twelve or thirteen, Anne joined the household of the seigneur de Riou in 1533; less than a year later Mary, eleven or twelve, was fostered with the de Bours family, related by marriage to the de Rious.[14]

The domestic, educational, and financial arrangements proved most satisfactory. The host families paid the girls' "finding" (room and board); the Lisles paid for clothing, jewelry, and pocket money and exchanged with the guardians the usual gifts of hawks, dogs, horses, clothing and food.[15] The arrangements proved economical for Lady Lisle. By Honor's first husband's will, each Basset girl was to receive £6:13:4 yearly for expenses; a bill from Mme de Bours for the three and a half years Mary spent with her shows that she had about £15 in expenses, leaving £8 or £9 for extras out of the roughly £24 she would have had for those years. Her expenses were mostly for clothing of the usual black, with a white girdle, gold thread, furs, ribbon, violet for sleeves, and seed pearls for a headdress. Mary also ran up some small gambling debts. The girls, especially Mary, showed concern for the expenses their family incurred, but Lady Lisle wrote "I think the cost of you well employed" (*LL*, 3:133–140, 215–217 and letters no. 570, 626, 590, 590a).

Though requests seemed extravagant at times, the girls were learning a sense of appropriate style. Anne apologized for the cost of gowns, cloaks, and jewelry, but "it is not possible to do otherwise, there are so many little trifling things which are here necessary which are not needed in England, and one must do as others do" (*LL*, 3: nos. 571, 578). "Trifles" could be lavish: Mary once thanked Honor for seven score pearls. But when Anne needed a jeweled strip, Mme de Riou thriftily purchased one that could be used as a headband or at the waist and sent Honor the bill (*LL*, 3: nos. 578, 584, 585). Other requests were mundane. Mary's garments were well mended, but she lacked sleeves; Honor always sent hose cloth, explaining that no one in Calais had the measurement for the girls' hose, since they had grown so much (*LL*, 3: nos. 583, 587, 590, 590a, 592).

The girls' education was the conventional one for country gentlewomen. They visited each other's households, played cards (hence the gambling debts), embroidered, learned manners, played the lute, spinet and virginals, and learned to read, write, and converse in French—all directed toward court placement and a desirable marriage. Apparently, Lady Lisle enjoyed proof that her children's educational programs were working. Anne and Mary dictated or wrote letters to her in French; in response to a scolding from her mother three years after she left France, Anne confided that she could write French but not English and had to find someone to take dictation (*LL*, 3: nos. 549, 550, and 5: no. 1126).[16]

Women took to the new form of letter writing as a personal medium of interaction, and it proved an effective tool in the power women exerted through their networks.[17] From a distance, Honor thus exerted moral as well as financial guidance over her daughters. She sent Anne three crowns and Mme de Riou assured her that "she doth not squander them, but employeth them right honestly for her small needs and in good works, and should I perceive that she doth otherwise I would advertise you thereof" (*LL*, 3: no. 593). When Mary needed money to pay gambling debts, Honor wrote Mme de Bours:

> I am content that she play when ye shall command her; but I fear she shall give her mind too much to play. It will come soon enough to her. I would she should ply her work, the lute and the virginals, but I refer it all to your goodness. (*LL*, 3: no. 583a)

Young women easily adopted the conversational style, as can be seen in Mary's letter to her sister Philippa in Calais, which suggests that Honor had reason to worry about Mary's gambling:

> My good sister and friend, I greatly desire to hear good news of you and my other sisters. If I may have my wish I would be every day an hour with you, that I might teach you to speak French. I enjoy myself so much here in this country that I should be right well content, if that I could often see my lady my mother, never to return to England.
>
> I send you a purse of green velvet, a little pot for my sister Frances [Lord Lisle's eldest daughter], also a gospel to my sister Katharine, and a parroquet to my lord my father, because he maketh much of a bird. I beg of you, my sister to have the goodness to present it to him, and to entreat him to send me some pretty thing for this Easter. He hath yet not sent me anything, although I have never forgot him.
>
> There is a gentleman here who is called Philip, and for love of your name he sendeth you a little basket. I have promised him a bow. I pray you to be a mean to my lady that she send it him by this bearer. I owe a pair of shoes to the gentlewoman who seeth to my wants which I lost at play with her. I greatly wish that my mother would send them to her. I have not yet given any present to the chamberer of Madame. I were right glad to have something to give to her.
>
> Recommending me as well and as humbly as I may to your good favour, to the good favor of my sister Frances, and to that of my sister Katharine and to all the gentlewomen of my lady my mother.... I pray our Lord to give you a good husband, and that very soon. (*LL*, 3: no. 588)

This chatty, affectionate letter is full of the pleasures of daily life and the exchange of small gifts. It teasingly suggests romance for an older sister who is looking for a husband and presents a gift to her stepsister,

soon to be her sister-in-law. To the family patriarch she sends a
flattering gift for a man with a keen eye for a bird. Mary's relations
with her stepfather and his daughter were obviously close, with no
tensions.[18] The girls also wrote faithfully to their mother, expressing
love for their family and greeting household members. When it
seemed Honor was carrying a Plantagenet heir, Mary wished she
could be present at the birth "to warm his swaddling clouts for the
babe." Anne and Mary visited each other in their French households;
their brother James, at school in Paris, visited them more than once
(*LL*, 3: nos. 594, 597, 201). While the girls were happy in their French
homes, emotional ties to the natal family remained strong.

Strong attachments to the foster families do appear in the letters.
In 1534, about six months after her arrival, Anne wrote that M. and
Mme de Riou treated her so well that "had I been their natural
daughter they could not better nor more gently have entreated me."
Monsieur wrote of Anne at the same time: "I ensure you she doth
conduct herself at all times with right honest and virtuous demeanour,
and sheweth plainly that she hath been well nurtured" (*LL*, 3: no.
571, 572).[19] There seemed to be a competition in making the English
girls feel at home; after a month, Mme de Bours wrote to Lord Lisle
about Mary's health and her pleasure with her:

> I find her of such an excellent disposition that I love her as if she
> were my daughter, and she is beloved of all them that see her. It
> maketh me not a little proud that they should say she is fairer than
> Mistress Anne.

Mary had not yet learned much French, but she had a good will to
learn (*LL*, 3: no. 574).

The French noblewomen's pleasure in the girls' company did not
diminish but seemed to increase with time. Mme de Riou took Anne
with her on a 300-mile journey to be at the laying-in of Madame's
daughter. On completing the journey, which involved visits to
illustrious country estates, Madame wrote that Anne had made a
good impression with everyone (*LL*, 3: no. 585). After two years,
Mme de Bours wrote that Mary "well deserveth to be cherished."
When M. de Bours suddenly died, Madame asked Mary to write
her mother to find out if she objected to having Mary dress in
mourning; ever sympathetic, Honor did not. In return, Mme de
Bours made sure that Mary's education and accomplishments were
not hidden by mourning. When the French queen visited Abbeville,

Mme de Riou acted as deputy for her sister Mme de Bours and Mary, in court attire, was presented to the queen (*LL*, 3: nos. 617–19).

Parting with the girls was difficult for the foster mothers. Mme de Riou wrote of Anne that she could not "conceive greater pleasure than to have her with me, and I shall be very sorry when she must return"(*LL*, 3: nos. 576, 581). After three years Anne returned to Calais while her mother worked with Husee to place her at court, though her ties to the de Rious continued (*LL*, 5: no. 1126). Mme de Bours' parting from Mary was even more anguished. Mary had been with her for three and a half years, longer than Anne was with Mme de Riou; Mme de Riou had a second family of young children, but Mme de Bours had only two grown children, a daughter married and with a child, and a son, heir to his estate and unmarried. She enjoyed the companionship of Mary, a well-connected English girl younger than her children. She wrote of Mary as beautiful, tall, affectionate, and accomplished in music, French, and fine dress:

> I could not cherish her more tenderly were she my own daughter. I have found her so entirely obedient that it is impossible to express to you the natural goodness of disposition that is in her. (*LL*, 3: no. 626)

Mary was a comfort to her guardian and, as we shall see, perhaps already a love interest for Madame's son. Mary and Mme de Bours parted reluctantly (*LL*, 3: nos. 622, 623, 623a, 626–27), but the time had come for Mary to seek a service position in England.

The fostering arrangements removed the two girls from their natal family in their early teens, but separation did not weaken their affection for parents, siblings, or stepsisters. The loss of their natal father seems to have come early enough in their lives that Lord Lisle could in some measure replace him. The fostering arrangement was an affectionate one but recognized on all sides to be temporary. Not all such arrangements resulted in strong mutual bonds, but the Lisles made an effort to select compatible foster parents for their daughters and sons and to keep the arrangement mutually agreeable with the exchange of gifts, services, and tokens of esteem.

PHASE THREE: SERVICE POSITIONS

For Tudor noble parents, as for those of the Middle Ages, appropriate service stations were not menial but rather opportunities for continued training and contacts that could lead to profitable marriages. Desirable service positions, even if the family had to pay the finding, included those in the household of a powerful noble family, a prominent cleric, or the king's high officers. Other choice positions, as in the household or government of Calais, ensured a living and provided training. In securing a suitable position for children or wards, adults called upon networks of kin and friends to solicit their influence.[20] Again, not only the patriarch's networks were important but also those of the mother.

Honor and Arthur had high aspirations for their children. The Basset girls had dowries of £66:13:4, a typical sum for the time, so that marriage within the gentry class was guaranteed. Honor hoped to put the youngest three into court as ladies-in-waiting to the queen or Princess Mary[21] or, failing that, into noble households. Well-placed female kin were enlisted to help: Honor's niece the countess of Sussex, another "niece" (really a cousin) the countess of Salisbury, and the countess of Rutland, wife of Arthur's cousin. Mrs. Arundell, who became Lady Sussex, was Honor's sister's daughter, and Honor must have reasoned that if her niece could make such a brilliant marriage as a Maid of Honor, Anne or Katharine could as well. Placing a daughter in such a position was so much a function of the female network that when Husee approached his male connections at court, he was reprimanded, "for it is thought by my Lady of Sussex and other of your lady's very friends that it is no meet suit for any man to move such matter, but only for such ladies and women as be your friends" (LL, 4: no. 896).

The initial response of Honor's lady relatives, however, was that at fifteen or sixteen, Anne was too young for the court. Undaunted, Honor proposed the next older daughter, Katharine, but there were no openings for a Maid of Honor, and there matters rested for a year (LL, 4: 104–107, no. 863). To further the endeavor, plans were set afoot to place Anne or Katharine in the household of Lady Sussex or some other lady "that the King and Queen may see her" (LL, 4: nos. 867, 868a, 870a). Strategies and maneuverings finally fell into place through gifts of quail. Jane Seymour, then queen, was pregnant and doted on quail, readily available around Calais. The Lisles duly contacted their French friends, and, many shipments of quail later, Husee could write:

> Madam, upon Thursday last the Queen being at dinner, my Lady Rutland and my Lady Sussex being waiters on her Grace, her Grace chanced, eating of the quails, to common of your ladyship and of your daughters: so that such communication was uttered by the said ii ladies that her Grace made grant to have one of your daughters; and the matter thus concluded that your ladyship shall send them both over, for her Grace will first see them and know their manners, fashions and conditions, and take which of them shall like her Grace best.

The queen proposed to pay wages and livery, but the one chosen would have to provide the rest for herself. The girls would stay with Lady Sussex and Lady Rutland, and the one not selected as a Maid of Honor would enter the household of the king's sister, the duchess of Suffolk. The effort had taken a year and a half.

Such dazzling prospects required preparation. The girls were to be at court in six weeks, dressed for the part. Husee did not recommend major expenditure because the one selected would have the further expense of court attire. But they were to have "ii honest changes," one satin, one damask. External appearances were not the only concern; the prudent Husee also advised on the young women's behavior. The message is such as one would find in a medieval book of manners:

> And for as much as they shall now go upon making and marring, it shall please your ladyship to exhort them to be sober, sad, wise and discreet and lowly above all thing, and to be obedient, and governed and ruled by my Lady Rutland and my Lady Sussex… and to serve God and to be virtuous, for that is much regarded, to serve God well and to be sober of tongue.

He added that he knew they were well reared but pointed out the practical advantages, since the court was "full of pride, envy, indignation and mocking, scorning and derision." Furthermore, if they were to be a credit to the family, they must not disgrace their kin at court. He urged that a good exhortation about their behavior and prospects from "your ladyship's mouth" before they left "will stick nigh their stomachs." Husee's recommendations give vivid context to Polonius's advice to Laertes; one imagines that such solemn scenes were typical of parental admonitions to adolescents as they went off to make their debuts in the world.[22]

Gifts of quail for the queen continued, and Husee urged that the girls be sent over soon, as one of the Maids of Honor was to be married and a place would be available. They arrived on September 15, 1537 (*LL*, 4: nos. 888-895). The arrangements for the girls at court give an intimate idea of the care and concern that the two young matrons provided for their kinswoman's daughters:

> My Lady of Sussex hath given Mrs. Anne a kirtle of crimson damask and sleeves of the same, and also she hath promised Mrs. Katharine a gown of taffeta, so that she is very good and loving to them; and Mrs Anne lieth in her chamber, and Mrs. Katharine in my Lady Rutland's chamber. (*LL*, 4: no. 895)

Noblewomen attending the queen had chambers in which they could keep two female companions; they could add one, but the limit was three. Thus, each of the women took in one of the girls while they waited for the queen's decision.

When the queen had seen the girls, she chose Anne. The investment in "finishing" her in a French household had reaped the desired dividend. As a Maid of Honor, she would receive a wage of £10 a year and livery (a Christmas cloth allowance, and proper attire for coronations and other ceremonies). She would have chamber space, candles and fire materials but would have to provide her own bed. She would also pay for her servant, but her meals and those of the servant were provided.

The matter of dress was essential for the aspiring courtier. Initially, the queen allowed Anne to wear French apparel, but she had to wear an English velvet bonnet and frontlet. Lady Sussex lent the bonnet; Husee personally felt the French hood was more becoming, "but the Queen's pleasure must needs be filled." Both girls needed new gowns and Lady Sussex oversaw the conversion of old gowns into kirtles. Anne's office required her to wear black satin or velvet with pearl edges or tawny satin; Katharine, who was to stay with Lady Rutland, did not need a prescribed outfit but did have to dress the courtier's part (*LL*, 4: 194–96, nos. 895, 896, 900).

Discussion of appropriate behavior continued. At first, Husee was confident Honor need not worry about the girls' demeanor: "the gentlewomen are of a good judgment and hath fine wits, so that I trust there shall be no fault found in them." But Anne's high spirits apparently led to criticism from Lady Sussex and others. Still, Husee was able to write that "Mrs. Anne is clearly altered, and in manner no fault can be found in her"(*LL*, 4: nos. 895, 906). Despite this one slip, Anne did remarkably well in her court career. Her beauty and grace recommended themselves to Henry VIII, who approved Queen Jane's choice. Her appointment, however, lasted only a month: she began her duties just as Jane took to her chamber before childbirth, and within twelve days of Prince Edward's arrival, the queen was dead (*LL*, 4:175–182).

The loss of his third queen did not discourage Henry from promising to retain Anne as a Maid of Honor for his next; she served all his later wives. In the interim she stayed with Lady Sussex and was at court as much as possible to remind Henry of herself and her wage. As usual her mother took an active role: gifts to Henry of quail, peas, and Honor's fine conserves were forthcoming. In 1539, on the verge of his marriage to Anne of Cleves, Anne wrote to her mother that she had presented Honor's conserves to the king, who liked them and asked for more of the damson ones. Her mother also recommended loyalty to the king—needless advice to a now-seasoned courtier (*LL*, 5: nos. 1427, 1513, 1558, 1620, 1653). Anne appreciated her mother's efforts to secure her preferment, thanking her for being "so good a mother unto me as to see me set forward, to your great cost and charge." But no doubt her beauty and accomplishments went far to ensure Henry's favor. A notable woman at court wrote in 1538 (when Anne was perhaps eighteen) that she "is as fair a gentlewoman, and as well made, as any that I know, and as gentle and as well behaveth herself that every body praiseth her that seeth her; and there is no doubt but she shall come to some great marriage" (*LL*, 5: no. 1201). Some speculated it might be with Henry himself (*LL*, 5:66).

We must leave the brilliant and beautiful daughter and turn to the more usual career pattern of the elder and apparently less accomplished and attractive Katharine. While Honor continued to push for a court preferment for her, Katharine stayed with Lady Rutland, Arthur's cousin's wife. Honor also pursued a place for her in Lord Hertford's household, but as he was a family enemy, Katharine enlisted Husee's support to remain with the Rutlands (*LL*, 5:433–34, 439, no. 1379). Husee, more comfortable with the less luminous Basset children, was moved by her arguments:

> I have been in hand with Mrs. Katharine, whom I perceive is loath
> to displease your ladyship, for she remitteth the ordering to your

> ladyship. I see well that she is loath to depart from my Lady Rutland, and fain would she be for her most preferment. She reconeth it better to be with my Lady Rutland, (in case she being with Lady Hertford) should be taken but as her woman; for my Lady Rutland doth not so take her nor use her. She is content to follow your ladyship's mind, and unless it might be for her great advancement I know well she would be loath to go from my Lady Rutland.

Husee could not have found a better time to argue for the current arrangement, which he thought best for all. He regarded Lady Rutland as a social arbiter, well placed at court; he also had a high regard for Katharine's judgment. Furthermore, in the same paragraph he says he has secured a "woman" for Honor, clearly alluding to the inferior position Katharine would occupy in the Hertford household (*LL*, 5: no. 1396a).[23]

As with the attachment that developed between the two girls and their French foster mothers, Katharine's relationship with Lady Rutland became a warm one. Lady Rutland had written that "Mrs. Katharine shall be as welcome to her while she liveth as her own daughter." Honor allowed the arrangement to continue and sent a pretty letter and a songbird to Lord Hertford thanking him for his kindness (*LL*, 5: nos. 1393, 1404, 1405, 1435). With the rumor that the king would marry Anne of Cleves, Katharine wrote her mother asking her to secure her an appointment in the new queen's household. Again Lady Rutland offered advice and support, and in 1540 Katharine was taken into Queen Anne's household though she never became a Maid of Honor, partly because of the marriage's short duration (*LL*, 5: no. 1574 and 6:276–77, nos. 1636, 1649–50, 1653).

For women, the service career usually ended with marriage, but the Basset girls did not marry young. Anne, whose court career lasted through all Henry VIII's later marriages, then received an annuity and married at thirty-three; Katharine was in her late twenties or perhaps thirties. Both married rather better than their sisters, so the strategy of fostering them in noble households worked as their parents had planned. Mary would likely have married as well had not Lord Lisle been arrested. Bridget, after her convent upbringing, married at perhaps twenty-five.[24]

THE RISKS OF STEPMOTHERS AND FOSTER MOTHERS

Accepting responsibility for children of a former marriage or taking in foster children posed risks to the surrogate mother as well as the children and adolescents; the Verney letters, for instance, paint a picture of reluctance to take on the burden of additional children.[25] The problems that could arise were many. The close, familial living arrangements in extended households could encourage romances among young people that were invariably awkward for all concerned. Margery Paston's marriage to Richard Calle is a well-known example; the Lisle letters also record the intimacies that developed. Lady Weston wrote to Lady Lisle asking if she needed a young gentlewoman in her service. The woman, aged twenty-six, came from a gentry family but "she did cast love to a young man, a servant of my husband, and he likewise to her, which young man had nothing; but there was no promise of matrimony." The man was dismissed, and Lady Weston was trying to place the young woman elsewhere (*LL*, 1: no. xxxi).

More serious was the secret marriage contract Mary Basset made with Gabriel de Montmorency, seigneur de Bours. The letters indicate that the attraction began while Mary was fostered with his mother. After exchanging gifts and letters in the spring of 1540, he made several trips to Calais to speak of marriage. The visit could not have come at a worse time; Lord Lisle had just been arrested. Honor Lisle, Mary, and Philippa were questioned and it came out that Mary and Gabriel had entered into a secret contract of marriage. Since Mary needed the king's permission to marry a Frenchman, these private actions were highly irregular; as it was a desirable marriage, suspicion of complicity with the young couple naturally fell on the Lisles. At first Honor claimed she had put off the suitor, saying he must speak with Lord Lisle, but further questioning revealed that Mary had told her mother and sisters of the engagement. Worse yet, when the interrogation began, Mary and Honor's gentlewoman threw the incriminating love letters into the latrine. The contract increased the suspicions that had led to Lord Lisle's arrest; implicated because she knew of the contract but did not stop it, Honor was arrested with her daughters. Political circumstances crushed the romance. Mary later married a West Country gentleman (*LL*, 6: 139–48).

Stepchildren could also prove a nuisance. The Plantagenet daughters caused no problems, but Jane and Thomasine Basset, the daughters of Honor's first husband, were a constant strain. For such spinsters, the normal life course was as supernumeraries in various relatives' homes. Jane, however, wanted to be keeper of the Basset manor house in Devon. She moved her possessions there, but also wanted to take the great book of deeds and charters to which she had no right and which Honor wanted kept safe because of sundry lawsuits. Jane did manage to take Honor's dower agreement (*LL*, 3: 35–43, no. 513). Having established herself, hired a maidservant and secured an aggressive dog, Jane informed Honor that she needed more room and income; she moved from one cow pasturing in the park to three cows and a horse and expected from Honor a buck each year, or at least a doe. Such a tyrant had Jane become that Thomasine went to live with a married sister, sneaking out at dawn when Jane was asleep. Jane saw her sister's departure as part of a plot to force her into one of her married sister's households (*LL*, 3: 45–66, nos. 513–24).

As this essay privileges one set of letters over others, it cannot completely dispel negative images of foster and stepmothers; if the negative side of fostering does not appear in the Lisle letters, it does in those of the Pastons and Plumptons.[26] But the letters do call attention to subjects that deserve more study. Assumptions that all such arrangements were directed to the support of patriarchy require critical reappraisal. The importance of female networks in fostering and other areas was greater than has been documented. And the importance of kinship networks, foster parents, and stepparents in furthering the careers of youth has been underestimated.

NOTES

1. Peter Laslett, *Family Life and Illicit Love in Earlier Generations* (Cambridge, 1977), chap. 4, notes that one-sixth or more of American children under eighteen live in one-parent families, either through death or divorce. In the reconstitution of a seventeenth-century village population, 32 percent of children were orphans, more without a father than a mother. Men usually remarried quickly after a wife's death; widows usually did not remarry as often but I found that 75 pecent of London citizens' widows with children remarried. As this information was recorded when the children's wardship was determined, it probably represents underreporting (Barbara A. Hanawalt, "Remarriage as an Option for Urban and Rural Widows in Late Medieval England," in *Wife and Widow in Medieval England,* ed. Sue Sheridan Walker [Ann Arbor, 1993], pp. 141–64).

2. *The Italian Relation of England: A Relation of the Island of England,* ed. C.A. Sneyd, Camden Society 37 (1847), p. 24. Historians who quote this visitor's negative views on fostering generally reach the same conclusions he did. See H.S. Bennett, *The Pastons and Their England* (Cambridge, 1922), pp. 79–80, 82–83; Lawrence Stone, *The Family, Sex and Marriage in England, 1500–1800* (New York, 1977), pp. 105–07. A particularly mindless repetition of the myth is in Barbara Kaye Greenleaf, *Children through the Ages: A History of Childhood* (New York, 1978), pp. 32–37, paraphrasing Philippe Ariès, *Centuries of Childhood: A Social History of the Family,* trans. Robert Baldick (London, 1962). Even an opponent of this view for early modern England, Linda A. Pollock, *Forgotten Children: Parent-child Relations from 1500–1900* (Cambridge, 1983) does not consider the nurturing role surrogates might play. On fostering from the viewpoint of the receiving household, see Kate Mertes, *The English Noble Household, 1250–1600* (Oxford, 1988), pp. 174–75.

3. Stone, *Family, Sex and Marriage,* pp. 105–07, speaks of closer bonds to wet-nurses than to mothers, and characterizes wetnurses as "mercenary"; Lloyd DeMause, *The History of Childhood* (New York, 1974), pp. 32–36, considers wet-nursing abandonment. In fact there is scant evidence for the use of wetnurses in England. I found virtually none for fourteenth- and fifteenth-century London (Barbara A. Hanawalt, *Growing Up in Medieval London: The Experience of Childhood in History* [New York, 1993], pp. 51–58); Pollock, *Forgotten Children,* found none for their extensive use outside the upper classes.

4. Miriam Slater, *Family Life in the Seventeenth Century: The Verneys of Claydon House* (London, 1984), pp. 56–57, sees fostering as typical of the patriarchal family. Diane Willen, "Women and Religion in Early Modern England," in *Women in Reformation and Counter-Reformation Europe,* ed. Sherrin Marshall (Bloomington, IN, 1989), pp. 140–41, criticizes both overemphasis on patriarchy and the thesis of Joan Kelly's essay on women in the Renaissance: "Did Women Have a Renaissance?" *Women, History, and Theory* (Chicago, 1984), pp. 19–50. The Lisle letters do not speak to the debate over whether women had a Renaissance, since the Lisle daughters were trained for court and eventually for marriage.

5. Hanawalt, *Growing Up in Medieval London,* pp. 129–53; eadem, *The Ties That Bound: Peasant Families in Medieval England* (New York, 1986), pp. 75–78.

6. Barbara A. Hanawalt, "Lady Honor Lisle's Networks of Influence," in *Women and Power in the Middle Ages,* eds. Mary Erler and Maryanne Kowaleski (Athens, GA, 1988), pp. 188–214, explores the establishment of a woman's networks. Barbara J. Harris, "Property, Power, and Personal Relations: Elite Mothers and Sons in Yorkist and Early Tudor England," *Signs,* 15 (1990), 606–32, includes Honor Lisle and her sons, emphasizing natural mothers rather than fostering. In "Women and Politics in Early

Tudor England," *The Historical Journal* 33 (1990), 259– 81, Harris discusses women who negotiated fostering arrangements as well as marriages for their children.

7. *The Lisle Letters*, 6 vols., ed. Muriel St. Clare Byrne (Chicago, 1981), hereafter: *LL*. The letters are preserved in the Public Record Office; some were edited in *Calendars of State Papers, Domestic*. The Paston, Stonor, and Plumpton letters also refer to fostering, but here I use only the Lisle letters.

8. On gentry families combined by remarriage, Stone, *Family, Sex and Marriage*, pp. 44–45. John Basset was born Oct. 26, 1518; James, probably the last child, in 1526/7. Philippa was the oldest, perhaps born in 1516. Katharine was probably born in 1517 or 1519–20. Anne was born c. 1521, Mary and George between 1522 and 1525.

9. Ruth Kelso, *Doctrine for the Lady of the Renaissance* (Urbana, IL, 1956) discusses books of advice for women including the humanist Vives' work for Katherine of Aragon. See also Retha M. Warnicke, *Women of the English Renaissance and Reformation* (Westport, CT, 1983). The education of princes and male courtiers was a favorite theme of the Renaissance and the adolescent training of many males can be documented; in contrast, books of manners for females and scant evidence for their lives leave one wondering about women's real adolescent experience.

10. The alternative, committing a daughter to a nunnery, was neither cheap nor necessarily desirable. Eileen Power, *Medieval English Nunneries* (Cambridge, 1922), discusses the expense of entering a nunnery and women's lives in them. Barbara J. Harris, "A New Look at the Reformation: Aristocratic Women and Nunneries," *Journal of British Studies* 32 (1992), 89–98, finds that men preferred to marry off daughters rather than see them enter nunneries. Thus there were few elite women in the nunneries.

11. Harris, "Women and Nunneries," finds that noblewomen showed little interest in nunneries, neither entering them nor endowing them. She does not consider whether they used them as the Lisles did, but that Bridget was the most prestigious child at St Mary's indicates they did not. Probably Arthur and Honor would not have placed Bridget in a convent were they not living abroad.

12. Debate on the use of vocabulary to distinguish children of different ages and developmental stages stems from Ariès' claim (*Centuries of Childhood*, pp. 18–32, 411) that childhood and adolescence did not exist until the early modern period because the labels did not have the same meaning then as now; James A. Schultz, "Medieval Adolescence: The Claims of History and the Silence of German Narrative," *Speculum* 66 (1991), 519–39, has sought to support Ariès. But any reader of the "ages of man" literature knows that the argument is fallacious. See, e.g., J. A. Burrow, *The Ages of Man: A Study in Medieval Writing and Thought* (Oxford, 1988).

13. For a reflective view of Anne Boleyn's early years and fostering at the Burgundian and French courts, see Retha M. Warnicke, *The Rise and Fall of Anne Boleyn* (New York, 1989), pp. 6–28; compare Eric Ives, *Anne Boleyn* (Oxford, 1986), pp. 22–46. Arthur Lisle knew French, and like Thomas Boleyn had considerable diplomatic experience; Honor Lisle knew Anne Boleyn and was among the masked beauties with Anne and her kinswomen at one of Henry VIII's meetings with the French king (Ives, *Anne Boleyn*, p. 200). Both Honor and Arthur would thus have known the value of a French education for the advancement of both sons and daughters.

14. Thirteen was a typical age because the young women were to serve as "decorative foils" to their mistresses. They were to learn to dress, play musical instruments and sing, converse easily, and generally make themselves desirable for marriage or Maids of Honor in a royal court (Warnike, *Rise and Fall of Anne Boleyn*, pp. 12–13).

15. Hanawalt, "Honor Lisle's Networks," pp. 194–95. Exchanges with foster parents were of particular importance to preserve goodwill and to ensure good treatment of the children.

16. The boys also demonstrated their skills: John wrote a Latin letter and George showed his acquisition of a good hand. Only forty-seven letters survive from Lady Lisle's children: Katharine (three), John (three), George (two), Anne (ten), Mary (thirteen), and James (sixteen).

17. More than brothers and fathers, these women, and others whose letters are not preserved, could use letters to convey emotions and maintain networks at a distance. Letter writing for women could provide distance without formality, and intimacy without embarrassing or dangerous confrontation. In some respects the letters, because they were unpublished, played a role similar to seventeenth-century autobiographies. See Mary Beth Rose, "Gender, Genre, and History: Seventeenth-Century English Women and the Art of Autobiography," in *Women in the Middle Ages and the Renaissance*, ed. Mary Beth Rose (Syracuse, NY, 1986), pp. 245–78. See also Joan Ferrante, "Public Postures and Private Maneuvers: Roles Medieval Women Play," in *Women and Power in the Middle Ages*, pp. 221–28.

18. *LL*, 3: no. 609, is from Mary to Philippa thanking her for a New Year's gift and sending greetings from the de Rious to Anne. Apparently, Mary received little from Arthur in this period; he sent her a demi-ducat at New Year's and promised a gown, but in March she asked Honor to remind him of the gown (no. 615). In *LL*, 4:193–97, no. 899, a correspondent obviously accepts that Arthur is much engaged in the Basset girls' interests.

19. Margaret of Austria wrote in similar terms to Thomas Boleyn about his daughter: "I find her so bright and pleasant for her young age that I am more beholden to you for sending her to me than you are to me" (Ives, *Anne Boleyn*, p. 23).

20. Byrne discusses service and its meaning for Tudor England in *LL*, 3: 1–35.

21. Warnicke, *Rise and Fall of Anne Boleyn*, p. 13, comments that Thomas Boleyn's aim was for his daughter to become a Maid of Honor to the queen of England, not queen herself.

22. *LL*, 4: 887, remarkable for its succinct layout of the patronage system, dress, and behavior accompanying such an appointment. The Lisles were well served by Husee; he, of course, had his own reasons to wish that the girls were exemplary because his reputation at court was also at stake. Ives, *Anne Boleyn*, pp. 3–21, has a superb discussion of the court's heated atmosphere.

23. Though one might construe the arrangement as a move toward peace-making, Husee advised the Lisles to introduce a servant or adviser as informant in the Hertford household. Either as hostage or informer, Katharine would have been in a very uncomfortable position.

24. For the chief protagonists' fates, *LL*, 6:271–90. Marriage was not for every woman. One-sixth to one-quarter of women remained single in the sixteenth century; the average age at marriage for women was 26, for men 17 to 29 (J. Hajnal, "European Marriage Patterns in Perspective," in *Population in History: Essays in Historical Demography*, eds. D. V. Glass and D. E. C. Eversley [Chicago, 1965], pp. 101–43). Stone, *Family, Sex, and Marriage*, pp. 47–49, found a similar pattern of age at marriage for peers; 4 percent of peers' daughters did not marry in the late sixteenth century.

25. Slater, *Family Life in the Seventeenth Century*, pp. 132–38. Mertes, *English Noble Household*, pp. 174–75, suggests the fostering period might coincide with the life stage when the family itself had young children, causing friction within the household. Honor evidently did not foster children in her household, but her expanded household did include young men connected with the garrison and governing of Calais; to an extent they became her responsibility as well as Lord Lisle's.

26. Bennett, *The Pastons*, pp. 82–86.

LOOKING FOR GRANDMOTHER:
THE PASTONS AND THEIR COUNTERPARTS
IN LATE MEDIEVAL ENGLAND[1]

Joel T. Rosenthal

The Paston Letters *record the activities of Agnes and Margaret Paston, two active fifteenth-century English grandmothers. Other sources supplement the picture with tales of anomie and isolation, the old women's household as the center of socialization for young girls, and grandmothers as lynchpins between the family's past identity and current enterprises.*

Family dynamics and relationships within the kinship network are among the more mysterious, as well as the more complex, issues that social historians feel called upon to tackle. Within the space bounded and governed by these "socially constructed" forces lie some critical problems: definitions of identity, of personality and social affect, and of the strength of the imprint of our early coding among others. Some of these mysteries have been tackled by recent scholarship. Others, however, have either defied us or have remained beyond the pale of our focused curiosity.

The three-generation family—the triad of grandparents, parents, and children—is elusive, to say the least. Because such a unit or three-tier aggregation was demographically improbable and because of the male-directed nature of descent and inheritance and refinement sources, the links between the first and the third generation are hard to track or assess. I have tried elsewhere to gauge the incidence or frequency of three-generation links and to estimate the strength of and the feeling behind some of these links.[2] But the material has been more quantitative and genealogical than personal or qualitative. Furthermore, most of what we learn about grandparent-grandchild relationships pertains to grandfathers, and it usually is approached in terms of their formal rather than intimate or individualized links with grandchildren whom we know because they were the old men's heirs.

What about grand*mothers*? When we pose this question we can think of a "grandmother" as a person, an institution, and finally a function or an activity—as in the verb "to grandmother." In the mythology of family life, she is frequently depicted as a major figure. Whether we look at "primitive society," at working class and immigrant life with the bonding of alternate generations, at the complex legacies of ethnicity and the oral tradition, or at popular culture as transmitted through the media, the grandmother is apt to emerge as an emotional and functional focal point of the kin group.[3] She is a caretaker; she may move into the children's home if widowhood or disability so dictate; she transmits the lore of the elders to the young; she is the matriarchal lynchpin around whom ceremonies and rituals revolve. Whether we set her in the kitchen with an infant on her lap or in a retirement community or on an excursion of "senior citizens," she is a key element in the family unit.

So we situate her today. But how much of this role can we run back to late medieval England? How many of her roles—real or fictitious—can we identify and explicate for family life in earlier centuries?[4]

One striking characteristic of the grandmother in that earlier world is that she is not readily found. Even when working with sources that proclaim her presence, one finds her hard to identify. The *Inquisitions Post Mortem* offer glimpses of (aged) widows, now the subject of inquiries regarding dower holdings and next of kin, but such findings are thin, even with their bits of hard data. Nor do wills offer much richer fare.

And yet, despite these awkward and ill-marked turns of the road, there is no doubt that grandmothers were sometimes waiting to be heard, could we but pick up their voices. To help in this search we turn—as many have done before us—to the letters of the Paston family from Norfolk, written between 1425 and 1495. "Grandmothers and grandmothering in the Paston family" has a comforting ring, conjuring up visions of a deep text of affective interaction, of rich splashes of color on the tapestry of lived experience. A close look yields less than we might hope. What was the Paston record in regard to its women and their three-generation overlap?

Between the death of William Paston I in 1444 and Margaret Paston in 1484 we have two instances of grandmothers (and grandchildren) within the patriarchal line: Agnes, née Berry, and the more familiar Margaret, née Maultby.[5] Agnes comes first, in chronology and in the depth of experience as a grandmother. Agnes survived William I by 35 years; since her first grandchild by John I had been born in 1442, she had some 37 years as a grandmother before her death in 1479.[6] During this span her son John I and his wife Margaret produced seven children who survived and grew to adulthood, links in a three-generation family. Margaret, by contrast, was a grandmother for less than a decade, between the birth of Christopher (who died in infancy) or of William IV (born 1479–80) and her own death in 1484. The full tale of the grandmothers comprised more than these hard facts, but we should begin here. What can we extract from the letters regarding the two women and their three-generation links?

For Agnes, we have the thirteen letters and nine miscellaneous documents she wrote between 1440 and 1465; all but the first emanate from her long stretch as a widow and grandmother. In addition, we have three letters written to her between 1445 and the early 1460s, none of much value. But finally, and of considerable importance, we have a reasonable body of other peoples' letters in which she figures. From this material what information, and how much, can we extract regarding her contact with her grandchildren and her role—perceived or imposed—as a grandparent? What can we piece together about her concern for the third generation? And because the letters are a two-way glass, what do the other letter writers say about Agnes in the context of her role as matriarch and grandmother over a long period of time?

Agnes' own letters lack buried treasure. In her own letters and those written to her, mostly from her years of widowhood, there is no mention of grandchildren as individuals or of her role or capacity as a grandmother. But in some of the numerous letters between other correspondents in which she is mentioned or discussed—especially in some that passed between the second generation (mainly her daughter-in-law Margaret) and the third generation, her grandsons (John II and John III)—she receives considerable attention as a woman who mattered to those who depended upon her or who were called upon to heed her voice and her activities.[7]

By the time we reach a useful letter we are at 1462; Agnes had been a grandmother for almost two decades, a widow since 1444, and was almost the last survivor of her own generation. The references to her in younger relatives' letters fall into two categories: those that relate to her role in family affairs and those with a strong personal note (often not a hard and fast distinction). Business before pleasure. Between 1468 and 1478 four letters convey news of her role in family affairs. John III wrote to his brother John II in March 1468 about Agnes' trip to London (with their mother Margaret, Agnes' daughter-in-law) to press their side in the eternal property quarrels: "My lady and my grantdam be com to London for the same mater, wherfor it wer well do that the jugys wer enformyd of your mater before they spak wyth theym" (*PLP*, 1:538). A year later we find Margaret writing to John II about a visit with Agnes to the bishop of Norwich, Walter Lyhert, in the family's abortive efforts to block the marriage of daughter Margery to Richard Calle. Margaret says that Agnes was as forward as she in this unsavory business, and Margaret stressed to John that it had been a joint effort: "letyng yow wete that on Thurysday last my moder and I hwere wyth my lord of Norwych, and desyerd hym that he woold nomore do in the matere towscheyng yowr syster." And when Margery stood by her guns, the two women were partners in distress: "Thes leud worddys gereue me and here grandam as myche as alle the remnawnte." Margaret's decision to end relations with her daughter was made while, "I was wyth my moder at here plase wan sche [Margery] was exameynd...." Shame and scandal made the women act with one heart and mind (*PLP*, 1:341–42).[8]

In 1473, John II wrote to ask his mother about his being cut from his father's will. His grandmother and uncle had told him that his share of the estate had fallen short of his expectations (*PLP*, 1:466).[9] And in the last of the four letters business is mixed with the personal, as family honor was invoked to justify another round in the endless pursuit of land and inheritance. John II tells John III that it behooves them to pursue their interest in the manor of Oxenhed (Oxnead, Norfolk), for their grandmother's sake: "Item, bothe ye ande I most nedys take thys matere as owre owne, and it weere for noon other cawse butt for owre goode grawntdames sake" (*PLP*, 1:511).[10]

Other letters between these correspondents offer a more domestic or affectionate dimension, perhaps needed because of Agnes' long-running quarrel with her son John I over old William's estate and John's inordinate share thereof, largely at the expense of his brothers. In 1462, when John III was on military service in the North, he asked his brother (John II) to convey his best tidings to his grandmother and to cousin Clere: "I pray yow let my grandam and my cosyn Cler haue knolage how that I desyiryd yow to let hem haue knowlage of the tydyngys in thy letyr, for I promysyd for to send them tydyngys" (*PLP*, 1:524). This went with a similar commission regarding his parents. A few months later Margaret told her husband that John II had returned from his travels but that the boy's grandmother was making (too) much of his return (*PLP*, 1:284–85).[11] Since relations between John I and John II were strained, we do not know if Margaret was trying to coax her unyielding husband into a more pliable stance, like that taken by old Agnes, or whether she was siding with her husband and distancing herself from what she might have considered her mother-in-law's too indulgent behavior towards a wayward youth.

In 1463 it was Margaret who was playing the role of peace maker between husband and eldest son. This time a long letter to John II reminds him that his family duties include keeping in touch with his grandmother: "Your grandam wold fayne her sum tydyngys from yow. It were welle do that ye sent a letter to hyr howe ye do as astely as ye may" (*PLP*, 1:288). By 1470 John I was dead, and Margaret's letter to John II came with presents from his grandmother: "I send you be the berere her—of all the syluer vessell that your graundam maketh so mych of, which she seid I had of myn husbond and myn husbond shuld haue had it of his fadere"; she goes on to indicate that the presents she received from her mother-in-law never quite lived up to their supposed value (*PLP*, 1:350). In 1474 we have John II sending mixed news to his mother: "Blessynd be Good my grauntdam is amendyd by suche tyme as myn oncle W. come hyddre, but my yongest cosyn Margret, hys doghtre, is ded and beryed er he come hom" (*PLP*, 1:478). The last letter of this group, from Margaret to John III, instructs him—now the eldest surviving son—to convey best wishes to the old lady: "Recommaund me to yowyr grauntdam. I wold she war her in Norffolk as well at es as evyr I sy hyr, and as lytyll rewlyd be hyr son as evyr she was, and than I wold hope that we alle shuld far the bettyr for hyr" (*PLP*, 1:374).[12]

Together these disconnected snippets construct a picture of Agnes' continuing presence and of her powerful and often difficult personality. The pieces are thin as a full biography but they convey an image of a vigorous old lady, actively (or aggressively) involved in her own affairs and in those of others until near her death. The Agnes who emerges fits neatly into the larger patterns of Paston behavior and ego: everyone wanted to be involved in everything. The mere existence of the letters—with so many recipients and so many different writers—indicates how Pastons, over the decades, were concerned to be kept abreast.

But the principles that determine inclusion or exclusion in the letters reflect more than tone of voice and style of discourse. Because they center on the patriarchal quest for land and social position, the letters concentrate on the chain of Paston to Paston; whole batches of letters barely acknowledge the collateral lines and the kinsmen and women who had moved away from the mainstream. Thus it is consonant with the purposes of the collection that the letters say virtually nothing of Agnes' involvement with her grandchildren from farther afield, that is, with those not caught up in the quarrels and lawsuits that constitute the bread and butter of the correspondence.

Agnes and William had five children who survived infancy. We noted her sustained and seemingly warm contacts with the two eldest sons of her first son, her grandsons John II and John III, plus her active role in working against the marriage of her granddaughter Margery to Richard Calle, the family's bailiff. But of her son William—married to no less than Anne Beaufort, a daughter of the duke of Somerset—the letters say nothing. The Paston–Beaufort marriage produced at least two daughters, one of whom married the earl of Westmorland's heir in a match arranged by Margaret Beaufort, Henry VII's mother.[13] This is an interesting topic *not* to mention. Neither does Agnes refer to her youngest child, Elizabeth, beyond the early problem of finding her a husband. She was successively wife and widow of Robert Poynings (of the peerage family) and of Sir George Brown, and a mother by both husbands. Whatever the ties between Agnes-as-mother and these children and their children, households, and influential friends, no traces are found in *The Letters*. The letters focus on the struggles to preserve the Paston and Berry inheritance and to implement the (supposed) provisions of the Fastolf will; even children who married outwards, albeit upwards, were relegated to the realms of silence in our records.

The intrafamilial silence that surrounds Agnes is compounded by the fact that we only have preliminary drafts of her will rather than the final version that went to probate. Her daughter-in-law Margaret's will indicates that family ties otherwise unmentioned, even pointedly ignored, could be the center of some attention at the end. The drafts of Agnes' will mostly reveal her protracted concern with the fact that John I had come away with the lion's share, and his brothers William and Clement with not nearly enough, from the will of William I, their father. This enduring quarrel becomes a rich family text but one with little focus on grandchildren.[14] What we do get from Agnes are striking reminiscences and reflections upon her role as mother, memories of William's deathbed drama thirty-five years before,[15] and of her own prospects when faced with death. As with many widows who survived husbands by so many years, the end was a nostalgic time to reemphasize bonds of husband and wife, not just with prayers but even—given the formulaic nature of a will— with anecdote. In her last letter to her son (in 1465: John I died in 1466) Agnes recalled her husband: "Youre fader sayde, 'In lityl bysynes lyeth myche rest.' This worlde is but a thorugh-fare and ful of woo, and whan we departe ther-fro, rigth nouyght bere wyth vs but oure good dedys and ylle" (*PLP*, 1:43–44).

When Agnes turned to her own death and burial, she put herself firmly in the setting of family traditions and the customary recipients of largesse (and she remembered that she had two families). She and William had subsidized a "perpetuall masse" at the White Friars, Norwich. Beyond that, bequests were to go "to the mendinge of the chappell of Our Ladie" in that house, "whereas Sir Thomas Gerbredge my grandfather and Dame Elizabeth his wife and Sir Edmond Bery my father and Dame Alice his wife be buried, and Clement Paston my sonn."

If Agnes' words and influence reveal an aging but powerful presence over a long span of years, her daughter-in-law Margaret— generally the most central and expressive of the Paston women —is virtually invisible (and inaudible) in this role. Of course, Margaret only had a few years; her chance did not come until 1479 (the year of Agnes' death) and she died in 1484 (when her sons John II and Walter also died). None of the letters either to, from, or about Margaret from this short period tell anything of her three-generational role, one for which she had waited so long and for the realization of which she had expended so much energy. But as a counterpoise, Margaret left a will that opens a very wide door (*PLP*, 1:382–89). It is a mine of information about grandchildren, fleshing out genealogy and giving guidance to ties and sentiments that are otherwise hidden. From such a controlling personality as Margaret, the will is a strongly personal statement.

When she made her will, four of her children were still alive; all come in for some mention. As for the next generation—the children of the children—seven grandchildren are among the beneficiaries. They were the children of four of her children, of whom two were alive, two dead. Edmund's son Robert (plus Edmund's wife), along with William and Elizabeth, children of John III, receive conventional bequests. Beyond these three grandchildren, whose parents were alive, her bequests show some variation. The deceased John II left a bastard daughter Custance, remembered by the grandmother with ten marks, "whan she is xx yer of age." Three grandchildren from the much-cursed marriage of Margery and Richard Calle, probably youngsters who had by then outlived their mother, are serial beneficiaries; that is, the bequests went to the second (William) and the third (Richard) if the first (John) died without heirs. The bequest to the Calle children was only for £20, and it could not be claimed until the beneficiary had reached the age of twenty-four—four years beyond the waiting time for their cousin Custance.

Margaret's will, especially when set against the singlemindedness of her many letters, is as loquacious and comprehensive an instance of grandmother-grandchild communication as we find in the fifteenth century, one sided though it is. That it comes at the end—after years of active epistolary life in which Margaret never even alluded to these grandchildren—should make us reflect on the many realms of life that never became topics reflected in written sources even of private and personal communication. When we set the examples of her strong Paston family bonding against the fact that she requested burial at Mawteby with her natal family, rather than with the in-laws with whom she had been so involved for almost four decades, we have an intriguing tangle. It is a warning against easy generalizations about how lives were lived and identities framed.[16]

***

The data from Agnes and Margaret Paston actually provide a fair amount of information about how two long-lived women/grandmothers played their roles. The survival of pertinent information is sketchy, needless to say, and much of what we know rests on a few crucial statements, the survival of a few key documents. Nevertheless, these returns lead us to suggest a rich tapestry of the world of grandmothering, little though it has been preserved.

What more can we learn about grandmothers and grandmothering if we turn farther afield? It is likely that the returns will be thin; no other families have left such a rich archive, and few offer documentation on two successive matriarchs. Since Margaret Paston's will contained so many riches, parallel wills from numerous fifteenth century widows, many of them elderly and many of them, presumably, grandmothers, demand our attention.

Though the number of such wills is too small to enable us to talk of percentages or employ the "usuallies" and the "not infrequentlies" beloved of social historians, we find wills similar to Margaret's regarding the relation to grandchildren. Margaret Blackburn, widow of Nicholas, former lord mayor of York, was in the mainstream when she said: "Lego Nichilao Blakburn, filio meo, x li…et Roberto Blakburn, filio suo, decem marcas," though the number of grandchildren named and the amount left them put her way above the median.[17] Euphemia Langton scattered a small shower of personal and household goods upon her son's five sons while distributing a great pile of such stuff to many recipients via the clauses of a long will.[18]

There are variations, but when the third generation is mentioned, few testators stray far. Dionisia Holme of Beverley made it quick and easy: "Dionisiae Thorpp j togam de scarlette syngle. Cuilibet alii sex filiorum et filiarum praedictorum Willelmi Eland et Johannae j peciam albam stantem."[19] Catherine Fitzwilliam, once a gentlewoman of the countess of Cambridge, remembered two granddaughters: Katherine, "filiae primogenitae eorundem Ricardi and Elizabethae," was to receive "unum sigillum de aurio cum cruce de auro." One notch down, Katherine's sister ("sorori suae") was remembered with "j annulum de auro cum lapide rubio infra."[20]

There is little here that is unfamiliar or new after Agnes Paston's family role and Margaret Paston's will. The hurdle we cannot readily surmount in trying to assess these benefactions, like the links behind them, is that they come bereft of much context of relationship. Not only is family genealogy missing (in terms of the total of living children and grandchildren), but also any insight into the choices that governed recipients and benefactions. There is a range of other questions about testamentary links between grandmothers and grandchildren: were the children of daughters preferred to those of sons? were girls preferred by their grandmothers over their brothers? what proportion of all grandchildren were included among the beneficiaries?[21]

Even an elaborate will that reflects the last wishes of a woman who lived life at the top of the pyramid leaves questions. When Cecily Neville, dowager duchess of York and mother of Edward IV and Richard III, died in 1495 she, like Agnes Paston, was a relic of an earlier generation; in her case the deaths of immediate relatives had also left her a tragic if still dominant figure. Her will, perhaps due to political discretion (and Cecily's age), was steered strongly towards descendants of the third generation; Cecily was a grandmother with a passion for this role, judging from her final utterances. There are bequests to the queen (her granddaughter), to four other grandchildren—daughters of Edward IV and Elizabeth Wydeville, and to three grandchildren from a daughter's marriage into the de la Pole family. Two men, grandsons-by-marriage, were remembered, Henry VII being one of them. In addition, two great-grandsons receive bequests: Arthur, Prince of Wales, and his brother Henry, duke of York. Though Cecily's pattern of benefaction was governed by mortality and demography, it also indicates a strong grandmother-identity. Few fifteenth-century wills, whether from men or women, include so many third-generation descendants, and almost none reaches down to children of the fourth generation.[22]

**

There are two other topics to touch. One concerns the dowager household as a unit for socialization and intergenerational bonding. In the domestic arrangements of elderly women with adequate economic and physical resources we can locate opportunities for contact between grandmother and granddaughter. The networking of older women and young girls was vital for parties at both ends of the life cycle—whether the old and the young were closely related by blood or not. At a lesser social level the widow-cum-grandmother who lived with her children or who shared the home under some quasi-contractual agreement, assumed a comparable set of obligations regarding the young girls.[23]

This aspect of domesticity and socialization—as when Lady Pole took in Elizabeth Paston as her paying guest-cum-apprentice—is hardly in dispute. But what strikes us, coming by way of the Pastons, is how little relevant material emerges from the letters. The news that Paston recipients awaited was not likely to contain many details of "normal" patterns of domestic and family life; then as now, news leans towards the anomalous, the scandalous, and the sensational. We learn of the beatings administered to Elizabeth when she resisted marriage proposals, and we note that she was held in virtual house arrest. Agnes' comments are contained in a "memorandum of errands," and they also contain her thoughts about getting daughter Elizabeth out on her own, plus a note of the sums owed "Lady Pole" (duchess of Suffolk) for Elizabeth's keep (*PLP*, 1:40–41). When Margery made the love match with Richard Calle that sent her mother and grandmother to the bishop of Norwich, we may ask who had been looking after whom, even though the courtship might have been conducted by heavy looks and casual touches, right under the noses of mother, father, and (even) grandmother.

Whatever was going on and whether the children would have preferred to stay home or to escape to some other domestic unit, the role of grandmother's household as a training center for the young girls has to be judged another topic about which the Pastons did not choose to write. The awareness of her presence, even warmth of feeling, in the letters of John II and John III indicate that Agnes was close to their lives. Had these common experiences and memories taken root in London (where she lived with her son William at least part of the time) or at their East Anglian residences or on prolonged visits and holiday seasons? Or was the feeling inculcated through injunctions about doing the right thing towards one's elders?

The last topic we turn to is a sober one, and here we turn to the *Stonor Letters* rather than to the Pastons. Some of our inquiry has concerned old women, grandmothers by virtue of their years and their luck in the fertility stakes, burdened with the inescapable problems of the years. In the *Stonor Letters* we get glimpses of an old lady who is a subject of concern in several letters between her granddaughter's betrothed and his soon-to-be mother-in-law. In December 1477, Thomas Betson told Elizabeth Stonor (the mother-in-law) that "I spake unto my lady, your modyr…and she wold scarsely oppyn hir mouthe unto me; she is displesid and I know nat whereffore, with owte hir old sekenes be fallen on hir ageyn; God send hir ones a mery contenaunce, and a ffrendely tonnge." Was old Margaret Croke angry with young Thomas, displeased with the proposed marriage, or was she really in bad shape?[24]

When Thomas wrote in June 1478, he had better news: "My lady, your modyr, is in good helthe and ffareth well, and she sendeth you gods blissyng and hirs."[25] But a month later it was less cheerful: "I mette with my lady, your modyr, and God wote she made me right sullen chere with her countenaunce whyles I was with hir: me thought it longe till I was departed." She belabored Thomas with a repetitious tale that may have originated with his recounting it to her: "she brayke me to off the tayle I told hir betwene the vicar that was and hir; she said the vicar never ffared well set he tooke it so mych to hart." It was a dispiriting afternoon: "I had no joye to tary with hir. She is a ffyn mery woman, but ye shall nat know it nor yit ffynd it, nor none of youres by that I se in her." And when the old lady pays a visit it sheds no joy: "yff my lady, your modyr, mete my cossen Anne she will say no more but 'Godes blissynge have ye and myne,' and so goo hir waye fforthe as thow she had no joye of hir. Whanne ye come to London I shall tell you more."[26]

These excerpts are, admittedly, a thin wedge with which to open the doors of anomie and withdrawal. And yet, from a world that has left few such reflections, these painful and belabored communications provide a rare look at the inner and personal problems of a life now moving towards its natural end. Such a course must have been common for many women who had outlasted husbands and (as had Cecily of York) many of their children. These excerpts show the old lady's indifference to the world of her grandchildren, or perhaps they reflect a sporadic or self-absorbed concern. Not even the imminent prospect of great-grandchildren seems to have made much difference. From our distance it is easy to offer a diagnosis: dementia, depression, anger, the melancholy that accompanies isolation.

There are few data and few insights into the problems of personality change and gerontology. We are inclined to practice medicine, or psychology, without a license, and we note her isolation even when she was situated within a tightly-knit and communicating family unit. When we think of how easily control can slip away from the aged, we are more sympathetic to the heavy-handed behavior of the aging Agnes Paston. From a therapeutic perspective it was good news that she was still sufficiently engaged to command that her grandson drop her a note while he was wandering around the North on the king's business.

***

A few points have emerged. This essay is "about" the Paston family, an unlovely bunch. Two modern scholars who have treated them in depth have come away with a distinct bias against their leading figures; much of what sympathy is expressed is for those beleaguered daughters and feckless sons, Pastons who had fallen from grace.[27] Their usual demeanor helps reveal the dynamics of daily life among the pushy upper-middling classes. The three-generational forms of family interaction, seen exclusively in terms of the old women (as the men followed form and died first), add another dimension to the relationships. The presence (or absence) of grandmothers, and the need for a particular stance in dealing with them, was clearly part of the arsenal utilized by the young and the middle-aged when alarms were sounded. Agnes, in particular, elevated grandmothering into a sustained and protracted institution; her special status was another of the facts of life with which others had to cope in a tradition-bound, hierarchical social structure.

The second conclusion is "about" old women. We rarely see them as much more than the object of an *Inquisition Post Mortem* or, in a will, as the final arbiter of bequests, driving the engine of posthumous social control. The stages, crises, and contours of their lives are especially hard to fathom. Though we are never going to know all that much about the role and identity of the grandmother in this long-gone and reticent world, we can add nuances to the tale of the life course and of lived experience. Old people, like all others, had multiple identities and played numerous parts. Little of this multiplicity stands out; for old women, any additional context in which we can set them is all to the good. Coming to them as grandmothers offers a set of criteria by which to judge them, a list of challenges and problems by which to assess how they coped and reacted.

In some ways we are talking here about "three-generation consciousness." We have seen such consciousness and awareness in Agnes' dealings with those of the next and the next-plus-one generation. It also emerges in the memoranda for the preparation of her will, a reference to her own grandmother and grandfather. Such consciousness is likewise found in Margaret's will, as it is in her reference to clauses and bequests that had originated as far back as her grandfather's will. The Paston children, in turn, picked it up; old William's father (Clement), as well as William himself, were elements in the world they sought to re-create, building blocks towards the traditions they invented and then scrambled hard to realize.[28] I have argued elsewhere that the fifteenth-century family was in some ways a vertical construct, with space for previous generations as well as for the as-yet unborn who eventually would be expected to carry out conditional clauses just coming into being.[29]

If this transcendental view of how people framed their identities and egos within their family and social circles has any validity, then the case for turning one's thoughts to grandparents and/or grandchildren is stronger. If there are few signs of sentimentality in such relationships and few indications that they were a *sine qua non* for the fulfillment of a long life, we can assert that at least the presence, possible use of, and opportunity to manipulate the children's children were not the least privilege of a Paston grandmother. Why would Agnes or Margaret (or Cecily Neville) choose to pass up such an opportunity, one that had required years of waiting but that now—when the moment finally came—called for little special training and no great stretch of emotional fabric or personal comfort? There was much more take than give in being a grandmother, especially being a rich and widowed grandmother no longer "covered" by a patriarchal spouse. It was mostly a one-way street, and the powerful position of the old lady was the dominant factor in the relationship.

If our sources tilt us in this direction, towards her power and influence, another voice whispers that the aged are often marginalized, with their dismay and anger expressed in petulance rather than in a discourse of reciprocity. Maybe Agnes Paston should have given old Margaret Croke some advice about self-assertion. And maybe Margaret Croke might have reminded Agnes Paston how lucky she was to be rich, in good health, and surrounded by grandchildren who—whether they liked it or not—took account of her wishes and kept an eye on her welfare.

NOTES

1. I wish to express my appreciation to the editors of this volume for inviting me to contribute this paper; the invitation spurred me to organize my thoughts on a topic that has beckoned for some time. Various writings by John C. Parsons, including some not yet in print, have been immensely suggestive. Thanks to D.C. Samuels for help in getting the "final" version to be a final version. I wish to pay tribute to the memory of H.S. Bennett, who, as a visiting professor at the University of Chicago, first alerted me to the fascination of the Pastons. And finally, a debt to Colin Richmond, who in recent years has reminded us of how much there still is to say about the Pastons as a family.

2. J.T. Rosenthal, "When Did You Last See Your Grandfather?" in *Politics, Society, and Religion,* ed. Rowena E. Archer (Stroud, Glos., 1995).

3. Though grandparents, and especially grandmothers, figure in so much literature on the family, there is little work devoted primarily or specifically to the special role and relations of third-generation survivors, at least not until we come to contemporary geriatric studies and writing. For general material, see Michael Young and Peter Willmott, *Family and Kinship in East London* (Harmondsworth, 1965); Peter Townsend, *The Family Life of Old People* (Harmondsworth, 1957); M. Fortes, "The Developmental Cycle in Domestic Groups," in *Kinship,* ed. Jack Goody (Harmondsworth, 1971), pp. 85–98. The search for grandmothers reveals many interesting items; in a *New York Times* obituary of January 11, 1995 we learn that Sylvia B. Seaman, who died at ninety-four and whose early life included marching as a suffragist, had, "in the 1970s...resumed writing. ...including her last book, *How to be A Jewish Grandmother* (1979)." Two recent books that approach grandmothers from very different directions are Tracy E. Hyde, *The Single Grandmother* (Chicago, 1974), and Rosemary O. Joyce, *A Woman's Place: The Life History of a Rural Ohio Grandmother* (Columbus, OH, 1983).

4. Peter Laslett, *The World We Have Lost,* 2nd ed. (New York, 1971), esp. p. 103: "You could not with any confidence expect to see your grandchildren in the world we have lost."

5. Norman Davis, ed., *Paston Letters and Papers of the Fifteenth Century,* 2 vols. (Oxford, 1971–76), hereafter cited in the text parenthetically *PLP.* Various editors of the letters seem reluctant to offer a genealogical table of the family; I rely on that in Roger Virgoe, ed., *Private Life in the Fifteenth*

Century (New York, 1989), p. 22. See *PLP*, 1:lii–lxxiv for thumbnail biographical sketches and a family chronology.

6. For long widowhoods, J.T. Rosenthal, "Aristocratic Widows in Fifteenth Century England," in *Women and the Structure of Society*, eds. Barbara J. Harris and JoAnn K. McNamara (Durham NC, 1984), pp. 36–47, 259–60; Barbara A. Hanawalt, "The Widow's Mite: Provisions for Medieval London Widows," in *Upon My Husband's Death: Widows in the Literature of Histories of Medieval Europe*, ed. Louise Mirrer (Ann Arbor, 1992), pp. 21–45; Caroline M. Barron and Anne F. Sutton, ed., *Medieval London Widows, 1300–1500* (London, 1994), passim, for case studies and general reflections.

7. In deference to the allocation of different topics in this volume, I have avoided "mothering," in favor of the three-generational relationship implied by "grandmothering." One aspect of "mothering" that might merit study, however, is that of the mother-in-law/daughter-in-law relationship, figuring here as the tie that bound Agnes and Margaret for a long generation.

8. On marriage in this family, H.S. Bennett, *The Pastons and Their England*, 2nd ed. (Cambridge, 1932), pp. 27–41 (on marriage), 42–50 (on "The Love Story"); C.F. Richmond, "The Pastons Revisited: Marriage and the Family in Fifteenth Century England," *Bulletin of the Institute of Historical Research* 58 (1985), 25–36; Ann S. Haskell, "The Paston Women on Marriage in Fifteenth Century England," *Viator* 4 (1973), 459–71; Keith Dockray, "Why Did Fifteenth-Century English Gentry Marry?" in *Gentry and Lesser Nobility in Late Medieval Europe*, ed. Michael Jones (Gloucester, 1986), pp. 61–80.

9. John II is taxing his mother because she has not kept him abreast on this; he has been forced to learn the state of family matters from others. The fires of indignation and grievance run high: "My fadre, God have hys sowle, leffte me scant xi li. londe in rent, and ye [Margaret] leffe me as pleasythe yow, and my grauntdame at hyre plesure."

10. At this point Agnes has less than a year to live, and, as an old woman her end must have been predictably near. The boys, entering their thirties, were beginning to look beyond her: "Ye woote well thatt ther is an other entresse longyng to vsse afftre here [Agnes'] dysceasse." John charitably explains his brother's failure to respond to the latter's problems: "ye haue nowe wyffe and chylder, and so moche to kare fore thatt ye forgete me."

11. As with most of the longer letters, this one contains bits of news about different matters; the key family touch is (ll. 37–39), "My moder and many other folky makyth moche of your son John the older, and right glad of hys comyng hom, and lekyth reght welle hys demenyng."

12. The key news here appears in the fifth paragraph of what Davis prints as a five- or six-paragraph letter. Though it is likely that many of

the letters were composed over some (short) time span, rather than being written or dictated in just one sitting, the order of the news they convey and the relationship of the various topics to each other is worth further analysis.

13. Michael K. Jones and Malcolm G. Underwood, *The King's Mother: Lady Margaret Beaufort, Countess of Richmond and Derby* (Cambridge, 1992), p. 101. See *PLP*, 1:194 for William's will, in which he names both Margaret Beaufort and "my nevew" Edward Poynings among the executors. At his death in 1496 William had outlived Anne Beaufort, and in his will he remembers his two daughters, Agnes (named for her paternal grandmother?) and Elizabeth.

14. For the drafts of Agnes' will: *PLP*, 1:44–45 (draft of a will, September 16, 1466); 45–47 (part of a will, probably 1466); 47–48 (part of a will, probably 1466); and 49 for an extract from a will written no later than 1479.

15. *PLP*, 1:44–47. In three of the snippets Davis prints, Agnes recalls the scene near William's end: the summoning of the children and others, the working out of the terms, and the other scenes of the drama. Her narrative powers are of note: *PLP*, 1:45: "my seyd husband, lyyng sek on hijs bede, sent fore me…to here hijs wyll rede. And in owre presens all he began…." On the irony of William's death bed and final dispositions as a seminal event in family history (and mythology), Colin Richmond, *The Paston Family in the Fifteenth Century: The First Phase* (Cambridge, 1990), chap. 6, "The Deathbed of William Paston and Its Consequences," pp. 167–205.

16. As Agnes remembered her grandparents' burial site in the draft of her will, so Margaret referred to business that went back to her grandfather's time, possibly for a generation or two before that: *PLP*, 1:222: "Syre Robert of Mawthby and Ser John and myn grawnsyre, and dyverse other of myn awnceterys."

17. James Raine, Jr., ed., *T[estamenta] E[boracensia]*, vols. 2 and 3, Surtees Society vols. 30, 45 (1855, 1865), pp. 47–49: the probate date is April 29, 1435. We may not find the Pastons so hardhearted, could we compare them to many others of comparable status; the widow's bequest here to her son really means that she is excusing him a debt of £10 that she had coming. The son Nicholas also had two daughters, mentioned later in the will and slated to receive some wool cloth. In addition, the testator (and widow and grandmother) Margaret had two other children who received bequests and whose children *also* were beneficiaries. There was a daughter Isabel who had several sons, each of whom got ten marks, and a daughter Alice with a son John, singled out by his grandmother for a cash bequest of £10 "et xij cocliaria argenti signata cum R et N."

18. *TE*, 2:259: the will was probated November 24, 1463. *TE*, 2:214: for Isabel Kerr following a similar course. The way in which Kerr's

grandchildren are identified, and the order in which they are listed, is also fairly standard: first her son is named, then the son's son, and then the son's son's sister (as explained in the will)—so our order of learning of the recipients is that of son, then grandson, and lastly granddaughter.

19. *TE*, 3:183 (probated August 10, 1471).

20. *TE*, 3:227 (probated at Doncaster, May 30, 1477).

21. There is another whole set of questions about grandmother-daughter-grandchildren relationships that depend to a considerable extent on propinquity and that could be best answered at the level of manorial and village life, had we the data. These touch such matters as the mother's presence and help at confinements, with babysitting while the mother worked in or outside the house, godparenting, the teaching of domestic skills, and more of this sort. They pertain to mothers helping daughters (and daughters-in-law?) and to mothers socializing the next generation into the responsibilities of parenting: the topic is treated for fathers and sons and mothers and daughters in Barbara A. Hanawalt, *The Ties That Bound: Peasant Families in Medieval England* (New York, 1988).

22. John G. Nichols and John Bruce, eds., *Wills from Doctors' Commons*, Camden Society 83 (1862), pp. 1–8.

23. Jennifer C. Ward, *English Noblewomen in the Later Middle Ages* (London, 1992); Kate Mertes, *The English Noble Household, 1250–1600* (Oxford, 1988); *A Collection of Ordinances for the Royal Household* (London, 1790); all these give some introduction to primary and secondary sources by means of which this large topic can be approached. For a near equivalent from the other end of the social spectrum, Elaine Clark, "Some Aspects of Social Security in Medieval England," *Journal of Family History* 7 (1982), 307–32.

24. Charles L. Kingsford, ed., *[The] Stonor Letters and Papers, 1290–1483*, Camden Society, third series 29–30 (1919). The letter cited here is no. 185 (2:28). Kingsford gives a genealogy of the Stonors at 1:vi, and a discussion of the family at 1:xxvii–viii. For a detailed and illuminating study of Margaret Croke, see Kay Lacy, "Margaret Croke (d. 1491)," in Barron and Sutton, *Medieval London Widows*, pp. 143–64.

25. *Stonor Letters*, 2:55, no. 217 (June 24, 1478). Now Margaret is more outgoing, and she expresses interest in the recovery of Elizabeth Croke's husband (her son-in-law): "She is very glad of his recovery, and she prayed God to send hym good helth."

26. *Stonor Letters*, 2:64, no. 224 (July 31, 1478).

27. Bennett, *Pastons and Their England*, p. 33: in treating marriage and the family Bennett remarks that Margaret's "own children were treated with considerable severity, and the harsh genius of Agnes still dominated the Pastons' ideas of the education of children." But the younger woman was an apt student: "Both Agnes and Margaret are seen in their worst light in their dealings with their daughters. Agnes was never a genial woman"

(p. 79). Colin Richmond's acerbic views of the late medieval gentry in general and the Pastons in particular have been sprinkled through innumerable articles and reviews in recent years; the general Richmond line is that the Pastons were on a par, for greed and self-interest, with the people who have run the British government since 1980. Robin DuBoulay used to comment in his seminar at the Institute of Historical Research that if a more amiable family than the Pastons had left a letter collection, much of our view of fifteenth-century family life might be altered, and considerably for the better.

28. *PLP*, 1:503 (ll. 14–17) and 1:624-25 (ll. 47 ff.) for further glimpses of this (and we have already noted Margaret's reference, *PLP*, 1:222). In the letter in which John II tells John III that they must fight to keep Oxnead for grandmother's sake, he goes on to recount an incident that—whatever other problems it raises—reveals a politically correct stance against "age-ism": "yonge William Brandon is in warde and arestyd fore thatt he scholde have by force ravysshtyd and swyvyd an olde jentylwoman, and yitt was nott therwyth easyd but swyvyd hyr oldest dowtre and than wolde have swyvyd the othere sustre bothe, wher-fore men sey fowle off hym, that he wolde ete the henne and alle her chekynnys."

29. J.T. Rosenthal, *Patriarchy and Families of Privilege in Fifteenth Century England* (Philadelphia, 1991).

THE EMPRESS MATILDA AND HER SONS

Marjorie Chibnall

The Empress Matilda had good relations with all three of her sons, but made her life's work the task of securing Henry's inheritance in England and Normandy. She had a strong influence on his training, and he showed great respect for her.

Medieval biographers rarely discussed their subjects' views on child-rearing, unless they were candidates for canonization. So even if an early biography of King Henry I's daughter, the Empress Matilda, had survived,[1] it is unlikely that we would have had any glimpses into her family life like those that can be found in the *vita* of her grandmother, St. Margaret of Scotland.[2] Moreover, the empress had to bring up her three sons in troubled times. Even the eldest was not yet three when the death of her father, King Henry I, plunged her into a war to win and retain her inheritance; and for more than twelve years her life was spent in castles under constant danger of attack. Her family life has to be pieced together from casual references in chronicles, charters, and occasional letters. Since she had no daughters, her own upbringing could not have provided an example to imitate, and she cannot have seen a great deal of her granddaughters when they were in the care of her strong-willed daughter-in-law Eleanor of Aquitaine though in their adult lives Matilda was held up to them as a model of courage and fortitude.[3]

No children survived from her first marriage with the emperor Henry V. Born in 1102, and betrothed when she was seven years old, she went to Germany in 1110 to be educated in German customs and language. Just before her twelfth birthday she was married at Worms in a ceremony of unparallelled pomp and brilliance.[4] Thereafter she either traveled with her husband in his journeys throughout Germany and Italy as far as Rome, or acted on his behalf in some part of his wide empire while he was campaigning elsewhere.[5] Her work and adventures as the consort of a German emperor are important in forming an assessment of her character, and the way she was likely to face pregnancy and motherhood later. One chronicler, Hermann of Tournai, wrote (without specifying a date) that she bore a child who lived only a short time.[6] Probably there is some truth in the story, since King Henry could scarcely have pinned his hopes on her as his heir if she had been believed to be sterile. There is no means of knowing whether she had other unsuccessful pregnancies. But the evidence shows that she carried out her arduous duties as required: she crossed the Brenner Pass in March 1116 before the snows had melted, accompanied her husband to Rome across war-torn Italy and assisted him in the government of the Matildine lands in Tuscany. When rebellion in Germany took him back across the Alps, she remained with the army in northern Italy, acting as regent and presiding over courts for nearly two years. Her later life in Germany was equally active and hazardous until her husband died in May 1125, leaving her a childless widow of twenty-three.[7]

Twelfth-century kings and their consorts undertook duties and faced hazards which, though at times different, were perhaps equally perilous for both sexes. Warfare took its toll of the men, childbirth of the women. Both were trained to perform duties that were arduous and to accept danger as a part of life. No doubt they took reasonable precautions; military practice was to engage in pitched battles only as a last resort, but as any leader who shrank from a necessary encounter could expect to get a bad press from jongleurs and chroniclers, and leaders often campaigned even when sick or wounded.[8] While it is clear that Henry I's wife, Queen Matilda, was careful to be at her manor of Sutton Courtenay near Abingdon, where she could count on the attendance of a skilled physician, Abbot Faritius of Abingdon, for the birth of her daughter the later empress, no duties called for her elsewhere at the time.[9] Whatever the state of health experienced by the empress herself in her constant traveling, all we know is that she had work to do and she did it. This at least gives us a clue to her later actions, as heir to the English throne and as mother of a future king.[10]

Henry I's only legitimate son drowned in 1120 when the White Ship sank. As soon as the Empress Matilda was widowed in 1125, the king brought her back to England, made her his heir, and in 1128 arranged a marriage with Geoffrey Plantagenet, count of Anjou, who was almost ten years her junior.[11] Like all royal marriages at the time, the union was politically motivated. A male heir was needed, and young Geoffrey, as the most powerful of Normandy's neighbors, was a desirable ally. Affection between the parties would have been a bonus, but it was not expected and, as far as the evidence goes, never existed. The marriage started roughly, and for a time Matilda returned to her father.[12] But by 1131 she was back in Anjou, and the couple, as ill matched personally as they were well matched politically, settled down to a partnership in government. Their reward came when, on March 4, 1133, a son was born at Le Mans. On March 25, he was baptized Henry in the cathedral by Guy of Ploermel, bishop of Le Mans.[13] Matilda gratefully offered a pall to St. Julian, patron saint of the cathedral, and her joyful father gave an annual rent in England. Perhaps because Matilda was being groomed as King Henry's heir— indeed, she had more in common with him than with her husband— she joined him shortly after he came to Normandy on August 2, 1133. She was with her father at Rouen when her second son, Geoffrey, was born at Pentecost 1134. It was a difficult birth and nearly cost Matilda her life. Robert of Torigni, a monk of Bec-Hellouin, told how she wished if she died to be buried in the abbey of Bec-Hellouin, and how she insisted in spite of her father's wish that should she be buried in Rouen Cathedral, her soul would never rest in peace unless her body lay in that abbey.[14]

She recovered and remained for a time in Normandy with her father who, as Henry of Huntingdon relates, was rejoicing in his two grandsons.[15] Their birth, however, in time brought strained relations with Henry's son-in-law. According to Robert of Torigni, Count Geoffrey wished the king to do fealty to him and his wife for all the castles in Normandy and England. This probably exaggerates a quarrel due to Henry's refusal to relinquish the castles in the marches in Normandy and Maine which had been Matilda's dowry,[16] but whatever the cause, the result of the quarrel was that Matilda was in Anjou or Maine with her husband when her father died on December 1, 1135 at Lyons-la-Forêt.[17] Her cousin, Stephen of Blois, count of Mortain, who had sworn with the other Norman barons to accept her as Henry's heir,[18] was married to Matilda of Boulogne, and held her county of Boulogne and extensive English honors *jure uxoris*.[19] He was in Boulogne when news of his uncle's death reached him. From the port of Wissant it was an easy journey to England, and merchant ships constantly plied to and fro.[20] Stephen, disregarding his oath, made at once for England, where he could count on the support of vassals of the honor of Boulogne in the southeast. He persuaded the Londoners to accept him as king and, with the backing of his brother, Bishop Henry of Winchester, he was crowned king on December 22, three weeks after the old king's death.[21]

Matilda was with her husband Geoffrey in his lands either in Maine or Anjou. The news of her father's death must have taken a day or two longer to reach her, and she was further from England than was Stephen in Boulogne. In Normandy, she had a right to her dowry castles, including the mighty fortress of Argentan, which her father had kept in his own hand until his death; she had revenues from the forest of Gouffern, but no fiefs or vassals and nothing in England.[22] She went at once to Argentan, accompanied by whatever escort Geoffrey was able to provide for her. He himself followed as soon as possible with reinforcements, accompanied by his vassal William Talvas of Bellême, who wished to claim his father's former castles in Normandy.[23] At Argentan the castellan, Wigan the Marshall, received Matilda as his liege lady, and handed over the castles of Argentan, Exmes and Domfront. Unfortunately Geoffrey's troops so alienated the Normans by living on the country that they became embroiled in local conflicts, and had to withdraw without doing anything to advance Matilda's cause.[24] Further progress was impossible without them, for the Norman barons ignored Matilda's rights and, after debating whether to offer the crown to Stephen's elder brother Theobald, heard of Stephen's coup and accepted it as a *fait accompli* for the sake of peace. Even Matilda's illegitimate half-brother, Robert Earl of Gloucester, after possibly suggesting the boy Henry—then not quite three years old—as a future king,[25] fell in line with the rest. Of the Norman barons, only Rabel of Tancarville at Lillebonne in the Seine valley took Matilda's part, and he was too far away to help her.[26] Far from "staying put," as has been alleged,[27] she had immediately advanced as far as she could into Normandy. She had no chance of reaching the coast, controlled no port, and had no vassals in England. Her only hope was to wait until her husband could bring reinforcements and renew his attempt to help her fight her way forward. He was able to protect her rear by granting the castles of Ambriéres, Gorron and Châtillon-sur-Colmont in Maine to Juhel de Mayenne on condition that he would help to recover the inheritance of his wife and sons. Geoffrey was unable to return to Normandy until September 1136, and this invasion was again a failure.[28]

Matilda had become pregnant shortly before King Henry's death, but there was no question of her pregnancy deterring her from going immediately to England to demand her inheritance, since political and military circumstances alone made it impossible for her to get even as far as the Channel. She went as far as she could, and held out in a dangerous advance post far into Normandy, with the courage and resolution that might have been expected of her from her previous career. She bore her third son, William, at Argentan on July 22, 1136.[29] Some two months later, she led a force of about two hundred men to help her husband at the siege of Le Sap during his unsuccessful invasion.[30] She was the centre of resistance in the dangerous outpost of Argentan until enough support rallied to make a crossing to England possible.[31] In all this, as in the remainder of her career, she acted as might be expected of a woman who, as Arnulf of Lisieux wrote, showed no sign of feminine weakness.[32]

In normal circumstances, young boys might have remained in their mother's household until they were about old enough to begin training for the masculine arts of war and hunting, at the age of about seven.[33] But the life of a queen or female regent for an heir was rarely normal, and Matilda's position was exceptionally difficult. The whereabouts of her children is uncertain until all three of them added their crosses together with hers to one of Geoffrey Plantagenet's charters making concessions to the citizens of Saumur in June 1138. Geoffrey granted it before the doors of Saint-Pierre-de-la-Couture in Le Mans, and took it to his wife at Carrouges, a castle near Argentan. There she and her sons Henry and William added their crosses, before it was taken back to Saumur. Her second son, Geoffrey, was being brought up there in the house of Goscelin *Rotonardi*, and there he added his cross.[34] So we know that Henry and William were then with their mother in Normandy. William, not quite two years old, had almost certainly been there with his mother since his birth; it was later said that she had a special affection for him. Henry's movements are less certain; his father may have kept him in Anjou for greater security and sent him into Normandy only after Matilda's position had been strengthened when her half-brother Robert Earl of Gloucester joined her cause.[35] Young Geoffrey, on the other hand, remained in Anjou. This is probably because it was prudent to keep one of the boys out of the fighting line. It would be tendentious and probably wrong to suppose that his difficult birth had alienated the affections of his mother. Nevertheless, among her three sons, he must have been the one whom, for whatever reason, she knew the least.

William and Geoffrey then disappear from the sources for ten years. All three boys remained with their father when Matilda crossed the Channel in September 1139 to challenge Stephen on English soil. But after Stephen's defeat and capture in 1141, and Matilda's precarious acceptance as "lady of the English,"[36] she began to associate young Henry's name with hers in charters.[37] Her advantage did not last long; Stephen was free before Christmas 1141 and by the end of 1142 she had been driven out of Oxford and had settled herself in the very strong castle of Devizes. There she remained for five years, at the center of resistance, while her half-brothers and loyal supporters campaigned on her behalf.[38] Her chief consolation was the arrival of her eldest son Henry, whom Geoffrey Plantagenet, fully occupied in conquering Normandy, sent to join her.[39] At nine, Henry was of an age to live in a male household, and we know that much of his time during his first visit to England was spent at Bristol with his uncle Earl Robert. But from time to time he visited his mother at Devizes, added his name to her charters, and received the homage of some supporters.[40] From her, no doubt, he learnt something of the arts of government which had been taught to her by her masterful father and her first husband, the emperor.

All Henry I's children had been well educated, and Matilda's education as a child bride had been continued at Trier, where she had been taught the German language.[41] Her first language was French and she also knew Latin.[42] Her son Henry became a good linguist: Walter Map claimed, somewhat extravagantly, that "he knew all the tongues used from the French sea to the Jordan, but spoke only Latin and French."[43] Earl Robert was a cultured man and in Bristol provided good tutors for his nephew, including a certain Master Matthew and Adelard of Bath, who dedicated a treatise on the astrolabe to him.[44] His father, Geoffrey, was equally solicitous for his education when they were together. William of Conches, a member of Count Geoffrey's household, praised the count for encouraging the boys from their earliest years in the study of letters rather than in games of dice, so giving him a lasting love of learning.[45]

In 1148 Matilda returned to Normandy;[46] the following year, Henry was knighted at Carlisle by her uncle King David of Scotland and took control personally of the struggle for the English throne.[47] Matilda meanwhile settled just outside Rouen, where a royal residence had been built in the park of Quevilly and the monks of Bec had a priory, Notre-Dame-du-Pré.[48] Like her mother Queen Matilda, whose last years were spent at Westminster, she kept a little court and carried on the duties of her station in a semi-monastic retirement.[49] Whatever share she may have had in the upbringing and education of her sons was now behind her. She remained, however, an influence not only in the government of Normandy, where Henry needed her help, but also in the lives of all three young men. No ruling family is ever without some power struggles and even open quarrels; on two occasions, young Geoffrey rebelled against his brother Henry. Yet Matilda seems as far as we know to have had the interests of all three at heart and to have maintained good relationships with all of them.

Henry's power and wealth increased spectacularly in the years between 1150 and 1154. First he was invested with the duchy of Normandy by his father, and when his father died in September 1151, Henry became count of Anjou. In 1152, he married Eleanor of Aquitaine, the divorced wife of the king of France, and acquired her vast inheritance. He was still fighting to win the succession to the English throne; but by the time Stephen died in 1154 Henry had been recognised as his heir.[50] The same years, however, had been less fortunate for young Geoffrey, who considered himself unfairly set aside. He was said to have tried unsuccessfully to kidnap Eleanor before her marriage to his brother.[51] When King Louis, outraged at the marriage of his vassal Henry without his consent, invaded Normandy, Geoffrey joined forces with him.[52] The attack failed, and the brothers apparently became reconciled. It is even possible that Henry allowed Geoffrey to look after some of his interests in Anjou during his final attack on Stephen the following year, though his younger brother William was probably in charge of the Norman frontier.[53] The next positive news we have of Geoffrey is that he and Sulpicius of Amboise, the castellan of Chaumont who had rebelled against Theobald V of Blois,[54] were prisoners in Theobald's hands. Sulpicius died in captivity and at this point Matilda intervened and persuaded Henry that he must secure Geoffrey's release though

Theobald was insisting on the dismantling of the castle of Chaumont before he would grant it. The episode is known only from a confused account in the chronicle of the lords of Amboise,[55] but it is important as showing Matilda as a peace-maker in the family, for it must have been she who persuaded Henry to agree to a concession he would not willingly have made otherwise. The reconciliation between the brothers lasted a few years; after news came of King Stephen's death, Geoffrey, together with his mother and William, was among those consulted by Henry when he stopped at Rouen on his way to England for coronation.[56]

This, however, was not the end of Geoffrey's trouble-making. He claimed that his father, who had granted him only three castles when he died, wished him to inherit Anjou if Henry ever won the English crown.[57] Even if this were true, it would not have justified his earlier disloyalty, when Henry's future hung in the balance and his pardon by his brother might reasonably have been held to cancel any pre-existing claim. Whatever the truth about the elder Geoffrey's intentions on his death-bed, young Geoffrey took part in a second unsuccessful rebellion in 1156, demanding Anjou as his rightful inheritance.[58] Once again he was pardoned, but persuaded to part with two of his castles in return for an annual pension.[59] A second pardon may seem surprising, and it is tempting to see the hand of Matilda in the settlement. She was with all three sons in Rouen in 1156/7,[60] and there was evidently a family council at the time of the reconciliation. The affairs of Nantes were probably discussed at the same time: apparently on the advice of Henry II, the citizens of Nantes had rebelled against their lord and chose Geoffrey as their new lord. As long as Matilda lived, all family quarrels were in the end resolved amicably, but within five years of her death this changed drastically. If her voice was decisive, however, her motives remain enigmatic. She certainly wished for peace in the family, but she had made the task of securing her eldest son's inheritance her life work, and her later actions were to show that she would not countenance any disparagement of him. She may have had in mind how her father had worn down the resistance of his brother Robert Curthose, after Curthose's attacks, by inducing him to part with his territorial claims in exchange for a pension and only imprisoned him for his own safety as a last resort.[61] Her earlier intervention on Geoffrey's behalf when he was languishing in Theobald's dungeon may have been

motivated purely by maternal concern, nevertheless she may also
have been aware, with her shrewd political judgement, that it was
desirable to placate Theobald of Blois and have him as an ally. Since
Geoffrey died prematurely on July 26, 1158, only a year after being
offered the lordship of Nantes by the Bretons,[62] it will never be known
if he would have continued to be a thorn in Henry II's side or if so
what Matilda's response would have been.

Both she and Henry were able to count on the support and loyalty
of William, her youngest son. Shortly after winning the English
throne, Henry conceived a wild scheme for conquering an Irish
kingdom with papal consent and giving it to William. Matilda
prudently advised against the idea; Henry's hands were full enough
already, and Ireland was unlikely to submit on demand.[63] Instead,
William was enriched with extensive estates. By 1159, when Henry
gave him a substantial part of the escheated estates of King Stephen's
son, William of Blois, in East Anglia and Sussex, he held land in
fifteen counties and was one of the richest men in England. He also
held the vicomté of Dieppe, and had a household staffed with
distinguished administrators. His income was between £1000 and
£1700 a year, and he supported his brother with unwavering loyalty.[64]
But he was frustrated in his wish to marry the countess of Warenne,
widowed in 1160. Thomas Becket, archbishop of Canterbury, refused
to sanction the marriage on the grounds of consanguinity, and,
though Henry II's own parents had been more closely related, the
king did not attempt to secure a papal dispensation, which might in
any case have been difficult on account of the papal schism. Stephen
of Rouen, in a bitter passage in the *Draco normannicus*, charged
Becket with animosity towards William and attributed the young
man's death in January 1164 to his disappointment and sorrow.
William had gone straight to his mother at Rouen and had died
there. He was buried in the priory of Notre-Dame-du-Pré, among
the monks of Bec, who were her friends as well as his own.[65] Six
years later, according to the chronicler William FitzStephen, one of
Becket's murderers struck down the archbishop with the words, "Take
this, for the love of my Lord William the king's brother."[66] Matilda's
sorrow and bitterness must have been even greater than Stephen of
Rouen's, but she did not allow them to hamper her efforts at peace
making between her son Henry and Becket when she was called
upon to attempt arbitration of their dispute.

The evidence on the whole suggests that Matilda's feelings for her younger sons amounted to no more than normal maternal solicitude for Geoffrey but to genuine affection for William, who turned to her at the time of his greatest sorrow. But Henry, her eldest son, was always her first consideration. She was a woman who had learnt to discipline even her strongest feelings and never permit them to cloud her shrewd political judgment. From the time in 1141 or 1142 when she gave up all hope of being crowned queen of England, all her efforts were directed toward helping Henry to secure and hold the whole of his inheritance in England and Normandy. He reciprocated by treating her with reverence all her life. In their joint charters, her name always preceded his even after he became king of England.[67] Even if this was because, despite his personal informality,[68] he acknowledged her love of ceremonial (which allowed a dowager empress to take precedence over the king), his personal respect for her was genuine. He relied on her judgment, and was willing to leave her as his deputy to issue writs, hear cases, and confirm Church elections when the task of governing his vast domains took him away from Normandy.[69] But, not surprisingly, as he grew older and more experienced in government, he built up his own circle of advisors: young men with a deep knowledge of laws.[70]

The first occasion on which he is known to have rejected his mother's advice was over the election of Thomas Becket as archbishop of Canterbury. Matilda advised against it. Her experience in Germany with Archbishop Adalbert of Mainz must have taught her that a devoted chancellor may turn into an archbishop more devoted to his church than to his former master, but she was over-ruled.[71] No doubt Becket's rigid opposition to the marriage of her youngest son did nothing to shake her distrust of him. But there was no open rift with Henry, and she did not allow any grudge against Becket to distort her judgement. When a bitter quarrel broke out between Henry and Becket both sides tried to win her support. Her son sent his envoy, John of Oxford, to blacken Becket's character; and a few days later Nicholas, the prior of the hospital of Mont-Saint-Jacques at Rouen arrived to plead Becket's cause.[72] John of Oxford arrived first, and Matilda lent him a ready ear. When Prior Nicholas came three days later she refused to see him, perhaps remembering Becket's proud obstinacy and thwarting of her son William's hopes for marriage. But if Walter Map is to be trusted,[73] Matilda had advised her son never to act on the advice of others without himself looking at the situation; she would not have been true to herself had she not heard both sides. At the third attempt, Nicholas was admitted to a remarkably frank private interview. After hearing the letters he had brought, Matilda confessed that she regretted what she had already written to her son who, she said, concealed his relations with the Church from her because he knew that she rated the freedom of the church higher than the royal will. She wrote again to Henry, asking him to let her know his intentions in writing; when she knew them, she would do her utmost to bring about peace. Later, when Prior Nicholas brought the Constitutions of Clarendon to her, she frankly expressed her views on the Church, blaming the bishops for some things while upholding the royal dignity. To Becket, however, she put her son's case forcefully, and showed clearly that she would not allow any liberties of the church to conflict with ancient and accepted royal customs, and she urged him not to be governed by pride.[74] What she wrote to her son we do not know: her attempted mediation between two strong-willed and obstinate men may have been doomed to failure anyway. Even had she lived, she might not have been able to avert the final tragedy. This, however, was a very rare failure. She continued to be consulted on matters of government and at the end of her life succeeded in preventing a minor quarrel arising from a dispute about the collection of money for the Holy Land from degenerating into armed conflict.[75] Whether or not she approved of the campaign Henry began against Brittany in 1167,[76] she did not live long enough to make her objections known. On September 10, 1167 she died at Rouen, and was buried as she wished with her son's consent, before the high altar in the abbey of Bec-Hellouin. Her devoted friend, the monk-poet Stephen of Rouen, who attended her funeral, personally carried the news to Henry in Brittany, and Henry returned immediately to Normandy.[77] During the years she lived among the monks of Bec at Le Pré, she came to be regarded as their spiritual mother, and bequeathed much of her material wealth to them.[78] Possibly her panegyrist Stephen of Rouen did not exaggerate when he claimed that she loved the monks as if they were her own children.

Matilda's two younger sons had died before her. By the time of her death, however, she had achieved her life's great ambition: she saw her son Henry firmly established as duke of Normandy and king of England. In him, her maternal and royal ambitions were fulfilled.

NOTES

1. A *Vita* said to have been written by Arnulf of Liseux has been lost. See Marjorie Chibnall, *The Empress Matilda: Queen Consort, Queen Mother and Lady of the English* (Oxford, 1991), p. 3.

2. Lois L. Huneycutt, "The Idea of the Perfect Princess: The *Life of St Margaret* in the Reign of Matilda II (1100–1118)," *Anglo-Norman Studies* 12 (1989–90), 81–97.

3. *Radulfi de Diceto Decani Lundoniensis opera historica*, ed. W. Stubbs, 2 vols. Rolls Series 68 (London, 1876), 2:15–18; Edmond-René Labande, "Les filles d'Aliénor d'Aquitaine: étude comparative," *Cahiers de civilisation médiévale* 29 (1986), 105–12.

4. Chibnall, *Empress Matilda*, pp. 16–17, 22–26.

5. Gerold Meyer von Knonau, ed., *Jahrbücher des deutschen Reiches unter Heinrich IV und Heinrich V*, 7 vols. (Leipzig, 1890–1909), 6:116–21, 282–83, 288–90, 358; vii, 77–78, 97–98, 142, 146–47, 270–74, 321–22, and *passim*; Chibnall, *Empress Matilda*, pp. 27–41.

6. Hermann of Tournai, *Liber de restauratione monasterii S. Martini Tornacensis*, MGH SS xiv, 274–327, at 282.

7. Meyer von Knonau, *Jahrbücher*, vii, 322–23; Chibnall, *Empress Matilda*, p. 40.

8. Guillaume de Poitiers, *Histoire de Guillaume le Conquérant*, ed. Raymonde Foreville (Paris, 1952), pp. 212–15.

9. Chibnall, *Empress Matilda*, p. 9.

10. This digression has been made necessary by Elisabeth van Houts' suggestion that Matilda was deterred from taking action to secure the throne in 1135 because she was pregnant and might have been feeling too sick to cross the Channel ("Women in Medieval History and Literature," *JMH* 20 [1994], 277–92). Van Houts comments, "one's own gender experiences color one's interpretation of the past," but these experiences must be kept in balance with an assessment of other factors, including individual character and the very real differences in culture, both between centuries and between times of peace and times of war, when even ordinary individuals achieve the seemingly impossible. Matilda's career shows her to have been, in courage and resolution, at least equal to her uncle William Rufus, who insisted on crossing the Channel in a storm to deal with a crisis in Maine, saying he had never heard of a king being drowned (William of Malmesbury, *De gestis regum Anglorum*, 2 vols., ed. W. Stubbs, Rolls series 90 [1887–89], 2:373). Matilda was every inch an empress and might have

replied in like words to any effort to deter her from crossing the Channel,
had political and military circumstances allowed her to reach the Channel
before Stephen was crowned.

11. Chibnall, *Empress Matilda*, pp. 43–44, 50–56.

12. Chibnall, *Empress Matilda*, pp. 57–58.

13. Chibnall, *Empress Matilda*, pp. 59–61.

14. *The Chronicle of Robert of Torigni*, ed. Richard Howlett in
Chronicles of the Reigns of Stephen, Henry II and Richard I, 4 vols., Rolls
Series 82 (London, 1884–89), 4:123–24; *The Gesta Normannorum Ducum
of William of Jumièges, Orderic Vitalis and Robert of Torigni*, ed. Elisabeth
van Houts, 2 vols. (Oxford, 1992–95), 2:242–47. I am grateful to Dr. van
Houts for lending me the proofs of this volume before publication.

15. *Henrici Archidiaconi Huntendunensis historia anglorum*, ed.
Thomas Arnold, Rolls Series 74 (London, 1879), p. 253.

16. Robert of Torigni, *Chronicle*, p. 128; Marjorie Chibnall,
"Normandy," in Edmund King, ed., *The Anarchy of King Stephen's Reign*
(Oxford, 1994), pp. 93–115, at p. 96.

17. *The Ecclesiastical History of Orderic Vitalis*, ed. Marjorie Chibnall,
6 vols. (Oxford, 1969–80), 6:448–49; *The Historia Novella of William of
Malmesbury*, ed. K.R. Potter (Edinburgh, 1955), pp. 13–14.

18. C. Warren Hollister, "The Anglo-Norman Succession Debate of
1126: Prelude to Stephen's Anarchy," *JMH* 1 (1975), 19–39, rpt. in Hollister,
Monarchy, Magnates and Institutions in the Anglo-Norman World (London
and Ronceverte, 1986), pp. 145–69.

19. J. Horace Round, "The Counts of Boulogne as English Lords,"
in Round, *Studies in Peerage and Family History* (Westminster, 1901), pp.
147–80, at pp. 163–73.

20. R.H.C. Davis, *King Stephen, 1135–1154*, 3rd edn. (London and
New York, 1990), p. 9.

21. Davis, *King Stephen*, pp. 16–17.

22. Chibnall, "Normandy," p. 97.

23. Orderic Vitalis, *Historia ecclesiastica*, 6:454–55.

24. Orderic, *Historia ecclesiastica*, 6:454–57; Torigni, *Chronicle*, p. 128.

25. Orderic, *Historia ecclesiastica*, 6:454–55; Torigni, *Chronicle*, pp.
128–29; *Gesta Stephani*, ed. K.R. Potter, rev. R.H.C. Davis (Oxford, 1976),
pp. 12–15.

26. Orderic, *Historia ecclesiastica*, 6:482–85; Chibnall, "Normandy,"
pp. 96–97.

27. Van Houts, "Women," p. 288.

28. Orderic, *Historia Ecclesiastica*, 6:466–75; Torigni, *Chronicle*, p.
128.

29. *Chronicae Sancti Albini Andegauensis*, in Paul Marchegay and
Émile Mabille, eds., *Chroniques des églises d'Anjou* (Paris, 1869), p. 34.

30. Orderic, *Historia ecclesiastica*, 6:472–73.

31. Chibnall, *Empress Matilda*, pp. 67–68, 72–74.

32. The epitaph by Arnulf of Lisieux contains the lines, "Virtutum titulis humani culmen honoris/ Excessit mulier, nil mulieris habens" (*PL*, vol. 101, col. 199).

33. For the education of the children of the nobility, see Frank Barlow, *William Rufus* (London, 1983), pp. 15–16.

34. Léopold Delisle and Élie Berger, *Recueil des actes de Henry II*, 4 vols. (Paris, 1909–17), 1: no. 1.*

35. Davis, *King Stephen*, pp. 34–35; Chibnall, *Empress Matilda*, pp. 73–74.

36. Davis, *King Stephen*, pp. 48–53.

37. Marjorie Chibnall, "Charters of the Empress," in George Garnett and John Hudson, eds., *Law and Government in Medieval England and Normandy* (Cambridge, 1994), pp. 276–98, at pp. 288–89.

38. Chibnall, *Empress Matilda*, pp. 117–27.

39. Chibnall, *Empress Matilda*, pp. 116–17; Davis, *King Stephen*, p. 69.

40. Chibnall, *Empress Matilda*, pp. 144–45.

41. Torigni, *Chronicle*, pp. 218–19.

42. When Nicholas of Mont-Saint-Jacques brought the Constitutions of Clarendon to her, she told him to read them to her in Latin and explain them in French (Chibnall, *Empress Matilda*, p. 170).

43. Walter Map, *De nugis curialium*, ed. M. R. James, rev. C.N. L. Brooke and R.A.B. Mynors (Oxford, 1983), pp. 476–77.

44. C.H. Haskins, "Henry II as a Patron of Literature," in A.G. Little and F.M. Powicke, eds., *Essays in Medieval History Presented to T.F. Tout* (Manchester, 1925), pp. 72–73.

45. R.L. Poole, *Illustrations of the History of Medieval Thought* (London, 1884), pp. 129–30, 347–48.

46. Chibnall, *Empress Matilda*, pp. 148–49.

47. Davis, *King Stephen*, pp. 104–07.

48. *The "Draco Normannicus" of Étienne de Rouen*, in *Chronicles of the Reigns of Stephen, Henry II and Richard I*, ed. Howlett, 2:712–14.

49. William of Malmesbury, *De gestis regum*, 2:494–95.

50. Marjorie Chibnall, "L'avènement au pouvoir d'Henri II," *Cahiers de civilisation médiévale*, 37 (1994), 43–48; J.C. Holt, "1153: The Treaty of Winchester," in King, ed., *Anarchy of King Stephen's Reign*, pp. 291–316.

51. W.L. Warren, *Henry II* (London and Berkeley, CA, 1973), p. 45.

52. Torigni, *Chronicle*, pp. 165–66.

53. I owe the information about William fitz Empress to Professor T.K. Keefe, to whom I wish to express my gratitude.

54. Chibnall, "Normandy," 110, 113; Jean Dunbabin, *France in the Making, 843–1180* (Oxford, 1985), pp. 231, 250, 334–35.

55. *Gesta Ambaziensium Dominorum*, in *Chroniques des comtes d'Anjou et des seigneurs d'Amboise*, eds. Louis Halphen and René Poupardin (Paris, 1915), pp. 127–31.

56. Torigni, *Chronicle*, pp. 180–81.

57. Count Geoffrey's bequests and intentions have been the subject of debate. Torigni, *Chronicle*, p. 163, states that before his death, the count gave Anjou to Henry, and four castles to Geoffrey (evidently a slip; at p. 189 Torigni names only three). William of Newburgh, *Chronicles*, ed. Howlett, 1:112–14, names the same castles but asserts that on his deathbed, Count Geoffrey specified that if Henry established his claim to England and Normandy, Geoffrey should have Anjou; and that Henry, who had not been present at the deathbed, was forced to swear before hearing the terms of the bequest that he would abide by them. There is also an ambiguous reference in John of Salisbury's *Letters*. Newburgh's version is accepted by, e.g., J. C. Holt, "The End of the Anglo-Norman Realm," *Proceedings of the British Academy* 61 (1975), 240, and T.K. Keefe, "Geoffrey Plantagenet's Will and the Angevin Succession," *Albion* 6 (1974), 266–74; but questioned by others, including Warren, *Henry II*, p. 42, and John Le Patourel, *Feudal Empires: Norman and Plantagenet* (London, 1984), ch. 9. Whatever the truth of the story—evidently put about by young Geoffrey—clearly he considered himself badly treated by his elder brother.

58. Torigni, *Chronicle*, pp. 189–90.

59. Torigni, *Chronicle*, pp. 189–90 says that by an agreement in July 1156, he was allowed to keep Loudun and to receive an annual pension of 2000 Angevin *livres*. See also William of Newburgh, *Chronicles*, ed. Howlett, 1:113–14.

60. *Calendar of Documents preserved in France*, ed. J.H. Round (London, 1899), no. 681.

61. C.W. David, *Robert Curthose* (Cambridge, MA, 1920), pp. 134–49, 179.

62. Patrick Galliou and Michael Jones, *The Bretons* (Oxford, 1991), p. 194. Henry II successfully claimed the overlordship of Nantes after Geoffrey's death.

63. Torigni, *Chronicle*, p. 186.

64. Thomas K. Keefe, "Place-Date Distribution of Royal Charters and the Historical Geography of Patronage Strategies at the Court of King Henry II Plantagenet," *The Haskins Society Journal* 1 (1990), 179–88, at 185–87.

65. Étienne of Rouen, *Draco Normannicus*, p. 676.

66. J. C. Robertson, ed., *Materials for the History of Thomas Becket*, 7 vols., Rolls Series 67 (London, 1875–85), 3:142; the remark is attributed to Richard le Bret.

67. Chibnall, "Charters," p. 290.

68. Warren, *Henry II*, pp. 78–79.

69. Chibnall, *Empress Matilda*, pp. 160–61; Delisle and Berger, *Recueil des actes d'Henri II*, 1:169–70. Delisle considered that in Normandy at least, Henry relied on Matilda rather than on his wife. There is unfortunately not a shred of evidence to throw light on the relations between Matilda and her daughter-in-law.

70. Paul Hyams, "Henri II comme juriste eut-il une politique de réforme?" *Cahiers de civilisation médiévale* 37 (1994), 85–89.

71. *Materials for the History of Thomas Becket*, 5:410; Chibnall, *Empress Matilda*, p. 167.

72. *Materials for the History of Thomas Becket*, 5:144–51.

73. Map, *De nugis curialium*, p. 479.

74. *Materials for the History of Thomas Becket*, 6:128–29.

75. Chibnall, *Empress Matilda*, p. 173.

76. Peter Johannek suggests she was critical of her son's behavior at this time: "König Arthur und die Plantagenets," *Frühmittelalterliche Studien* 21 (1987), 384–87.

77. Étienne of Rouen, *Draco normannicus*, p. 596.

78. Étienne of Rouen, *Draco normannicus*, p. 712. Lists of her gifts to Bec-Hellouin are edited by Howlett among the *Additamenta* to *Draco normannicus*, pp. 758–60, and by A. A. Porée, *Histoire de l'abbaye du Bec*, 2 vols. (Évreux, 1902), 1:650–51. See also Chibnall, *Empress Matilda*, p. 18.

PUBLIC LIVES, PRIVATE TIES:
ROYAL MOTHERS IN ENGLAND AND SCOTLAND,
1070–1204[1]

Lois L. Huneycutt

Narrative sources present a different picture of medieval maternal-child relationships from other evidence, invoked in current debate, that was never meant to reflect the quality or quantity of familial affection.

O ver three decades have passed since Philippe Ariès posited that medieval people did not recognize childhood as a distinct phase in the human lifecycle. Although Ariès saw the medieval attitude toward children as benign, or at worst indifferent, scholars responding to the questions he raised sometimes painted an even gloomier picture, seeing the European Middle Ages as an era dominated by neglect and even outright abuse of the youngest members of society. Perhaps the most extreme statement of this belief came in 1970 from Lloyd DeMause, who described pre-modern childhood as "a nightmare from which we have only recently begun to awaken."[2] In reaction to such extreme positions, scholars have analyzed differences between modern and pre-modern familial structures, and have industriously quarried evidence for the quantity and quality of family affection in the European past. Accepting Ariès' premises, some scholars searched for the period in which the modern nuclear family, with its "affective qualities," was born, and many accepted the conclusions in Lawrence Stone's 1977 study, *The Family, Sex, and Marriage in England, 1500–1800.* Stone places the development of the modern, nuclear family in the late early modern period and found the sixteenth-century family to have been an "unemotional, authoritarian institution" in which "affective relationships seem generally to have been cool, and those that existed were widely diffused rather than concentrated on members of the nuclear family."

Thus, the pre-modern family, with its open-lineage inheritance structures, existed primarily for the purpose of acquiring, holding, and transmitting property.[3] Reaction to Stone and Ariès has generated enormous debate, with a bibliography too extensive to be discussed here. In general, however, the debate has benefited medievalists by asking new questions of old sources and opening up previously untapped evidence to investigation of both the structure and the experiences of the medieval family.[4]

Studies of pre-modern childhood have plundered iconography, liturgy, saints' lives, miracle collections, household expense accounts, and even coroner's inquests; medievalists in the past two decades have shown, as Shulamith Shahar concludes, "that a concept of childhood existed in the Central and Late Middle Ages, that scholarly acknowledgement of the existence of several stages of childhood was not merely theoretical and that parents invested both material and emotional resources in their children." Parents were capable of distinguishing different stages in child development, and many even enjoyed the company of infants and small children, although, as is true today, others did not. And, even though a small child's life was precarious, a child's death was generally a traumatic experience for its family.[5] Nevertheless, the myth of medieval indifference to children persists, and a generation of medievalists has been subjected to continuing debate over whether medieval parents loved their children.

In placing myself with those who see the pre-modern family within affective as well as property-transmitting terms, I do not, of course, claim that the medieval family was exactly like its modern counterpart or that family structure across time, distance, and the social spectrum was identical or even similar. Nor do I believe that our work is complete. For instance, despite the wealth of sources available for the study of dynastic strategies and child-rearing techniques among the royal families of medieval Europe, these families *as families* have attracted relatively little attention from social historians. Avoidance of the families of kings is understandable, for one of the tenets of the social history movement has been that the lives of royalty and the upper aristocracy are atypical of the great majority of those who lived in the medieval centuries. There are, however, lessons to be learned when the tools and methods of the social historian are applied to those for whom traditional sources are richest. For instance, scrutiny of the lives of medieval queens has opened new windows into cultural attitudes toward femininity, ethnicity, sexuality, fertility and religious devotion, to name but a few areas covered in recent studies of medieval queenship. These studies show that understanding the queen's role is essential to uncovering the political, ecclesiastical, administrative, and cultural history of the Middle Ages.[6] The success of these studies suggests that royal sources might also reveal much about attitudes toward children and childhood. The examination is particularly timely in that just as the queen has emerged as a powerful actor in the public realm, her success in the private realm has been questioned. In a 1988 article, written while he was researching a biography of King John of England, Ralph V. Turner examined relationships among Queen Eleanor of Aquitaine and her children. Acknowledging that "we can hardly expect any direct evidence with which to determine the depth of Eleanor's maternal instincts," he argued that indirect evidence, such as long separations of parent and child in the formative years, the use of wet-nurses and tutors, and the practice of fostering all led to poor relationships between the Angevin queen and her children.[7] Extrapolating from the case of Eleanor and her family, which he assumed to be typical of royal and aristocratic families, Turner contended that "the pattern of aristocratic child-rearing seemed almost aimed at placing children at a distance from their parents, both physically and emotionally." In general, he concluded, "the psychological investment of English royalty in their children does not seem very great."[8] But unlike adherents of Ariès and Stone, Turner did not blame the medieval era for Eleanor's seeming neglect of her children. Although he did claim that "medieval men and women had no notion that one's character is indelibly shaped in earliest childhood," he located the real problem in the aristocratic lifestyle, contending that women of the upper classes, busy with public responsibilities, have never seen childrearing as something that demanded their personal attention. In a second article examining childrearing among Anglo-Norman royalty, Turner again pointed to the employment of parental substitutes as evidence of a lack of personal involvement by parents in the rearing of their royal offspring. Extending his comparison to present-day society, Turner concluded that

> medieval women's lack of time for child-care should arouse sympathy today, not condemnation, for modern women face a similar dilemma. Just as Anglo-Norman queens had little time for children amid the

work of supervising their households and acting as regents for absent husbands, so American women today find economic pressures preventing them from finding time for their children.[9]

Turner's belief that a woman with responsibility in the public arena cannot be an effective parent is inherently threatening, and not just for those of us who study medieval queens with some sympathy. In effect, Turner argues that a parent's "psychological investment" in a child hinges on that parent's personal involvement with its day-to-day care and that the degree of love or affection between parent and child is directly proportionate to the amount of time they spend together. His conclusions are at odds with those of many scholars such as Nicholas Orme, whose study of the education of English royal and aristocratic children from the eleventh to the fifteenth century led him to conclude that "the employment of deputies does not mean that parents took no active role in the rearing of their children—far from it." Pointing out that parents carefully organized the education of their sons and daughters, chose the masters and mistresses, and laid plans for the future marriages and careers of their children, Orme concluded that, unlike the salaries of nurses, tutors, and the like, a parent's influence and time with his or her children are not likely to show up in royal account books and thus "we must be careful not to underestimate the impact that it may have had."[10]

Orme's point about the nature of our sources is a crucial one. We are not often made privy to the feelings of any medieval parent, even of a royal mother. Traditional documents that allow insight into the operations of the royal court are largely financial in nature; they can show how resources were collected and expended, but their emphasis is entirely public. When studying Eleanor of Aquitaine's interaction with her young children, we are limited to such documents, which are susceptible to widely-varying interpretations, a point to which I shall return at the conclusion of this essay.

There are, however, sources other than financial records and wills that can provide glimpes into the childhood experiences of members of the Anglo-Norman royal family. The maternal ancestors of Queen Eleanor's husband, King Henry II, particularly his great-grandmother Margaret, the Anglo-Saxon queen of Scotland from c. 1070 to 1093, left behind an unusual number of private documents. These documents show several generations of close and loving interaction between Margaret and her children and among her children and their own children. Of course, there is always some danger in relying on individual cases as "typical" or "atypical" of an era. For the Middle Ages, the very fact that a family left substantial documentation renders it immediately suspect. Nevertheless, if our theories are to have any validity, they must conform to the experiences of real people. And in conjunction with Turner's evidence about the Angevins, the study of Margaret of Scotland's family should prove valuable, if only as a counterbalance to Eleanor's—for, if Eleanor's children were especially fractious, Margaret's appear to have been unusually devoted in their familial relationships. As a second point of contrast, Margaret has enjoyed almost universal approbation from medieval and modern commentators alike, while Eleanor's career has been nothing if not controversial. As a check to the extreme positions presented in the careers of Margaret and Eleanor, I will also mention briefly the career of Margaret's daughter Matilda II (queen to Henry I, 1100–1118) before returning to present an alternative interpretation of the evidence for Eleanor of Aquitaine's maternal role.

Margaret of Scotland was the only grandchild of Edmund Ironside to produce legitimate offspring; it is through her that occupants of the English throne trace their lineage back to the pre-Conquest line.[11] Margaret and her siblings fled England after the Normans arrived, landing in Scotland where King Malcolm Canmore was said to have been overwhelmed by Margaret's beauty and virtue.[12] They were married by 1070, and all indicators point to a happy union. Margaret was an effective and successful queen, particularly in directing ecclesiastical matters. For instance, two letters from contemporary churchmen witness her desire to lead the Scots, who still clung to Celtic customs, into line with the universal Church.[13] But we are fortunate that for Margaret, we are not forced to rely on the usual public documents. Sometime between 1104 and 1107, a biography of Margaret was written at the request of her daughter, Queen Matilda II. This biography, called "simple but exquisite" by David Knowles and "touching, in some ways beautiful," by Robert L. Ritchie, derives much of its charm from the fact that it is an entirely personal document.[14] Matilda had been sent from home at an early age, perhaps around six, to be educated in England under the supervision of Queen Margaret's sister, a nun at Romsey Abbey. It is unclear whether Matilda ever saw her mother again; if she did, it was probably only once, for perhaps four months.[15] The author of the biography claims that Matilda commissioned the work after she became queen of England so that, even though she knew her mother's outward appearance only slightly, she might have a full account of her virtues (*VM*, prologue, p. 324b). Matilda took care to find the right person to write the biography. The author's prologue, addressed to her, claims that "you said you entrusted this task to me on account of my great familiarity with her, and because you heard that I had access to her private thoughts" (*VM*, prologue, p. 324b). In the course of the work the author recounts conversations he had with the queen and describes the interaction between the king and his wife, and the queen and her children. He also provides Matilda with an account of Margaret's public activities.

I have argued elsewhere that the biography was written to be a teaching tool for Matilda rather than as a hagiographical account of Margaret's life.[16] It cannot be taken as straight history, either, for the author may have exaggerated Margaret's reforms or their effectiveness in order to encourage Matilda to imitate her mother. It obviously provides an idealized portrait. It was, after all, written some ten years after Margaret's death by a monk who admired her greatly. There is, however, no reason to doubt the genuineness of either the description of the queen's public life or the extensive scenes portraying her family life. At the very least, the text provides insight into ideals of proper queenly and motherly behavior at the turn of the twelfth century; as we shall see, that era accepted and expected that a woman could be both queen and mother and that she could succeed in both roles.

The author of Margaret's biography left little doubt that her days were filled with royal responsibilities. He described both her direct and indirect influence in the public sphere: "All things which were fitting were carried out by order of the prudent queen; by her counsel the laws of the kingdom were put in order, divine religion was augmented by her industry, and the people rejoiced in the prosperity of affairs" (*VM*, chap. 1, p. 325b, para. 6). Margaret brought sacred relics into Scotland and built churches to house them; she also repaired existing churches, including the early Christian shrine on Iona. Pilgrims coming to worship at the shrine of St. Andrew took advantage of ferry services and housing provided by the queen. Margaret introduced previously unknown luxuries into Scotland and, in so doing, increased trade coming into the kingdom. Malcolm had such respect for her wisdom that "he dreaded to displease the queen in any manner, but rather used to rush to comply with her wishes and prudent plans in all things" (*VM*, chap. 2, p. 326b, para. 11). She accomplished her improvements with such care that, even though the king's processions became more splendid and his retinue increased, none of his courtiers dared to harm the poor or the rustics of the kingdom. Margaret is even portrayed presiding over an ecclesiastical council—no doubt assisted by the three monks Archbishop Lanfranc had sent from Canterbury at her request. During the council, she debated the correct manner of calculating Lent and Easter, rules for observing the Sabbath, marriage customs, and proper preparation for taking the Eucharist.[17] Her other activities were no less beneficent. She secretly arranged to pay the ransoms of English captives taken during Scottish raids. The queen took proper care of the realm's poor, so much so that she had to be restrained from over-lavish almsgiving. Eager to set the right example, she personally fed the hungry and washed the feet of paupers every day during Lent. Independent documentation of her biographer's claims is rare, but the available evidence tends to corroborate his characterization of Margaret as a true partner in ruling Scotland, busy "among the tumult of lawsuits, and the manifold cares of the kingdom" (*VM*, chap. 2, p. 326a, para. 10).

So far, we have a picture of Margaret engaged in the kinds of activities that we are coming to recognize as typical of the eleventh and twelfth centuries, activities that Turner believed barred queens and other noblewomen from active involvement in their children's lives. Yet, motherhood was central to the functions of the medieval queen, whose primary duty was always to produce an heir to the throne. This duty was often the focus of early medieval coronation ceremonies, which stress the queen's fertility as a blessing to the kingdom.[18] Certainly the image of "queen as mother" pervades medieval writing for and about queens: her biographer calls Margaret the "most pious mother" of Scotland, "from whom no one went away empty-handed," a metaphor echoed a generation later in a suppliant's letter to Matilda addressing her as the "mother of all England" (*VM*, chap. 3, p. 328c, para. 18).[19] But in this family at least, motherhood was not empty symbolism. If we examine Margaret's *vita* further, we find that she was no less successful in her private life than she was in her public role as queen of Scotland. She genuinely seems to have enjoyed the company of small children. One of her Lenten charities was to bring nine orphaned babies into the palace, where she held them on her knees and fed them specially-prepared "soft foods, the kind infants of that age love" with the same spoons she herself used (*VM*, chap. 3, p. 329a, para. 22). According to her biographer, Margaret's care for her own children was "no less than that she expended on herself," and she diligently tried to introduce them to "honest manners" (*VM*, chap. 1, p. 325d, para. 9). Margaret was harsh by modern standards, believing in the proverb that "he who spares the rod hates the child," but the author leaves no doubt that she was motivated by true concern for her children's characters. And her methods were evidently successful: we may doubt the author's claim that the eight children never fought among themselves, but his pride in them is clear as he writes that "because of the religious zeal of their mother, the children's manners were far better than those of other children who were much older than they were." Margaret had her children brought to her "very often" and taught them the precepts of the Christian faith "using words suitable to their age and understanding" (*VM*, chap. 1, p. 325d, para. 9). These statements leave little doubt that some people in the Middle Ages had at least rudimentary ideas about child development. In one episode, Margaret is quoted talking with her children, speaking tenderly and addressing them as *viscera mea*—"my flesh," or literally, "my guts" (*VM*, chap. 1, p. 325e, para. 9).

Like innumerable medieval parents, Margaret had to face the prospect of death knowing that she was leaving behind children too young to fend for themselves. The author recognized the closeness of the family and shows that her children returned her love. Her eldest son predeceased her by three days, killed with his father while on a raid in England; Edmund, the second son, arrived home after the raid, to find Margaret herself mortally ill:

> He had come to tell his mother that his father had been killed, along with his older brother, and now he found his mother, whom he especially loved, to be about to die! He knew not whom he should mourn first! But above all, the departure of his very sweet mother pierced him with bitter pain, when he saw her about to die before his very eyes! (*VM*, chap. 4, p. 330f, para. 31)

On her deathbed, Margaret spelled out her concern for her younger children, three of them not yet into their teens. Recognizing the little ones' primary needs, she made the biographer promise to act as a father, teacher, and caretaker to them, admonishing him above all, "see that you expend them love" (*VM*, chap. 4, p. 330b, para. 27).

We do not know the immediate fate of these children. A rival line of kings seized the Scottish throne on Malcolm's death, and later sources claim that Margaret's brother took the children into England, where they were placed in the care of relatives.[20] The younger sons soon turned up at the English court of William Rufus, and Matilda and Henry seem to have known each other before their marriage, so perhaps she visited court as well. As a group, the children did not do too badly for themselves: three of the sons became kings of Scotland, Matilda became queen of England, and the younger daughter Mary was married to Eustace, count of Boulogne.[21] Margaret's five younger children remained close throughout their adult lives, despite long periods of physical separation. Whether this is because of their upbringing or their shared experience of adversity after their parents' death cannot be known, but Queen Margaret's children certainly did not suffer from any lack of "psychological investment" on the part of their parents.

Nor did Margaret's grandchildren, among whom were the son and daughter of Matilda, queen of England from 1100 to 1118. We are not as fortunate in our sources when looking at Matilda in her maternal role, since nothing like the biography of Margaret exists for her. Nevertheless, a look at the public documents shows that she also divided her concern between her public and private roles and ultimately succeeded at both. The case of Matilda will have to stand for all of Margaret's children, for space does not allow us to explore at any length the adult interactions among Margaret's children nor their later memories of their childhood, but I will point out that all the children eagerly commemorated their parents in their pious benefactions, and that they also generously commemorated each other. They were also liberal in endowing each other with estates and in promoting each other's welfare.[22]

Margaret's daughter, Queen Matilda, evidently learned much from her mother's example, even though they spent little time together. Matilda was an active queen, who at the age of twenty did not hesitate to testify to her eligibility for marriage before an entire episcopal council. Once married, she served as a member of Henry's *curia regis,* attesting his charters and acting as his regent during his periodic trips to Normandy. She issued charters, judged lawsuits and criminal cases, and controlled a substantial demesne. She shared in governing the kingdom, once referring to the Exchequer as "my court and the court of my husband."[23] The records show her granting fairs and augmentations of fairs, appointing abbots, and providing safe conducts, all matters which only someone invested with regal authority could have handled. She corresponded with many of the leading ecclesiastical figures of her day, using these men as both spiritual and political counselors. Matilda was also a generous benefactor: she corresponded with many of the leading bishops of Europe, patronized numerous ecclesiastical houses and established Holy Trinity Aldgate, one of England's first houses of Augustinian canons. She was particularly generous to the city of London, building hospitals, bridges, and a bathhouse along the wharves.[24] And, though the sources are scantier about her private life, Matilda was also concerned about her two children, Matilda and William. She was almost certainly involved in the negotiations that led to the younger Matilda's marriage to the German Emperor Henry V.[25] She also had some personal interest in her children's education. One account in the records of the Augustinian Priory at Merton may be more typical than surviving documentation leads us to believe and certainly demonstrates that at least one royal mother realized that childrens' early experiences could shape their character. According to the Merton chronicler, Matilda was fond of Merton's founder, Gilbert the Sheriff, and often visited him to see the progress of his foundation while it was being built. She usually brought along her young son, William, and saw that he enjoyed himself on his visits, hoping that William's childhood memories of playing on the grounds would induce him to remain a lifelong patron of Merton Priory.[26]

Although Matilda was never canonized, as her mother was, chroniclers writing soon after her death reported "signs" occurring at her tomb on a regular basis. She is invariably referred to as "Matilda the Good Queen" or "Matilda of Blessed Memory" during the two centuries that followed her death. Perhaps the sermon preached by Roger of Salisbury at her funeral in 1118 sums up contemporary opinion best: "from the time when England was first subject to kings, out of all the queens one will not be found like her, and neither will a similar queen be found in the ages to come, whose memory will be so praised, and whose name will be blessed through the ages."[27]

Contemporary writers were quick to see parallels and connections between Matilda's actitivies and those of her mother. Some modern historians have questioned how great an influence Margaret could have been, given their long separation and Matilda's admittedly weak memories.[28] Matilda may have idealized her early years, but she also may have retained stronger memories, or at least impressions, than has been assumed. A look at the sources shows that Matilda chose to link herself with her mother at every opportunity. As Matilda's impeccable lineage was probably chief among the reasons she was chosen as Henry I's queen, part of her interest in her mother must have arisen from the blood link Margaret provided to the Anglo-Saxon kings. But the number of references to Margaret in literature written for Matilda is too great to be explained away as mere antiquarian interest. In addition to the *Vita Margaritae* itself, Elisabeth van Houts has collected eight poems by at least three different authors, written either for Matilda or as epitaphs shortly after her death. Most of these poets were writing to gain Matilda's favor and patronage, so they were willing to write what she wanted to hear. All eight poems mention Margaret, usually to evoke Matilda's illustrious ancestry, but one describes its subject as "having all things of her mother," so much so that though Margaret was enclosed in her sepulchre, she continued to illuminate the English realms with her merits.[29] We have already seen, through Matilda's belief that William's childhood memories would influence his later behavior, that she knew that early childhood was an important stage in an individual's development. Could that knowledge have arisen from Matilda's memories of the happy family life she had known with her parents in Scotland, an early life that she prized enough to have it incorporated into the biography that served as a textbook for several generations of Margaret's descendants?

It is now time to return to the crucial problem of the sources and their interpretation. It is not often that we are allowed a glimpse into the private life of the palace such as the *Vita Margaritae* allows. In most cases, we have only the records of the political and administrative sides of royal activity. Financial records, which for England exist in part from the mid-twelfth century, sometimes allow us to reconstruct the households and itineraries of royal children, and historians have used such itineraries to estimate the amount of time royal children and their parents spent together. Returning to the evidence for Eleanor of Aquitaine and her children, we must admit that separations were frequent. Turner's reconstruction of Eleanor's itinerary shows that she left England to visit Normandy and Anjou in the summer of 1156, taking her oldest living son, Henry, and her daughter Matilda, both under two years old. On another trip to Normandy, in 1160, she took Matilda but not her younger sons, three and two; by this time Henry, now five, was already in the hands of tutors and probably remained at home.[30] Between 1163 and 1165 Eleanor was traveling in England, taking one or two of the children but never all of them at once. She did spend the spring of 1165 at Winchester with all but young Henry. In May of that year, five months pregnant, she crossed to the Continent with Matilda, nine, and Richard, eight; the other children, except Henry, joined her within a few months after a daughter was born that fall. In 1167, Eleanor and Matilda, now eleven, sailed to England where Eleanor gave birth to John. Eleanor may have chosen to take Matilda with her knowing that within a few months the girl would leave the family to be married in Germany. Between 1168 and 1174, Eleanor's movements are unclear, but it appears that she was traveling in Aquitaine; during this period, the two youngest children lived for a time with the nuns at Fontevrault Abbey. Eleanor's middle daughter and namesake left at age nine to join her Castilian fiancé. The youngest daughter, Joan, was not sent to Sicily for marriage until she was thirteen.[31]

Evaluation of the "psychological investment" that Eleanor of Aquitaine made in her children during their formative years rests largely on the above evidence. Turner pointed to the frequent separations to conclude that Eleanor "had hardly shone as an exemplar of maternal devotion during her children's early years," but I believe an alternative interpretation is possible: from the above itinerary, it seems that Eleanor did try to have her children with her as often as possible, even at times when it must have been quite inconvenient. Of course, it would have been foolhardy in the extreme to take all the children with her on a Channel crossing; few in her circle would have forgotten that a shipwreck some forty years earlier had cost Henry I his only legitimate son. It would have been easier, cheaper, and safer to leave them in England under the care of competent deputies—easier, that is, if Eleanor had little or no emotional attachment to her children. No one without a "psychological investment" in a child would willingly choose to journey from England to the South of France in the company of two toddlers, especially given twelfth-century traveling conditions. The relationships between Eleanor and her children, once they became adults, seem to have been characterized by genuine concern and affection, and it is difficult to believe that the devotion shown her by her adult sons and daughters did not grow out of childhood experience, experience that simply left no record in the account books and annals of the court.

Chroniclers and bookkeepers were interested in events of a public nature. They often failed to record the births and deaths of royal children, but this did not mean that society did not recognize the existence of children—merely that those children did not become important to historians of the period until they were old enough to influence political events. The chroniclers' indifference, however, cannot and should not be taken as evidence that royal parents shared their attitudes. Frequent separations of mother and child, the use of tutors and nurses, and early entry into adult roles are all hallmarks of medieval royal childhood; all are vastly different from the way we raise our children today. It cannot be denied that childhood was much shorter and generally less sentimentalized in the Middle Ages than in the modern world. Yet the fact that medieval children appear in adult roles at sometimes startlingly early ages does not necessarily indicate ignorance, indifference, or cruelty on the part of medieval parents. On the contrary, parents were often desperate to insure the well-being of their offspring, to provide them with foster parents, parental surrogates and other adult protectors in the case of their own early demise. We need not assert that medieval children were unwanted and unloved, nor that medieval childhood was generally unhappy, much less the "nightmare" that modern theorists have posited. Nor do we have to believe that busy aristocratic mothers typically had little interest in or involvement with their small children. We have not yet uncovered enough evidence of the proper kind to reconstruct a "typical" royal or aristocratic childhood before the fifteenth century. Eleanor of Aquitaine, with her vast and widely separated holdings, may have been an unusually remote royal mother; Margaret of Scotland and her children may have been unusually close. Or, the private ties between Eleanor and her children may elude us—as Margaret of Scotland's itinerary does. Because of the widely different nature of the sources available to us, we cannot meaningfully compare the "psychological investments" of a Margaret and an Eleanor. We are left with a comparison of the records themselves, and this comparison has shown that the need for caution in attempting to discern the private motives of medieval parents from the types of documents that are normally available to us. Margaret's biographer explicitly describes her deathbed fear that her absence would deprive her children of the love she expended on them. Might we not reasonably conclude, from Eleanor's attempts to have her children with her, that she feared the same for her own small children?

NOTES

1. I was privileged to read a version of this essay at the February 1995 meeting of the Illinois Medieval Association. I wish to thank the organizers, presenters, and audience at that meeting who helped to sharpen its focus over the course of the two-day forum dedicated to medieval children and families.

2. Philippe Ariès, *L'enfant et la vie familale sous l'Ancien Régime* (Paris, 1960), trans. Robert Baldick as *Centuries of Childhood: A Social History of Family Life* (New York, 1962); Lloyd DeMause, "The Evolution of Childhood," in his *The History of Childhood* (New York, 1974), pp. 1–73, at p. 1.

3. Lawrence Stone, *The Family, Sex, and Marriage in England, 1500–1800* (New York, 1977), p. 5.

4. Several studies stand out for scholarly merit and common sense. See Shulamith Shahar, "Infants, Infant Care and Attitudes Toward Infancy in Medieval Lives of Saints," *JMH* 10 (1982), 281–309; Barbara Hanawalt, *The Ties that Bound: Peasant Families in Medieval England* (Oxford, 1986); Mary Martin McLaughlin, "Survivors and Surrogates: Children and Parents from the Ninth to the Thirteenth Centuries," in DeMause, *History of Childhood*, pp. 101–82. Shahar's *Childhood in the Middle Ages*, trans. Chaya Galai (London and New York, 1990) has become the standard work on the subject.

5. Shahar, *Childhood in the Middle Ages*, pp. 1, 149–55.

6. See John Carmi Parsons, ed., *Medieval Queenship* (New York, 1993); Pauline Stafford, "The King's Wife in Wessex, 800–1066," *Past and Present* 91 (1981), 3–27, and eadem, *Queens, Concubines and Dowagers: The King's Wife in the Early Middle Ages* (Athens, GA, 1983); Suzanne Fonay Wemple, *Women in Frankish Society: Marriage and the Cloister 500–900* (Philadelphia, 1985); Lois L. Huneycutt, "Intercession and the High-Medieval Queen: The *Esther* Topos," and John Carmi Parsons, "The

Queen's Intercession in Thirteenth-Century England," both in *Power of the Weak,* eds. S. B. MacLean and J. E. Carpenter (Urbana, IL, 1995). As background to the present essay, see Lois L. Huneycutt, "The Idea of the Perfect Princess: The Life of St. Margaret in the Reign of Matilda II (1100–1118)," *Anglo-Norman Studies* 12 (1990), 81–97. Mary Erler and Maryanne Kowaleski, eds., *Women and Power in the Middle Ages* (Athens, GA, 1988), contains several essays on queenship, as does Derek Baker, ed., *Medieval Women. Essays Edited and Presented to R.M.T. Hill,* Studies in Church History Subsidia 1 (Oxford, 1978). Marion Facinger's "A Study of Medieval Queenship: Capetian France, 987–1237," *Studies in Medieval and Renaissance History* 5 (1968), 1–48, remains a valuable starting place for the study of French queens.

7. Ralph V. Turner, "Eleanor of Aquitaine and Her Children: An Inquiry into Medieval Family Attachment," *JMH* 14 (1988), 321–35, at 323.

8. Turner, "Eleanor of Aquitaine and her Children," 325. Turner's discussion of John's childhood in *King John* (London and New York, 1994) is more subtle and perhaps less tendentious, though he repeats (p. 27) the assertion quoted above. "Psychological investment" and "emotional capital" are ubiquitous phrases in the discussion of familial affection in pre-modern times. I reluctantly perpetuate the tradition, while wondering if the use of such terms may not force us to think of personal relationships in economic terms and conclude that love and affection are nonrenewable resources.

9. Turner, "The Children of Anglo-Norman Royalty and Their Upbringing," *Medieval Prosopography* 11 (1990), 17–44, esp. 32.

10. Nicholas Orme, *From Childhood to Chivalry: The Education of English Kings and Aristocracy, 1066–1530* (London, 1984), pp. 16–17.

11. Margaret and Malcolm III of Scotland's elder daughter, Matilda (also known as Edith) married in 1100 King Henry I of England (r. 1100–1135). Henry and Matilda's daughter, also Matilda, married Count Geoffrey of Anjou. The eldest son of Geoffrey and the younger Matilda married Eleanor of Aquitaine and ruled England as King Henry II from 1154 to 1189.

12. Turgot, "Vita S. Margaritae reginae Scotiae," *AASS,* June, vol. 2, June 10, pp. 324a–31a, at chap. 1, p. 325a–b, par. 6. The "Vita" is hereafter parenthetically cited as *VM*; all translations are my own.

13. See Helen Clover and Margaret Gibson, eds., *The Letters of Lanfranc, Archbishop of Canterbury* (Oxford, 1979), no. 50, at p. 150; and "Epistolae Theobaldi Stampiensis," *PL,* 163:765.

14. David Knowles, *The Monastic Order in England 943–1216,* 2nd edn. (Cambridge, 1966), p. 170; Robert L. Ritchie, *The Normans in Scotland* (Edinburgh, 1954), p. 399.

15. In the late summer of 1093, Matilda was removed from the nunnery at Wilton by her father, outraged that she, valuable to him in creating marriage alliances, had been seen wearing a nun's habit. Her whereabouts from August 1093 to November 1100 are unknown, although

a visit to Scotland is not unlikely. She had not returned to the convent by February 1094, when Anselm of Canterbury asked the bishop of Salisbury to have her returned. See Lois L. Huneycutt, "'Another Esther in our own times:' Matilda II and the Creation of a Queenly Ideal in Anglo-Norman England" (Ph.D. diss., University of California, Santa Barbara, 1992), pp. 72–81.

16. Huneycutt, "Perfect Princess," 81–97.

17. *Letters of Lanfranc,* ed. Clover and Gibson, p. 150.

18. The oldest surviving *ordo* for a queen's consecration was written by Hincmar, bishop of Rheims, for Judith, daughter of Charles the Bald, when she became queen of England ("Coronatio Iudithae Karoli II filiae," *MGH Capitularia 2, Capitularia regum francorum* [Munich, 1883, repr. 1960], pp. 425–27). For modern discussion of the fertility trope, see, among others, Janet Nelson, "Inauguration Rituals," in her *Politics and Ritual in Early Medieval Europe* (London and Ronceverte, 1986), pp. 283–307, at p. 296.

19. For the letter, see Herbert of Norwich, *Epistolae Heribert de Losinga,* ed. Robert Anstruther (Caxton Society, 1846; rprt. New York, 1969), no. 25. See also Lois L. Huneycutt, "Images of Medieval Queenship," *The Haskins Society Journal: Studies in Medieval History* 1 (London, 1989), 61–71.

20. Huneycutt, "Another Esther," p. 74. See also John of Fordun, *Chronica gentis scottorum,* book 5, section 21, quoted in *Early Sources of Scottish History,* ed. Alan Orr Anderson, 2 vols. (Edinburgh, 1922), 2:86, note 1.

21. Edgar, r. 1097–1107, Alexander 1107–24, David 1124–53. Mary wed Eustace, count of Boulogne, and was survived by a daughter, also Matilda, countess in her own right and queen of England upon the accession (1135) of her husband, Stephen of Blois.

22. Matilda is recorded as helping to arrange the advantageous marriages of her sister Mary and brother David. Contemporaries seemed to recognize the special bonds among Margaret's children. When King Edgar died in 1107, Matilda's correspondent Bishop Ivo of Chartres wrote to assure her that Edgar, known for his piety, would ascend quickly to Heaven. David spent much time at Henry I's court and was also close to Matilda, who took it upon herself to further David's spiritual progress. She once called him to her chamber and asked him to help her wash the feet of some lepers she had brought into the palace; David good-naturedly refused, but the lesson stayed with him. When Matilda died in 1118, David endowed her chamberlain with some of his English holdings and arranged that some of the profits of those holdings would go toward an annual memorial service for the soul of his sister and their parents. See Huneycutt, "Another Esther," pp. 142, 160.

23. The charter in question records Abbot Faritius of Abingdon's appearance at the Michaelmas Exchequer accounting of 1111 to have a land dispute adjudicated. The queen, presiding in King Henry's absence, referred to the court as *"curia domini mei et mea."* See *Chronica monasterii de Abingdon,* 2 vols., ed. Joseph Stevenson, Rolls Series 2 (London, 1858), 2:116–17.

24. Huneycutt, "Another Esther," chaps. 4, 5.

25. A letter from Henry V to Matilda, thanking her for previous favors and seeking continued help, appears to be related to the marriage negotiations. See "Udalrici codex," *Monumenta germanica historiae,* Bibliotheca rerum germanicarum, Monumenta Bambergensia 5, ed. Philip Jaffé (Berlin, 1869, reprt. 1964), no. 142, discussed by Karl J. Leyser, "England and the Empire in the Early Twelfth Century," *Transactions of the Royal Historical Society,* 5th series 10 (1960), 41–84, reprt. in Leyser, *Medieval Germany and its Neighbors, 900–1250* (London, 1982), pp. 191–214.

26. M.L. Colker, "Latin Texts Concerning Gilbert, Founder of Merton Priory," *Studia monastica* 12 (1970), 241–72.

27. *Liber Monasterii de Hyda,* ed. E. Edwards, Rolls Series 45 (London, 1866, reprt. 1964), pp. 312–13 (my translation).

28. E.g., Derek Baker, "A Nursery of Saints: St. Margaret of Scotland Revisited," in his *Medieval Women,* pp. 119–41, esp. pp. 131–32.

29. Elisabeth van Houts, "Latin Poetry and the Anglo-Norman Court: The Carmen de Hastingae Proelio," *JMH* 15 (1989), 39–62; André Boutemy, "Notice sur le recueil poétique du manuscrit Cotton Vitellius A xii du British Museum," *Latomus* 1 (1937), 7, note 10.

30. Eleanor's most recent biographer believes that young Henry did accompany Eleanor on a channel crossing in 1160 but cites no source (D.D.R. Owen, *Eleanor of Aquitaine: Queen and Legend* [Oxford, 1993], p. 48).

31. Turner, "Eleanor of Aquitaine and Her Children," 324–25.

ADELA OF BLOIS
AS MOTHER AND COUNTESS

Kimberly A. LoPrete

Noblewomen played critical roles in the affairs of men related to them by blood and marriage. Countess Adela governed her husband's domains and raised their children, moved by concern for their well-being as well as by political expediency.

Writing in the decade after the monastic retirement in 1120 of the Countess Adela of Blois, Chartres, and Meaux, the Anglo-Norman monk-historian, Orderic Vitalis, described her as "a praiseworthy mistress" who "honorably governed her husband's county after his pilgrimage and skillfully educated her young sons in the defense of holy church." Elsewhere in his narrative Orderic noted diverse domestic and lordly deeds of this "noble mother" and "wise and spirited woman" who ruled as countess for over twenty years, during her husband's absences on crusade and after his death in battle at Ramla.[1] Orderic's pairing of Adela's wifely and maternal roles with her comital governance was not unusual for contemporary commentators on her life;[2] she lived at a time when positions of political authority were transmitted through noble families and much political activity involved shifting familial alliances and their members' claims to lands and offices, both of which could be transmitted through women. As mothers in ruling families played integral (if subordinate) roles, even domestic activities allowed them to act with acknowledged political authority, especially when circumstances dictated that they performed administrative, judicial, and other governing tasks for absent husbands or inexperienced heirs.[3]

More noteworthy is Orderic's pairing of Adela's governance with her role as an educator of future rulers. Orderic thus highlights aristocratic mothers' poorly-documented activities as the ruling elite's instructors in the values and behavioral expectations attendant on status and rank.[4] As a ruling mother and countess, Adela could teach through the example of her own behavior;[5] but she had been educated in Latin letters and, in turn, saw to it that several of her children received at least the rudiments of a literary education. Following Orderic's lead, I will explore how Adela, building on her experiences as a literate bride whose marriage furthered the political aims of her natal and affinal families, oversaw her children's education while grooming them for specific socio-political roles amidst shifting, family-based power politics. However restrictive these roles may seem to modern westerners, preparing children for them need not have been achieved without concern for individual physical and emotional well-being. Indeed, fostering in children a sense of the contributions they could make to the welfare of those upon whom they depended for survival and social standing could have increased the children's sense of self-worth.[6]

By presenting sources overlooked in published accounts, this essay will on one level increase knowledge of Adela's relations with her children. Even so, extant sources remain inadequate for thorough reconstruction of Adela's day-to-day relations with her children or her emotional bonds to family members. The historian interested in assessing Adela's handling of the roles of mother and countess must, of course, extrapolate from this meager evidentiary base in terms of what is known of prevailing sociocultural contexts and attitudes to mothering and children. Yet for Adela's lifetime, those contexts remain multifaceted and elusive. As the synthetic studies of medieval motherhood by Clarissa Atkinson and medieval childhood by Shulamith Shahar reveal, there was no one set of cultural attitudes or material circumstances shared even by all noble parents in northern France, while evidence of all sorts remains scarce and biased toward registering public behaviors until the latter half of the twelfth century.[7] Despite claims to the contrary—usually by nonspecialists— medievalists have argued convincingly that children in the Middle Ages were widely regarded as human beings with needs and proclivities different from those of adults, that strong, positive, affective bonds could be forged between noble spouses or mothers and children, and that aristocratic parents invested in their children, both psychologically and materially.[8]

What I have not seen presented, despite contrary assertions, is evidence that noble mothers' delegation of primary childcare to non-kin domestic familiars or family members living elsewhere necessarily precluded oversight of designated caregivers, concern for children cared for by others, or routine (if perforce intermittent) personal contact between mothers and children.[9] As little can be known of the day-to-day and affective lives of even prominent and politically active mothers, generalizing assumptions combined with arguments from silence are especially weak. Nor has convincing evidence been adduced to show that such mothers' administrative or political activities, even when they involved children, necessarily impeded the formation of positive emotional bonds between mother and child. Whether a mother's political interests would eventually converge with, or diverge from, those of her children depended on complex and changing factors; but any mother of Adela's time who hoped to further her interests through her children would have been ill-advised to neglect them or to alienate their affections. A sense of common interest and mutual obligation could be inculcated from childhood in sons as well as daughters. Primogenital succession, while favored, was not universally practiced by noble families, and daughters were frequently married to forge alliances; if a daughter was to foster her natal family's interests in a new household, she would need to identify with them.[10] On another level, then, this essay explores indications that political or economic expediency, while important, were only two of several factors Adela weighed when she took decisions affecting her children's lives. Her actions show how noble mothers, as living links joining two family groups, could move to the center of affairs of men related to them by blood and marriage.

Adela was the youngest daughter and second-to-youngest of the nine or ten children born to William the Conqueror and his wife Matilda of Flanders.[11] Little is known of the upbringing of Adela and her brothers or sisters, but it does appear that some of them received the rudiments of a literary education. Three tutors were hired for Adela's brother Robert Curthose, and her brothers William Rufus and Henry were also said to have been formally instructed.[12] Her sister Cecilia, dedicated to God as a child at the pre-Conquest family foundation of Holy Trinity, Caen, was educated there by a well-known master and was a noted patron of Latin letters.[13] Another literate sister, a consecrated virgin, was buried at Holy Trinity and may have lived there for a time.[14] Contemporary attestations of Adela's Latinity predate her marriage; clerical authors later praised her skills and sent her Latin compositions of diverse *genre*, length, and complexity, and she once sightread a Latin label identifying St. Helen's relics to a crowd gathered to witness their translation.[15] No direct evidence indicates how she gained her knowledge of Latin. But given her parents' concern for their children's education, her mother's travels (especially in Normandy) to assist William's rule, and Holy Trinity's place in the education of Adela's sister(s), I would suggest she was entrusted to the nuns there and was educated either by her sister's tutor or other clerics.[16]

Whatever the course of Adela's early years, marriage was a defining moment in her life. Ceremonially betrothed at Breteuil perhaps by 1080, she married by 1085; her wedding at Chartres may have taken place around her fifteenth birthday (c. 1083). Adela's husband was Stephen-Henry, eldest son and designated primary heir to Count Thibaud III of Blois, Chartres, Meaux, and Troyes. As was common for aristocratic couples at this time, pragmatic and political considerations made the choice of spouse more an arrangement among parents than a matter of sentiment between partners; Adela's marriage was meant to assure continued cooperation between the Anglo-Normans and the Thibaudians against the counts of Anjou, who were continuing efforts to extend their power and influence in Normandy and Blois-Chartres.[17]

Despite the arranged marriage and an age difference of at least eighteen years, Adela and Stephen-Henry appear to have evolved a cooperative relationship grounded in mutual respect, if not personal affection. After 1089, when Stephen-Henry became count of Blois, Chartres and Meaux, Adela was routinely consulted by him, joined with him in all aspects of comital administration, and, on occasion, took decisions independently or implemented joint decisions.[18] While on crusade, Stephen-Henry sent Adela letters corroborating the documentary evidence that he routinely confided in his wife.[19] It is hard to assess the personal sentiment behind these letters' use of *amica* and *dilecta*; they were really penned by Stephen's chaplain, and such conventional expressions of affection were routinely applied to allies, faithful followers, or dependents.[20] Commonplace recourse to the language of love to describe a range of sociopolitical relations need not, however, devalue signs of intimacy in these letters, especially as the affection thought natural in nuclear family relations provided the ideal base for the bonds uniting larger social groups. A memorable vignette penned by Orderic long after Stephen returned to France shows Adela, between conjugal caresses, urging her aged and war-worn husband to return to the Holy Land.[21] As he was hardly a bedchamber earwitness, Orderic's report must be seen as his invention, not Adela's "speech"; still, its plausibility depends on his audience's assumption that this couple did share intimate moments. Their engendering of at least six to eight children in some fifteen years implies a degree of sexual compatibility that lends credence to the story's premise and suggests Stephen and Adela enjoyed each other's company.[22]

The comital couple, like many of their noble peers, named their children to honor maternal relatives of higher status than paternal kin:[23] their first son for Adela's father, their best-attested daughter for Adela's mother. Younger sons and another daughter bore customary Thibaudian names—Thibaud, Odo, Stephen, Henry, and (perhaps) Agnes. Little can be known of Adela's physiological experience of motherhood. As her eldest son seems to have been born c. 1087–88, it appears she bore most of her children in her twenties, perhaps into her thirties. References to physicians in her entourage and to her patronage of medical practitioners suggest that she, like her sister-in-law Matilda II of England, would have been attended by doctors at childbirth.[24] It cannot be known whether Adela nursed her children, but her travels across the Thibaudian domains from 1089 and her growing role in comital affairs from 1092, suggest she delegated day-to-day childcare to members of her household.

Delegated childcare need not imply lack of affection for children. As there are periods of three or four years in which nothing is recorded of her activities, public or domestic, yet during which she appears to have borne children, it would be rash to assume that she shared no intimate moments with family members. And without contradictory evidence, it would also be rash to assume she provided no oversight to the primary caregivers, or that she was unconcerned for her children's well-being, especially as indirect indications of her concern do exist. Charter attestations of her sons Odo and Stephen in their childhoods suggest that they, at least, were raised chiefly at one of the family's principal residences and were not routinely obliged, as young children, to accompany other family members in administrative perambulations. Odo, who was probably always frail and died in his early teens, was evidently provided with professional medical attendants perhaps recruited through Adela's patronage of physicians; she also endowed anniversary prayers for his soul.[25] Thus, Odo seems to have been the object of her solicitude in life and in death, even if obligations kept her from providing that care personally.

Adela's youngest son, Henry, was dedicated to God as a young child, a conventional form of family piety.[26] It is interesting that she offered her last, seemingly healthy, son; she apparently did not see cloistering as a way to avoid caring for sickly children (such as Odo) or to limit the number of children with claims on family lands and honors. Status concerns perhaps played a role in Adela's choice for her son of the Cluniac order, the most prestigious and internationally influential order of the day. All sources agree Henry made his profession at Cluny itself, but his appearance in 1111 as a monk of the Thibaudian supported house of La Charité-sur-Loire suggests Adela first entrusted him to the Cluniacs there, near Thibaudian domains in northern Berry where she could conveniently visit him when in that area. Odo Arpin, La Charité's prior by c. 1107, had moreover fought beside Stephen-Henry at Ramla; crusading ties perhaps recommended the house for Stephen-Henry's son.[27] Adela could thus be assured that her husband's soul would be prayed for and that Henry would be raised and educated in a manner befitting his status.[28] Still, perhaps out of maternal concern, it appears she arranged for him to spend his early years at a house where she easily could visit him. He could have transferred to Cluny to take his formal vows at the age of consent (fourteen or fifteen).

Like her own mother, Adela saw that tutors were hired to train her sons who were being groomed for secular careers. In c. 1101, Thibaud had with him a *magister* Burdinus, of whom nothing else is known.[29] Thibaud and Stephen were likely also grounded in Latin letters by one Geoffrey, a monk from Saint-Évroul in Normandy trained in the liberal arts at Orléans. The chronicle claiming that Geoffrey tutored Thibaud and Stephen is heavily re-worked, but it is by no means unlikely that Adela would choose a well-educated French-born tutor from a Norman monastery.[30] In 1107, Adela granted to Sainte-Foi, Coulommiers, seven *hospites* formerly belonging to William Normandus, *magister* of one of her sons (probably Stephen).[31] Nothing else is known of this tutor, though his *cognomen* implies Norman origins. Stephen's presence at his mother's and brothers' side in 1102 and 1109–10 and this 1107 reference to a tutor indicate that he spent his childhood in the Thibaudian domains and was not sent to his maternal uncle's court in England until his mid-teens.[32] Thibaud appears to have been entrusted to his paternal uncle, Count Hugh of Troyes, by c. 1103, when he was ten or slightly older. Hugh and his wife were then childless after almost a decade of marriage, and grooming a nephew as Hugh's potential heir would serve both the Thibaudians and Adela: Hugh's office and lands could be kept in Thibaudian hands, and Adela was relieved of her son's martial training. Thibaud still visited her and was attested in her entourage outside Châteaudun in 1104.[33]

While these tutors' duties are not specified, Geoffrey, surely, was fluent in Latin and was unlikely to have overseen training in horsemanship or other worldly skills, which could have been imparted by other tutors or male relatives. Any tutor could easily have instructed other children in the area, moreover, and formal instruction in Latin by a learned tutor could be supplemented by vernacular oral teaching from household clerics, jongleurs, or Adela herself. The tenor of such teaching is now lost to historians. But precisely because circumstances prevented one noble mother from personally instructing her teen-aged son in what she thought he must do to attain worldly and Heavenly rewards, Dhuoda, in the ninth century, composed a manual of advice for her son. Her work, while surely unknown to Adela, nonetheless allows access to noble mothers' vision of their roles as educators and the complex contours of their advice. Comparison with didactic literature directed to eleventh- and twelfth-century lay courts shows the enduring relevance of Dhuoda's key themes, especially "family relations, social order, and the connection between religious and military responsibility."[34] A literate mother versed in the moral thought of her day and experienced in marriage politics and estate management, Dhuoda voiced—in words that were written down—concerns and advice that could well have been echoed by Adela two hundred and fifty years later. According to Orderic, such oral teaching, comprised of Biblical and hagiographical tales of "holy knights," augmented by legends of Carolingian warrior-heroes, was dispensed by the chaplain at Hugh of Avranches' court to barons, knights, and noble boys; Orderic also refers to jongleurs who sang to lay audiences of ancient warriors' deeds.[35] Several jongleurs are

attested in Adela's entourage as well as household clerics who could
have instructed as well as entertained her children.[36]

Hugh of Sainte-Marie, a monk at Fleury-sur-Loire, presented to
Adela in 1109–10 two versions of his "Ecclesiastical History Plus Deeds
of the Romans and Franks." Explicitly stating his intent to instruct
learned and unlearned lay people in proper behavior by examples
from the deeds of ancient emperors and men beloved of God, Hugh
placed his narrative within a centuries-old tradition of historical texts
written by learned churchmen for lay rulers' instruction.[37] As Paul
the Deacon's *Historia Romana* and the second volume of Freculphus
of Lisieux's history testify, such works were often directed to future
rulers' mothers because of their critical roles in their sons' education.[38]
Hugh noted the popularity at lay courts of vernacular recitals of
Charlemagne's deeds, and he included, in a work meant for a mother
and countess, Einhard's passages on Charlemagne listening to
readings from the deeds of the ancients and Augustine's *City of God*,
on Charlemagne's patronage of scholars and his insistence that both
sons and daughters be instructed in the liberal arts. Adela's eldest
son was married and living elsewhere when she received Hugh's work,
but Thibaud and Stephen were still attested in her entourage. Marked
for secular careers, they were of an age to learn from Hugh's moral
teaching masked as history, even if Adela had to translate and retell
his vignettes. Hugh's examples of learned, astute, and morally sound
women also made his work suitable for Adela's daughter(s), if they
were raised at her court.[39]

Because of his lackluster adult career, Adela's oldest son, William,
has received little attention. William was groomed as his father's
principal heir and was likely instructed beside his brothers. In 1100,
over fifty, Stephen-Henry returned to the Holy Land; but first, he
and Adela took measures to assure a smooth devolution of power
should he not return from his second voyage. The comital title was
conferred on William, and, to display his new status he was associated
in comital acts on a tour of the Thibaudian domains.[40] He came of
age by 1103, when he resorted to violent threats to disrupt Adela's
efforts to resolve her dispute with the canons of Chartres cathedral.
The only source for this episode, Bishop Ivo of Chartres, blamed
William's advisors and refrained from excommunicating him.
William continued, moreover, to appear with the comital title, albeit
in roles subordinate to Adela, as late as 1106–07.[41] But after 1107,

William vanished from family acts, while Thibaud was knighted and appeared with the comital title. It thus appears that in 1107 Adela replaced William with Thibaud as Stephen's primary heir, though for a time Thibaud still frequented Hugh of Troyes' court.[42]

Why Adela set William aside (when about twenty and already married) cannot be determined. An English historian in the 1190s claimed he was "deficient in intelligence as well as degenerate"; a mid-thirteenth-century Cistercian chronicler in Champagne, who apparently conflated two of Adela's sons, stated that the eldest, Odo(!), a stammerer with no valor, was not allowed to succeed his father because he wed the lord of Sully's daughter.[43] Odo may have been a weakly stammerer, but William's ability to rally the men of Chartres in 1103 suggests rather a certain eloquence and assertiveness. Such behavior may not have been very astute, and vowing to kill the canons while harassing the bishop suggests a lack of moral rectitude, but Adela had already seized the canons' goods, and Thibaud later forced Ivo's successor into exile after pillaging his estates.[44] Orderic, the only contemporary to assess William, called him "a good and peaceful man, blessed with children and wealth."[45] Only Bishop Ivo's account of William's actions in 1103 contradicts Orderic, and one violent act need not imply a deep-seated character defect.

William did marry the Sully heiress, but contemporary documents indicate that Adela herself arranged the marriage to brace the Thibaudian position in northern Berry. The Thibaudians, in fact, recovered Sully and its dependencies in 1100; William's marriage, by November 1104, was intended to assure comital rule there as King Philip I moved to secure viscomital rights in Dun and Bourges in 1100–04. In light of William's behavior in 1103, moreover, Adela may have wished to give him an independent income prior to assumption of his full inheritance.[46] The Thibaudian recovery of Sully and William's later appearance with the comital title show that his marriage was not a formal disinheritance. Why Adela displaced him will probably never be known. Perhaps Orderic caught William's personality very well—perhaps he did prefer a good life amid a growing family to the arduous life of a leading prince, or perhaps he was merely less able than Thibaud as a leader of men. Nothing implies he did anything but acquiesce in Adela's choice of wife and her decision to deprive him of his father's counties; indeed, several of his children owed their careers to family ties with the rulers of England

and Normandy.[47] William's marriage and Thibaud's calm substitution as heir imply that Adela ably balanced politics and individual proclivities among her sons to assure Thibaudian rule in northern Berry in 1104 and in 1107 to ascertain that her husband would be succeeded by the son deemed the more likely to prove an effective ruler.

From 1107, then, Thibaud was groomed as his father's primary heir. His role in comital governance increased, especially in the new century's war-torn second decade. Still, Adela continued to exercise authority independently of him and to determine the contours of Thibaudian relations with neighboring princes; her behind-the-scenes diplomacy was critical to Thibaudian–Anglo-Norman victories in 1113 and 1119. It thus appears that Adela, like her male peers, associated her designated heir(s) in rule prior to her retirement and without giving up her authority as countess. Such association gave an heir active training and provided support for a ruler, such as Adela, who was obliged to govern widespread domains.[48] Adela apparently did not try to find Thibaud a wife, likely because the Thibaudian–Anglo-Norman alliance confirmed by her own marriage continued to serve comital interests. Perhaps she felt that a wife's presence might confuse relations with her son; with William siring sons and Stephen in the wings, there was no urgent need for Thibaud to marry. He did so only in his early thirties, after Adela retired; his choice of wife was evidently motivated more by status concerns than alliance formation.[49]

Multiple sons improved the odds that one would live to sire a male heir, but grown sons could dispute family lands and honors. Adela's plans for her son Stephen probably evolved as he matured and family circumstances changed. Hugh of Troyes' second wife did not bear a child until the 1120s, and until then the possibility remained that Stephen might replace Thibaud as Hugh's heir. After 1103–08, during which time no record of Stephen survives, he appears, in his mid-teens, with Adela and Thibaud in 1109–10.[50] Then, in 1111, armed hostilities erupted between the Thibaudians (allied with Adela's brother Henry I of England, duke of Normandy) and the Capetian Louis VI (allied with the count of Anjou). During this round of warfare Stephen was knighted by Henry I and fought his first battles. Whether out of Henry's sense of obligation to his nephew, his gratitude to Adela for support in Normandy, her hope that Stephen be provided for without further dividing the Thibaudian lands, or a combination thereof, Henry also gave Stephen the Norman county of Mortain and the honor of Eye in Suffolk. When conflict resumed in 1116–19, Henry granted Thibaud five castles in Maine and Perche; with his assent, Thibaud then granted them to Stephen in exchange for his share in the paternal inheritance. Clearly, Stephen still had some claim on his father's lands, but when the Thibaudian–Anglo-Norman alliance created an opportunity for territorial gain, he received the newly-acquired castles so as not to diminish Thibaud's inheritance. Several of these castles were later given to the count of Anjou as the price of peace, but Stephen's future as a major landholder in the Anglo-Norman realm was assured; after Adela retired, Henry arranged for him to marry the count of Boulogne's heiress, with wide lands in England.[51] Adela had been a prime mover in reactivating the Thibaudian–Anglo-Norman alliance; that one result was to earn her third adult son an honorable place in the world, while avoiding a succession dispute between her sons, should not be overlooked.

As Adela was well aware, women represented important capital in a world of family-based politics; thus the Thibaudian–Anglo-Norman alliance also affected her daughters. In the wake of the Thibaudian–Anglo-Norman victories in 1113, her daughter Matilda married Henry I's ward Richard, earl of Chester and viscount of Avranches. Son of a powerful baron who had been Henry I's early supporter, Richard was a most suitable husband for Adela's daughter. The marriage assured his loyalty to Henry and the Thibaudians in the troubled years 1116–19; as members of Henry's inner circle, with lands and honors on both sides of the Channel, Richard and Matilda could expect a glorious future. But both drowned with Henry's son in November 1120, five to eight years after they married and before they had produced a viable child.[52]

Adela's other daughters or step-daughters were married to important castellans to secure their loyalty during the 1111–13 hostilities. One, whose name is unknown, married Milo II of Bray-sur-Seine, who held Bray from the senior Thibaudian line and stood to inherit the viscounty of Troyes from his mother. His paternal uncle had been royal seneschal while his cousins held castles from, and had other ties to, the Capetians; in 1109–10, he acquired Montlhéry from Louis VI. By offering Milo a daughter in marriage, Adela won his support in her conflicts with Louis. As Milo had not canonically divorced a first wife, this marriage was annulled—but not before it served its political purpose.[53] The fate of this anonymous (step-)daughter is unknown.

A second (step-)daughter, Agnes, married another prominent castellan who held honors from both Thibaudians and Capetians: Hugh III of Le Puiset, viscount of Chartres. The marriage cannot be dated precisely, but circumstances suggest the context of the 1111–13 fighting. Hugh came of age c. 1108 and proceeded to loot monasteries near Le Puiset, a castle he held from the Capetians. Early in 1111, Adela appealed to Louis VI, who with Thibaud took Le Puiset and wrecked Hugh's castle; Hugh was confined by Louis, but soon released. By the end of 1111, hostilities had broken out between Louis and the Thibaudians, and Hugh now fought for the Thibaudians. What induced him to support Thibaud? In 1112 Hugh, at Chartres, confirmed grants at Adela's behest, and she may have agreed at that time to press the claims to the castle of Corbeil Hugh had ostensibly renounced to gain his release from Louis. Marriage to Thibaudian's sister would confirm his support.[54]

Adela thus arranged marriages for four of her children when politics dictated astute alliance building. The spouses of three of them were from viscomital families with long-standing ties to the Thibaudians; the daughter who married outside the Thibaudian domains wed a prominent member of her maternal uncle's court. Two sons found worthy wives on their own; though one was helped by Adela's brother. One son was professed at the most renowned monastery in Europe, and his career too was promoted by his maternal uncle. Willing and able to use her family's children as political pawns, Adela still tried to ensure that their adult lives would not be strikingly unlike that which they might have known as children. Milo and Hugh's familial and feudal ties to the Capetians and Thibaudians put them among the most eminent men of noncomital rank in northern France; their ties to the Thibaudian domains allowed their wives to remain in touch with their natal family. Both houses had produced crusaders: Milo's father fell at Ramla; Hugh's father at Antioch. By 1111, moreover, all three daughters were at least fifteen years old; whether Adela might have married them off earlier had such crises arisen when they were younger cannot be determined.

When Adela retired to Marcigny in 1120 she could be assured that her fostering of the Thibaudian–Anglo-Norman alliance had benefited her affinal family and that her living children were well-placed to prosper as adults. Her actions show how, at a time when political power was grounded in families, noblewomen's roles as daughters and mothers involved them in "public" affairs through relations to parents, husbands, and children. To posit sharp distinctions between "domestic/maternal" and "public/political" concerns thus leads to fundamental misapprehensions of the continuum of experience for such women, wed for "political" reasons and moved from the role of daughter to those of wife and mother. I use the term "family" here because, despite any growing identity with patrilineal descent groups, European kinship remained fundamentally bilateral in that maternal and paternal relations were considered equally when applying incest rules and women could transmit status, lands, and claims to office from natal families to husbands and offspring. Nonincestuous marriage was valorized on the grounds of spreading love through ever-expanding kin groups, while the political and material standing of patrilineal descent groups could be preserved or improved through relations with maternal kin.[55] Adela, a king's daughter, transmitted the highest social status to her children; as the mother of a count's heirs, she took measures affecting her affinal family's lands and honors, and used natal family ties to foster the well-being of her children and the Thibaudian family, of which she was the effective head for over twenty years.

While little is known of Adela's feelings for her husband or children, she appears to have developed relationships grounded in mutual trust and affection for them. She also evidently provided her children with professional medical care and with instruction geared to individual needs and the adult roles for which she was grooming them. Some of that instruction was apparently dispensed by Adela herself, through the example of her own behavior or through moral tales she related to them. It seems that all her sons but one spent their childhoods at the family's principal residences; her daughters were likely raised with them. Only in their early to mid-teens were two sons sent to relatives' courts to be groomed for adult roles, but they still had contact with their mother. Her youngest son enjoyed the stability of a convent easily accessible to her visits. Clearly, she did not consider her children's futures only on the basis of political expediency. Concern for social status appears to have been important to her conception of their future well-being; but it appears she allowed for individual needs, proclivities, and desires, especially for William, Thibaud, and Odo. No evidence suggests her children were less than satisfied with the direction she gave their lives. In light of these details of Adela's management of the Thibaudian household, unknown to Orderic, his praise of her as mother and countess, precious as it is, sounds muted indeed.

NOTES

1. Orderic Vitalis, *Historia ecclesiastica,* ed. and trans. Marjorie Chibnall, 6 vols. (Oxford, 1969–80), 11.5 (ed. Chibnall, 6:42-44); 10.20 (5:324); 11.15 (6:156–58); 8.24 (4:300); 5.19 (3:182); 11.12 (6:68–72); 5.11 (3:116); my translation varies slightly from Chibnall's. For an overview of Adela's life, see my "The Anglo-Norman Card of Adela of Blois," *Albion* 22 (1990), 569–89; extended discussion is in my doctoral dissertation, "A Female Ruler in Feudal Society: Adela of Blois (ca. 1067–ca. 1137)," 2 vols., University of Chicago, 1992.

2. André Boutemy, "Deux pièces inédites du manuscrit 749 de Douai," *Latomus* 2 (1938), 126; Ivo of Chartres, ep. 134, *PL* 162:145; Hildebert of Lavardin, eps. 1³, 3⁸, *PL* 171:144–45, 288–89; Osbert of Clare, ep. 15, ed. E.W. Williamson, *The Letters of Osbert of Clare* (London, 1929), pp. 84–85; and Robert of Torigni, "Additions to William of Jumièges," 8.39, ed. Jean Marx, *Guillaume de Jumièges, "Gesta Normannorum ducem," édition critique* (Paris, 1914), p. 331.

3. For orientation to sociopolitical structures underlying women's powers, Jo Ann McNamara and Suzanne Wemple, "The Power of Women through the Family in Medieval Europe, 500–1100," rev. repr. in *Women and Power in the Middle Ages,* eds. Mary Erler and Maryanne Kowaleski (Athens, GA, 1988), pp. 89–96; Janet L. Nelson, "The Problematic in the Private," *Social History* 15 (1990), 355–64; Pauline Stafford, *Queens, Concubines, and Dowagers: The King's Wife in the Early Middle Ages* (Athens, GA, 1983); Karl J. Leyser, *Rule and Conflict in an Early Medieval Society: Ottonian Saxony* (Oxford, 1979), pp. 49–73; Walter Berschin, "Herrscher, 'Richter,' Ritter, Frauen: Die Laienstände nach Bonizo [von Sutri]," in *Love and Marriage in the Twelfth Century,* eds.W. Van Hoecke and A. Welkenhuysen, Mediaevalia Lovaniensia ser. 1, studia 8 (Louvain, 1981), pp. 116–29; John Carmi Parsons, ed., *Medieval Queenship* (New York, 1993).

4. Janet L. Nelson, "Women and the Word in the Earlier Middle Ages," *Studies in Church History* 27 (1990), 69–78; Rosamond McKitterick, *The Carolingians and the Written Word* (Cambridge, 1989), pp. 223–70; Shulamith Shahar, *Childhood in the Middle Ages* (London, 1990), pp. 116–17, 210, 217–18.

5. Kimberly A. LoPrete, "Adela of Blois and Ivo of Chartres: Piety, Politics, and the Peace in the Diocese of Chartres," *Anglo-Norman Studies* 14 (1991), 131–52; Caroline W. Bynum, *Docere Verbo et Exemplo: An Aspect of Twelfth-Century Spirituality* (Missoula, MT, 1979), pp. 77–98, 181–99; C. Stephen Jaeger, *The Origins of Courtliness: Civilizing Trends and the Formation of Courtly Ideals, 939–1210* (Philadelphia, 1985), pp. 210–26.

6. In addition to works cited in n. 8, see Caroline W. Bynum, "Did the Twelfth Century Discover the Individual?" in her *Jesus as Mother: Studies in the Spirituality of the High Middle Ages* (Berkeley, CA, 1982), pp. 82–109; Nancy F. Partner, "No Sex, No Gender," *Speculum* 68 (1993), 419–43; and John C. Parsons, "Mothers, Daughters, Marriage, Power: Some Plantagenet Evidence, 1150–1500," in Parsons, *Medieval Queenship*, pp. 72–78.

7. Clarissa W. Atkinson, *The Oldest Vocation: Christian Motherhood in the Middle Ages* (Ithaca, 1991); Shahar, *Childhood*, esp. pp. 1–31, 77–120.

8. For summaries and critiques, see Mary Martin McLaughlin, "Survivors and Surrogates: Children and Parents from the Ninth to the Thirteenth Centuries," in *The History of Childhood*, ed. Lloyd DeMause (New York, 1974), pp. 101–81; David Herlihy, "The Making of the Medieval Family: Symmetry, Structure, and Sentiment," *Journal of Family History* 8 (1983), 122–29; Jerome Kroll and Bernard Bachrach, "Child Care and Child Abuse in Early Medieval Europe," *Journal of the American Academy of Child Psychiatry* 25 (1986), 562–68; Ralph V. Turner, "Eleanor of Aquitaine and her Children: An Inquiry into Medieval Family Attachment," *JMH* 14 (1988), 321–22; Shahar, *Childhood*, pp. 1–7; Atkinson, *Oldest Vocation*, pp. 66–74, 115–29.

9. For assertion with inconclusive evidence, Turner, "Eleanor," pp. 324–27, 331–33; idem, "The Children of Anglo-Norman Royalty and their Upbringing," *Medieval Prosopography* 11 (1990), 23–25, 27, 40–44. Cf. Lois Huneycutt's essay in this volume.

10. See the perceptive comments by Parsons, "Mothers," pp. 69–75.

11. Godfrey of Rheims, "Ad Ingelrannum," in "Trois oeuvres inédites de Godefroid de Reims," ed. André Boutemy, *Revue du moyen âge latin* 3 (1947), 343, ll. 127–37; corroborated by Ivo, ep. 5, *Yves de Chartres, Correspondance,* ed. and trans. Jean Leclercq (Paris, 1949), p. 14.

12. Charles W. David, *Robert Curthose, Duke of Normandy* (Cambridge, MA, 1920), p. 6; M. Dominica Legge, "L'influence littéraire de la cour d'Henri Beauclerc," in *Mélanges offerts à Rita Lejeune*, 2 vols. (Gembloux, 1969), 1:679–80; Frank Barlow, *William Rufus* (Berkeley, CA, 1983), pp. 18–22; Turner, "Children," 25–26.

13. Marie Fauroux, ed., *Recueil des actes des ducs de Normandie de 911 à 1066* (Caen, 1961), no. 231 (pp. 442–46). On the tutor, Arnoul de Choques, Raymonde Foreville, "L'école de Caen au XI siècle et les origines Normandes de l'université d'Oxford," in *Études médiévales offertes à M. Le Doyen Augustin Fliche* (Paris, 1952), p. 89, and eadem, "Un chef de la

première croisade: Arnoul Malecouronne," *Bulletin philologique et historique de Comité des Travaux Historiques et Scientifiques (1953–1954)* (1955), 377–90. For her patronage see Elisabeth van Houts, "Latin Poetry and the Anglo-Norman Court 1066–1135: The 'Carmen de Hastingae Proelio'," *JMH* 15 (1989), 46–47.

14. This would be Adelaide/Adeliza; see David C. Douglas, *William the Conqueror: The Norman Impact upon England* (Berkeley, CA, 1964), pp. 393–95; Léopold Delisle, *Les Rouleaux des morts du IXe au XVe siècle* (Paris, 1866), p. 181 (with reference to another sister, Matilda, buried at Holy Trinity); Anselm of Canterbury, ep. 10, *S. Anselmi cantuariensis Archiepiscopi, Opera omnia,* ed. Franciscus S. Schmitt, 6 vols. (Edinburgh, 1938–61), 3:113.

15. Godfrey of Rheims, ed. Boutemy, p. 343, ll. 115–38; Hildebert of Lavardin, eps. 1$^{3-4}$, 3^2, 3^8, *PL* 171:144–48, 284, 288–89; idem, *carmina* 10, 15, *Hildeberti Cenomannensis episcopi, carmina minora,* ed. A. Brian Scott (Leipzig, 1969), pp. 4–5; Baudry of Bourgueil, *carmina* 134–135, *Carmina,* ed. Karlheinz Hilbert (Heidelberg, 1979), pp. 144–88; Hugh of Fleury, *Hugonis Floriacensis chronicon,* ed. Bernard Rottendorff (Munster, 1638), pp. 1–181 (extracts ed. George Waitz, MGH SS 9:349–64, repr. *PL* 163:821–54); Notcher of Hautvillers, *Miracula sanctae Helenae apud Altumvillare,* in *Acta sanctorum ordinis Sancti Benedicti in saeculorum classes distributa,* saeculum IV/2, ed. Jean Mabillon (Paris, 1680), pp. 154–56.

16. For educating girls at monasteries, see Penelope D. Johnson, *Equal in Monastic Profession: Religious Women in Medieval France* (Chicago, 1991), pp. 20–23, 101, 144–45, 180, 248–49; for near-contemporary cases, see Leyser, *Rule and Conflict,* p. 55; Stafford, *Queens,* pp. 54–55; R.W. Southern, *Saint Anselm and His Biographer: A Study of Monastic Life and Thought, 1059–c.1130* (Cambridge, 1963), pp. 183–93; Abelard, "Historia calamitatum," ed. Joseph T. Muckle, *Mediaeval Studies* 12 (1950), 183–84; and Nicholas Orme, *From Childhood to Chivalry: The Education of the English Kings and Aristocracy, 1066–1530* (New York, 1984), pp. 45, 64–65.

17. Orderic, 5.11 (ed. Chibnall, 3:116); *Gesta Ambaziensium dominorum,* in *Chroniques des comtes d'Anjou et des seigneurs d'Amboise,* eds. Louis Halphen and René Poupardin (Paris, 1913), p. 96 and n. 1; René de Lespinasse, ed., *Cartulaire du prieuré de La Charité-sur-Loire (Nièvre), ordre de Cluny* (Paris, 1887), no. 94 (pp. 201–3), hereafter: *LCL*; LoPrete, "Anglo-Norman Card," 572–76. For royal mothers' involvement in daughters' marriages, and fifteen as a fitting age for marriages to be solemnized, see Parsons, "Mothers, Daughters," pp. 63–78.

18. *LCL,* no. 94 (pp. 201–3); LoPrete, "Female Ruler," 1:85–98, 109–27.

19. Heinrich Hagenmeyer, ed., *Die Kreuzzugsbriefe aus den Jahren 1088–1100* (Innsbruck, 1901), ep. 10 (p. 152).

20. Hagenmeyer, *Kreuzzugsbriefe*, epp. 4 (pp. 138–40), 10 (pp. 149–52). C. Stephen Jaeger, "L'Amour des rois: structure sociale d'une forme de sensibilité aristocratique," *Annales, E.S.C.* 46 (1991), 547–71; idem, *The Envy of Angels: Cathedral Schools and Social Ideals in Medieval Europe, 950–1200* (Philadelphia, 1994), pp. 103–6, 193. Monks called Adela *karissima, dulcissima, amatissima,* and *amatrix ferventissima* when memorializing her protection and benefactions (Émile Mabille, ed., *Cartulaire de Marmoutier pour le Dunois* [Châteaudun, 1874], nos. 67 [pp. 60–63], 76 [pp. 67–68], 161 [pp. 150–51]), hereafter *MD*.

21. Orderic, 10.20, ed. Chibnall, 5:324; for Stephen's decision to return under threat of sanctions, Orderic, 10.12, ed. Chibnall, 5:268.

22. Stephen fathered one known daughter, Emma, out of wedlock; that her second son was old enough to become treasurer of York Cathedral by 1114 indicates she was born before Stephen's marriage (R.L. Poole, "The Appointment and Deprivation of St. William, Archbishop of York," *EHR* 45 [1930], 273–77; Janet E. Burton, ed., *English Episcopal Acta V: York 1070–1154* [Oxford, 1988], pp. xxx, 123).

23. For examples, Jean Dunbabin, "What's in a Name? Philip, King of France," *Speculum* 68 (1993), 949–50; Theodore Evergates, *Feudal Society in the Bailliage of Troyes under the Counts of Champagne* (Baltimore, 1975), pp. 112, 241 n. 26; David Herlihy, "Land, Family, and Women in Continental Europe, 701–1200," in *Women in Medieval Society,* ed., Susan M. Stuard (Philadelphia, 1976), pp. 16–23; David Crouch, *The Image of Aristocracy in Britain, 1000–1300* (London, 1992), p. 10.

24. *Miracula sancti Agili, resbacensis abbatis* 1, ed. AASS, Aug., 6:591; Benjamin E. C. Guérard, ed., *Cartulaire de l'abbaye de Saint-Père de Chartres,* 2 vols. (Paris, 1840), 2: nos. 57 (pp. 309–10), 60 (pp. 454–45), hereafter: *SPC*; Baudry, *carmen* 134, ll. 1255–1342 (ed. Hilbert, pp. 181–85); LoPrete, "Adela and Ivo," p. 145 nn. 63–64; Edward J. Kealy, *Medieval Medicus: A Social History of Anglo-Norman Medicine* (Baltimore, 1981), pp. 18–19, 193–96. For birth dates of Adela's children see LoPrete, "Female Ruler," 1:109–11, 176–77.

25. For Odo's medical attendant, see *SPC*, 2: no. 60 (pp. 454–55); for his anniversary, see Paris, BN, MS latin 12878, no. 352 (fol. 306r); René Merlet and the abbot Clerval, eds., *Un manuscrit chartrain du XI siècle* (Chartres, 1893), p. 149. For Stephen, see below, nn. 31–32.

26. Joseph H. Lynch, *Simoniacal Entry into Religious Life from 1000 to 1260: A Social, Economic and Legal Study* (Columbus, OH, 1976), pp. 36–60; John E. Boswell, "*Expositio* and *Oblatio*: The Abandonment of Children in the Ancient and Medieval Family," *American Historical Review* 89 (1984), 17–18, 22–23, 31–33; Shahar, *Childhood*, pp. 191–93.

27. Lena Voss, *Heinrich von Blois: Bishof von Winchester (1129–1171)* (Berlin, 1932), pp. 3–4; for 1111, *LCL*, no. 48 (p. 124). For his profession, see Orderic, 5.11, ed. Chibnall, 3:116; and William of Newburgh, *Historia rerum Anglicarum*, 1.4, ed. Richard Howlett in *Chronicles of the Reigns of*

Stephen, Henry II and Richard I, 2 vols. RS 82 (London, 1884–85), 1:31. On Thibaudian Cluniac patronage, see Auguste Bernard and Alexandre Bruel, eds., *Recueil des chartes de l'abbaye de Cluny*, 6 vols. (Paris, 1876– 1903), no. 3557 (at 4:685–86), hereafter: *Cluny*; Paris, BN, MS fr. 12021, pp. 8–10; Michel Bur, *La formation du comté de Champagne, v. 950–v. 1150* (Nancy, 1979), p. 224; *LCL*, nos. 6 (p. 26), 94 (pp. 201–3); Nicolaus Camuzat, *Promptuarium sacrarum antiquitatum Tricassinae dioecesis* (Troyes: Natalus Moreau, 1610), fols. 373v–75.

28. For Henry's career after Adela retired, see David Knowles, *The Monastic Order in England* (Cambridge, 1941), pp. 282–93; M.J. Franklin, ed., *English Episcopal Acta VIII: Winchester, 1070–1204* (Oxford, 1993), pp. xxxv–xlix; Henry once made a donation for the souls of his mother, maternal uncle, and brother, in that order (ibid., no. 113 [pp. 77–78]).

29. Eugène de Lépinois and Lucien Merlet, eds., *Cartulaire de Notre-Dame de Chartres*, 3 vols. (Chartres, 1862–65), 1: no. 24 (at p. 107), hereafter: *NDC*.

30. The "pseudo-Ingulf" chronicle, a thirteenth- or fourteenth-century continuation of an earlier chronicle, was reworked in the fifteenth; see *Continuatio ad historiam Ingulphi*, ed. [William Fulman] in *Rerum anglicarum scriptorum veterum*, vol. 1 (Oxford: Sheldonian Theater, 1684), p. 121; William G. Searle, *Ingulf and the "Historia Croylandensis": An Investigation Attempted* (Cambridge, 1894); Henri d'Arbois de Jubainville, *Histoire des ducs et des comtes de Champagne*, 6 vols. (Paris, 1859–66), 2:268–70; Orderic, 4, ed. Chibnall, 2:xxv–xxix, 344–46. Other details at this point in the chronicle are neither implausible nor contradicted by other evidence.

31. J.J. Champollion-Figéac, ed., *Documents historiques inédits tirés des collections manuscrits de la Bibliothèque Royale et des archives ou des bibliothèques départementales*, vol. 2 (Paris, 1843), no. 3 (at p. 6). That the *hospites* were once William's was omitted in the copy of this act for the monks' mother house (Gustave Desjardins, ed., *Cartulaire de l'abbaye de Conques en Rouergue* [Paris, 1879], no. 485 [at pp. 352–53], hereafter: Conques), but it is in the early twelfth-century Coulommiers copy drawn up at the time of Adela's donation (Arch. dépt. Seine-et- Marne, H.824). When Thibaud confirmed this grant, he specified that William was *magister fratris mei* (Champollion-Figeac, *Documents historiques*, 2: no. 8 [at p. 15]).

32. Jacques Laurent, ed., *Cartulaires de l'abbaye de Molesme, ancien diocèse de Langres, 916–1250*, 2 vols. (Paris, 1907–1911), 2: no. 18 (pp. 25–26), 26 (pp. 31–32), hereafter: *Molesme* [1102 at Coulommiers]; V. Bigot, ed., *Histoire abrégée de l'abbaye de Saint-Florentin de Bonneval [1715]* (Châteaudun, 1875), pp. 57–58 [1109]; Jean Dufour, ed., *Recueil des actes de Louis VI, roi de France (1108–1137)*, 3 vols. (Paris, 1992–), 1: no. 46 (pp. 86–90) [1110]; see also R.H.C. Davis, *King Stephen, 1135–1154*, 3rd edn. (New York, 1990), p. 7.

33. Louis Paris, ed., *Histoire de l'abbaye d' Avenay*, 2 vols. (Rheims, 1879), 2: no. 4 (pp. 72–73); *Molesme*, 2: no. 19 (pp. 26–28); see also LoPrete, "Anglo-Norman Card," 576. For Thibaud in 1104, see *MD*, no. 77 (pp. 68–71).

34. Dhuoda, *Liber Manualis*, ed. and trans. Pierre Riché in *Dhuoda, Manuel pour mon fils: Introduction, texte critique, notes*, 2nd edn. (Paris, 1991); quotation is from *Handbook for William: A Carolingian Woman's Counsel for Her Son by Dhuoda*, trans. Carol Neel (Lincoln, NB, 1991), p. xii. See also Jaeger, *Courtliness*, pp. 127–75, 195–254; Orme, *Childhood to Chivalry*, pp. 112–80; Shahar, *Childhood*, pp. 209–24; and M. T. Clanchy, *From Memory to Written Record: England 1066–1307* (London, 1979), pp. 177–201.

35. Orderic, 6.2 and 6.3, ed. Chibnall, 3:216–18; see also works cited in n. 34.

36. For *Goffredus joculator* in 1101 see *MD*, no. 67 (pp. 60–62); before 1120 Adela gave to the monks of Sainte-Foi, Coulommiers, the daughters and grandchildren of the *joculator* Radulfus along with Arnulfus *joculator* with his wife and children (Arch. dépt. Seine-et-Marne, H.824; Thibaud's 1132 confirmation is Champollion-Figeac, ed., *Documents historiques*, 2: no. 8 (pp. 14–17).

37. *PL* 163:821–22; see also Karl F. Werner, "Gott, Herrscher und Historiograph: Der Geschichtsschreiber als Interpret des Wirkens Gottes in der Welt und Ratgeber der Könige (4. bis 12. Jahrhundert), in *"Deus qui mutat tempora": Menschen und Institutionen im Wandel des Mittelalters; Festschrift für Alfons Becker*, eds., E.-D. Hehl, H. Seibert and F. Staab (Sigmaringen, 1987), pp. 1–31.

38. MGH AA 2:4–5 and MGH Epist. 5:319–20; see also Joan M. Ferrante, "The Education of Women in the Middle Ages in Theory, Fact, and Fantasy," in *Beyond their Sex: Learned Women of the European Past*, ed. Patricia A. Labalme (New York, 1980), pp. 10–15.

39. *PL* 163: 851b, 849–50, 822c respectively; see also Rottendorff's edition of Hugh (above, n. 15), pp. 1, 29–30, 37–8, 72, 77, 87, 95, 100–1, 106, 116, 120, 122, 124–26, 129–30, 133, 139–44, 146, 150–51, 157, 165, 171, 173–74, 176–77, 179. I addressed the issue of exemplary woman rulers in Hugh's history in an unpublished paper presented to the Medieval Academy of America in 1992.

40. Arch. dépt. Eure-et-Loir, H.613; and Émile-Epiphanius Morel, ed., *Cartulaire de l'abbaye de Saint–Corneille de Compiègne*, 3 vols. (Montdidier, 1904–78), 1: no. 23 (pp. 54–55), hereafter: *SCC*; see *NDC* 1: no. 24 (p. 107) for William with comital title c. 1101. See also Andrew W. Lewis, "Anticipatory Association of the Heir in Early Capetian France," *American Historical Review*, 83 (1978), 911–25 (though his Thibaudian chronology must be revised in light of these documents, unknown to him).

41. Ivo, epp. 134, 136, ed. *PL* 162:144–45; LoPrete, "Adela and Ivo," 147–48. For William's appearances as count, *SPC*, 2: no. 14 (pp. 411–12); *MD*, no. 77 (pp. 68–71); M. Gemähling, *Monographie de l'abbaye de Saint-Satur près Sancerre (Cher)* (Paris, 1867), no. 2 (pp. 137–38); Jean Martin-Demézil, "Les Forêts du comté de Blois jusqu'à la fin XIVe siècle," *Mémoires de la Société des Sciences et Lettres de Loir-et-Cher* 35 (1963), 197–203, no. 2; Jacques Depoin, ed., *Recueil de chartes et documents de Saint-Martin-des-Champs, monastère parisien*, 1 (Paris, 1912), nos. 96–97 (pp. 156–59), hereafter: *SMC*; Noël Mars, *Histoire du royal monastère de Sainct-Lomer de Blois de l'ordre de Sainct-Benoist* [1646], ed. Alexandre Dupré (Blois, 1869), pp. 142–45.

42. *MD*, no. 78 (pp. 68–71); and *Conques*, no. 485 (pp. 352–53); *Molesme*, 2: no. 173 (pp. 321–23) [1108].

43. William of Newburgh, *Historia*, 1.4, ed. Howlett, 1:31; Aubry of Troisfontaines, *Chronicon*, MGH SS 23:25.

44. Ivo, ep. 134, ed. *PL* 162:144; for Adela's plundering, see Ivo, ep. 121, *PL* 162:134; for Thibaud in 1115–1116, see *Vita altera beati Roberti de Arbrissello* 3.13–15, *AASS*, Feb. vol. 3:615–16.

45. Orderic, 5.11 and 11.5, ed. Chibnall, 3:116, 6:42.

46. For Thibaudian recovery of Sully, see Paul Marchegay, ed., *Cartulaire du prieuré bénédictin de Saint-Gondon-sur-Loire (866–1172)* (Les Roches-Baritaud, 1879), nos. 8 (pp. 25–26), 10 (p. 29). For Philip, Robert-Henri Bautier, "La Prise en charge du Berry par le roi Philippe Iᵉʳ et les antecedents de cette politique de Hugues le Grand à Robert le Pieux," in *"Media in Francia": Recueil de mélanges offert à Karl Ferdinand Werner* (Paris, 1989), pp. 44–46, 49–60. For the marriage, see Gemähling, *Sancerre*, no. 2 (pp. 137–38). See also LoPrete, "Female Ruler," 1:242–56.

47. William had at least five children (Orderic, 7.9, 11.5, 13.24, ed. Chibnall, 4:46, 6:42, 6:536 and n. 1; and Robert of Torigni, "Additions," 8, ed. Marx, p. 318).

48. LoPrete, "Anglo-Norman Card," 570, 583–88; Lewis, "Anticipatory Association," 911–22.

49. Thibaud wed Matilda, daughter of the duke of Carinthia, by 1123 according to Bur, *Champagne*, p. 285, though he is mistaken on the date of Adela's retirement, six or seven months before the White Ship sank (Hugh the Chanter, *History of the Church of York*, ed. and trans. Charles Johnson, rev. Michael Brett, C.N.L. Brooke, and M. Winterbottom [Oxford, 1990], p. 154).

50. Arbois de Jubainville, *Histoire*, 2:105–10; Hugh remarried 1110–1114. For Stephen's attestations in 1109–10, see n. 32.

51. Orderic, 11.5, 12.4, 12.15, ed. Chibnall, 6:42, 6:196, 6:224; Davis, *King Stephen*, pp. 7–9.

52. G.E.C., 3:164–66, dates the marriage 1115 but no evidence is cited. Richard attested more acts of Henry in 1113 than any other year, suggesting

he married shortly thereafter (Charlotte A. Newman, *The Anglo-Norman Nobility in the Reign of Henry I: The Second Generation* [Philadelphia, 1988], p. 185). For their deaths, see Orderic, 12.6, ed. Chibnall, 6:304.

53. Suger, *Vita Ludovici Grossi regis*, 19 and 23, *Suger: Vie de Louis VI Le Gros*, ed. and trans. Henri Waquet (Paris, 1929), pp. 148, 172; Ivo, ep. 238, *PL* 162:246.

54. Arbois de Jubainville, *Histoire*, 2:189; Suger, 19–21, ed. Waquet, pp. 130–42, 150–52; René Merlet, ed., *Cartulaire de Saint-Jean-en-Vallée de Chartres* (Chartres, 1906), no. 14 (p. 9); Adolphe de Dion, "Le Puiset aux XIᵉ et XIIᵉ siècles," *Mémoires de la Société archéologique d'Eure-et-Loir*, 9 (1889), 29. One of Agnes' sons made an ecclesiastical career in England during the reign of his maternal uncle, King Stephen; in 1153 he became bishop of Durham (G. V. Scammell, *Hugh de Puiset, Bishop of Durham* [Cambridge, 1956], p. 310, no. 11).

55. Constance B. Bouchard, "Consanguinity and Noble Marriages in the Tenth and Eleventh Centuries," *Speculum* 56 (1981), 268–73; Jack Goody, *The Development of the Family and Marriage in Europe* (Cambridge, 1983), pp. 134–46, 222–39; James A. Brundage, *Law, Sex, and Christian Society in Medieval Europe* (Chicago, 1987), pp. 187–203, 214–45, 256–92, 331–41; Alexander C. Murray, *Germanic Kinship Structure: Studies in Law and Society in Antiquity and the Early Middle Ages* (Toronto, 1983); Donald A. Bullough, "Early Medieval Social Groupings: The Terminology of Kinship," *Past and Present* 45 (1969), 3–18; Karl J. Leyser, "Maternal Kin in Early Medieval Germany, a Reply," *Past and Present* 49 (1970), 126–34; and Herlihy, "Making" (as in n. 8), 116–30.

BERENGUELA OF CASTILE'S POLITICAL MOTHERHOOD:

THE MANAGEMENT OF SEXUALITY, MARRIAGE, AND SUCCESSION[1]

Miriam Shadis

Queen Berenguela negotiated and exploited a patriarchal society. Through management of her son Fernando III's sexual morality and the arrangement of her children's marriages, she preserved and promoted the Castilian royal lineage.

Queen Berenguela of Castile and León (1180–1246) typifies the medieval elite woman whose ordained role in life was to be a wife and mother. The political circumstances of her native Castile, however, complicated and even enhanced Berenguela's reproductive responsibilities. As the eldest daughter of Alfonso VIII and Leonor of England, Berenguela was, at different points in her young life, the presumed heir to the throne.[2] This may have been one reason why she was an attractive bride for her father's cousin, King Alfonso IX of León, whom Berenguela married in 1197 without the necessary papal dispensation. As a result of this blatant disregard of the canons forbidding consanguineous marriage, she was forced by Pope Innocent III to separate from her husband. Before their separation, however, Berenguela and Alfonso produced five children: Leonor, who died in infancy; Fernando; Berenguela; Constanza; and Alfonso. Once separated from Alfonso IX, Berenguela's anomalous position—neither wife nor widow—lent her independence and flexibility. When she returned to her parents' court in 1204, she was a young mother with four small children over whom, it is important to note, she maintained control: her relations with Alfonso were characterized by tension as each struggled for political and familial dominance, and her main source of power became her access to, and relations with, her children. In the interests of the crown to which she was entitled and of her own lineage, Berenguela organized the political and reproductive lives of the three of her children who married and of other members of her family as well.[3]

Thirteen years later, after the deaths of her parents and both her adolescent brothers, she found herself elevated "by right of inheritance" to the Castilian throne.[4] Though fascinating, the story of what followed will be dealt with only briefly here, for Berenguela abdicated almost immediately—certainly, within months—in favor of her son Fernando. Abdication did not, however, mean that she gave up power. Her renunciation in fact framed and defined her grasp on political power, a grasp which remained firm until her death in 1246; abdication left her free to act as the king's mother—a significant role for any queen. Mother and son were occupied for several years by political rebellions attendant on the transfer of power from the minority of Berenguela's brother Enrique I to Fernando's reign; with peace restored by 1219, Berenguela turned her attention to securing the future.

MARRIAGE AND THE MANAGEMENT OF SEXUALITY

The arrangement of her children's marriages was an important aspect of Berenguela's role as a mother; she used marriage to build and block alliances, to gain heirs and to prevent others from gaining heirs, to control her children's sexuality, and to maintain a level of propriety for the monarchy. Marriage was thus both a privilege and a tool which Berenguela used to secure the future of her family's authority and power, continuing in her children the patterns of her own early life.

Berenguela arranged the marriages of her children Fernando, Alfonso, and Berenguela; all played specific, timely roles in confirming the Castilians' place in local, Peninsular, and European politics. Implicitly identifying reproduction as a political tool, Berenguela sabotaged the marriages of her son's main political competitors, his half-sisters, through the marriage of her own daughter; this, and the maternal negotiations between Berenguela and Alfonso IX's first wife Teresa of Portugal (likewise divorced from him) over Teresa's daughters' struggles to claim the kingdom of León, illustrate how these mothers both defended and exploited their daughters. But Berenguela also is recorded to have observed Christian precepts about marriage to an almost astonishing degree when it came to arranging the marriages of her oldest son, Fernando. As did other promoters of Christian ideology, Berenguela saw marriage as a remedy for (male) incontinence.[5] The importance of the king's sexuality and his mother's relationship to it is more than anecdotal; understanding royal mothers as active guardians of their children's morality contributes to the definition of medieval motherhood and also has interesting implications for understanding royal power. The political motherhood of this energetic and savvy woman reconfigures the traditional nexus of marriage, procreation, sexuality, and succession.

Though few royal children married without consideration of the kingdom's needs, the most important marriages Berenguela arranged were, of course, those of her kingly son. Fernando's successive unions with appropriate women would be the key to the success of Berenguela's lineage. Once Fernando had been accepted as king of Castile and his enemies more or less subdued, his mother took it upon herself to find her son a suitable wife. The author of the Cronica Latina says that Berenguela's "total intent and desire was to procure honor for her son in every way possible."[6] She surveyed the available noblewomen of Europe and settled upon Beatriz of Swabia, whom she considered to "surpass all of the others of Christendom in the nobility of her lineage." Beatriz was the daughter of Philip, duke of Swabia (already deceased), and granddaughter of the Emperors Frederick Barbarossa and Isaac II Angelos of Constantinople. The reigning German emperor, Frederick II, was her guardian, and it must have been he who kept Berenguela's ambassadors waiting for four months while the marriage was negotiated sometime in the autumn of 1218.[7]

The historian Julio González suggests that the idea to marry Beatriz came from Berenguela's sister Blanche, later Queen of France, who would have had in mind the reinforcement of the alliance between her father-in-law Philip Augustus and Frederick II against Otto IV of Brunswick and King John of England. González further speculates that the negotiations were carried out by Constanza, Frederick II's Aragonese wife, who was Berenguela's and Blanche's cousin.[8] This theory implies continuous correspondence between the sisters and a fairly active role on Blanche's part at the French court even before Philip Augustus' death. But if not completely farfetched, González's theory does not seem the simplest explanation, nor the most probable, given that in 1218 Blanche was only the foreign wife of the Capetian heir. Since the marriage of Fernando and Beatriz echoed a failed attempt to connect the two dynasties a generation before, when Berenguela was betrothed to Beatriz's uncle, Conrad of Rothenburg,[9] it is more likely that Berenguela hoped the marriage would strengthen the Castilian connection with the Holy Roman Empire as well as provide heirs to perpetuate her family's hold on the Castilian crown. The ability to command a spouse from a geographically distant and politically important family may have served to elevate Berenguela's and Fernando's status; Berenguela was not forced to choose a wife for her son from a local royal or noble family merely for the sake of appeasement as was the case in her marriage to Alfonso IX of León.[10] Positing such a motivation for this marriage highlights Berenguela's own shift in personal power. Originally, she herself served as a "trophy" in her betrothal to Conrad; her status shifted as she ended up a sort of illegitimate appeasement bride for Alfonso IX of León, but later, as queen and queen mother of Castile, she was able to command an exotic trophy for her son—and herself. Thus, Berenguela perpetuated, through her son's marriage, her father's policies on the preservation of family power and dynasty building, and Fernando's marriage furthered the Castilians' international interest.[11]

As part of the preliminaries to his marriage, on November 27, 1219, Fernando knighted himself at the convent of Las Huelgas.[12] This ceremony and the wedding which followed it confirmed Fernando's status as an adult and, thus, as a full-fledged king;[13] the two rituals went hand in hand for royal men entering adulthood. Berenguela took part in the knighting by unbuckling Fernando's sword after he had taken it from the altar and put it on. She thus filled the role of a sponsor and completed her abdication as she conferred her own sovereignty upon him.[14] Legitimized by her status as a monarch, Berenguela stretches but does not cross gendered boundaries; the startling combination of masculine and feminine roles reminds us of her essential share in achieving and preserving the Castilian crown. Here the traditional role of sponsor was overlaid by her maternity: as Fernando's mother, she literally and symbolically helped him to become king. Her participation in this event symbolizes for us the continued cooperation of mother and son and undoubtedly symbolized to those present a permanent symbiotic relationship between mother and son. Fernando's initiation into adulthood did not, therefore, presume a necessary separation or independence from his mother. Three days later, Fernando and Beatriz married in the old Romanesque cathedral of Burgos. The knighting and the wedding provided an opportunity to assemble the important nobles who owed him allegiance, and after the wedding a parliament was held, over which Berenguela presided. Again, her presence and involvement were essential to the processes of legitimation, and not only for the sake of ritual or ceremony; the records of the parliament show Fernando under Berenguela's direction and give us a glimpse of Castile's political future and Berenguela's place in it. These rituals—knighting, wedding, and parliament—served to reiterate to those present Fernando's legitimate status as king of Castile.[15]

Fernando's marriage to Beatriz, so carefully planned and orchestrated by his mother—it was she who greeted the bride upon her arrival in Castile[16]—in no way displaced Berenguela as a dominant figure at the Castilian court. In choosing a bride for her son, she continued her duties as a mother, ensuring the reproduction of her family. She herself could not, or would not, have more children, but she could make sure that her son did. Berenguela had borne five children in six years; she could expect her daughter-in-law to do no less. Beatriz's reproductive task was far more important than any imperial goals harbored by the Castilians, and her fifteen-year marriage to Fernando produced at least nine children; Alfonso, Fadrique, Fernando, Enrique, Felipe, Sancho, Manuel, Leonor, and Berenguela lived beyond infancy.

All medieval ruling families relied upon marriage alliances to provide structural bases for their power, and the Castilians were no exception. For Berenguela, contracting successful marriages for her children was thus an essential part of her commitment to good government as well as to strengthening her family. Yet as a mother, she was committed to her children's marriages in ways that went beyond the purely structural aspects of political alliances. Her concerns reveal the degree to which her responsibilities as a mother and as a queen were imbued with a Christian ethic that matched her desire for power. As regarded marriage, this ethic was manifest in her concern that Fernando's sexual behavior be appropriate to his status as a Christian king. Considering human nature and the at times infamous sexual behavior adopted by the great, perhaps Berenguela's worries were not unfounded.[17] Certainly she was not alone as a royal mother in her preoccupation with her son's continence; her sister Blanche is well known for her attention to Louis IX's personal life.[18] At the very least, it appears that royal mothers were the (self-) appointed guardians of their sons' sexual morality.[19]

Berenguela's attention to Fernando's morals thus assumes a political dimension, for despite Beatriz's glorious ancestry, the perpetuation of the royal lineage was not the primary reason given for her marriage to Fernando. Rather, it was rationalized by the need to combat general anxiety about the king's potential promiscuity, which, if left unchecked, might prevent him from carrying out his sovereign duties effectively. When Fernando first married, according to his chancellor de Rada, archbishop of Toledo, Berenguela sought a wife for her son as she "always wished to protect him from illicit [women]," for it was "inappropriate for such a great prince to be dissipated in extraordinary wantonness."[20] De Rada's rationalization for the marriage may seem bizarre, for marriage would normally be seen as a matter of course for a young king eager to perpetuate his family's lineage and to secure his place as a serious participant in European affairs. Perhaps Fernando's status was enhanced by his distinctly exogamous relationship to Beatriz and by her kinship to the Roman and Byzantine emperors; judging from de Rada's account, however, there would also have been the sense that instead of dissipating himself, Fernando would increase his status and that of his lineage through intercourse with her. Berenguela's concern for Fernando's sexual behavior was thus of both a political and eugenic nature, though presented as Christian morality by the chroniclers who recorded it. Significantly, the rationale of Berenguela's concern for her son's purity was also applied to Fernando's second marriage, at the age of thirty-seven or so, to Jeanne de Ponthieu. By that time the Castilian succession seemed secure; Fernando had seven sons and two daughters when Beatriz died in November 1235, and when he married Jeanne in 1237, his heir, Alfonso, was aged sixteen. As it would be difficult to argue that Fernando's second marriage was needed to guarantee the future of the lineage, Berenguela's alleged concern for her son's chastity takes on new meaning. Fernando's second marriage also gives us a good picture of the intricacies involved in Berenguela's efforts to enhance her son's power and prestige, for the marriage touched upon issues of sexual and canonical propriety, inheritance, blocked alliances, and sisterly favors.

After Beatriz died, according to de Rada and the compilers of the Primera Crónica General, Berenguela was once again concerned that Fernando might "diminish his nobility" by consorting with illicit women.[21] Therefore she again took it upon herself to find her son an appropriate bride, who turned out to be Jeanne, the daughter and heir of Countess Marie of Ponthieu and her husband, Simon de Dammartin. It seems that in arranging this marriage, Berenguela was doing her sister Blanche a favor. In 1225, the countess and count of Ponthieu had come to terms with Blanche's husband Louis VIII over their allegiance to the French crown. An important part of this agreement was that Marie and Simon agreed not to marry any of their children during the next two years without the French king's permission, nor would they ever marry any of their children to the king's enemies.[22] When in 1234 Blanche heard of Jeanne de Ponthieu's potential marriage to Henry III of England, she reacted quickly, for Henry (concerned about Louis IX's marriage to Marguerite of Provence) hoped that a marriage to Jeanne would solidify his power among French nobles opposing Blanche and Louis. Gonzalez suggests that Blanche put forward Jeanne as a suitable bride for her nephew;[23] given the variety of rationales for the marriage, it is possible that Berenguela and Blanche did cooperate in this venture. By settling Jeanne on Fernando, Blanche was looking out for Louis' interest; he preserved control over his vassals and an upper hand over Henry III, while Fernando's seven sons left little likelihood that a future king of Castile would become count of Ponthieu.[24] Fernando, on his part, preserved his moral purity and status. Thus, even though Fernando and Jeanne also faced the impediment of consanguinity, political interest won out as the marriage allowed both sisters to achieve their goals for their sons.

Countless anecdotes demonstrate that medieval kings did not necessarily enter into marriage to satisfy their sexual desires, and the preservation of chastity was not a reason generally given for medieval kings to enter into marriage. Furthermore, the desire for children as a justification for marriage would hardly be worth mentioning in terms of dynastic necessity; this was a standard explanation in terms of canonical interest in what was otherwise a decidedly secular institution.[25] The cases of Fernando and Louis IX may, then, reveal tensions between the requirement that the king perpetuate his lineage and yet present himself as a sacred, even saintly figure. Chroniclers confronted with this problem perhaps resolved their confusion by emphasizing the king's mother's arrangement of his marriages and her concern for his chastity; next to kings' crusades and efforts at "good government," praising the monarch's private life demonstrated what a good Christian he was and thus perhaps served the chroniclers' rhetorical strategies. The issue begs the question of the Castilian kings' sacrality and asks why these two queens at just this particular time were so actively concerned with their sons' sexual behavior and its relation to government. It also invites critical exploration of royal mother's relations with their sons and of the influences that shaped their attitudes toward their sons' sexuality. At any rate, the effectiveness of Berenguela's intervention in Fernando's personal life appears incontestable; unlike his father, Alfonso IX, and his son, Alfonso X, Fernando had no known children out of wedlock.

Berenguela's attentions to Fernando's sexual propriety are all the more striking when one considers the case of her younger son, the infante Alfonso, lord of Molina. There seems to be absolutely no recorded concern on Berenguela's part that her younger son "diminish his nobility," and certainly Alfonso took no pains to follow his brother's example: married three times, he fathered at least eleven children, more than half of them born out of wedlock. It is noteworthy that several of Alfonso's natural children played significant roles in Iberian society—for example, Juan Alfonso, bishop of Palencia, and Berenguela Alfonso, mistress of Jaime I of Aragon.[26] As the infante Alfonso was a loyal friend of the court throughout the reigns of his brother and nephew until he died in 1272, the scant concern shown by either Berenguela or Fernando over his sexual behavior is remarkable and throws into even more prominent relief Fernando's situation as a chaste king. (Berenguela's sister Blanche, likewise, appears to have been little concerned for her younger sons' continence, suggesting that sexual misconduct on the part of cadets was of no consequence. The chroniclers say little about this; no rationale save politics is given for cadets' marriages.)

Though he was apparently not the focus for his mother's concerns about sexuality, Alfonso did not escape her matrimonial machinations. His first marriage signalled the end of a major rebellion and brought the royal family a significant patrimony. Five years after his accession to the throne of Castile in 1217, Fernando III still had to contend with attacks and rebellions by the powerful Lara family. After the successful siege of the castle of Zafra, held by the Lara Gonzalo Pérez de Molina, in the autumn of 1223, Berenguela negotiated a peace with the lord of Molina that was sealed with the marriage of the infante Alfonso to Mafalda, Gonzalo Pérez's daughter. Mafalda's brother Pedro was disinherited and Alfonso became lord of Molina upon his father-in-law's death, around 1240. In 1242 Berenguela received the convent of Buenafuente as a gift from the Archbishop de Rada on condition that she found a convent there dedicated to the Virgin. A few days later she ceded the monastery to Alfonso, clearly as a gift to the Molina patrimony, but through her son, she kept the monastery well within the royal sphere of influence. The whole process bound the Lara more tightly to the future of the royal family.[27]

PROCREATION AND SUCCESSION

Any medieval noble marriage might involve all the considerations outlined thus far: a desire for heirs, originating or blocking political alliances, concern for moral behavior. Another marriage negotiated by Berenguela provides a case study epitomizing the issues mothers faced in assuring the success of their lineage, particularly emphasizing the political roles of reproduction and the function of daughters as potential mothers and marriage pawns.

In 1217, when Berenguela abdicated the Castilian throne to Fernando, all of the terms outlined in previous treaties regarding Fernando's rights in León changed, at least as far as his father Alfonso IX was concerned. None of those treaties had recognized that Fernando might become king of Castile.[28] While it had certainly been Alfonso IX's ambition to obtain that throne for himself, he was not inclined to see his son ruling it, at least not while he himself still lived. Furthermore, in a strange separation of personal interest and lineage, Alfonso now seemed intent on assuring that the kingdoms of León and Castile should never be united under his son, once his acknowledged heir.[29] After an unsuccessful military effort to remove Fernando and Berenguela from power, Alfonso set about installing as his de facto heirs in León his daughters Sancha and Dulce, the surviving children of his first marriage to Teresa of Portugal. In fact, because of royal daughters' potential in medieval Iberia to fulfil their parents' expectations not only through marriage but possibly through inheritance, three of the daughters of Alfonso IX—Sancha, Dulce, and their half-sister Berenguela—became pawns in the effort to secure that kingdom's throne for a male heir.

In January 1217, Alfonso endowed Sancha and Dulce with a series of properties and incomes.[30] Shortly thereafter, the infantas became noticeably active at their father's court. Their presence in the public sphere could be attributed to their new access to property, but it also coincided with their half-brother's accession to the throne of Castile, and I believe it was part of their father's program to establish them as his heirs in León. Their new prominence was announced when Sancha and Dulce confirmed their father's gift to the Order of Calatrava on May 28, 1217; their names appear immediately after Alfonso's, above his seal and above the list of clerical and secular witnesses: "I, the infanta Doña Sancha, daughter of the king of León, confirm"; and Dulce likewise. They confirmed again the next day, and again their names headed the list of nobles. This type of confirmation continued into 1228 and was quite unusual; even former queens of León did not confirm royal documents in this fashion.[31] In May 1219, Alfonso included Sancha and Dulce in a concession to the council of León in the same manner in which he had previously included his wives and sons: "I Alfonso ... with my daughters the infanta Doña Sancha and the infanta Doña Dulce, [et cetera....]"[32] Two months later, a treaty between Alfonso and the king of Portugal contained the first explicit reference that the king of León intended his daughters to rule after him:

> ...if the king of León should predecease the king of Portugal, the king of Portugal ought to maintain the same pact with the daughters of the king of León, the infantas Doña Sancha and Doña Dulce, in the same manner as with the king of León, their father.

Alfonso made further statements that he expected his agreements to be kept with his daughters after his death and consistently included the infantas in the intitulation of his documents between 1217 and 1230, when he died.[33]

Alfonso's naming of both Sancha and Dulce as heirs is problematic because it is not clear how they were expected to co-rule. It seems that Alfonso intended for at least one of them to marry and to legitimize her claim to power through her husband and offspring. Despite the sworn support of various Leonese knights and nobles for Alfonso's daughters, Alfonso's plans for his kingdom would be seriously jeopardized unless he managed to find a husband for at least one of his daughters, and this, as we will see, he endeavored to do. If both married, probably the rule of primogeniture would prevail, though again that might depend on the relative strength of potential husbands and the fertility of the individual woman. Alfonso recognized this problem when he made a typical concession to the Order of Santiago with his daughters' consent; he noted that the Order would carry out the terms of the agreement for "me and my above named daughters and their progeny, or the progeny of one of them if the other has none...."[34] Clearly, it had become imperative for Alfonso IX that Sancha and Dulce should marry and bear children, preferably sons, who could inherit the throne.

As a result, it seems that by 1224 a potential marriage had been negotiated for either Sancha or Dulce with the aging crusader-knight Jean of Brienne, former king of Jerusalem. I have found no specific reference to negotiations for the marriage; González speculates it was arranged by a legate from Rome around 1222, and the Cronica Latina tells us that in 1224 "the king of Jerusalem Jean, en route to Santiago, came to take in marriage one of the daughters of the king of León, with whom was promised to him the kingdom of León."[35] The lack of a paper trail for these negotiations is hardly surprising, due to the scantiness of surviving documents in general, and the fact that the proposed marriage never took place. Furthermore, unlike other marriage negotiations, this one was not the result of pacification or treaty, and thus might not have required the amount of written preparation other marriage contracts received. The purpose of Jean's journey to León, moreover, was purportedly a pilgrimage, which might indicate a desire for secrecy on the part of the Leonese court; this makes some sense in light of what followed, for Alfonso's plans were destined to be thwarted by his former wife Berenguela, who arranged that instead of marrying Sancha or Dulce, Jean de Brienne would leave the Iberian peninsula as the husband of her daughter Berenguela.

The chronicler de Rada and subsequently the Primera Crónica General, have little to say about the marriage of Jean de Brienne to this daughter of Alfonso IX and Berenguela.[36] En route to Santiago,

Jean sent messengers to Queen Berenguela and her son Fernando, seeking an audience. Accordingly, he went to Toledo, where

> he was received with honor, and contracted a marriage with them, with the daughter of the queen and sister of the king Fernando....The queen doña Berenguela, looking into the future, as a prudent woman foreseeing the impediment that the said king of Jerusalem could cause her son the king don Fernando concerning the right that he had to the kingdom of León, if the aforementioned king [Jean] contracted a marriage with either of the daughters of the king of León, whom he had by queen doña Teresa, and if he were to remain in that kingdom—chose to give the said king her daughter, Berenguela by name, as a wife.[37]

Clearly it was in Berenguela's best interest to prevent the marriages of Sancha or Dulce to any man who might have the strength to claim the Leonese throne. Jean de Brienne had already had a similar success with the kingdom of Jerusalem, whose heiress he married.[38] Berenguela meant to enforce the terms of the treaty of Cabreros, which named her son Fernando as heir to the kingdom of León. How to entice Jean away from another potential kingdom? Her daughter Berenguela came with no such bargain; it is not at all clear what her dowry was to be.[39] She was less than twenty-four years old, somewhat but not significantly younger than her half-sisters; perhaps on that account she appealed to the eighty-year-old knight.[40] It is possible, moreover, that having met Queen Berenguela and her son Fernando, Jean saw that he was up against a powerful team with strong, if not completely legitimate, claims to the Leonese throne and that as an aging, foreign consort, his chances against them would be slim. Queen Berenguela, moreover, promised Jean that they would conclude negotiations on his return from his pilgrimage.[41] This escape clause suggests Berenguela's ultimate goal was less to marry off her daughter than to prevent the marriages of her son's chief rivals, his half-sisters. By marrying her daughter to Sancha's or Dulce's intended bridegroom, Berenguela prevented them from claiming power through any potential heirs. The infanta Berenguela fulfilled her function as a royal daughter as her mother had done twenty-five years before but at the expense of Sancha's or Dulce's opportunity to assume that same function: to marry and perpetuate her lineage's hold on power.

SUCCESSION AND INTERVENTION

The next challenge to the security of the Castilian royal lineage came with Alfonso IX's death in 1230. The struggle for the throne of León became a contest between mothers, as Berenguela competed with Teresa of Portugal, her predecessor as queen of León. This contest for political control provides an opportunity to study female power dynamics. It is a particularly rich episode for theoretical and feminist inquiry, as we have an example of one woman encouraging others to lay aside their claims to power and authority in favor of a more "legitimate," that is, male, authority—Fernando. The problems of female exploitation of patriarchy and the complex intertwining of male and female power must be reckoned with in any analysis of this event.

Alfonso IX died in September 1230, leaving Sancha and Dulce to contend with their powerful half-brother and his formidable mother. Fernando had better military resources than his sisters and the support of most of the powerful men in the kingdom of León, despite the nobles' earlier promises to Alfonso. Nonetheless, Sancha and Dulce made a serious attempt to fulfil their father's plans for them. Upon hearing of his death, they went immediately to the nearby city of Astorga but were refused entry. They moved on "with indignation" to León, where the bishop and the people of the town were willing to receive the persons of the infantas but not their knights or armed retainers. They had a similar experience at Benavente and finally went to Zamora where, with their mother Teresa, they were taken in.[42]

In Castile, Fernando learned that Alfonso had left the kingdom of León to the infantas and went to Toledo to take counsel with Berenguela, Archbishop de Rada, and other nobles. Matching Teresa move for move, his mother urged him with "maternal solicitude" to "hasten to receive his father's kingdom," lest "by chance delay would bring about some disorder."[43] The Castilians then quickly crossed the Sierra de Guadarrama and made their way through the borderlands of Medina del Campo and the towns of León. Though Berenguela had been separated from her husband for twenty-four years, she retained lands in León where she was recognized as queen, and her status probably aided Fernando's campaign. Meanwhile, as the partisan de Rada tells us, "Sancha and Dulce prepared their rebellion with their accomplices." Fernando successfully besieged the city of León, and there "by the bishops and all of the citizens he was elevated to the highest dignity of the kingdom of León, the clergy and the people singing the Te Deum harmoniously and joyfully."[44]

By that time Teresa, Sancha, Dulce and their partisans had come to Villalobos. From there they asked to meet Berenguela in her town of Valencia, to which she agreed.[45] De Rada adds that despite the fact that Fernando's partisans were not in favor of this, Berenguela so feared the consequences of war, especially for the poor, that she went to meet Teresa. At Valencia the two mothers negotiated a peace, which was signed on December 11 in Benavente.[46] The settlement endowed Sancha and Dulce with the enormous sum of thirty thousand maravedís annually for the rest of their lives as well as various castles and towns. Provisions were made for the possibility that they might marry, be widowed, repudiated, or divorced or that either one or both might join a religious order. For their part, Sancha and Dulce agreed to give up their claims to León and their noble alliances as well. They agreed, furthermore, to destroy any charters or other records in which Alfonso named them his heirs.[47] The sisters were essentially disabled from legitimately claiming any authority in León other than as the king's sisters. Fernando and Berenguela were attempting to undo Alfonso IX's effort to document his desire that his daughters succeed him—illustrating just how important that documentation was. De Rada compared Berenguela's negotiation here to her abdication, emphasizing the legal propriety of these actions, which resulted in the coronation of her son first as king of Castile and then as king of León: "and in this matter the skillful attention of the noble queen engaged [itself] so greatly that with no less grace did she give the king her son this kingdom than [she gave him] the kingdom of Castile, which belonged to her by law of inheritance."[48] The treaty reinforced Fernando's position as a legitimate ruler, one who came by force of law and not simply by force of arms. More than a strategically maternalistic feeling for the poor of León, the need to assert Fernando's legal position reveals the rationale for Berenguela's meeting with Teresa: her strategy was to achieve the throne for her son by the most secure means.

Despite Fernando's claims and military strength, his half-sisters held out for what was promised them. It must have been clear to them that Fernando and his mother could take León by force, but I think that Sancha and Dulce realized, too, that they had legitimate claims to the throne of León—and they knew that Berenguela and Fernando understood this. If the force of law indeed held a higher place than the force of arms in this military, feudal[istic] society, then perhaps these women were, in this particular situation, at an advantage in their disadvantage. Denied (at least in theory) access to the force of arms, it became imperative that they saw their legal advantages and used the tools available to them, which were associated with contractual arrangements: specifically, the art of negotiation.[49] I would not go so far as to argue that Sancha and Dulce thought that they could actually prevail over Berenguela and Fernando but rather that, by negotiating with them, they might retain at the very least their father's initial settlement and perhaps some of their royal privileges. Like Fernando with his mother, Sancha and Dulce were guided in their decisions by their mother Teresa: it was she who met with Berenguela and perhaps she who suggested and agreed to the terms of her daughters' concession.

Teresa's role takes on new significance when we realize that neither Sancha nor Dulce was married, nor did they have any children. Born between 1190 and 1196, they were at least thirty-four in 1230; they would be effective as queens only if they could produce heirs, so they must have been perceived to be still fertile. Most of the women noted in this article bore children well into their thirties, save Berenguela who was unmarried after age twenty-four, but perhaps the infantas' age led some Leonese nobles to reconsider promises to Alfonso IX. As unmarried women, they were vulnerable, not because they had no man to defend their interests but because they were not mothers, and as long as they remained unwed, they were unlikely to become legitimate mothers any time soon. Why they needed their mother to represent them when they were over thirty years old can only be surmised, but I assume it was for at least one of the same reasons that Fernando needed Berenguela. We are thus given a glimpse of one of the duties of royal motherhood in this moment of meeting and negotiation. Berenguela and Teresa not only produced the future as mothers but decided it as queens when they negotiated the rights and privileges of their children. It must have been clear to them that Berenguela, the mother of a son, had the advantage; it remains an open question how Teresa saw the potential (and real) power of her daughters as she struggled to hand on her own power as a royal mother to nonmothers.[50]

CONCLUSION

The attention given to securing the kingdom of León highlights critical strategies of one medieval mother. Berenguela's interactions with her sister Blanche of Castile, and her rival, Teresa of Portugal, not only suggest that sisterhood and engagement with the patriarchal order were crucial aspects of Berenguela's praxis of motherhood but also demonstrate that other women—in this case Blanche and Teresa—adopted similar strategies. Berenguela, Blanche, and Teresa served as their children's primary advisers; it is uncontested that through her office as regent, Blanche of Castile held a great deal of personal power and authority.[51] In the event that one of Alfonso IX's children, Sancha, Dulce, or Fernando III, should come to rule the kingdom of León, his or her mother would have a great deal of power, if not authority. This is, in fact, what happened with Berenguela who, I believe, sought personal power and who dedicated her life to expanding her family's power and her own. Clearly, either Berenguela or Teresa had much to gain personally by her children's royal inheritance. It is not clear what Teresa gained by negotiating her daughters' concessions to Fernando, except for their safety and the security of their property, probably the most a royal princess could hope for under such circumstances. In this sense Sancha and Dulce's "abdication" with their mother's support parallels Berenguela's earlier relinquishing of the regency in Castile during the minority of her brother Enrique I. Berenguela herself, on the other hand, appears to be successful in securing personal power, even as the chroniclers and Fernando himself recognize her "maternal solicitude" and devotion to Fernando's future. Though in other circumstances her sex would have been a handicap, her motherhood thus becomes a tool of her success and provokes a new consideration of the meaning of royal motherhood. With gender, then, motherhood becomes a "useful category of historical analysis."

We are not surprised by Berenguela's and Teresa's solution to the Leonese succession: Berenguela's personal history leads us to expect abdication from someone. We are perhaps surprised by Berenguela, freed at this moment from the constraints of gender though only by exploiting the infantas' gender-based weakness. Their abdication, forced by her, elicits re-evaluation of her "abdication" thirteen years earlier. The limits placed on the infantas are not comparable with Berenguela's continued exercise of royal power. Abdication meant different things for these women. For Berenguela, it was a strategy to conciliate the people of Castile and at the same time secure her power; for Sancha and Dulce, it was the failure of strategy but also the maintenance of the status quo. By abdicating, Berenguela seemed to have given up public authority in order to be powerful, but in reality, she in no way removed herself from the public sphere.[52] Sancha and Dulce's abdication did not enable them but offered them security. More important, their abdication, arranged by Berenguela for her son, achieved and confirmed a clearer path to power for the Castilian queen and her family.

This essay also suggests differences between motherhood and womanhood as routes to power, evidently with motherhood dependent upon womanhood but also surpassing it. It was as a mother that Berenguela had the most direct, socially legitimate access to public authority. Subject to certain social restrictions, Berenguela took advantage of the norms of motherhood in order to achieve her goals. As a woman, she threatened the social and political equilibrium. As the female link in a male line of succession—grandfather to grandson, uncle to nephew—she also provided the opportunity to restore equilibrium, which she did through her abdication. As a mother, for the enhancement of the prestige and power of her own son she negotiated the terms by which another mother acquiesced in the abdication of her daughters. Berenguela's rise to power demonstrates the complicated relationship of power to authority and the way in which gender served as a mechanism through which medieval society legitimated power and authority. Even though as a Castilian woman Berenguela could hold royal authority, her gender did not entitle her to exercise the power that ultimately legitimized such authority. Her strategies of abdication and collusion allowed her to circumvent the restrictions placed on her gender and even to take advantage of her gender and her motherhood in securing her main goals: the perpetuation of her personal power and her lineage through the kingship of her son.

NOTES

1. I am grateful to Nancy Caciola, Cynthia Chamberlin, and Joe McLaughlin, who carefully read this essay and made thoughtful suggestions. Any weaknesses of argument or infelicities of style are no fault of theirs.

2. Born c. 1180, Berenguela was heir to the Castilian throne until her brother Sancho's birth in 1181; he lived only three months and was not

followed by another brother until the birth of Fernando in 1189. Fernando's death in 1211 made the young Enrique (1204–1217) heir presumptive, with Berenguela after him.

3. I argue in "Piety, Politics and Power: The Patronage of Leonor of England and Her Daughters Berenguela of León and Blanche of Castile," in *The Cultural Patronage of Medieval Women*, ed. June Hall McCash (Athens, GA, 1995), pp. 202–27, that Berenguela's attention to lineage rested on a strong, involved identification with her natal family, and that her patronage has a matrilineal genealogy. Her sense of lineage was not based solely on self-identification as her father's daughter but located Berenguela herself as an element of that lineage, complicating the "law of the father" with a new "law of the mother."

4. Rodrigo Ximénez de Rada, *[Historia] D[e] R[ebus] H[ispanie sive Historia Gothica]*, ed. Juan Fernández Valverde, *Corpus Christianorum*, Continuatio Medievalis (Turnholt, Brepols, 1987), 8.15 (at p. 297). In 1214 Berenguela briefly followed her mother as regent for her brother Enrique I, who succeeded their father Alfonso VIII in that year; she was soon pressured to abdicate by the powerful noble Alvaro de Lara. In 1217, after Enrique I's accidental death, Berenguela inherited the throne.

5. These secular reasons to contract marriage intersected with traditional Christian rationale on the purpose of marriage, particularly in terms of procreation. The essentially Augustinian goals of marriage, as distilled by twelfth-century decretalists, were to promote virtue through marital fidelity, to provide an appropriate environment in which to rear Christian children, and to promote love and mutual support within marriage (James A. Brundage, *Law, Sex, and Christian Society in Medieval Europe*, [Chicago, 1987], p. 235). It seems mothers had a strong interest in the achievement of both secular and religious goals. On the relationship of motherhood to the Christian rationales for marriage, see Clarissa W. Atkinson, *The Oldest Vocation: Christian Motherhood in the Middle Ages* (Ithaca, NY, 1991), p. 75. One could expand consideration of marriage to examine the placing of children and grandchildren in religious life, for such vocation paralleled marriage in the secular world and served many of the same functions. Constanza, Berenguela's only child not to marry, entered religious life at the favorite family institution, the Cistercian convent of Las Huelgas in Burgos.

6. Anon., *Crónica Latina de los Reyes de Castilla*, ed. Luis Charlo Brea (Cádiz, 1984), p. 58.

7. *Crónica Latina*, pp. 58–59; *DRH*, 9.10 (pp. 290–91). The only source which refers directly to the marriage agreement is Honorius III's 1222 confirmation of Beatriz's dower (Demetrio Mansilla, ed., *La documentacion Pontificia de Honorio III (1216–1227)* [Rome, 1965], no. 411). See also Luciano Serrano, *Don Mauricio, Obispo de Burgos y Fundador de su Catedral* (Madrid, 1922), p. 45.

8. Julio González, *Reinado y diplomas de Fernando III*, 3 vols. (Córdoba, 1980), 1:96–97. Fernando III's chief modern biographer, González, here relies on Serrano, *Don Mauricio*, pp. 42–43. González states that chronicles suggest that the idea for Fernando's marriage to Beatriz came from outside the court, but I have not located the source to which he may refer.

9. The betrothal was recorded in the Treaty of Seligenstadt, April 23, 1188 (Julio González, *El Reino de Castilla en la Epoca de Alfonso VIII*, 3 vols. [Madrid, 1960] 3: no. 99. See also Peter Rassow, *Die Prinzgemahl: Ein Pactum Matrimoniale aus dem Jahre 1188. Quellen und Studien zur Verfassungsgeschichte des Deutsches Reiches in Mittlealter und Neuzeit* (Weimar, 1950).

10. I am grateful to Judith Herrin and Cynthia Chamberlin for suggesting this line of speculation. The close kinship among the royal houses of Aragon, León, and Portugal, meant, moreover, that the problem of consanguinity was virtually insurmountable (Serrano, *Don Mauricio*, pp. 42–43).

11. In 1234, Alberic of Trois-Fontaines noted that Fernando petitioned the pope for permission to use the title emperor, "as had certain of his ancestors" (M. Bouquet, ed., *R[ecueil des] H[istoriens des Gaules et de la] F[rance]*, 24 vols. [Paris, 1738–1904] 12:614). The "ancestor" was his great-great-grandfather Alfonso VII, who styled himself emperor; by 1234 Fernando held nearly all of Alfonso VII's domains and was perhaps justified in seeking the title. His marriage into Beatriz' family, long associated with the German empire, perhaps inspired him in this endeavor.

12. It was a standard practice for Castilian kings to knight themselves; see Peter Linehan, *History and Historians of Medieval Spain* (Oxford, 1993), pp. 592–98.

13. Linking knighting and marriage isolates royalty from others of the elite, who, although knighted, might have to wait until they could afford to marry or entered an inheritance (Georges Duby, "Youth in Aristocratic Society," in *The Chivalrous Society*, ed. Georges Duby, trans. Cynthia Postan [Berkeley, CA, 1980], pp. 112–22.)

14. Enrique Florez, *Memorias de las Reinas Catolicas de España*, 2 vols. paginated as one (Madrid, 1761), p. 554, implies she buckled the swordbelt on Fernando after he donned a second "belt of knighthood," but *DRH*, 9.10 (p. 291), uses the verb "deaccinxit." It is troublesome to have only one reference to the moment, but Berenguela's participation is reported by the reliable de Rada, who was certainly present (repeated in Alfonso X, *Primera Crónica General de España,* ed. Ramón Menéndez Pidal, 2 vols. [Madrid, 1955], cap. 1034). Florez was likely confused by Berenguela's presence at the ritual as well as eighteenth-century knighting rituals which may have involved two separate belts. Teofilo Ruiz, "Unsacred Monarchy: The Kings of Castile in the Late Middle Ages," in *Rites of Power: Symbolism, Ritual,*

and Politics since the Middle Ages, ed. Sean Wilentz (Philadelphia, 1985), p. 124, may anachronistically apply a later *mentalité* about the conferral of royal power, perhaps being confused by the mechanical Santiago used by kings after the fourteenth century to avoid any *human* conferring power upon them (Linehan, *History and Historians,* pp. 593–4). Linehan also suggests (p. 595, notes 123–124) the appropriateness of Berenguela's unbuckling of Fernando's sword and so taking the role of chivalric godparent, or *padrina.* A significant social debt accrued with each stage of the knighting; Fernando had to be very careful about his choice of sponsor. Whom could he better trust than Berenguela? The conundrum of a woman conferring royal and chivalric authority was recognized by Berenguela's grandson Alfonso X, who forbade women's participation in the most significant part of these rituals, the knighting itself (Real Academia de la Historia, *Las siete partidas del rey don Alfonso el Sabio,* 2 vols. [Madrid, 1807, repr. 1972], 2.21.11). He did not, however, forbid women from *un*-buckling a knight's belt—and thus confirming knighthood; he must have been, albeit uncomfortably, fully aware of his grandmother's precedent.

15. *Crónica Latina,* p. 60, says that "Even in the old days, such a parliament had never been seen in the city of Burgos!" The published document nearest in time to the parliament is dated Burgos, December 12, 1219 (González, *Fernando III,* 2: no. 93). The dating clause of this document refers to Fernando's knighting and his wedding but not to the parliament, nor do the documents which follow. The witnesses to the document of December 12 are the usual familiars of the court. In other words, Fernando's documents tell us nothing regarding the parliament's activity. *Crónica Latina* (p. 60) and *DRH,* 9.10 (p. 291), however, say the parliament was attended by nobles, lords, knights, and important men of the kingdom. From the presence of noble women, Evelyn Procter assumes this parliament was purely ceremonial (*Curia and Cortès in Leon and Castile, 1072–1295* [Cambridge, 1980], pp. 77–78). I take this to mean that no official business was transacted. Given Berenguela's presence at assemblies generally, Procter's characterization of the parliament is perhaps misguided; later royal women, such as María de Molina, participated in full, genuine parliaments. Procter also notes that this was the same kind of parliament held at the marriage of Fernando's sister Berenguela to Jean of Brienne (see below). Given the complement of estates present and the expense involved, it seems rather frivolous not to have convened a working parliament.

16. *DRH,* 9.10 (p. 291); see also *Crónica Latina,* p. 59.

17. Proliferation of natural children—particularly when the security of a lineage was fragile—might "diminish the king's nobility" not only by lessening his moral stature but also by threatening to fragment his patrimony among competing illegitimate offspring. This does not, however, seem to have been the case in Castile. In fact, kings such as Alfonso IX of

León and his grandson, Alfonso X, relied upon natural sons and daughters when they could not always completely trust their legitimate children.

18. Louis's contemporary, Geoffrey of Beaulieu, says that when Blanche was faced with the hypothetical question whether Louis should "lie with a woman who was not his wife" to save himself from mortal illness, she replied that though she loved Louis above all mortals she would let him die rather than offend the Creator. Her response deeply impressed the young king or at least the French chroniclers (Geoffrey of Beaulieu, *RHF*, 20:4; Jean de Joinville, *Life of Saint Louis*, in R.B. Shaw, trans., *Chronicles of the Crusades* [Penguin, 1963], p. 182).

19. Atkinson, *Oldest Vocation*, pp. 174–181 notes saintly mothers who took personal responsibility for their children's moral behavior—e.g, the fourteenth-century St. Brigitta of Sweden.

20. *DRH*, 9.10 (p. 290). It is unclear whether Fernando was unchaste before marriage, though given the tendencies of the men in his family (especially his father, with whom he lived between 1214 and 1217), it would not be surprising if Fernando had some early experience with "illicit women." If true, this would suggest that Berenguela was less interested in preserving chastity than in reinforcing appropriate kingly behavior.

21. *DRH*, 9.18 (p. 300); the later *Primera Crónica General*, cap. 1048, implies, however, that it was at Fernando's instigation that his mother sought a new bride for him.

22. Alexandre Teulet, ed., *Layettes du trésor des chartes*, 6 vols. (Paris, 1863–1909), no. 1713 (July 1225). See also Élie Berger, *Histoire de Blanche de Castille, reine de France* (Paris, 1895), p. 201, and Jean Richard, *Saint Louis, Crusader King of France*, trans. Jean Burrell, abridged ed. Simon Lloyd (Cambridge, 1992), pp. 32, 56–57.

23. Undoubtedly, Blanche reminded the countess and count of Ponthieu of their previous agreement. Berger (*Histoire de Blanche de Castille*, p. 326) credits Blanche with impeding the marriage by alerting the pope to a consanguineous union but cites Matthew Paris, who does not mention Blanche in this case (Paris, *Chronica Majora*, ed. H. R. Luard, 6 vols., RS 57 [London, 1872–1884], 3: 327–28). See also *RHF*, 22:602b, and the papal prohibition of the marriage, April 27, 1236 (Léon Auvray, *Registres de Gregoire IX*, 4 vols. [Paris, 1890–1955], no. 3135), issued after Henry wed Eleanor of Provence. Interestingly, as with Fernando's first marriage, González credits the arrangement to those outside Berenguela's circle, though not beyond her sphere of influence (*Fernando III*, 1:114).

24. González, *Fernando III*, 1:114; Teulet, *Layettes*, nos. 2699–2700.

25. Brundage, *Law, Sex, and Christian Society*, pp. 235–40, 364–65.

26. Cynthia L. Chamberlin, "The 'Sainted Queen' and the 'Sin of Berenguela': Teresa Gil de Vidaure and Berenguela Alfonso in Documents of the Crown of Aragon, 1255–1272," in *Spain and the Mediterranean World of the Middle Ages: Studies in Honor of Robert I. Burns, S.J.*, ed. Larry J.

Simon (Leiden, 1995), pp. 303–21. On Juan Alfonso, see González, *Fernando III*, 1:88; Mansilla, *Iglesia castellano-leonesa,* no. 53 (p. 319); and Peter Linehan, *The Spanish Church and the Papacy in the Thirteenth Century* (Cambridge, 1971), p. 230.

27. On the peace of Zafra, see *DRH,* 9.11 (p. 292); *Crónica Latina,* p. 59, and *Primera Crónica General,* cap. 1035. For the Buenafuente affair, see María del Carmen Villar Romero, *Defensa y repoblación de la línea del Tajo en un lugar determinado de la provincia de Guadalajara: Monasterio de Santa María de Buenafuente* (Zaragoza, 1987), pp. 20–21, and appendix, document no. 19; González, *Fernando III,* 1:88, and 3: no. 703.

28. The treaties of Cabreros, Burgos, and Valladolid are dated respectively March 26, 1206, September 7, 1207, and June 27, 1209 (González, *Alfonso IX,* [Madrid, 1944], 2: nos. 205, 219, 251.

29. González, *Alfonso IX,* 1:170–78, surmises Alfonso was undecided whether to follow absolute primogeniture and name as heir the oldest child of his first marriage—Sancha—or the elder son of his second marriage. But in *Fernando III,* 1:247-49, González suggests Fernando III's legitimacy might have become an issue. As Alfonso IX's first marriage was also dissolved for consanguinity, however, Sancha's legitimacy was just as dubious. Moreover, when Alfonso IX and Berenguela separated, Pope Innocent III declared their children legitimate. Berenguela and Fernando sought a reaffirmation from Pope Honorius III in 1218 (Mansilla, *Honorio III,* no. 179 (p. 141). See also August Potthast, ed., *Regesta Pontificum Romanorum (1198–1304),* 2 vols. [Graz, 1874; repr. Berlin, 1957], no. 5866. On Fernando's legitimacy, compare note 49 below. Alfonso IX seems to have disregarded the rule of primogeniture by naming *both* daughters as heirs; even if he had named one, it would have been unprecedented to choose an elder daughter over a living son. González is apparently uncertain as to why Alfonso IX decided to pursue his daughters' inheritance; the king's behavior presents us with a very interesting turn of events that will remain a conundrum without more evidence.

30. A normal, protective measure to ensure Sancha and Dulce an income for life, especially should they not marry (González, *Alfonso IX,* 2: no. 342). At the time, the infantas were in their mid-twenties and, remarkably, single; in the event one married or died unmarried, the survivor would receive her sister's share. If both died or married and died childless, everything would revert to the kingdom.

31. González, *Alfonso IX,* 2: nos. 346 and 347; documents confirmed by Sancha and Dulce also include nos. 411 (1221) and 523 (1228). If these seem few, it is important to bear in mind the paucity of extant Leonese documents and the fact that many, especially later ones, do not retain their witness lists.

32. González, *Alfonso IX,* 2: no. 372.

33. González, *Alfonso IX*, 2: respectively nos. 373 (the king of Portugal was Sancha and Dulce's maternal cousin Alfonso II [González, *Fernando III*, 1:247–49]), and 415 (Gil Manríquez's promise to Alfonso IX to defend the castle of Villalobos for the king and the infantas, and for the sisters after Alfonso's death; if Manríquez predeceased Alfonso, his heirs would observe the agreement with Sancha and Dulce. It seems Manríquez kept his promise; as noted below, Villalobos was where Sancha, Dulce, and Teresa took refuge during the attempt to retain the Leonese throne after Alfonso IX's death).

34. González, *Alfonso IX*, 2: no. 620. An unpublished charter from the Cathedral of Salamanca shows that Sancha and Dulce were recognized as heirs outside of the king's court: ". . . Regnante Rege dompno Alfonso cum filiabus suis infantibus dompna Sancia et dompna dulcia in legion, gallecia, asturiis et Extremadura." (Madrid, Archivo Histórico Nacional, Clero, carpeta 1881, nos. 17, 18 [December 16 and 18, 1223]).

35. González, *Fernando III*, 1:250–51, citing *Crónica Latina,* p. 61.

36. De Rada merely states that the infanta married Jean de Brienne, regent of the kingdom of Jerusalem (*DRH,* 7.13 [p. 247]).

37. *Crónica Latina*, p. 61.

38. Marie de Montferrat (d. 1219); their only daughter Yolande, queen of Jerusalem (d. 1228), was the second wife of Emperor Frederick II.

39. *Crónica Latina,* p. 61, states that when they left Castile after the wedding, the infanta and her husband were given a "generous gift" and commended to God.

40. The infanta died before her husband, but, given the disparity in their ages it is likely that in 1224 she (and her mother) expected early widowhood would leave her free to contract another marriage or to remain single and enjoy a noble widow's power and influence. That the union endured and produced heirs could not have been foreseen in 1224. The infanta had five children: Maria, Berenguela, Alfonso, Luis, and Jean, who maintained contact with their Castilian kin (*Fernando III*, 1:252 note 94; R.L. Wolff, "Mortgage and Redemption of an Emperor's Son: Castile and the Latin Empire of Constantinople," *Speculum* 29 (1954), 47, note 6).

41. *Crónica Latina*, p. 61.

42. *Crónica Latina*, p. 84. It is unclear whether Teresa was with her daughters when they learned of Alfonso IX's death or joined them later. Did her presence encourage the Zamorans to open their gates to the sisters?

43. *DRH,* 9.14 (p. 285); see also *Crónica Latina,* p. 84.

44. *DRH,* 9.14–15 (p. 296). Lucas of Túy adds that Fernando entered the city with his mother (*Crónica de España*, ed. Julio Puyol [Madrid, 1926], p. 426). See also González, *Fernando III*, 1:256.

45. *Crónica Latina,* p. 85.

46. *DRH,* 9.15 (p. 296). González, *Fernando III,* 2: no. 270, is the queens' agreement settled between Fernando and his half-sisters. The author

of the *Crónica Latina*, p. 85, notes the queens' role in arranging peace and appears to have seen the document; his description echoes its language almost verbatim. In fact, Derek Lomax suggests ("The Authorship of the *Chronique Latine des Rois de Castille*," *Bulletin of Hispanic Studies* 40 [1963], 205-11) that the *Crónica*'s author may have been Juan of Osma, Fernando's chancellor under Rodrigo Ximénez de Rada.

47. González, *Fernando III*, 2: no. 270. Of course, evidence for Alfonso's wishes survives. Perhaps Fernando and Berenguela meant only to invalidate the documents; perhaps Sancha and Dulce still hoped they might one day make good their claims. Very likely the surviving records were in the hands of those not bound by the agreement.

48. *DRH*, 9.15 (p. 297).

49. That the infantas were denied access to arms in fact and theory is shown by the city of Leon's acceptance of them but not their knights; other towns which refused them probably did so on the same terms. Force of arms was crucial to Fernando's success in the kingdom of León, but ultimately his legitimation was achieved by his mother's negotiations, which undid Alfonso IX's will, as documented 1217-1230. Clearly all three claimants had hereditary right. Ruiz' analysis ("Unsacred Kingship," p. 122), doubts Fernando's canonical legitimacy; Ruiz says no attempts were made to legitimize him but evidently missed Berenguela's and Fernando's contacts with Innocent III and Honorius III (see note 29), and the treaties that recognized Fernando as heir to León. I also question if Sancha and Dulce had "better" claims to the throne; perhaps they held the moral high ground, but unfortunately for them, it appears that Alfonso IX had promised at least three of his children that each could succeed him.

50. Once again, women took responsibility for working out peace. This moment parallels others in which women, especially mothers, are credited with (and sometimes blamed for) compromise in the face of violence. Berenguela's mother, Leonor, was credited with arranging Berenguela's necessary but consanguineous marriage to Alfonso IX; other queens often intervened on daughters' behalf in difficult family or more broadly public situations (John Carmi Parsons, "Mothers, Daughters, Marriage, Power: Some Plantagenet Evidence, 1150-1500," in idem, ed., *Medieval Queenship*, [New York, 1993], pp. 63-78).

51. André Poulet, "Capetian Women and the Regency: The Genesis of a Vocation," in *Medieval Queenship*, ed. Parsons, pp. 93-116.

52. For abdication as a female maneuver to secure some level of power, see Elaine Tuttle Hansen, "The Powers of Silence: The Case of the Clerk's Griselda," in *Women and Power in the Middle Ages*, eds. Mary Erler and Maryane Kowaleski (Athens, GA, 1988), pp. 230-49.

THE FAMILY ROMANCE
OF GUIBERT OF NOGENT:
HIS STORY/HER STORY

Nancy F. Partner

This essay on Guibert's memoir uses a psychoanalytic approach to decode the deep plot of this twelfth-century narrative that offers rare and unusual insight into the dynamics of medieval family life.

HIS STORY

> Since I have for some time said nothing about my mother, who was my sole personal possession among all the goods I had in the world, it is proper that I should briefly touch upon a good life's better end.[1]

The first section of Abbot Guibert of Nogent's three-part book about his life belongs to that special class of expression which clamours to tell things it does not quite know. Almost unique in medieval Latin literature for accepting the invitation and moral permission offered by Augustine's *Confessions*, Guibert's book also confesses (from the first word of its first sentence) incessantly, insistently, a shade misleadingly. So much confession: "I confess the wickedness I did in childhood and in youth, wickedness that yet boils up in my mature years, and my ingrained love of crookedness…; I am forever sinning, and between sins returning to Thee, fleeing from goodness and forsaking it" (35–36). So little detail. This generalized and hypertrophied anguish ("my soul…bedded itself in baskets full of dung") was conventional; even Augustine is inexplicit about his desires and behavior after his boyhood theft of pears. Self-castigation and compunction in addressing God links the Augustinian exemplar to Guibert's version generically; the specific influence of

Augustine's sheltering authority is seen in Guibert's freedom to discuss at length his childhood, his feelings, and most of all, his mother. But Augustine did tell us the name of his mother; it was his concubine's name he censored. Guibert suppressed his mother's name, and in doing that he was also following Augustine's example, although he surely did not know it.

One small, telling result of this constraint on direct naming is that Guibert must rely on the noun and possessive pronoun of relation: "my mother" virtually becomes her name and lifelong identity. Even before marriage and Guibert's birth, in all her relations of life and activities unrelated to him, she remains connected to her youngest and last child as "my mother." Thus, when he begins his final passages about her with the startling description of "my mother" as "my sole personal possession among all the goods I had in the world," he has reached a culminating state of proprietorship after repeated possessory acts. As a monk, Guibert was not supposed to possess worldly goods, and a mother is hardly a renounceable possession. He might say that his own mother was his only personal belonging in the sense of a unique attribute, but at the time to which he refers he had at least one living brother, so she was not precisely "his" alone even in the progenerative sense he seems to imply. It is a curious remark, odd in its complacent matter-of-factness, and in its narrative function: confirming his unshared ownership before bringing her "good life" to its "better end." But "my mother," "my sole personal possession," does make coherent narrative sense because that is how Guibert consistently told her story.[2] Her story is his, because he is its only author. In telling her story, he takes full possession of her and confesses himself most freely.

Guibert wrote his confessional memoir in 1115, aged about fifty-one; his mother's death seems to have been between 1107 and 1110. He had been a monk or at least resident in a Benedictine monastery since he was thirteen, and abbot of Nogent for eleven years; he was an accomplished scholar and author of secular and theological works.[3] Book I of his memoir covers his life from birth in 1064 until 1104 when he was offered the abbacy of Nogent, but it relates his mother's life from her marriage—an unclear number of years before Guibert's birth. His sources are an overlapped and seamlessly merged combination of personal observation, strongly retained emotion, and what must be anecdotes retold many times by his mother. The most striking narrative characteristic of this book is the degree to which he tells *her experiences* as his memories.

He begins in formal propriety. Chapter 1 invokes the Augustinian confession motif, the "I" who confesses unreservedly to the God who knows all: "Whenever I call to mind my persistence in unclean things, O Lord, and how Thou didst always grant remorse for them, I am amazed at the long-suffering of Thy compassion…"(35). Chapter 2 introduces some individuality of experience in the benefits a gracious God showered on this undeserving soul: Guibert's "birth, wealth, and appearance," dubious goods that foster lust and pride and are subject to change, a flaw. But they are quintessential gifts because: "no one achieves by his own efforts his parentage or good looks…" (Wealth drops out, unnoticed.) Next, he thanks God for the logically prior gift: "a mother who was beautiful, yet chaste, modest, and steeped in the fear of the Lord."

The motif of physical beauty, as an empty and carnal show, immediately requires apology and explanation, for beauty is praiseworthy if accompanied by moral purity. Though as a transitory thing in humans its worth is diminished, even transient beauty reflects the eternal beauty which is divine (38–39).[4] It is a convoluted argument, faintly bizarre to have begun and awkward to end. Fortunately, Guibert locates an exegetical path out of this encroaching wilderness of contemplation of female beauty in *Romans* 1:20: "'The invisible things of God are clearly seen, being understood by the things that are made,' says the Apostle." Perhaps the most useful cliche of medieval culture, *Romans* 1:20 was the proof-text of all literary and historical hermeneutics, whether linking the "invisibilia" of allegorical meaning to the literal text in Augustine's *Doctrina Christiana,* or connecting the moral "invisibilia" to earthly event in John of Salisbury's history of the papal court. *Romans* 1:20, the interpreter's friend, seems to summarize the exegetical center, the very experience of meaning at the heart of the intelligible medieval universe. It was the hermeneutic paradigm which promised to guide right-minded readers reliably from the carnal distractions of the *littera* to moral stability in the *invisibilia*. Guibert offers a coherent but unusual application: his mother was notably beautiful in body but in her exceptional case this visible beauty was an accurate indicator of her inner beauty, the *invisibilia* of moral virtue and pure mind. Angels too are beautiful, he notes. Guibert is confusingly associated in this condition, for while he remarks that no man can acquire his parents or his good looks by his own efforts, his own outward beauty covered a sinful interior.

After introductory variations on this theme, Guibert offers his main topic: "Let us turn now to my own life." Before we do, we might first consider how to read a life written in such insistently self-interpreting language. Guibert, in a manner by then traditional, even banal, suggests a search like Augustine's for what is hidden but present in the manifest *littera* of human life—the spiritual drama of bewildered sin yearning for redemption through self-knowledge. "How could I catch even a glimpse of Thee if my eyes were blind to see myself?"(37). He does his best to work out that exercise of conscience and consciousness; even allowing for the era's conventions, he seems a sin-stricken man. But for all Guibert's self-exposure, he maintains a steady control over its meaning. Confessional language in twelfth-century prose was a self-interpreting medium. Such moral binaries of body/spirit, lust/chastity, worldly/otherworldly, and so forth, placed the range of human emotion and behavior in predictable, static moral categories. Thus Guibert, in phrases of self-rebuke at once sincere and trite: "And in what does despair consist, if not in throwing oneself deliberately into the pigsty of every outrageous lust?"(37). This energetic language insists on preempting its own interpretation; he who can speak of throwing himself into a pigsty of lust is already his own confessor and penitent, always already far ahead of his reader.

The overheated imagery has a self-cancelling effect on the modern reader who knows this man led a singularly constrained life. It becomes easy to forget that interpretation is an activity of translation, not paraphrase. Gross images like pigsties of lust and baskets of dung are too much meaning and none at all. We need a new language, a non-twelfth-century language, which respects the reality of the carnal letter but which opens onto a new realm of "invisible things." We have such a language in psychoanalytic exegesis which, addressed to the palimpsest of human experience, works in remarkable harmony with the medieval feeling for the location of truth. It is our only fully evolved system for deciphering the secular allegory of polysemous narrative language. The psychoanalytic premise which assumes the existence of layers of unseen, unseeable, permanently forgotten experience pressing on consciousness which can be recaptured only in translation, figuration, and allegory, allows as medieval exegesis allowed, things to be what they seem *and* what they do not seem to be, without contradiction. Language is itself the expression of such doubled and displaced meanings.[5] This essay offers a reading of Guibert's language, not as point for point symbolism—an incorrect psychoanalytic technique—but as its narrative structure suggests a personal allegory locked inside the consciously remembered life story.

Thus, in a provisional way, I notice that even Guibert's emphatic commonplace that no man can acquire good looks or his parents by his own efforts is not necessarily fixed in one literal commonsensical meaning only. In life, no one gets to choose his appearance or parents, but Guibert's *life* is not present to us; what we have is Guibert's book, his life story, a text which is experience in the way that all experience becomes a text once it is told: heightened, suppressed, shaped into narrative and channeled into expressive language which is never passively transparent on reality. All kinds of things denied to life itself may be achieved by one's own efforts in the story of one's life .

Guibert begins at his beginning, with his birth as his mother's last-born child, in a scene reminiscent of the birth of Tristram Shandy. Guibert describes her long and difficult labor lasting almost all of Good Friday and into Holy Saturday:

> Racked by pains long endured, and her tortures increasing as her hour drew near, when she thought I had at last in natural course come to birth, instead I was returned within the womb (41).

At this failed delivery, with the infant retracted back into the body of the weakened woman, despair gripped husband, kin, and friends in attendance; they rushed to an altar of the Virgin and dedicated the child to a life of religious service if only she would assist the birth. "At once a weak little being, almost an abortion, was born," a wretched-looking tiny baby, like a little corpse, like a premature birth. The attendants were concerned only that the mother was still alive; at his baptism women made cruel jokes.[6] In Guibert's analysis, all these things were the visible signs of his sinful nature (41–42). Eight months later his father died. No information is offered about his death, only the flat statement, with a suggestion that this was another of God's gifts to Guibert since the father would probably have broken his vow and kept his son in secular life. Guibert's mother raised him at home and never remarried (44).

Though heavily moralized, the birth episode is set in a recognizable social world with husband and kin waiting anxiously through a dangerous labor and birth. There is a sense of direct witness in Guibert's second-hand memories, of distraught people helplessly watching, so that extraordinary details—the infant almost emerged then retracted back into the mother's body; the father rushing off to bargain for miraculous intervention; the callous reactions to a feeble baby not expected to live—become absorbed in the writer's own experience and subject to his imaginative control. He chose to write these scenes as if he had been present as an observing adult. Guibert omits entirely the next six or seven years when he would have had some memories of his own of life with his mother ("and so [she] brought me up" covers some six years), and resumes in the next sentence when she brought a private teacher into the household to begin Guibert's education. He describes his life for the next six years in some detail.[7] By Chapter 7, he is about twelve years old and we have learned that he was beaten often, allowed no holidays, and despised his master's inadequate learning; he knew that master and mother were competing for his loyalty, and he knew how to manipulate his mother's feelings (44–50). From this point, the narrative structure is strange yet suggestive, though not in immediately apparent ways.

Chapters 1 and 2 introduce two main characters: first the narrator; next, his mother. He is good-looking, well-born, mired in sin; she is beautiful, chaste, and pious. Guibert is born, at dramatic length, in Chapter 3. His father dies perfunctorily in the first lines of Chapter 4. Eight chapters later in Chapter 12, Guibert is born again—not spiritually but literally: he tells another version of his birth story, and in the next chapter, his father dies again.

The narrative sequence of Book I which takes the author from birth to the abbacy of Nogent is halting, digressing; the chronology is vulnerable to stronger impulses. Guibert was a writer who composed without revision or written plan, following memory and impulse.[8] But a pattern emerges in the first fifteen chapters which get him to age twelve and past. The topics of the first seven chapters are: mother's beauty; Guibert's birth; his early education at home with widowed mother and private tutor; his mother's failed effort to secure a benefice for him before he was twelve years old. The years covered are 1064 to about 1075. Only much later in Book I, not in the next chapter, do we learn what happened next. It was the single most crushing disaster of Guibert's youth: when he was twelve, his mother who defied convention by keeping him at home with her for so long abandoned him. Always deeply pious, she retired to a semi-monastic life in 1076, apparently without consulting or warning her son. Guibert was shattered by her desertion; some forty years later, he describes himself at age twelve as "a little child" left to suffer as if "utterly an orphan with no one at all on whom to depend." He was well-connected, but "there was no one to give me the loving care a little child needs at such an age." All this she knew: "she knew that I would be condemned to such neglect...." "She knew for certain that she was a cruel and unnatural mother...." Love and fear of God had hardened her heart. His abandonment was made complete when his teacher also left to be a monk, and Guibert lapsed into depression and resentful misbehavior. Eventually he followed his tutor into the same monastery and began his adult career (74).[9]

But when Guibert tells us his life story the first time and approaches the events of his twelfth year, the narrative line derails and comes to a halt. Chapter 7 should relate the events of that year, but drifts off into oblique meandering digressions about sin and the need for church reform, instructive examples of conversions, and the moral condition of the age.[10] After four digressing chapters, he tells the story over in a new way that lets him plunge forward and through the devastating year of abandonment. Starting again, he chooses a new beginning point. "After these lengthy accounts I return to Thee, my God, to speak of the conversion of that good woman, my mother" (63). Instead of the physical event of his birth, he begins with the necessary precondition that turned a beautiful virgin into his mother: her betrothal "when hardly of marriageable age," lovely, noble, and already so filled with a dread of sin that the thought of sudden death obsessed her (63). His parents were married but his father was impotent and could not consummate the marriage for three years (extended in the next paragraph to seven, and later, "seven years and more").[11] Guibert repeats the gossip that blamed witchcraft practiced by an envious would-be mother-in-law. After a time, everyone knew the situation and many tried to take advantage of it—to dissolve the marriage, take control of property, drive away the young wife, or seduce her. Nasty gossip was incessant but no scandal touched his mother's reputation. Other married women in his degenerate age, the mature writer reflects, are wanton, sensual, and corrupt—nearly all of them, in fact. His mother's prolonged virginity was God's gift ("O Lord, that virginity which Thou didst in wondrous fashion prolong in her..."); a gift rather extorted from God, we might think, by her formidable lifelong concern with sexual purity.[12] But this virgin body with the power of functional castration was assailed by enmity, threats, social humiliation, and loss of honour. Guibert as narrator is fully present, aware and sensitive to her plight. And her married virginity lengthens each time he mentions it.

He conflates time drastically. Chapter 12 covers the entire time of his parent's marriage from betrothal to the death of his father. They had other children: three brothers are mentioned briefly in the book in offhand or hostile ways, but none is allowed into this chapter where, in narrative and real time, they must have been born. In Guibert's narrative they are never born—more to the point, never conceived. Only he is. We never know their ages in relation to his, where *they* lived after their father died. In Guibert's story, only he and his teacher seem to occupy his mother's house after her husband dies, though incidental remarks hint at a fullish household of women and men servants, chaplains, visitors. Such narrative attention and inattention is unsurprising; what is more curious is the fact that in Guibert's narrative, his mother remains a virgin wife until his conception. He said earlier that no man can choose his looks or his parents; but apparently he can do away with his male siblings easily enough. He can "write them out."

In Guibert's characteristic style of delayed and displaced vital information, we learn later in the book, way out of its chronological place, more about his father's impotence. Long after his father's narrative death (indeed, twice over) Guibert tells how the husband overcame impotence (and probably his fear of his beautiful, forbidding wife) by siring a child by another woman (94).[13] But in Chapter 12 where the marriage story is told, his mother's virginity ends differently. The witchcraft that had prevented sexual intercourse was inexplicably broken; everything follows in condensed, timeless order:

> When that bewitchment was broken by a certain old woman, my mother submitted to the duties of a wife as faithfully as she had kept her virginity when she was assailed by so many attacks. In other ways she was truly fortunate, but she laid herself open not so much to endless misery as to mourning when she, whose goodness was

ever growing, gave birth to an evil son who (in my own person) grew
worse and worse (67–68).[14]

In these two sentences of overstrained syntax, forced into tropes of
untranslatable parallelism which obscure and involute already obscure
sense, Guibert's mother loses her virginity, conceives and gives birth
to him. The Latin shows this syntactical/metaphorical impasse better,
but no more clearly:

> Cassatis, inquam, per anum quamdam illis pravis artibus, ea fide
> thalamorum officio deservivit, qua diutinam virginem sub tantarum
> animadversionum pulsatione servavit. Felix nempe alias in eo se
> infinitae non tam miseriae quam miserabilitati addixit, quod tunc
> bona, et multo magis postmodum bona semper malum, et meipso
> deteriorem semper ediderit.[15]

The power of achieving the condition for successful intercourse is
taken from his father and awarded to an anonymous old woman.
His mother, of her sole will and moral decision, seems to have entered
the marriage bed and (in the same verb) undertook the activities
performed there (*thalamorum officio*)—alone. She then compromised
her well-being and purity by producing a morally tainted son. *She* is
the subject of all the verbs, as well as the object: she submitted
(herself); she had preserved (her virginity); she sacrificed; she gave
birth. All the action is reflexive and she is the sole acknowledged
actor. No time elapses between her first (narrative) intercourse and
Guibert's birth. And the only persons present in this tiny, intensely
conflated scene are the mother and son—himself emphatically
present in the intensified pronoun, *meipso*.

Not only is the husband, rightful possessor of the woman, banished
from the marriage bed and birth (so unlike the first, populated
version), the only male present is Guibert, the infant whose dramatic
birth nearly killed his mother when he emerged from her, then
retracted, then emerged again. Why does he insist so often that he
was born in a state of profound sin? He has told it plainly enough.
In a psychoanalytic exegesis which reads the symbolic tropes of the
language of desire, the reverse grammar of unadmitted desire,
Guibert's infant body, witnessed and recorded in the unmistakeable
motions of intercourse, becomes symbolically, by the metonymy of
whole for part, the penis which alone initiated his mother into sexual
knowledge and impregnated her with himself.

And then he (narratively) killed his father, the rival who punished the son with castration by dedicating him to a religious life at the very moment of his birth. His mother is widowed again in the next chapter, the father brushed aside in a subordinate clause: "now after the death of my father...."[16] These strangely accented birth scenes vary the primal scene; it is not the parents who are seen in intercourse, but the son and mother. Accurately describing the timeless time and placeless space of the libidinous unconscious, Guibert's narrative achieves oedipal bliss in a text composed of malleable fragments of family history, molded by desire and the pressure of repressed but never forgotten secrets, into a narrative which confesses itself, in universal code, not as a family history but as the classic family romance. This paradigm of guilty desires, never satisfied and never expiated, is an emotionally constructed scenario which not only expresses a fantasy of gratification but also an infantile *explanation* of actual life according to an emotional logic.[17] In Guibert's case, reality presented him with no father and a mother who seemed everything most desirable, but also forbidding and overwhelming.

Every repeated time Guibert points to his mother's beauty, he confesses the object of his desire and points to the source of his own beauty, the visible sign of their deep, undiluted connection. As a girl, she was pretty; rich men pursued her when news of her unconsummated marriage got about; as a widow "the beauty of her face and form remained undimmed"(71); when she later adopted strict religious observance, "she still had much beauty and showed no sign of age"(75). He persistently marvels that her beauty never degraded her character into carnality, as if personal beauty should make the *possessor* lustful rather than inspire lust in others.[18] In a complicated maneuver of projection and self-censure, he always erotizes *her*: "Although God had given her such great good looks, [she acted] as though she were unaware of her beauty, and she cherished her widowhood as if, unable to bear them, she had always loathed a wife's bedtime duties"(92). He too enjoyed the equivocal gift of beauty: his "outward comeliness"(68) concealed "heaps of filth"(79), but his worldly kin thought his good looks added to his chances of success.

His elaborate prefatory platitude that "no one achieves by his own efforts his parentage or good looks" is the key to the inner plot of his confession. Concealed in the reverse grammar of repressed desire is: "I impregnated my mother with myself, and (so) I look just like her." So he condemned himself to emotional confusion and anxiety, for such forbidden triumphs exact a heavy price. Even writing his life long after his mother's death, Guibert could not describe her abandonment of him until his feelings found a way to encode his ultimate claim to her, as well as his undimmed anger and fear, for she was a woman dangerous for men to approach, and determined to be possessed by none. After the oedipal paradise of early childhood, Guibert's mother was lost to him several times: when she brought another man into her household and gave him father-like powers of discipline over the boy; when she gave her confidences to the tutor, excluding her son; when she abandoned him at age twelve and left him to depression and resentful misbehavior. After she died, he could reclaim her by writing her life into his, take revenge on the teacher by denigrating his ability and insulting him at luxurious length, and relive his oedipal triumph as he reduced his father to an impotent bystander in life and a pathetic, tortured shade in purgatory after death. John Benton noted Guibert's fascinated horror with the things he found loathsome: sexual uncleanness, excrementory humiliations, castration, forbidden knowledge of magic and divination.[19] In the twice-told birth account and Guibert's truism on the human condition I have tried to find the core narrative of this psychic plot. I stress that such psychoanalytic exegesis does not reduce, absorb, and replace the more expansive public story of a man's adult life in the world, but it does, I hope, turn the conventional ideogram of "medieval abbot" into a man.

The price of Guibert's secret victory in the competition for his mother, object of so many men's desire, was that he had acquired the secret virtuoso's hypersensitive suspicions of (others') sexual debasement; he was proud and ambitious, but not straightforward or confident. These traits did not dominate or destroy his life; he was merely neurotic among the legions of the normally neurotic, and he clearly learned to sublimate a good deal of energy into the proper concerns of his competitive literary and religious life. As he grew older his world and attention expanded appropriately. One might even say that his early vanquishing of his father in the most primal of competitions, whatever other conflicts it created, made him edgily competitive with men all his life, and this impulse guided his most successful efforts to gain attention, namely the literary production which eventually won him election to an abbacy.[20]

Psychoanalytic theory is culturally economical in that it retains the elements of desire and its trajectories in their traditional central place in Western thought since Augustine, and outlines a new, intelligible language for a fragmented world which no longer speaks one theological language. The literal signs of an invisible reality point inward to a shared and permanent world of desire and its objects, negotiated anew by each soul. The unresolved drama fixed timelessly in the unconscious center of Guibert's life finds its dignity in the universal drama of all human life: moved by desire, thwarted by reality.

*****

HER STORY

> In great fear of God and with no less love of all her kin and especially of the poor, this woman wisely ruled our household and our property (72).

If Guibert's story speaks insistently of sex, his mother's story speaks of gender. Guibert may celebrate her moral and personal distinction but his social vocabulary aligns her with all other women by marking the stages of her life by her relations to the dominant man of each phase: "When hardly of marriageable age, she was given to my father, a mere youth, by the provision of my grandfather" (63–64), or "as a maiden of tender years, or in her married life, or as a widow with a wider range of activities…" (75). "She" is harder to locate since she has lost her name and become the narrator's "personal possession" and been absorbed in his life narrative. Yet this book is, in its complicated ways, a representation of actual lives and in it, we do learn the life careers of its two major characters. Many of the key events of her life are told by Guibert with a participant's confidence and immediacy which can only be explained as the result of detailed confidences, many times repeated. *His* early memories had been formed to an intense degree by the impress of her personality, and he knows his family history only in her emphatically marked version.

The son's secret confession is inscribed in the mother's reminiscences. His story is a variant of paradise lost; hers is of prolonged trials of submission, mortification, loss, followed by courageous seizing of opportunity and the attainment of self-determination: paradise regained. Her victories were not easily won and some of the dramatic events of her life have the sound of favorite war stories told long after the campaign. The years of her life until her widowhood (how useful it would be to know how many there were) were lived in conformity to the requirements of her sex and class: custody of her was transferred by her father to a husband at an early age (again, what Guibert considers hardly marriageable remains imprecise); she moved away from her kin to live with her husband. The childhood horror of sin, especially the kinds occasioned by physical beauty, and lifelong revulsion from sex which Guibert mentions suggest that she did not identify her own ideals and ambitions with her marriage. Three or seven years of marital continence with a (temporarily) impotent husband also suggest deep reluctance and distaste for her situation. Even if this woman's revulsion from sex had other and more personal roots, as it must have had, she was an uneasy, reluctant player in the inflexible script of aristocratic family life.

The unyielding gender constructions of medieval Europe stand out in high relief around aristocratic women. These persons who lived within the social umbrella of power and privilege, sustained in luxury by the labor of others, sharers in unearned honors, expected neither to fight nor to labor, look to us (and perhaps themselves) the least powerful and most constricted of all medieval society. More than the daughters of any other class, the noble girl was likely to serve in a strange household, unable to command wages or change her employer. She was far more likely to have her marriage arranged for her, with minimum regard to her preferences and at an earlier age than lower-class girls; her success or failure in childbearing was more likely to affect her husband's regard for her, threatening even her security as a legal wife and attracting the hostile interference of his relations into her marriage. Familial interest in her sexuality's potential for inheritance-disrupting betrayal or dynasty-bolstering continuity exposed this most inward aspect of personality to public pressures, turning sex into gender.

The woman with every enumerated quality of mind and body except a name, "my mother," stands as historical proof-text of ideas about sexual renunciation most persuasively explained by Peter

Brown, who argues that the insistence on maintaining virginity or resuming continence should not be seen entirely in the negative terms of revulsion, rejection of body and pleasure, but also as the severing of a bondage to the oppressions of the social world, a positive striving for autonomy, self-direction, psychic wholeness and choice.[21] However moralized her self-understanding in conventional dicta of sin and purity, "my mother" shows us, albeit through her son's self-involved mind, how acutely a medieval woman could understand sex and gender, understand how personal sexuality and social expectation met in struggle and conflict, and how she might use that inchoate knowledge for purposes that might as well be called feminist.

Guibert's triumphal year was his first year of life; so, too, it was hers. With evident satisfaction and admiration, he tells how she foiled her in-law's hostile plans, evaded remarriage, kept control of her son and property, and consolidated her position as head of household. "Now, after the death of my father, although the beauty of her face and form remained undimmed, and I, scarcely half a year old, gave her reason enough for anxiety, she resolved to continue in her widowhood" (70). Her husband's kin took legal action against her in what seems a feudal court. Summoned to meet them, she took her stand in the church before the crucifix. When one litigant came to find her, she insisted on justice being done there: "stretching out her hand toward the image of the crucified Lord, she replied, 'This is my Lord, this is the advocate under whose protection I will plead.'" She won that round.[22] Remarriage was urged by her late husband's greedy, powerful nephew to make her life more pleasant, "since you have sufficient youth and beauty," and to allow the husband's kin to raise his children. She countered that argument with a "quite crafty" reply: "...your uncle was of very noble descent. Since God has taken him away, Hymen shall not repeat his rites over me, my lord, unless a marriage with some much greater noble shall offer itself." This *was* clever. She was only of the middling nobility and noblewomen invariably married in their own rank or a bit down. The annoyed nephew could do nothing to sway her. The fulcrum of power in her miniature feudal state was her own continent body.

And so, as Guibert says, "this woman wisely ruled our household and our property" (70–72), a household whose chief members were celibate men: son, tutor, chaplains. With a married woman's freedom from parental guardianship, a widow's freedom from her spouse, a mother's control over her minor child, and proprietary use of dower and perhaps feudal property, this determined woman achieved a rare degree of effective power. She was quite aware of her personal social authority and used it. When she insisted that her son's tutor drop his other pupils and devote himself exclusively to Guibert, everyone complied because of "their respect for my mother, as well as her power" (46); when she tried to buy Guibert a benefice she "bargained with the lord of the castle" (52) who controlled the living; when she decided to leave her home and create an idiosyncratic semi-monastic way of life, she was helped by Bishop Guy of Beauvais (73), and she eventually persuaded the abbot of St. Germer of Fly to let her take monastic vows without entering a convent, against reiterated canon law (133–34). After years of a generic "woman's life," she surely enjoyed having her own way.

"The priests have placed a cross in her loins," one of her dependents was heard to say (little Guibert was eavesdropping), but I doubt that she minded this kind of gossip (73). With her continence in constant public view, she maintained a strictness of observance and generosity to the poor that reinforced her autonomy and authority. Her son knew she wore haircloth beneath her beautiful gowns (72). For all her contrition and worry about sin, to the modern reader she seems a tough-minded, manipulative woman; she was domineering and had a habit of having dramatic dream visions that justified her decisions for herself and others, if there was opposition.[23] This does not impugn her sincerity. Sincerity and strategy sometimes coincide nicely, and clever people recognize their opportunities.

Guibert's mother never demonstrated any inclination to "leave the world" in the common understanding of entering a monastery or hermitage. Guibert frequently if passingly alludes to her constant contact with family and friends, her beautiful clothes, and delicate-tasting food (necessary for her health, he adds). A regular part of her moral exercise consisted of self-critical examination of the frivolous, worldly conversations she had just enjoyed with her guests. Even after she left the marital home and resided in her small house near the monastery at Fly—dressing in shabby black, worn shoes, her beautiful hair cut short—her social life continued unabated, "especially men and women of noble rank took pleasure in conversing with her."[24] Her religious retirement took place in a house built especially for her with a pious older woman who was her social inferior; the personal obedience to authority involved in true monastic life was clearly unacceptable to her. Her religious activities were frequent, engrossing, and perfectly sincere, but she wanted her life in the secular world, on her own terms.

She also—and this is a crucial aspect of her conflicted sexuality and her clever manipulation of gender relations—showed no real distaste for male companionship. She seemd to have recoiled from the emotional and bodily impact of sex itself and this feeling was reinforced by the mortifying inequalities of marriage, the dangers of childbirth, and her religion's linkage of sex with sin. But that does not mean that she disliked the company of men who could not threaten her. She chose the tutor for her son and insisted that this man give up his pupils and be entirely dependent on her; he became the chief adult male of her household, the surrogate father of her son, and her intimate confidant and friend. Guibert admits that she confided her dreams to the tutor; he was the one who had the house at Fly built for her; he entered the monastery at Fly when she moved there; and he was the weeping friend at her death bed. After her own fashion, she does seem to have remarried.

In whatever terms they translated their world's standards for judging male and female character, Guibert and his mother collaborated in seeing *her* as embodying a standard that placed her alone among women, and alone above men. She emerges, in her son's book, as a triumph of gender. In a society that customarily read femaleness as: sexual, febrile, carnal, inferior, emotional, fickle, cowardly, weak, private, penetrated, she resisted by accepting that code for all *other women*, as she taught her son to think, and defining herself as the striking exception. Her lifelong resistance to sexuality was the core of her aggressive adoption of the masculine counter-code: cool, continent, spiritual, rational, brave, stable, self-governing, public, powerful. Tracing the gender code of Guibert's book is instructive. Men (especially the laity) are predominantly faithless, lazy, brutal, lying, ignorant, hypocritical, adulterous, greedy; (Other) Women are frivolous, vain, seductive, untrustworthy, sensual, worldly, impious. Only "my mother" combines the feminine ideals of piety, modesty, chastity, dutifulness, and steadfastness, with the masculine values of self-control, pride, courage, honor, and reputation. We see in her an exceptionally neat instance of how repudiation of sex can effectively reorganize gender (and why her son was left with little ground to claim for himself).

But even under the sternest denial, sex will speak. One crucial event intervenes between the strangely coded passage of sexual initiation in Chapter 12 and the second (narrative) death of Evrard, husband and father. It constitutes the only elaborately described event of the central years of her married life. For a time (about 1054, long before Guibert's birth), Evrard was away from home on military service (230–232). This was common enough among the feudal classes: men had to fulfill lengthy military obligations during which their wives became head of the household. This time, however, she heard that her husband had been taken prisoner by a powerful man, notorious for refusing to accept ransoms, who kept his prisoners captive for life, which meant death. Guibert recounts that she was half dead from sorrow, unable to eat, drink, or sleep as she contemplated her husband's probable death.

> In the dead of night, as she lay in her bed full of deep anxiety, since it is the habit of the Devil to invade souls weakened with grief, suddenly, while she lay awake, the Enemy himself lay upon her and by the burden of his weight almost crushed the life out of her. As she choked in the agony of her spirit and lost all use of her limbs, she was unable to make a single sound; completely silenced but with her reason free, she awaited aid from God alone (69–70).

Help came: a good spirit, perched on her bed, cried out until the demon raised himself from her body and the two spirits fought until the noise woke the maid servants. The demon fled, and the good spirit paused before he left; he "turned to her whom he had rescued and said, 'Take care to be a good woman.'" The servants found her white and weak, scarcely conscious but with a perfect recall and understanding of what had happened. She treasured that admonition "ready to be guided to a greater love, if with God's help the opportunity should occur later." And it did, as Guibert quickly notes, "after the death of my father," when she resolved never to remarry in spite of her undiminished beauty and relative youth.

Here surely is a quintessential "medieval" episode: knights, ransom, incubus, divine messenger, moral warnings, celibacy as spiritual ideal. The social-political framework is feudal; the cultural or interpretive frame are popular beliefs of medieval Christianity. Thus, a pious woman of eleventh-century France, under the stress of the presumptive loss of her husband, has a supernatural visitation of demonic rape and rescue by a good spirit who gives her moral advice, reinforcing her belief system. That, with more detail elaborating the leading motifs, would pass as a viable cultural paraphrase—a "medieval" interpretation. But is that really an adequate account of the episode's *meaning*? Does "have a supernatural experience" hold any real human or cultural meaning for us? Obviously, I don't think so, but where does one reach for more depth and conviction?

Why, after the cruel assault she had endured, should the departing good spirit turn on *her* with warnings to be "a *good woman*" unless the demonic rape were understood as a punishment for some moral crime? What could she have done, alone, merely running her household in chaste independence, to provoke this? Hearing that her husband was captured and not likely ever to return, the worst she could do was...smile, exult, then deny and disavow this murderous wish, disguise it as grief, and let the conflict issue in a hideously appropriate punishment in the marriage bed. Guibert's narrative is completely silent on her reactions when Evrard was ransomed and returned. The narrator skips forward, as perhaps the woman's associative memories did, to the husband's actual death years later. The missing logic suggests itself: he did not die when she wished him dead, so she was not the murderous "bad woman" of her sinful wishes. Penitent and absolved, she was free to benefit by his death, when it came, to become the "good woman" of her own ego ideal and deepest gratification: independent, dominant, chaste, and free.

Even stories built as tightly on the matrix of gender as that of "my mother" are only one side of a double discourse. Serious attention must be paid to sexuality which remains, always, private, mysteriously constructed, and in ironic energizing relation to the clear ambitions of the ego.[25] "My mother" who "wisely ruled" in her world shows us the public, successfully sublimated side of a personality that, given less strength and less luck, might otherwise have been bitter and failed. In this formidable woman, "my mother," the invisible things of the mind are truly shown in the book she and her son made.

NOTES

1. Guibert of Nogent's autobiographical book which he called the *Monodiae* (commonly cited as his *Memoirs*) is widely read in John F. Benton's 1970 translation (emended from that of C. C. Swinton Bland) with valuable annotation, introduction, and appendices; this edition is available as a Medieval Academy Reprint for Teaching: *Self and Society in Medieval France: The Memoirs of Abbot Guibert of Nogent* (Toronto, 1984), p. 132; all parenthetical references in the text are to this edition.

2. There is a minimal variation in the chapter in which Guibert discusses her early married life and tries to remember that she was not yet then his mother, but "his wife," Benton, *Self and Society*, p. 69.

3. Benton suggests a basic chronology of Guibert's life and literary career (*Self and Society*, Appendix I, pp. 229–39); the birth date in April 1064 which he persuasively argues for makes the best sense of crucial elements of the text. Guibert, pp. 132–34 (text and notes), offer hints of her date of death.

4. Benton, *Self and Society*, pp. 38–39, including the odd citation of Sallust's remark about Aurelia Orestilla about whom good men found nothing to praise except her beauty which Guibert inverts to apply to his mother about whom good men could praise everything including her beauty.

5. John Forrester's illuminating *Language and the Origins of Psychoanalysis* (New York, 1980) takes as its subject the fact that language is the central concern of psychoanalysis, especially in the multiple modes of personal and culturally located symbolizations.

6. Benton, *Self and Society*, pp. 41–42. He suggests that he was baptized the same day, probably indicating that he was not expected to live.

7. Benton, *Self and Society*, pp. 44–50, conflates six years of home education under the schoolmaster his mother had added to her household, reporting a mixture of severity, beatings, and affection from the man, moral strictness and material indulgence from his mother, and his own adroitness in manipulating the competing affections of both adults.

8. Benton, *Self and Society*, p. 2, notes Guibert's confidence in his spontaneous mode of composition left his writings open to unemended mistakes and involuted syntax: "for the composition of this or my other works, I did not prepare a draft on the wax tablets, but committed them to the written page in their final form as I thought them out"(91). For my purposes this unrevised mentally composed writing is usefully malleable to fugitive associations, displacements, and confessional impulses.

9. These moves and relocations actually reunited the little family: Guibert's mother had a house built for herself near the monastery of St Germer of Fly; the tutor entered the monastery as a monk and Guibert's mother persuaded the abbot to take in her thirteen-year-old son also; Benton, *Self and Society*, pp. 74–77.

10. A diagram of parallel chapters of Book I:

Chap. 3:	Birth of Guibert	Chap. 12:	Parent's marriage to birth of Guibert
Chap 4:	Father dies.	Chap. 13:	Father dies.
Chap 5/6:	Education to age 12.	Chap. 14:	Age 12 - mother abandons Guibert
Chap 7:	Attempt to buy benefice.	Chap. 15:	Guibert enters monastery.

11. Benton, *Self and Society*, p. 63–64: "His wife's virginity thus remained intact for three years [note one of the few references to 'his wife']"; p. 65: "yet for seven whole years"; and p. 67: "seven years and more...."

12. Guibert is adamant that the age of chastity and modesty ended with his mother's youth although he cannot seem to find anyone except his mother among her contemporaries who was pious and chaste. Benton, *Self and Society*, pp. 65–66.

13. Benton, *Self and Society*, p. 94; this information occurs in Chapter 18, at which time Guibert was a monk, and is placed in an explanatory aside to his description of his mother's vision of his father in purgatory—the only time the father's name, Evrard, is divulged.

14. Benton, *Self and Society*, p. 67. Both the affliction of this alleged ligature and its dissolution are among the most vague and inadequately treated elements of the story; the general suggestion is that someone was to blame and it was not his mother.

15. Guibert, *De Vita Sua*, Liber I, *PL* 156:859.

16. This death occurs twice in the following chapter, Benton, *Self and Society*, pp. 69–70: once in Guibert's characteristic mode of curt brush-off ("Now, after the death of my father..."); and once in a more elaborated metaphoric version discussed in this essay in the section on Guibert's mother.

17. The *locus classicus* for what is not one single fantasy in which a child rejects the reality of family life in favor of a more dominating, gratifying, self-congratulatory and glamorous version, but several related variants is Sigmund Freud's brief 1908 essay, "Family Romances" (*Standard Edition*, trans. James Strachey, vol. 9, pp. 235–41). The well-known term, family romance, refers to the fantasy constructions of young children who "explain" the circumstances of their lives to themselves to arrive at more gratifying conclusions; these seldom remembered fantasies whose function is to correct actual life to serve the child's erotic and ambitious aims typically include revenge, the eroticized mother, banishment of sibling and paternal rivals, rationalization of incestuous desire.

18. In classic love theory, love is a sickness contracted by looking too much at beauty in the opposite sex, as in the mock stern diagnostic instructions of Andreas Capellanus: "Love is a certain inborn suffering derived from the sight of and excessive meditation upon the beauty of the

opposite sex, which causes each one to wish above all things the embraces of the other...," Andreas Capellanus, *The Art of Courtly Love*, trans. John Jay Perry (New York, 1941), p. 28.

19. Benton's introductory essay points frankly to evidence to Guibert's lifelong obsessions, bodily revulsions, possible homosexual interest, "castration complex"; these are isolated points that do not hold together in narrative logic which is the essence of psychoanalytic reading. *Self and Society*, pp. 21–27.

20. Benton notices Guibert's pattern of non-confrontational competitiveness with other men. *Self and Society*, p. 20.

21. This complex of ideas for which Peter Brown has been the earliest and most articulate proponent is widely accepted in feminist medieval studies though often a bit reduced in complexity; Brown's interpretations are always grounded in a psychoanalytic base from which he moves outward to cultural analysis. A cogent short version is "Bodies and Minds: Sexuality and Renunciation in Early Christianity," in *Before Sexuality: The Construction of Erotic Experience in the Ancient Greek World*, eds. David M. Halperin, John J. Winkler, and Froma Zeitlin (Princeton, 1990), pp. 479–93; and the full treatment of the subject is the immensely rewarding study, *The Body and Society* (New York, 1988).

22. The property and legal issues are very ambiguous but the suit of the husband's kin may have been so weak because she was defending her right to dower, and maintaining personal custody of her last child must have been an element in her control of property.

23. A vision was the trump card in her insistence on receiving the nun's veil, against multiple arguments from her son, Anselm of Bec, and others. Benton, *Self and Society*, p. 134.

24. Benton, *Self and Society*, p. 40, for her avoidance of spreading the scandal she heard; p. 76, for her contrition after idle conversation.

25. I am grateful to Professor Daniel Boyarin for pointing out to me that the life story of Guibert's mother, moving as it does from severe sexual conflict to success and autonomy in the world, bears an interesting resemblance to that of Bertha Pappenheim, better known as "Anna O.," Josef Breuer's first "talking cure" patient. "Anna O." was no more analyzed than the eleventh-century woman, whose repeated family stories (as well as the personal myth-building that inform Guibert's book) may have had a therapeutic effect in themselves, and both women found success in energetic action and self-direction in the world outside the family. Daniel Boyarin's book on "Anna O." is forthcoming.

CONTRIBUTORS

Marjorie Chibnall is Emeritus Fellow of Clare Hall, Cambridge. Her publications include *The World of Orderic Vitalis* (Oxford, 1984), *Anglo-Norman England 1066–1166* (Oxford, 1986), *The Empress Matilda* (Oxford, 1991), and editions of *The Ecclesiastical History of Orderic Vitalis* (1969–80) and *The Historia Pontificalis of John of Salisbury* (1956). She is now preparing an edition of the *Gesta Guillelmi* of William of Poitiers, and writing two books, *The Normans* and *The Continuing Debate on the Norman Conquest*.

Susanna Greer Fein is an associate professor of English at Kent State University and holds a doctorate from Harvard. She has published many articles on English verse, edited *Rebels and Rivals: The Contestative Spirit in "The Canterbury Tales"* (Kalamazoo, MI, 1991), and was the principal compiler of the *Speculum Subject Index*, 1926–74. Her continuing research interests are medieval English manuscripts, religious lyrics, and alliterative verse, and she is currently editing the thirteenth-century *Love Rune* by Thomas of Hales and writing a chapter on the Harley lyrics for *A Manual of Writings in Middle English*.

Stephan Grundy graduated from Southern Methodist University in 1991 and completed his doctoral thesis entitled "The Cult of Odhinn: God of Death?" in the Department of Anglo-Saxon, Norse, and Celtic at Cambridge University in 1995. He is currently researching Viking Age burial customs at Uppsala University. He is the author of several books and novels, including the best-selling *Rhinegold* and the forthcoming *Attila's Treasure*.

Rosemary Drage Hale teaches in the religion department at Concordia University in Montréal. She is currently completing a book on medieval practices of *imitatio mariae* and mother mysticism. Her translations of fourteenth-century Dominican convent literature are forthcoming. Other translations and articles on medieval women mystics have appeared in *Word and Spirit, Mystics Quarterly, Vox Benedictina,* and *Vox Mystica: Essays in Honor of Valerie Lagorio.*

Barbara A. Hanawalt is a professor of History at the University of Minnesota. In addition to numerous articles, she has published *Crime and Conflict in Medieval England* (Cambridge, MA, 1979), *The Ties that Bound: Medieval*

English Peasant Families (New York and Oxford, 1986), and *Growing Up in Medieval London: The Experience of Childhood in History* (New York and Oxford, 1993). She has edited *Women and Work in Preindustrial Europe* (Bloomington, IN, 1986), *Chaucer's England: Literature in Historical Context* (Minneapolis, MN, 1992), and *City and Spectacle in Medieval Europe* (Minneapolis, MN, 1994).

Lois L. Huneycutt, an assistant professor of History at California State University, Hayward, received her Ph.D. from the University of California at Santa Barbara. Currently at work on a biographical study of Queen Matilda II (1100–1118), she has published articles in *Anglo-Norman Studies, History Today, The Haskins Society Journal,* and *Medieval Queenship,* edited by John C. Parsons.

Jenny Jochens was trained at the University of Copenhagen and in Paris. She is professor *emerita* of History at Towson State University and is currently pursuing research at Stofnun Árnamagnússonar in Reykjavík. She is the author of *Women in Old Norse Society* (Ithaca, NY, 1995) and *Old Norse Images of Women* (Philadelphia, 1996).

Felice Lifshitz received her Ph.D. from Columbia University in 1988 and is now associate Professor of History at Florida International University. She is the author of *The Norman Conquest of Pious Neustria: Historiographic Discourse and Saintly Relics, 684–1090* (Toronto, 1995) and of articles in such journals as *Revue d'Histoire Ecclésiastique, Journal of Medieval History, Viator, Early Medieval Europe, Analecta Bollandiana, Annales de Normandie* and *The Haskins Society Journal.* She has completed an English translation of Dudo of St. Quentin's *Gesta Normannorum* and is currently at work on a book entitled *The Metahistory of Evangelization: Matrons, Martyrs, and Apostles.*

Kimberly A. LoPrete received her Ph.D. from the University of Chicago and is currently a teaching and research Fellow in the Department of Mediaeval History at the University of St. Andrews. Her publications include articles on Adela of Blois. She is completing a book-length study on Adela as a female lord while continuing her research into the historical writing of Adela's contemporary, Hugh of Fleury.

William F. MacLehose is currently completing his Ph.D. in medieval history at The Johns Hopkins University. His dissertation, from which "Nurturing Danger" is adapted, consists of studies in the cultural themes of the endangered child in high medieval French and English society.

Maud Burnett McInerney is visiting assistant professor of English at Haverford College, where she teaches Middle English and Contemporary Women's Literature. She holds a Ph.D. in Comparative Literature with emphasis in English, Latin, and French from the University of California at Berkeley. She is the mother of James and Lucy.

Allyson Newton received her Ph.D. in English from Rice University in 1994 and is assistant professor of English at Asbury College, where she teaches Medieval and Renaissance Literature. Her essay, "At the Heart of Loss: Shakespeare's Enobarbus and the Rhetoric of Remembering," will soon be published in *Renaissance Papers*, and she is currently working on a book-length study of memory and consolation in Shakespeare.

John Carmi Parsons holds the Ph.D. in Medieval Studies from the University of Toronto and the Licenciate from the Pontifical Institute of Mediaeval Studies in Toronto. Currently Assistant Professor in the Department of History at the University of Toronto, he has published *Medieval Queenship* (New York, 1993), *Eleanor of Castile: Queen and Society in Thirteenth-Century England* (New York, 1995), and a series of articles on medieval English queenship and the history of the family in medieval England.

Nancy F. Partner is associate professor of History at McGill University. Other of her publications related to the subject of this volume are: "No Sex, No Gender" in the *Speculum* issue which she edited (published in book form as *Studying Medieval Women* [Cambridge, MA, 1993]); "Reading the book of Margery Kempe," in *Exemplaria* 3 (1991); "Did Mystics have Sex?, in *Desire and Discipline: Sex and Sexuality in the Premodern West*, eds. J. Murray and K. Eisenbichler (Toronto, 1996). She is working on a book about psychoanalytic theory and medieval minds.

Patricia Ann Quattrin received her Ph.D. in Medieval Literature from the Medieval Institute, University of Notre Dame. She translated several homilies for *Vercelli Manuscript: Translations from the Anglo-Saxon*, ed. Lewis Nicholson (Lanham, MD, 1991), and has completed two works: *Words and Works in the Vision of William Concerning Piers the Plowman,* and a translation and introduction to *Prick of Conscience*. She teaches in the English Department at Grand Valley State University, and is preparing a translation of Aelfric's homilies.

Joel T. Rosenthal holds his degrees from the University of Chicago, and teaches medieval history at the State University of New York, Stony Brook. His areas of interest are family structure, old age, and the social position of women in late medieval England.

Miriam Shadis received her Ph.D. in Medieval History from Duke University, with a dissertation entitled "Motherhood, Lineage, and Royal Power in Thirteenth-century Castile and France: Berenguela de León and Blanche de Castille." She currently holds an Arthur J. Ennis, O.S.A., postdoctoral fellowship in the Core Humanities Program at Villanova University.

Pamela Sheingorn is professor of history at Baruch College, City University of New York, and a member of the program in interdisciplinary medieval studies at the Graduate School, CUNY. She is the co-editor (with Kathleen Ashley) of *Interpreting Cultural Symbols: Saint Anne in Late Medieval Society* (Athens, GA, 1990) and the translator of *The Book of Sainte Foy* (Philadelphia, 1995).

Andrew Sprung received his Ph.D. from the University of Rochester in 1992 and has taught premodern English literature at D'Youville College in Buffalo since 1992. His articles, including studies of the mother's gaze in Chaucer's *Clerk's Tale* and in Shakespeare's sonnets, have appeared in *Exemplaria, American Imago, Mediaevalia,* and *Mystics Quarterly.*

Bonnie Wheeler is director of the Medieval Studies Program at Southern Methodist University. She writes about late medieval literature and culture, and is the editor of the quarterly *Arthuriana.*